The Tribute of Blood

A book in the series

LATIN AMERICA OTHERWISE

Languages, Empires, Nations

Series editors:

Walter D. Mignolo, Duke University

Irene Silverblatt, Duke University

Sonia Saldívar-Hull, University of California

at Los Angeles

The Tribute of Blood

ARMY, HONOR, RACE, AND NATION

IN BRAZIL, 1864–1945   Peter M. Beattie

DUKE UNIVERSITY PRESS

Durham & London

2001

2nd printing, 2007

© 2001 Duke University Press   All rights reserved

Printed in the United States of America on acid-free paper ∞

Designed by C. H. Westmoreland   Typeset in Carter & Cohn

Galliard with Franklin Gothic display by Keystone Typesetting, Inc.

Library of Congress Cataloging-in-Publication Data appear

on the last printed page of this book.

About the Series

Latin America Otherwise: Languages, Empires, Nations is a critical series. It aims to explore the emergence and consequences of concepts used to define "Latin America" while at the same time exploring the broad interplay of political, economic, and cultural practices that have shaped Latin American worlds. Latin America, at the crossroads of competing imperial designs and local responses, has been construed as a geocultural and geopolitical entity since the nineteenth century. This series provides a starting point to redefine Latin America as a configuration of political, linguistic, cultural, and economic intersections that demand a continuous reappraisal of the role of the Americas in history, and of the ongoing process of globalization and the relocation of people and cultures that have characterized Latin America's experience. *Latin America Otherwise: Languages, Empires, Nations* is a forum that confronts established geocultural constructions, that rethinks area studies and disciplinary boundaries, that assesses convictions of the academy and of public policy, and that, correspondingly, demands that the practices through which we produce knowledge and understanding about and from Latin America be subject to rigorous and critical scrutiny.

Colonial administration and the postcolonial nation-state in Latin America followed a different pattern when compared with colonized countries in Asia and Africa. The early decolonization from Spain and Portugal placed most Latin American countries in peculiar positions with emerging imperial powers such as England and France. Latin America's incipient nation-states, indirectly dependent on these dominant European powers, were in turn shaped by these relations. Peter M. Beattie's book traces the gloomy picture of eighty years of nation-state formation in Brazil, focusing on military history and race relations.

By telling the story of Domingos, the son of an Angolan slave and a Portuguese nobleman, Beattie unravels the conflicting intersections of the army code of honor, the racial prejudices underlying the value system of postcolonial Brazil, and the constitution of its civil society. In the forming Brazilian State, "whiteness" was associated with honor, prestige, and wealth. However, in the international order of the period under study, the distinction between Anglo and Latin whites was being made, as "whiteness" in Brazil was not the same as "whiteness" in the United States. This superb study of the relationships between honor, race, and the army in Brazil also offers a wealth of information and ideas on the configuration of racial prejudices in Latin countries during the second half of the nineteenth and the first half of the twentieth century.

To my mother,

Jean O'Connor Beattie

To the memories of my father,

Francis Martin Beattie

And my sister,

Natalie Childress Beattie

Man to the hills, woman to the shore.

— Gaelic proverb

Cuchulain stirred,

Starred on the horses of the sea, and heard

The cars of battle and his own name cried;

And fought with the invulnerable tide.

— W. B. Yeats, "Cuchulain's Fight with the Sea"

I shouldered a kind of manhood

Stepping in to lift the coffins

of dead relations.

— Seamus Heaney, "Funeral Rites"

Contents

Illustrations

Acknowledgments

This is a humble attempt to acknowledge the many humans and trees who over the years have played a role in bringing this project into the form of a book. Inspirations and insights came from many sources, and I borrowed from the work, comments, enthusiasm, and examples of many, only a fraction of whom I will be able to mention here. The cooperation, lending, and appropriation that goes into the making of a historical case study can never be given its due in laudatory footnotes or acknowledgments. But when only one author's name goes on the cover, he or she must struggle to make jalopy shibboleths appear as vibrant and new as the phrase "previously-owned cars." So be it. While I avow full title to any of this book's shortcomings, I share credit for whatever may be commendable herein with my numerous named and unnamed collaborators (why does that last word make it sound like we have committed a crime?).

This project first began to take shape during a pre-dissertation trip to Rio de Janeiro. Like many graduate students, I was unable to find substantial documentation to pursue the original project outlined in my proposal, and I began to feel like a fraud. I explained my frustration to Eliseu de Araújo Lima, the knowledgeable and implacable paladin of the Arquivo Nacional's consulting section. Eliseu graciously suggested that I might be interested in a new collection of military police inquiries that the archive staff was organizing. He introduced me to Antônio Carlos Gonçalves Valério, who headed the section organizing judicial papers. Antônio kindly allowed me to peruse the uncataloged collection, and I was instantly drawn to the rich detail and picaresque quality of these documents. I returned to the United States determined to develop a project on the social history of common Brazilian soldiers. I am deeply indebted to these dedicated archivists and many others who took the time to share documents, ideas, and coffee.

Professor Robert M. Levine of the University of Miami, Coral Gables, provided encouragement, advice, and insights that sharpened my analytical skills and guided me through bouts of vertigo during the twists and turns of the research and writing process. Dr. Eul Soo Pang first introduced me to Brazil as an undergraduate, and he changed my life in 1985 by organizing my first chance to study abroad at the Universidade Federal do Pernambuco in Recife, Brazil. Professors Mark D. Szuchman, José Carlos Sebe Bom Meihy, William C. Smith, and Steve Stein provided crucial guidance as my studies and this project gestated. Frank D. McCann, Vitor Izecksohn, Celso Castro, Jorge Luiz Prata de Souza, Glaúcia Pessoa, Hendrik Kraay, and Zach Morgan always shared their expertise and provided a critical sounding board for my ideas about the military. They generously divulged their knowledge of documentation and sources. I also benefited from conversations with Brazilian colleagues who work in a variety of other areas: Ana Maria Lugão Rios, Hebe Maria Mattos de Castro, Sheila Siqueira de Castro Faria, João Luís Ribeiro Fragoso, Marta de Abreu Estevez, Marcus Joaquim Maciel de Carvalho, Fernanda Batista Bicalho, Nisia Trindade Lima, Gilberto Hochman, and Gladys Sabina Ribeiro, among many others.

I also want to thank the outside reviewers of my manuscript who identified themselves, Dain Borges and Elizabeth Ann Kuznesof for their advice and many helpful corrections that saved me from mistakes and misrepresentations. At Duke University Press, editor Valerie Millholland, editorial associate Miriam Angress, assistant managing editor Patricia Mickelberry, and copyeditor Darcy Tromanhauser have patiently and graciously guided this novice through the entire publication process.

I thank my colleagues at Michigan State University (MSU) in the Department of History and the Center for Latin American and Caribbean Studies who have helped me to develop as an instructor, a historian, and a collaborator. I extend special thanks to David Walker and prayers for his son John Henry's rapid recovery. We welcome our two new colleagues in Latin American history, Javier Pescador and Laurent Dubois, in our efforts to develop a strong undergraduate and graduate program in Latin American history at MSU. I also thank the MSU graduate students who work in Latin American history and other fields for their insightful critiques of my work over the years.

Fellow graduate students at the University of Miami provided emotional and intellectual support from the start: Maria Elisa Fernandez (who generously helped me in ways too numerous to mention here), Graham

Andrew, Carmen Alvarez, Michael LaRosa, Alan Belitsky, German Mejía, Carlos Monge, Quélia Quaresma, Anthony Johnson, Cristina Mehrtens, and others.

I also drew on the generosity and wisdom of many others on both sides of the equator, including Roger Kittleson, Sue Ann Caulfield, Mark Hoffnagel, Jeff Lesser, Joel Wolfe, Katherine Diane McCann, Flávio Gomes, Gerald Greenfield, Gayle Trainer, Steve Williams, Jean Daudelin, Kenneth Serbin, Bert Barickman, Daryl Williams, Marco Antônio Pamplona, Joan Meznar, Nancy Naro, Maria Marta Batista Bicalho, Timothy Coates, Cecília Loreto Mariz, Carlos Eugênio Líbano Soares, and Brian Owensby. The staffs of the Arquivo Nacional (especially Sátiro Nunes), the Arquivo do Centro de Pesquisa e Documentação — Fundação Getúlio Vargas, the Arquivo Público do Estado de Pernambuco, the Arquivo Público do Estado do Rio de Janeiro, the Instituto Brasileiro de Geografia e Estatística, the Biblioteca Nacional, the Arquivo da Casa de Oswaldo Cruz, the Arquivo da Casa de Rui Barbosa, and the Arquivo do Instituto Histórico e Geográfico Brasileiro all gave patient and considered assistance.

Generous research and writing support came from the James R. Scobie Memorial Prize of the American Historical Association's Conference of Latin American History, a Theodore Parker pre-dissertation grant from the University of Miami, a Fulbright IIE Fellowship, a National Endowment for the Humanities grant, and my current employer, Michigan State University.

To Erica Windler, with whom I share a passion for Brazil and its history, I hope we have many years to *dividir, brincar,* and *amar.*

I dedicate this book to three remarkable people: to my mother, Jean O'Connor Beattie, and to the memories of my father, Francis Martin Beattie, and my sister, Natalie Childress Beattie. My parents encouraged me to pursue my interests, and gave me enough room to make my own mistakes and learn from them. I thank them for their enduring love, support, and patience (I know I sometimes tried it). My mom taught me to love reading by example and by taking me to the public library each week as a boy. I learned about communicating from my father's mischievous sociability. I miss his playful banter and caring jeers. My sister Natalie taught me how to swim before I have any memories of life. I still find it hard that I cannot speak to her and float in her well of good cheer and humor.

Author's Note

To diminish confusion when using the term "state," I have opted to capitalize "State" when referring to the overarching institutions of government. When I use "state," I refer to the provinces that were redesignated as
"states" under Brazil's republican 1891 Constitution. Because of changing
rules governing spelling in Brazilian Portuguese, I have preserved original
spellings of names as well as titles of books, documents, and articles in
most instances. In some cases, terms or names have been adopted to
contemporary spelling standards for clarity.

Where possible, I have tried to use the language of Brazilian historical
actors to describe racial and ethnic identities, but for the convenience of
certain types of analysis, I have at times used categories that would likely
have seemed alien to many of the individuals who appear in this study.
Terms such as "nonwhites" are utilized to distinguish those who identified
themselves or were identified by others as not being of "pure" European
descent. The term Afro-Brazilian is employed at times to distinguish those
with black African descent from those who did not recognize this racial
heritage as part of their own identity or who were perceived by others to
possess this heritage. Over centuries, Brazilians have devised a plethora of
racial categorizations that belie the simple binary categorizations that contemporary scholars attempt to impose. Most Brazilians of African descent
in the late 1800s would have much more readily emphasized black and
brown identities with myriad gradations within each grouping. It is important to note, however, that Brazilian historical actors themselves did
not always employ racial and ethnic terms consistently.

I would refer interested readers to Ada Ferrer's insightful and more
detailed discussion of these issues on the use of racial terms by North
American historians and other scholars in the introduction to her book
Insurgent Cuba. I would add to Professor Ferrer's analysis that similar
caution and attention should be paid to the use of terms for a variety of
social categories used to distinguish class, sexual, gender, and age identifi-

cations among others. I have tried to present the terms utilized by historical Brazilian actors with each of these categories, but as with race, some compromises had to be made for analytical reasons or the lack of a tight linguistic fit for Portuguese terms translated into English. For instance, most of the Brazilian poor in the late 1800s distinguished stratification among their ranks with the terms "protected" (those with a prominent patron) and "unprotected" (patronless poor). Brazilians tended to use these homegrown terms rather than, for example, the exotic language of Karl Marx to distinguish between the proletariat and the lumpen proletariat (even though many Brazilians came to be exposed to these terms by way of the Brazilian labor movement beginning in the late 1800s). Different terms and competing conceptions of class, racial, sexual, ethnic, gender, and age identities coexisted, and in most cases, they continue to coexist in contemporary Brazil. I share Professor Ferrer's hope that attention to these distinctions will lead scholars toward a fuller examination of how these unnatural identities were formed and remade "on the ground" in specific historical settings.

Scholars often use the term conscription as a synonym for impressment. The tendency to conflate the two terms is heightened by the fact that there is no equivalent of the noun form "conscript" for impressment. In the text, I at times reluctantly resort to neologisms such as "dragoonee" and "inductee" to avoid both this imprecision and more cumbersome phrases such as "men pressed into service." I am careful to distinguish between these two distinct types of recruitment for military mobilizations because they are so different that to confuse them is similar to equating indentured servitude and debt peonage. There were times when these two forms of recruitment overlapped. The Brazilian government called up a number of enrolled national guardsmen for service in the Paraguayan War (a method I would regard as a type of conscription), and when many failed to report for duty, it empowered recruitment agents to hunt down and press draft-dodging guardsmen.

Both conscription and impressment are ultimately coercive forms of tribute labor recruitment, but their methods and the meanings attributed to them are distinct. *Conscription* comes from Latin meaning "to enlist or to select from a list." This referred to the obligation of Roman citizens of the Republic (men who satisfied minimum property requirements) to enroll as able-bodied adults liable to be periodically called up for military service. Conversely, *impressment* describes coercive recruitment performed by police or press gangs. These agents most often targeted men without property, including vagrants and lawbreakers. Impressment did not rely on selecting men from an enrollment list, the act from which the term *conscription* derived its meaning. When reformers of the seventeenth and eighteenth centuries spoke of conscription, most understood it as an enrollment of mostly law-abiding male youths from which recruits would be selected for service on the basis of a lottery. I thank my colleague Professor John Eadie for his insights on the origins and practices surrounding conscription in the Roman Republic and Empire.

Finally, I have adopted ratios of the rate of exchange of the Brazilian currency the milréis to the U.S. dollar to estimate comprehensible values for the reader which take inflation into account. I made these estimates based on data compiled by my colleague Hendrik Kraay in appendix 4 of his dissertation, "Soldiers, Officers, and Society: The Army in Bahia, 1800–1889."

Abbreviations and Acronyms

Archival abbreviations are in the Bibliography section

ACB	*Os Annaes da Câmara do Brazil*
AM	Assuntos Militares
AMD	Autoridades Militares Diversos
ASB	*Os Annaes do Senado do Brazil*
col.	coleção
cx.	caixa
CSMJ	Conselho Suprema Militar de Justiça
CSSH	*Comparative Studies in Society and History*
doc.	documento
fo.	folha
fu.	fundo
FEB	Força Expedicionária Brasileira
GIFI	Grupo de Identificação de Fundos Internos
HAHR	*Hispanic American Historical Review*
JLAS	*Journal of Latin American Studies*
la.	lata
li.	livro
LBA	Liga Brasileira de Assistência
LAMB	Liga Anti-Militarista Brasileira
LARR	*Latin American Research Review*
LBR	*Luso-Brazilian Review*
LDN	Liga de Defensa Nacional
ma.	maço
NCO	Noncommissioned Officer
pa.	pasta
PRC	Partido Republicano Conservador
Pro.	Processo
Rio	The city of Rio de Janeiro
RRMGuC	*Relatório da Repartição dos Negócios do Ministério da Guerra apresentado ao Congresso*

RRMGUP	*Relatório da Repartição dos Negócios do Ministério da Guerra apresentado ao Parlamento*
se.	*seção*
SPCOA	Secretaria da Polícia da Côrte Ofícios com Annexos
STM	Suprema Tribunal Militar
WMC	War Ministry Correspondence

Introduction

Soldiers of Misfortune,

Soldiers by Lot

"Soldado de amor"   "Soldier of Love"
Sou soldado, sentei praça   I am a soldier, I enlisted
Na gentil tropa de amor;   In the gentle corps of love;
Jurei as suas bandeiras,   I swore an oath to its banners,
Nunca serei desertor.   I will never be a deserter.

— Domingos Caldas Barbosa,
Verse of an eighteenth-century song

Portuguese officials in Rio de Janeiro summarily punished the mulatto composer Domingos Caldas Barbosa in the early 1760s by forcing him to serve as a common soldier. This unwilling recruit later became the most popular troubadour of the eighteenth-century Portuguese empire. The veteran would mine his troubled past for inspiration, and his army experience supplied him with a powerful metaphor. Domingos Caldas Barbosa's life, race, and song provide a revealing introduction to this examination of army recruitment and enlisted service, which I use to explore the understudied world of Brazil's free poor and their interaction with the State from 1864 to 1945. Even though Domingos lived in colonial times, his legacy loomed large in the late 1800s when an independent Brazilian State attempted to reform military recruitment and abolish slavery.

The son of an Angolan slave and an unidentified Portuguese merchant, Domingos grew up in the city of Rio de Janeiro (hereafter, Rio) before this lushly forested and mountain-ringed tropical port became Brazil's colonial capital in 1763. The boy's father recognized Domingos as his natural son, manumitted him, and provided privileged Jesuit schooling.

I. Regions, States, and Capitals of Brazil in the early 1900s. Note that Acre was not a state, but it became a federal territory in 1904.

Despite the boy's education, however, "polite" Rio society did not accept him as an equal because of his color and birth status. These injustices apparently spurred the waggish pupil's lyrical and satirical talents. Some of his songs lightheartedly parodied the Portuguese by asserting superior aspects of Brazilian culture.[1] The bard's musical quips irked Portuguese authorities who viewed him as an impertinent and potentially dangerous mulatto, regardless of his father's station. Domingos's talents earned him a martial exile in the Sacramento military colony—a Portuguese coastal redoubt on Brazil's southern frontier near the mouth of the Rio de la Plata, then a strategic causeway for the Spanish empire's lucrative traffic in Andean silver. The musician served in Sacramento as a private until the Spaniards overtook it in 1762 during the Seven Years' War. Portuguese authorities had long favored Sacramento as a locale for the remission of "criminals" from more settled areas in order to populate and defend a strategic frontier long disputed with Spain. Authorities summarily dragooned (hence the English term "goon") many men, like Domingos, for military service.[2] Returning to Rio, Domingos obtained his discharge, and his patrons arranged a post as a priest for the veteran in Portugal. Adopting the name Loreno Selinuntino, this bard-priest gained renown among both nobles and commoners as a lyricist. His works mixed Afro-Brazilian and European styles and found a lasting popular response in Brazil where they influenced the evolution of popular music.[3]

In the late 1800s, the Brazilian literary critic Sílvio Romero followed the lead of romantic European scholars, namely the Brothers Grimm, who used folk traditions as building blocks to erect "authentic" national identities.[4] To this end, Romero transcribed an 1880s version of Domingos's songs preserved by unnamed popular troubadours. Domingos's lyrics had been popularized and modified as they passed from bard to bard, migrating with Brazil's anonymous troubadors. As Romero remarked, "Loreno's [Domingos] ditties were still alive in the voices of the folk."[5] By 1880, Domingos's work had long since become unfashionable for educated Brazilians who had retuned their musical tastes to the more "civilized" trends emanating from Paris, Vienna, and Rome. Romero reintroduced Domingos to literate Brazilians as a nationalist artifact excavated from folk culture. The elevation of a mulatto, much more a picaresque ex-private, to the status of a national cultural hero by a respected intellectual marked a new approach to the predominantly white elite's conceptions of *Brasilidade* (Brazilianness). Domingos's humorous jabs at the Portuguese and praise of Brazil dovetailed with Romero's nationalist sensibilities. Three decades after Romero published his folklore collection, Lima Barreto, a mulatto novelist and civilian army arsenal employee, demonstrated how Domingos had become a national icon in *Triste Fim de Policarpo Quaresma* (The Sad End of Policarpo Quaresma). The 1915 novel invokes the bard-priest's image to parody the militarist nationalism at the turn of the century.[6]

Rustic Brazil's oral tradition kept alive many of Domingos's songs because they communicated frustrations, hopes, and fears through references to symbols, practices, and identities familiar to the folk. One such song preserved by popular oral tradition was Domingos's "Soldier of Love," as sung by an unidentified musician in Sergipe's interior that Romero recorded,

Fui soldado, assentei praça	I was a soldier, I enlisted
No regimento do amor;	In the regiment of love;
Como assentei por meu gosto,	Because joining was to my liking,
Nunca serei desertor.	I will never be a deserter.

Why did bards and their audiences continue to identify with Domingos's use of enlisted army service as a metaphor to emphasize the strength of amorous sentiments? Since impressment (forced recruitment, not to be confused with conscription) continued into the 1900s, the allusion to enlisted service held a similar meaning for Brazilians more than a century later. Officials still summarily (that is, without trials) remanded malcontents, vagrants, and suspected criminals to serve as soldiers for mandatory stints of six years or more. Though Domingos had lived a relatively privileged life, he had rubbed shoulders with the less fortunate, and he empathized with their concerns. Poor families could ill afford to lose the labor of able-bodied men or adolescents through impressment. Most also recognized the harshness of a private's career which was repaid with low wages and even less esteem. Most civilians, rich or poor, associated a private's life with degradation. As an 1878 editorialist fumed, "What person considered 'decent' would dare walk through the streets arm in arm with a common soldier?"[7]

With some important exceptions, only extreme circumstances could impel most Brazilians to volunteer to serve as enlisted men. These perceptions lent contextual weight to Domingos's metaphor. An enlisted man's status was so low, that to volunteer and to vow never to desert the army lent a tongue-in-cheek grandeur to Domingos's dedication to his lover and his willingness to sacrifice for romantic love.

The theme of desertion held even wider connotations. It preoccupied army officers, civil authorities, lovers, employers, slave owners, spouses, and families. Soldiers often fled from harsh conditions and abuse by officers, noncommissioned officers (hereafter NCOs), or comrades, as did slaves and free workers from the mistreatment of masters, bosses, peers, overseers, spouses, and kin. Difficult circumstances, including impressment, forced or induced men to abandon their families. For others, volunteering helped them escape their oppressors. Flight often seemed an appropriate response to injustice. Free poor men treasured geographic mobility, a freedom that distinguished them from slaves, soldiers, convicts, and most women. Such mobility is a marker of manly competence in many patriarchal cultures.[8] Desertion, therefore, held a special meaning for the common citizens who crowded public squares, rural markets, and sites of religious pilgrimage to sing, listen, and dance to Domingos's songs.

The army played a role in the State's efforts to restrict the free poor's mobility and to redistribute population strategically. But the anonymous bards who reworded Domingos's song affirmed evasion as a kind of inalienable right. Compare the verse, "Because joining was to my liking, I will never be a deserter" to Domingos's original lines, "I swore faith to its banners, I will never be a deserter." The unknown troubadour's assertion of his willingness to enlist replaces Domingos's appeal to oaths sworn to a flag. This modified verse is significant because the expression "*assentei praça*" (I became an active duty soldier) connotes neither volunteering nor being dragooned; in either case, a soldier was required to swear an oath to the flag. The underlying logic of this verse implies that if necessity or coercion forced an individual to enlist, then that soldier would have the right to desert. Many Brazilians exercised their right to flee from family, jobs, unjust masters or bosses, impressment, or even life in "civilization" itself. Largely disenfranchised from formal jurisprudence and politics, the free poor and slaves frequently invoked this right by making protest votes with their feet.

While many forcibly recruited troops deserted, most remained in the ranks enduring Spartan conditions, grueling work hours, and at times, abusive treatment. But despite the hyperbole of some historians, the army was not a concentration camp.[9] Many Brazilian smallholders, squatters, plantation workers, vagrants, slaves, and urban migrants lived under still harsher conditions. For some, life in the army improved their situations. Most army volunteers enlisted to escape hunger, unemployment, homelessness, and sometimes even slavery.[10] Whether dragooned or compelled by circumstances to volunteer, these "soldiers of misfortune" formed the mainstay of Brazil's army through the early 1900s. Serving alongside them, some — perhaps one could call them "soldiers of love" — willingly chose the army career over other potential occupations. A few received education and rose in rank to become officers. While army service was a punishment for many, to others it offered narrow avenues of social mobility or at least temporary shelter.

From Brazil's colonial era through the early 1900s, military impressment made army enlisted service a semicoercive labor system and a protopenal institution. In part, the army took on roles other than defense because of the lack of intensive warfare that seriously threatened the property of Brazilian elites.[11] The army's role as a penal destination and police force constituted a more consistent part of its duties than did its ostensibly transcendent obligation: to guard Brazil from enemy invasions and to train men to fight "conventional" wars.

This study examines the impressment and enlisted service systems that gave meaning to Domingos's martial metaphors, and the State's struggle to reform those systems. During Brazil's most intense international conflict, the Paraguayan War (1864–1870), mobilization difficulties prompted the State to reform recruitment by adopting a limited conscription system, first legislated in 1874. But only in 1916, amid the uncertainties of World War I, would the State successfully conduct a draft. For decades, many factors undermined the realization of a draft based on the leveling ideal of universal male conscription: popular protests, political party rivalries, a lack of infrastructure, bureaucratic intransigence, regional disputes, patriarchal privileges, ideologies, and the army's role in penal justice. Between 1864 and 1945, the adoption of largely Prussian-inspired recruitment and enlisted service models accelerated clashes and compromises between modern and traditional practices, institutions, identities, and values in Brazil.

The 1916 draft lottery altered the average soldier's career by giving rise to a new type of enlisted man: the "soldier-by-lot." The draftee replaced the more picaresque soldier of misfortune as the army's source of manpower. The draft not only changed the common soldier's career and status, but important aspects of the army's role in larger society. These changes altered the context and meaning of Domingos's martial metaphor, and implied transformations in ideas of penology, citizenship, honor, masculinity, race, national identity, and the proper limits of public power. These interconnected themes provide baseline values from which to analyze the changing relationships between strata of the poor and the State.

Domingos's life provides important clues to the relationship between race, status, and enlisted military service. The mulatto composer's fortune was unusual but not unique in Brazil where African slaves and their descendants at times formed more than two-thirds of the colony's population. Earlier attempts to enslave native Indians could not satisfy the labor demands of Brazil's plantation agriculture. Europeans (mostly Portuguese men), Indians, and Africans frequently coupled in Brazil, forming a population characterized by racial mixture.

To enhance their control over this diverse population and legitimize their power, Portuguese authorities and Brazil's mostly "white" native-born elites envisioned themselves atop a "natural" racial hierarchy. Those of mixed race constituted the middle of this racial scale while African-born slaves held the bottom rungs. Though rife with exceptions and contradictions, this idea of racial hierarchy sought to divide the poor and slave populations along lines of race and ethnicity by providing some non-whites with privileges and status over others. Portuguese authorities also hoped to stymie the formation of a shared Brazilian national identity among diverse colonials by promoting loyalty to racial privilege. One should not assume that all of those at the bottom, middle, or top of this racial scale accepted uncritically these bigoted notions. Most colonials, however, associated whiteness with honor, prestige, power, and wealth.[12]

Masters certainly relied on violence to maintain their authority among slave and free poor populations. When slaves were ample and cheap, they cruelly worked many to death. But owners also found patronage a cost-effective and psychologically appealing means to control and motivate slave workers. For instance, Brazilians manumitted their slaves with more frequency than most of their counterparts in the Americas.[13] A minority of whites convinced of their superiority thus negotiated an uneasy rule over a primarily nonwhite populace of free poor people and slaves, in part by allowing some, like Domingos Caldas Barbosa, access to freedom and social mobility through patronage. A small minority of talented non-whites blessed with patronage became revered members of society, and some came to be considered "white," even if, like President Nilo Peçanha (1909–1910), they could not entirely escape jocular references to their African ancestry.[14]

No matter how successful, however, perceptions of race colored views on honor. Portuguese elites brought to their colonies ideals that attributed honor to those who possessed "pure blood" that granted prestige, opportunities, and legal privileges to those with a traceable noble lineage. Purity of blood originally distinguished nobles from commoners and, with even more force, "old Christians" from "new Christians" (converted Jews and Moors). In Brazil, especially in the eyes of Europeans, mixed racial status externalized a lack of pure blood. Moreover, Europeans and their descendants commonly associated mixed race with the lack of legitimate birth status consecrated by a Church-sanctioned marriage.[15] Thus, racial perceptions carried implications about the quality of one's moral character and claims to honor. Hallowed conceptions of honor, racial status, and moral character remained a major obstacle for recruitment reform partly because the low status of enlisted service prevented authorities from excluding black men and from segregating soldiers in the ranks on the basis of race in the late 1800s.

Roberto da Matta's pioneering work on the conceptual and linguistic realms defined by "the house and the street" enriches our understanding of honor's social geography. Brazilians associate the house with honor, order, marriage, safety, family, and private power while the street implies disgrace, chaos, illegitimacy, danger, vagrancy, and vulnerability to the vagaries of impersonal public authority. Some of da Matta's rather rigid divisions of house and street into separate spheres of "personal" versus "individualistic" social relations become problematic in explaining change over time. Clearly there were and are ambiguities in the conceptions of house and street, and differing views often cleaved along lines of race, class, gender, ethnicity, region, period, and circumstances. Even so, his insight provides an important key to unlock meanings attributed to a variety of social spaces.[16] An association with the street usually implied a threat to family honor, the fundamental building block of order in the letter and philosophy of Brazilian law. Wealthy and poor actors manipulated, disputed, and altered the meanings of this geographic vocabulary, but they shared a language suffused with these markers of status.[17]

Honor demanded that male household members defend their kin, their dependents, and themselves from the sexual aggressions of other males. To insure family honor, the home took on special social and legal significance. The home's violation was a grave insult to honor because it compromised the ability of male household members to shield their feminine kin and dependents from real or putative sexual aggressions. Thus, Brazilian law restricted daytime searches of homes and prohibited officials and strangers from entering them at night except when natural disasters threatened, crimes were in progress, or cries of help came from within.[18] Although the poor could not always trust authorities to respect their homes' inviolability, they nonetheless subscribed to this principle and vociferously protested when officials trespassed against it. Subsequently scholars have built on da Matta's insights to examine the State's expanding role in regulating private space.[19]

The attempts to implement a conscription lottery reveal a dispute over the proper boundaries between private and State power often expressed in terms of the house and street. To implement a draft, authorities needed to move the barracks, figuratively and literally, out of the dangerous world of the street.

If the heterosexual family home represented one end of a spectrum of values, army barracks stood on the opposite end. The very term for an army enlisted man, *praça*, derived from the Portuguese word for public square. The term linguistically located soldiers in the dishonorable and disorderly world of the street. In colonial times, the term *soldado* (private) was a frequent euphemism for an exiled convict from abroad, or simply an unmarried man. This usage acknowledged the exemption from military service that married men enjoyed, as well as the use of penal exiles to fill colonial regiments.[20]

In some ways, the barracks were a male equivalent of the bordello; both attempted to distance "dangerous" male and female "loners" from "honorable" family households.[21] Officials tried to congregate and watch over men considered a threat to the home's sanctity in the barracks, but officers were often unable to police their troops effectively. The army applied corporal punishments to disobedient soldiers, a practice that kept praças uncomfortably close to the "dishonorable" status of slaves. Like slaves, praças needed their superior's consent to maintain a private home, and unlike private homes, barracks segregated mostly unmarried men into crowded, common, and — it was presumed — promiscuous abodes, as did the slave quarters of large plantations. An 1872 medical thesis observed, "In the military . . . sodomy has developed to such an extent that rare are those who do not practice it." This scandalous remark shows how many felt that the barracks' sexual segregation and authoritarian nature made it a place of "perverse" sexual danger where some men were subject to humiliating, "womanly" sexual submission.[22]

To enforce a draft, public perceptions of soldiering had to be modified so that it could be seen as an honorable, manly duty, rather than an emasculating punishment. The ideology of the house remained a central, though squeaky and rusted hinge that tenaciously resisted efforts to swing open the door of the private realm to universal male conscription and other "progressive" reforms.

The predominant view that a praça rank implied disgrace did not mean that all Brazilians viewed soldiering this way. Even politicians took pains to note the law-abiding soldiers who resented serving with "degenerate" inductees.[23] A variety of competing conceptions of proper manhood prevailed in different socioeconomic groups and regions. Certainly most career praças, their families, and friends had a distinct perspective. Some could claim to have risked all to defend national honor. Many likely considered themselves morally superior to wealthier civilians who used their influence to avoid service and protect their clients. Praças could identify themselves with the fashionable European ideology of the "nation in arms" that considered the military a microcosm of a nation and the vessel of masculine honor.[24] Draft advocates hoped conscription would strengthen this perception.

Still other praças defied predominant ideals of proper manhood, proudly embracing the role of social transgressor as a "manly" statement of rugged individuality. Conceptions of manhood are complex and often contradictory. While some broadly perceived conceptions of proper manly behavior exist, individuals ultimately devise and adjust their own versions in accordance with their age, experience, circumstances, local culture, and capabilities, among other factors. Whereas horsemanship was a prominent measure of manly competence for poor men in cattle country, in urban areas it had less importance. The savvy urban poor man often lampooned the humble cowboy's "boy-like" bumpkinry as did the cowboy his city cousin's "effeminate" lack of riding skills. I myself experienced this ridicule from farm laborers who dubbed me a "city boy" when I mounted a swaybacked steed in rural Pernambuco, which refused to stop grazing despite my red-faced attempts to spur it into a gallop. The stories of praças provide telling examples of the competing conceptions of manhood that shaped barroom brawls and major political and social transitions. This study follows others that move beyond all-too-often unchallenged stereotypes of Latin American machismos, themselves partly a byproduct of nationalist and regional rhetorical jousting.[25]

In the late 1800s, the quasi-mystical conception of the armed forces as an embodiment of the nation or the "nation in arms" gained ground internationally. The rhetoric of universal conscription portrayed the ideal male citizen as a soldier who would willingly lay down his life for love of country to defend national honor. It lent new romance and respectability to soldiering. Universal male conscription implied social leveling as it would draw citizens from all social classes. This concept would have been considered poppycock by the hierarchy-minded ancien régime armies that often depended heavily on foreign mercenaries and encoded racial, ethnic, and class privileges.[26] Attempts to create a strong identification between armed forces, emerging nations, and common citizens have received relatively little scholarly attention. But in the late 1800s, many believed that French and Prussian armies clearly demonstrated the effectiveness of land-based militarism for galvanizing cultural, economic, and political unity. For many leaders around the world, victory in warfare came to represent a nation's superiority. Wars invited cross-cultural comparisons and a reassessment of status among nations. This status was consistently indexed to conceptions of national honor, race, and "virility."[27]

On the surface, this work may appear to be a top-down study of a central State asserting its authority through uniform bureaucratic practices. The analysis, however, looks beyond high politics as "the" center of power; it speaks to recent scholarship that emphasizes the limits as well as the effectiveness of a State's power to implement reform. Although the term "State" is often used as shorthand, this analysis recognizes that the State is multifaceted and that policies emerge in contexts of contestation within and outside public institutions.[28] The effectiveness of army reforms and discipline, for example, were uneven and colored by local conditions. As the legacy of Domingos's "Soldier of Love" indicates, the oral culture of the poor preserved alternative visions of their civic rights and responsibilities. Power rested only in part and many times uneasily on the formal legitimacy of political majorities and on the authority that law granted officers and other officials. Popular and elite resistance to impressment and to conscription illuminates these limitations. National authorities brokered reforms through local leaders and negotiated with the public formally and informally.

By the early 1900s, the widespread adoption of European military practices altered the internal structure and composition of the armed forces and transformed the military's role in civilian society. The character, pace, and results of military reforms varied from nation to nation, but the legacy of this martial reformation has proven more durable, uniform, and ubiquitous than efforts to emulate other European institutions. The Brazilian army provides an apt case study for an analysis of the transfer of modern disciplinary techniques from an industrial European setting to a labor-intensive agro-export economy. As Brazil slowly completed a transition from slave to wage labor from 1850 to 1888, service as an army enlisted man was identified with marginality and captivity. From the Paraguayan War (1864–70), when the Brazilian government resorted to manumitting slaves and convicts to fill depleted ranks, to the mobilization of a Brazilian expeditionary force to fight alongside the Allies in Italy during World War II, a remarkable transformation took place in the common soldier's career and station. Though the proportion of active-duty soldiers remained small in comparison to Europe's, the number of army troops were significant when compared to Brazil's prison, orphanage, asylum, and poor house populations. The army's preeminent role in managing State-legitimated violence magnified further the common Brazilian soldier's importance.

As stated earlier, in its broadest strokes, this study uses army enlisted recruitment and service to analyze the changing relationships between the Brazilian State and strata of the free poor from 1864 to 1945. The stories of Domingos and other praças demonstrate the complexity of these relationships. The army's role as a "disciplining institution" make it a logical point of departure for exploring the State's role during Brazil's slow transition from a coercive to a free labor regime.

I advance several new hypotheses about the army and how its recruitment policy functioned in Brazil. First, the army was the central institution in Brazil's fledgling penal justice system in the late 1800s. Beyond inducting petty criminals and vagrants, the army conducted police work, administered civil prisons and penal colonies, and ran one of the largest national networks of orphanages for boys. The army would slowly extricate itself from its central role in the penal justice system at the turn of the century. Most studies of Brazilian policing suggest that as slavery declined (1850 to 1888) and immigration increased through the early 1900s, the State's role in disciplining the free wage-labor force increased. However, these mostly regional studies do not take into account the army's retreat from penal justice. Without impressment, many state and local officials would be forced to spend more on police, prisons, poor houses, and orphanages just to maintain the status quo with regard to social control. In many areas, it is likely that the State's overall disciplinary capacity declined during the Old Republic (1889–1930).

Second, the draft transformed enlisted military service from a punitive to a preventative institution of social reform. Instead of policing family honor by pressing wayward males, conscription aimed to win over the hearts, minds, bodies, and even the genes of the honorable poor to the eugenic, nationalist cause.

Third, it took more than changes in the army's role in penal justice and improvements in the terms and conditions of enlisted service to build the broad consensus necessary to implement conscription. Impressment reinforced models of patriarchy and manhood that proved resistant to change. Enlisted service's association with marginal social status and criminality made the honorable poor unwilling to cooperate with conscription laws. To challenge the power of traditional patriarchal practices and ideas required the emergence of new ideologies, credible international and internal threats to the Brazilian central State's sovereignty, and new political strategies, organizations, and alliances. A complicated combination of factors first inhibited and later made the draft possible, including World War I, eugenics, millenarian rebellion, labor unrest, assassinations, political lobbying, and new public relations efforts, among others.

Fourth, all of these developments were subsumed by an overall trend toward a more universal Brazilian nationalism. The ideal if not the practice of universal male conscription made it increasingly possible for Brazilians of all classes to imagine they belonged to a homogenized and leveled citizenry; such imaginings, however illusory they may seem, would allow nationalism to take stronger hold among the populace. They also weakened the ideals of traditional racial, social, and gender hierarchies without debilitating them. The citizen-soldier willing to serve and, if necessary, give his life for love of country was central to remodeling gender roles in relation to honor and patriarchy in the early 1900s in Brazil and elsewhere.

An analysis of the response of Brazilians to the institution of conscription thus has broad implications for the study of patriarchy and state building. Since the mid-1800s, conscription and attendant military reforms have been perhaps the most significant, consistent, and pervasive institutional reforms to occur within an international restructuring of gender, family, and State roles. Like military reformism, Roberto da Matta's codification of the social spaces of house and street comes from a cultural and anthropological legacy in the study of honor that spans the Atlantic and beyond. These influences make the understudied topic of Brazilian conscription particularly important for comparative history. Conscription, moreover, provides a means of moving beyond the ideologies of honor, race, and nation to consider how States implemented concrete eugenic institutional policies aimed at regenerating their countries through their masculine youth.

Fifth, this work seeks to establish impressment and conscription as distinct fields within the study of coercive and tribute labor systems. Seldom do theorists compare impressment and conscription to other coercive labor systems such as slavery, debt peonage, corvée labor, prison labor, indentured servitude, and so on. This book, to my knowledge, is the first that explicitly focuses on impressment and conscription as transatlantic tribute labor systems intricately linked to other labor practices and relations in broader society.[29]

The book is divided into three parts. The first uses a narrative approach to examine enlisted recruitment, society, and politics from colonial times to the early 1900s. The second pauses from narration employing a thematic examination of how and why coercive recruitment worked in the absence of reform from 1850 to 1916. It also considers who the soldiers were, how they lived, and the army's role as a disciplining institution. The third returns to a narrative analysis of the events that led to conscription's implementation and enforcement through 1945 when Brazil mobilized troops to fight with the Allies in Europe.

I

IMPRESSMENT,

PENAL TRANSPORTATION,

DEFENSE, AND POLITICS,

1549–1905

Chapter 1

"Nabbing Time"

The Heritage of Portugal's

Gunpowder Empire,

1549–1864

When "nabbing time" came they [Marcolino's forefathers] hid themselves in the wilderness until the impressment gangs moved on. Around here it was all wilderness. . . . Men would jump and dive under the water and then hide themselves. Later they [the government] began the lottery. I was called up twice, but I never went to serve. — Marcolino Alves, Periá-Humberto de Campos, Maranhão

The notion of the uniform had a devastating effect upon Leandro's spirit; to be a soldier was at that time — and perhaps still is today — the worst thing that could befall a *man*. He thus promised sincerely that he would change his ways and try to find a position where he would be *protected* from any police whim coming from the terrible major [Vidigal]. Nevertheless, finding a job for someone who had never given a thought to such a thing up to a certain age, and to do so right away, was not the easiest of tasks. — Manuel Antônio de Almeida, *Memoirs of a Militia Sergeant* (emphasis added)

Early modern armies performed seemingly contradictory functions by enforcing royal law while collecting, watching over, and employing males considered criminal, menacing, or, at best, unproductive. Thus, some law breakers became law enforcement agents.[1] The use of penal exiles, volunteers, and mercenaries to man Portugal's colonial army would influence the Brazilian army's development, and over the long term, an analysis of troop enlistment illustrates recruitment's connection to broader colonial and Brazilian national projects. When elderly rustic folk like Marcolino

Alves reminisced about recruitment, they referred to it as "nabbing time" (*tempo de pegação*). This expression vividly reflects how the prey of man-hunts often viewed it. When army, police, or national guard moved through the countryside or into urban shantytowns, they sometimes met with violence. More often they found that all save young boys and old men had fled before them to avoid possible impressment.[2] Others, like the protagonist Leandro in the picaresque novel *Memoirs of a Militia Sergeant*, sought out jobs that would provide them "protection" from impressment.

In Brazil's patriarchal society, status was defined by conceptions of honor, and client-patron ties protected status up and down the social scale. The inability to protect oneself from impersonal authority indicated a lack of status. The deceitful and violent tactics used to press men into the army's ranks resembled those used to capture slaves in Africa and the Americas. As many poor free men defined their manhood and honor against stereotypes of slave status and comportment, impressment evoked a powerful stigma.[3] Even today, a private's rank carries the taint of humble origins. Perceptions of praça rank would change over time, but its association with humble status is rooted in a history of impressment, which is in turn linked to Portugal's penal transportation system and the hierarchies of Brazil's multi-racial slave society.

The Soldiers of Gunpowder Empires

When Portuguese caravels disgorged the first armed force of six hundred men on Brazil's shores in 1549, it included two hundred regular soldiers and four hundred *degredados* — individuals exiled for crimes ranging from blasphemy to murder.[4] Manning colonial regiments with some of Portugal's most threatening subjects formed an integral part of the crown's colonization strategy.

Portugal readily adapted the technological innovations of sail and fire-arms to become one of the first and most successful "gunpowder empires." Technology revolutionized warfare, changed the social composition of militaries, and opened new fronts of European expansion.[5] Gunpowder heralded the tactical ascendence of plebeian infantry over noble cavalry-men. These conquest- and trade-driven empires battled to keep security ex-penditures low by minimizing opportunity costs. Whenever possible they eschewed pressing productive members of society. Instead, most or much of their manpower came from the dangerous classes: vagrants, thieves, blasphemers, foreigners, debtors, drunks, orphans, migrants, tractable "savages," incautious adventurers, and hapless passersby.[6]

Military superiority allowed Portugal to perfect techniques of coercive labor recruitment to defend and develop its imperial possessions.[7] African and Amerindian slavery was the most lucrative of Portugal's coercive migratory labor strategies, but penal exile also played an important role. Colonial armies became destinations for penal transportation systems as men were sentenced to serve terms of exile abroad as praças.

Most "honorable" Portuguese peasants and artisans regarded enlisted service with scorn, in part because the army inducted vagrants and "criminals." The crown compounded this disdain with its consistent policy of paying a praça's meager wages tardily and then only in part. Portuguese ballads warned young maids that it would be better to die than to marry a private.[8] Some men went to great lengths to escape the clutches of recruiters by mutilating themselves.[9] Even so, others volunteered to escape penury or seek adventure. Agents had their greatest success in attracting volunteers when they could oil reluctant recruits with alcohol and make good on cash bounties for enlistment. With these incentives, they signed on men who desperately needed resources or who simply could not resist the temptation of a drinking spree. The lure of riches in India during the 1500s or a gold-rush in Brazil during the 1700s inspired *reinóis* (natives of Portugal) to volunteer for colonial duty. Economic downturns, family tragedies, or demographic pressures on the land could push poor reinóis to seek security in soldiering.

Frontier colonial garrisons, like Church mission towns, were important outposts for the dissemination of Portuguese culture and political domination. Some colonies, like Angola, did not attract voluntary migrants and depended on soldier-exiles to maintain a strategic Portuguese presence.[10] The opportunities offered by a praça's career oscillated over time and varied from outpost to outpost.[11] A few of the lucky and talented climbed the ranks and became officers.

Before further discussing impressment's role in colonization, it is helpful to make a brief digression to give the reader a more general sense of Brazil's regional diversity and to illuminate how geography, climate, politics, and economic production shaped differences in regional populations over a broad sweep of time. The northeast's lush coastal plains are ideal for

PORTUGAL'S GUNPOWDER EMPIRE

sugar cane cultivation, and its coastline thrusts eastward, giving privileged access to European and African shipping lanes [see figure 1]. These features made the northeast the hub of early colonization and development. Sugar production demanded intensive labor which led the Portuguese to depend first on Indian slaving but ultimately on large numbers of imported African slaves to perform the heavy work of cultivating and processing sugar cane. From the sixteenth century forward, racial intermixing created a predominately brown population in the northeast. The region's dry mountainous interior was not appropriate for large-scale agriculture, but it was amenable to animal husbandry and small-scale crop raising. After the 1870s, however, cataclysmic droughts periodically choked the hinterlands, driving thousands of parched backlanders to the humid coast. This coincided with a steady decline in the value of Brazil's sugar exports during the nineteenth century which crippled the northeast's economy; the region's coastal economy could not employ migrants from the hinterland. This established a characteristic migration pattern that continues to this day; the exodus of northeasterners to other regions of Brazil.

The southeast had played a backseat role to the sugar-producing northeast until precious metals and stones were discovered in the mountains of Minas Gerais in the late 1600s by Indian slavers and explorers from São Paulo. To regulate better the taxing of profitable gold exports, the Portuguese moved Brazil's colonial capital from the northeast city of Salvador to Rio in 1763. By the 1800s, the mining boom had subsided, but then the expansion of coffee production began. As in the mines of Minas Gerais, large numbers of African slaves performed the arduous labor in coffee cultivation and processing. Coffee plantations rapidly spread across the region's high planes from the province of Rio de Janeiro to São Paulo and southern Minas Gerais. By 1900, coffee accounted for 50 percent of Brazil's export earnings. In the northeast, Africans, Indians, and Europeans formed a racially mixed society, but in contrast, the southeast absorbed heavy doses of mostly European immigration in the late nineteenth and early twentieth century. After the abolition of slavery in 1888, Rio de Janeiro and São Paulo's coffee frontier and urban centers absorbed waves of immigrants from Italy, Spain, Portugal, and Japan along with smaller streams of Eastern Europeans and Syrio-Lebanese. In comparison, the region's other provinces received more modest numbers of European immigrants, but on the whole, the region came to have a far larger light-skinned population than did the northeast. The southeast's growing share of national population reflected its prosperity; it was by far the most populous region by the early 1900s.

Carved out of territory long disputed with Spain, the violent border-lands of the south had only been sparsely populated in the colonial era. In the late 1800s, homesteading incentives and State subsidized transportation attracted land-hungry and unemployed European immigrants. Germans, Italians, and Poles settled in isolated immigrant colonies where most preserved their native language and traditions. Internal migration, led by northeasterners (who had no access to the land grants available to some immigrants) added to the south's demographic growth. The mountains and grasslands of this fertile, temperate region produced timber, cattle, grain, rice, and wine. Its reliance on less labor-intensive forms of production required fewer African slaves, and its population was much more European than other regions by the early twentieth century.

Two unwieldy frontier states made up the central west region that, though sparsely populated in colonial times, demonstrated slow but steady growth after Independence. The fertile wetlands of Mato Grosso are traversed by navigable rivers, but moving to the east wetlands give way to the dry mountainous high plains that dominate Goiás before dipping into the Amazon basin to the north. Cattle raising, scattered mining, and the collection of *mate* tea leaves were the region's most important economic activities. The North comprises the larger part of the Amazon River basin. Fortunately for administrators, this region is crisscrossed with navigable waterways. A boom in rubber and cocoa stimulated population growth in the North during the late 1800s. The late-developing frontier regions of the North and the Central West received comparatively limited African and direct European immigration compared to other regions. The local Indian populations contributed more visibly to the culture and racial composition of these gargantuan frontier regions. Even so, they remained sparsely populated compared to other regions. From colonial times to the present, most of Brazil's population clung to the coast. Army praças served as an integral part of frontier settlement in all regions as well as in the defense and development of coastal urban centers.

Regional differences shaped the character of recruitment which also fluctuated between peace and wartime. War altered the norms governing recruitment, exposing parts of the "protected" poor population usually shielded from it. Duing its colonial rule in Brazil (1500–1822), Portugal often experienced shortages of volunteers. When the crown required men, it issued recruitment quotas to local Portuguese officials, who, backed by royal law, sought to protect married men from recruitment. A certifiable marriage was a mark of "honorable" status that the state used to classify plebeian subjects. Even without the benefit of modern statistics, authorities knew that single young men were the main perpetrators of crime and public disturbances. Married men were responsible for protecting and supporting their wives and children. By recruiting married men, the crown could be accused of exposing married women to ill repute by removing their natural male protectors from the household.

The number of pressed men and volunteers often failed to satisfy the crown's need for troops in the colonies. To resolve this shortage, the crown tapped into Portugal's convict populations. Accordingly, Portuguese courts came to prefer sentences of temporary or permanent exile in the 1500s, although judges reserved such sentences for serious civil and religious crimes: homicide, theft, kidnapping, blasphemy, sodomy, bigamy, Judaizing, and witchcraft. Portugal initiated penal exile or transportation systems to settle sparsely populated colonies, a practice France, England, Spain, and others would later imitate.[12]

Sentences of banishment reveal the importance attached to place in early modern Portugal. The ties of family, patronage, and status were often anchored in one's locality. Exile deprived an offender of the local social bonds developed over a lifetime or even generations. The importance of the hearth served as an obstacle to periodic imperial demands for a more mobile population, and sentences of penal exile proved an effective means of countering the ties of home. This is not to say that populations were not geographically mobile and that voluntary mobility did not offer advantages to the poor who were willing to take risks. Crown officials also worked to keep honorable subjects in place to facilitate order, production, and tax collection.

The crown relied heavily on sentences of penal exile as a frugal remedy to the court's mounting problems with crime at home. According to their crimes and the crown's needs, judges sentenced exiles to specific destinations. Circular letters from the crown instructed district officials weeks before the biannual fleet embarkation for India to "not only arrest such persons as live to the prejudice and scandal of the common weal by com-

mitting crimes, but also those who live in idleness." Timothy Coates estimates that from 1550 to 1720 Tribunals of Inquisition and royal courts
deported more than seventeen thousand degredados from Portugal to
Asia, Africa, and Brazil.[13]

Judges often specified that male offenders serve sentences of exile in
colonial battalions. Exiles without specific instructions could legally work
where they liked and move about freely within the designated jurisdiction.
Royal decrees show that in practice these rights were not always respected.
A 1692 royal missive informed the Viceroy of India that degregados who
had completed their sentence of exile should be denied passage home
"only when there is a need for more soldiers there."[14] Royal defense took
priority over juridical principles. Since a scarcity of labor characterized the
colonies, colonial officers could not make rigid distinctions between volunteers and exiles in the ranks. Criminals and volunteers were lumped
together, tainting all with the stigma of criminal exile.[15]

The association of criminal punishment and recruitment was in no way
unique to the Portuguese army. The most renowned eighteenth-century
military strategist, Frederick II of Prussia, preferred to dragoon the up-
rooted and refractory elements of society or to hire foreign mercenaries.
The shrewd "Sergeant-King" observed that the secret to managing such an
armed force was to ensure that soldiers feared their officers more than their
enemy.[16] While all ancien régime armies incorporated "criminals," what
may have distinguished Portugal from its European rivals was its willingness to press serious offenders, and its reluctance to use capital punishment. Portuguese courts sentenced some of the kingdom's most heinous
offenders to colonial army service, including some convicted of homicide.
The Spanish, French, and English applied capital punishment more liberally. Perhaps Portugal's relatively small population prompted it to utilize
even hardened felons as colonial soldiers and settlers.[17]

To help ensure that these volatile elements did not turn their arms on the
crown, the officer corps remained, in theory, a nobleman's preserve.[18]
European monarchs employed foreign mercenaries as an additional
hedge. Freebooters brought needed professionalism, and countervailed
the potential threat posed by arming the local dregs of society. Officials
often viewed mercenaries as more reliable troops for quelling internal
insurgency because, unlike native soldiers, they had few links to local
populations. If payment or other obligations were not fulfilled, however,

mercenaries could become riotous enemies. Soldiers of fortune held an uneasy check on the soldiers of misfortune and vice versa.

Portugal's relative geographic isolation and the far-flung character of its colonization favored the development of a navy, whereas the numerous conflicts between armies in the Continental heartland made northern Europe the natural laboratory for innovations in land-based warfare. A major reform of Portuguese land forces came in 1762 when Portugal entered the Seven Years' War (1756–63) allied with England and Prussia. Frederick the Great commissioned Count Wilhelm de Shaumbourg-Lippe to organize the Portuguese army and its operations against Spain. The count provided the Portuguese army with its first unified penal code in 1763. Eleven of the twenty-nine articles prescribed capital punishment for aggravated crimes ranging from wartime desertion to mutiny. Lesser offenses incurred floggings with the flat of a sword.[19] With modifications these draconian laws formed the basis of the Brazilian army's criminal code until 1899. One Brazilian cadet in the 1860s likened the articles to "twenty-nine swords of Damocles" suspended above every soldier's head.[20]

The penalties established by Count de Lippe were refined by the royal ordinances of 9 April 1805 to better coordinate Portuguese military justice with the penal transportation system. For instance, the prescribed sentence for third-time deserters included a minimum six-year exile in Portuguese India or Africa, and consequent loss of credit for time served.[21]

Estimating the number of penal exiles that Brazil received and determining how many of them served as soldiers requires further investigation. Likewise, there are no estimates of the volunteers, pressed men, and exiles in regular Portuguese army forces sent to Brazil. The proportion of each undoubtedly varied from garrison to garrison and over time.[22]

 Brazil's colonial army can best be understood as a collection of regional army battalions rather than an over-arching institution. With the exception of the Debatable Lands (territory disputed between Portugal and Spain in southern Brazil), colonial authorities coordinated their captaincy's (administrative districts) regiments with ample autonomy. Little rotation of men or officers occurred among the captaincies.[23] Ideally, regular battalions were to be replenished by remissions of Portuguese replacements. The royal government viewed reinóis as more reliable agents of royal policy because they supposedly identified with the crown's interests over local agendas. Despite administrative prejudice, however, Brazilian

battalions supplemented their ranks with local recruitment because Portugal did not supply enough troops.

When the 1700s gold rush began in Minas Gerais, the crown tightened immigration restrictions to Brazil. Part of this effort included a 1722 royal decree prohibiting the dispatch of exiles to Brazil. This temporarily cut off a source of army manpower, especially for the frontier outposts of Maranhão and Sacramento.[24] The viceroys of Rio de Janeiro, however, continued to transfer malefactors to frontier garrison towns and it is likely that others followed suit.[25] Despite the official bans, exiles from abroad continued to wash up on Brazil's shores. Indeed, the commander of Britain's first penal colonizing mission to Australia, Arthur Phillip, gained his first experience with convict transportation by delivering exiles from Portugal to Brazil in 1774.[26]

After Brazil's Independence (1822), the officer ranks included Portuguese- and Brazilian-born men, the latter outnumbering the former. The highest ranking officers normally began their careers as cadets, a status awarded to those who could prove they were the sons of army officers or nobility. Most officers, however, rose from the NCO ranks. Thus, the army allowed men of humble backgrounds a degree of social mobility in colonial and early imperial Brazil.[27]

Army recruitment in Brazil adopted the Portuguese practice of using the barracks as a penal dumping ground. Viceroys voiced strange amazement that Brazilians evinced an "inexplicable repugnance" for army enlisted service and frustration with the difficulties of raising men.[28] In Brazil, impressment was impeded and desertion facilitated by the vast wilderness that surrounded cities and plantations. The common expression "God is great but the wilderness is greater" (*Deus é grande mas o mato é maior*) captures well the popular wisdom of poor Brazilians who fled to the forests to avoid army service.

In some respects, however, Brazilian recruitment was distinct from the standard practices of the Portuguese military. In the late 1700s and early 1800s, authorities barred all slaves and free blacks from serving as praças while allowing free mulattos like Domingos Caldas Barbosa to serve. Similarly, before 1831 Brazil's militia units segregated soldiers into black, mulatto, and white battalions.[29] But these restrictions were scrapped after the first decade of Independence, although in some regions restrictions against the African-born continued.[30] Thus, the army's lower ranks integrated whites with free people of African and Indian ancestry, but most praças were of mixed race. A loosely organized third-line of defense, the *ordenanças,* incorporated all free males of military age who did not serve in the army, navy, or militia.

At times, regular Portuguese and irregular Brazilian forces fused into a single fighting force.[31] A prime example occurred when the crown augmented its forces in southern Brazil to counter Spanish encroachment on its borderlands during the Seven Years' War. As Count de Lippe reorganized the Portuguese army in Europe, the crown called up colonial forces to Brazil's far south. The crown ordered captaincies from Rio de Janeiro southward to mobilize troops. Only about one-third of the 6,368 soldiers fielded were Portuguese. Two of five Brazilians mobilized came from the then relatively poor captaincy of São Paulo.[32] While recruitment in São Paulo began with appeals to loyalty and promises of pay, pensions, and uniforms, few volunteered. Authorities soon turned to pressing São Paulo's sparse population of some 80,000 free inhabitants. The captaincy's Portuguese-born governor drew up recruitment lists based on ordenança rolls. When the coastal São Paulo town of Ubatuba did not produce the required recruits, the governor demanded that officials levy the entire population of able-bodied adult males, bachelors and married men alike. Obviously the rules that normally governed impressment by protecting married men were violated. *Paulistas* took to the hills. Crown officials denigrated recruitment fugitives as "aquilombados" (residents of runaway slave communities) equating the status of poor free men with unruly slaves. When threats failed, officials arrived with royal permission to imprison families, burn homes, and confiscate fugitives' property. Bounty hunters who captured fugitives were to be reimbursed with their captive's property. Meanwhile, the captaincy's few convicts were mustered into the ranks.[33]

The mobilization did not limit itself to men. The crown specifically sought to enlist women to settle in Iguatemi, a new Portuguese army colony founded near Brazil's modern day border with Paraguay. São Paulo's governor called on municipalities to recruit women of questionable reputation still able to bear children. Officials hoped women in Iguatemi would stem desertion and stimulate population growth. However, disease and enemy attack eventually drove these unwilling settlers from the insalubrious site.[34]

The Portuguese crown continued to employ similar methods in Brazil, if on a smaller scale, to secure its vast unsettled borderlands and strategically redistribute population. The members of the Portuguese Court, however, soon found themselves the victims of exile during the Napoleonic invasion of Iberia. With support from their ally Britain, the court relocated to Rio in 1808 and opened Brazil's ports to free trade. Only fourteen years later, Prince Pedro I would declare Brazil's Independence from Portugal and usurp his father King Dom João VI's most important colonial possession. João had returned to Portugal in 1821 to attempt to settle disputes with a Portuguese Parliament that hoped to reassert mercantilist control over colonial commerce in Brazil. In the intervening years, Brazil had become a major trading partner with Britain, and the British supported and quickly recognized the new Independent Brazilian nation to secure access to this vital market for English merchants. Pockets of loyalist military resistance in Bahia and Piauí would be quickly quelled. Brazilians won their independence without the need for large scale troop mobilizations that might have destabilized the plantation and slavery systems, unlike the Spanish American Wars of Independence that armed significant numbers of nonwhite soldiers and saw the emergence of large numbers of nonwhite officers, even generals.[35]

The Brazilian Imperial Army

The army established by Brazil's first monarch, Pedro I, resembled its mother institution. Pedro, who took interest in military matters, molded his officer corps to foster an aristocratic society. The emperor engendered loyalty through patronage and promotions; similarly, he punished disloyalty by withholding patronage.[36] Promotions to senior officer ranks continued to be heavily influenced by ascribed rather than achieved status. Geographic origin, wealth, and familial connections often counted more than professional abilities, experience, and education. Rivalries within and over the army illuminate the importance that recruitment, officer advancement, and nativism played in the fledgling empire.

Many Portuguese-born officers garrisoned in Brazil supported Pedro and continued to hold high ranks in Brazil's new army.[37] Brazilian-born officers resented what they perceived as the emperor's favoritism toward Portuguese officers and bureaucrats. Pedro also created elite honor guards in key provinces composed of men from privileged social stations. These honor guards could hardly be described as regular forces because they were required to muster only four times a year, but their creation underscored the low esteem of service in regular battalions.

Recognition as a cadet continued to be a fast track to the Brazilian army's upper echelons. In 1820, King Dom João VI extended eligibility for cadet status to the sons of civil servants and commissioned militia officers. In practice, even these requirements were relaxed as the century progressed. By the mid-1800s, most officers came from Brazil's middle sectors rather than families of the landed elite.[38] A few select officers received professional training as engineers at the national military academy first established in 1810. For those lacking a technical education, the cadet career was an apprenticeship of arms. Cadets technically held a praça rank until receiving a commission, but cadet status augmented their pay and protected them from the humiliation of corporal punishment.

The new emperor feared his father's restoration, even though most soldiers and officers supported Independence. Independence did not improve the popularity of army service or alter its character, rather, it may have detracted from the army's public image. One senator recalled that in Minas Gerais in 1824, "Militia men, who had been called up to celebrate the feast of the Body of Christ came from Mariana and other points to Ouro Preto, were after the procession . . . marched to Rio. This administrative action contributed much to making military life even more hated because . . . [it] had been an act of betrayal to call up militia men for a procession and afterwards . . . pressing them for army service."[39] These underhanded means of recruiting men normally "protected" from impressment led some contemporaries to compare praças to slaves.[40] Adding insult to injury, Eurocentric prejudice and recruitment difficulties led Pedro to recruit northern European mercenaries. He imported German and Irish mercenaries for his campaign to wrest the Debatable Lands from Argentina. His detractors described the mercenaries as the foreign henchmen of an emperor with absolutist pretensions.[41] Though some Portuguese-born had remained in the army's enlisted ranks, foreign consuls shielded their immigrant citizens from impressment, even gaining the release of some contracted abroad as mercenaries.[42]

The 1824 Constitution had altered the authorities responsible for recruitment by creating the elected post of justice of the peace. Justices also enjoyed the power to supervise labor contracts. While the Constitution enumerated free Brazilians' rights, in practice, impressment curtailed them. An 1822 imperial decree emphasized that impressment should target those who lived in "criminal idleness." Like ancien régime armies, the State tried to stop impressment from disrupting "productive" free laborers by targeting the unprotected poor. The law exempted married men, only sons, seamen, merchants, students, and the overseers of plantations and cattle ranches. As long as cowboys, carpenters, government employees, commercial employees, tailors, and fishermen actively plied their trades and demonstrated good behavior, they also enjoyed immunity from impressment.[43] Because they were the valued property of the wealthy, slaves were exempted, but in some dire emergencies, officials armed bondsmen on a limited scale.[44]

When locally elected justices of the peace assumed office in 1828, they took charge of recruitment, formerly the prerogative of the now defunct colonial post of captain major.[45] Powerful planters or their surrogates typically won election as justices, bolstering the power of the propertied members of society, although competition to control this new office created a new source of conflict between rival landowners. Nonetheless, by controlling justices, local potentates enhanced their control over the free poor.[46]

Those left subject to impressment included mostly under- and unemployed unskilled laborers. Once dragooned, the onus of proving one's exemption was on the recruit. Inductees remained confined in recruit depositories or local jails until proven exempt. They had to hope that patrons or relatives had the money and contacts to register an official petition with the provincial governor verifying an exemption. Many managed to obtain their discharge through tedious official channels, but others did not. To justify their actions, police often stated that pressed men had transgressed community values. An 1847 letter from a police delegate in the small coastal town of Barra Mansa, Rio de Janeiro was typical: "I am sending 4 recruits. . . . [Even though some are married men] they do not provide their wives any protection and wander like vagrants through this municipality without seeking any employment. Furthermore they create disorders and steal livestock. Thus, I thought it convenient to press them for army service."[47]

Those common Brazilians who supported losing factions in local revolts also faced impressment to the army. This likely fate made many plebeian rebels more reluctant to lay down their arms than their leaders.[48] Unlike Portuguese courts, those in Brazil refrained from remitting felons convicted of serious crimes, such as homicide, for peacetime army service. If apprehended, these offenders would likely face trial and prison sentences. Some victims of press gangs, however, were held in docked ships at night and used to perform public works during the day.[49]

Brazil's war with Argentina over the Debatable Lands (1825–28) revealed the contradictions of military mobilization in an independent slaveholding society. Slaveowning interests opposed the costly war over territory that had little in common with the rest of Brazil. Brazil's Cisplatine province, modern-day Uruguay, had few slaves and mostly Spanish- or Guarani-speaking residents; its soil was better suited to ranching than plantation agriculture. These economic and social differences, combined with the region's republican sentiments, led most Brazilian slavocrats to favor peaceful succession of the Cisplatine province when the Spanish-speaking majority opted to join the Argentine confederation.

When Pedro declared war on Argentina in 1825, plantation owners attempted to obstruct recruitment through Parliament, but even so, many men were pressed. The army mushroomed from a force of 6,000 to more than 20,000 between 1824 and 1827. Pedro sidestepped legislators by borrowing funds from Brazil's newly formed national bank and employing foreign mercenaries. The poor showing of Brazil's army in the campaign besmirched its reputation, and Pedro's stubbornness in conducting it cost him political support. Meanwhile, popular resentment toward foreign mercenaries grew in the capital. Rio's residents badgered foreign soldiers, and in turn the mercenaries' bullying and drunken brawling resulted in riots in July 1828. Brazilian troops eventually restored order, and Parliament forced Pedro to disband his mercenaries.[50] By then, Pedro had little choice but to accept British mediation with Argentina, which resulted in the creation of Uruguay as a buffer state. Despite peace, the army's forces grew to 33,276 by 1829.[51]

Pedro's preference for foreign mercenaries and the perception that he privileged Portuguese-born officers earned him the ire of many Brazilian officers and praças. Turning their backs on the emperor, most Brazilian-born officers and troops supported Parliament's initiatives. Meanwhile, the capital was amok with street fighting between nativists and a burgeoning Portuguese community. To escape the repressive reign of Dom Miguel in Lisbon, hundreds of Portuguese fled to Rio in the late 1820s. Brazilian republican radicals such as Antônio Borges da Fonseca ardently criticized Pedro. Borges fanned the flames of Lusophobia in Rio with his republican newspaper and led nativist gangs in attacks on the Portuguese quarter, deriving support from Brazilian-born enlisted men in Rio's garrisons. Street fighting between nativist and Portuguese gangs peaked in March 1831.[52]

As parliamentary leaders called for more stringent measures to contain the violence, Pedro sought a showdown with the legislature. He rearranged his Council of State (the monarch's council of advisors) without Parliament's approval. Many soldiers joined outraged civilians in Rio's streets to protest the emperor's defiance of Parliament. Lacking the necessary popular and military support to defend his position, Pedro I abdicated his throne in favor of his five-year-old son on April 7, 1831. To quell the revolutionary hopes of republican radicals, legislators quickly recognized Pedro II as emperor and organized a parliamentary regency to rule in the boy's stead.

In July 1831, republican radicals staged a riotous protest in the capital intended to topple the regency government. Many army praças took to the streets to support the republican cause, but most of their officers remained royalist. Even though the republican putsch failed, it demonstrated the threat that inducting the unprotected poor into the army could pose to the propertied classes who by and large favored monarchy.[53]

The seditious activities of praças, most of whom came from racially mixed backgrounds, frightened the privileged, whether affiliated with the emerging Conservative or Liberal parties. The regency found substantial parliamentary support for its proposals to restructure military institutions. To reduce the army's power, the Liberal politicians (they referred to themselves as "moderates" in the 1800s) who dominated the new regency halved the army's active duty forces to 14,342 men. Parliament dismissed troops involved in uprisings, eliminated many regular units, and transferred others to frontier redoubts. By May 1832, most regular troops had vanished from Rio. By 1835, the war minister reported that the army had only 4,642 praças. Parliament also abrogated the colonial civil militia organized by racial and occupational categories. As a new counterweight to the imperial army's power, the Liberals instituted a National Guard. Ironically, the regency sought to preserve monarchy with a quintessentially republican institution.[54]

Individuals who satisfied restrictive property requirements could be elected national guard officers. Those who satisfied the relatively modest requirement of 200$000 *milréis* annual income were eligible for guard service. Parliament intended these policies to "whiten" the militia to insure that men of property were armed and prepared to suppress insurrection by the darker-skinned majority (free and slave).[55] Political bosses avidly sought commissions as guard officers to nominate their free clients to guard posts, protecting them from military recruitment.[56] Guard officers, who in most instances were influential landowners, sometimes falsely vouched for their clients' claims to incomes of 200$000 milréis (approximately forty U.S. dollars in the 1830s), bypassing property requirements. This alleged income made the client eligible to vote, giving patrons additional political leverage. This arrangement formed the cornerstone of the *coronel* (colonel) system, so termed because of the guard rank commonly held by political bosses. It became the basic unit of political organization in imperial Brazil. In *coronelismo,* a political boss was granted virtual carte blanche over local affairs as long as he produced a large majority of votes from his district for the dominant provincial party. Because there was no secret vote, *coronéis* could threaten to press men who bucked their authority. Under Pedro II's rule (1840–89), coronéis were in turn held in check by the tendency to centralize political power in Rio, and the political system tended to support status quo in the military.[57] Most coronéis feared that a strong army would impinge on their autonomy; therefore they opposed meaningful army reform.

The military reforms of the 1830s, however, fueled regional tensions. Two decades of insurrection ensued after Pedro I's abdication and the Regency's far-reaching military reorganization: the Cabanos War in Pernambuco (1832–35), the Cabanagem in Pará (1835–40), the Sabinada in Bahia (1837–38), the Balaiada in Maranhão (1838–41), the Farroupilha in Rio Grande do Sul (1835–45), and the Praieira Revolution in Pernambuco (1848–49). The character of these revolts varied, but the luxury of hindsight indicates that they eventually unleashed a challenge by disenfranchised groups to the nation-building project of slavocratic interests. While inter-elite disputes often precipitated the outbreak of revolts, these movements ultimately served to mobilize disadvantaged groups: slaves, Indians, and free poor men of all races.[58]

Difficulties in mobilizing troops to quell regional rebellion elicited a series of efforts to adjust the 1822 recruitment law. In August 1837, Parliament passed legislation that permitted inductees to provide substitutes and allowed the wealthy to pay 400$000 milréis (approximately eight U.S. dollars in the 1830s) for exemptions. To make mobilization more efficient, Parliament farmed out recruitment to authorized agents who worked in tandem with civil authorities. At first, only army officers could become contracted agents paid 4$000 milréis per recruit. Parliament passed subsequent adjustments to this measure in 1841, 1848, and 1852, but none substantially altered the system.[59]

By 1837, popular challenges to the regency prompted the government's Liberal leader, Padre Diogo Antonio Feijó, to resign, which spurred a conservative reaction. Retrenchment on federalist policies had already begun under Liberal rule, but the new Conservative regent, Pedro de Araújo Lima, accelerated the pace of centralization. Part of this effort involved limiting local control over recruitment and the National Guard. During the 1830s, many northeastern provinces created the post of municipal prefect to check the power of justices of the peace. Parliament selected governors from an elected short-list, and in turn governors nominated prefects. In many cases, governors awarded recruitment prerogatives to prefects, undermining the justices' authority.[60] By the early 1840s, every province passed laws making guard officer ranks appointed rather than elected offices. Cuts in army personnel and the dissolution of colonial militia units alienated many men with military skills, who were subsequently prone to foment insurgency in part as a bid to regain lost status.[61]

Parliament relied on its weakened imperial army to stifle rebellion. The small army had to depend on support from local opponents of rebellious factions. Even so, some army personnel fought against factions supported by the imperial government. This indicates the strong regional and provincial identity of many officers and troops who placed their ideological, regional, or factional loyalties above their allegiance to Rio's high command. Both rebels and loyalists relied on a mix of impressment, voluntarism, and venality to augment their forces.[62] The army, however, had the added edge of pressing extra troops from areas undisturbed by revolt.

Maranhão's Balaiada Rebellion exhibits the links between impressment and insurrection. In 1838, the Liberal party, which had controlled Maranhão's politics since 1822, was defeated in fraudulent elections called by the new Conservative Parliament in Rio. Winning control of Maranhão's legislature, Conservatives promulgated the post of prefect and nominated their cadres to the post in towns across the province. They stripped jurisdiction over recruitment from justices of the peace and awarded it to prefects. They also followed Pernambuco's lead by appointing rather than electing National Guard officers. These acts soon ignited a major conflict. On December 13, 1838, cowhand Raimundo Gomes Vieira raided the prison in the Vila da Manga with nine co-conspirators. They freed Raimundo's brother and others pressed as army recruits. Raimundo then convinced the local national guard troops to join the uprising. Rebel demands included due process according to the Constitution, expulsion of Portuguese-born citizens, the elimination of prefects, and amnesty for rebel forces. The first of these demands sought to curb impressment abuses. This revolt shows how partisan politics and the need to raise troops to suppress revolts could generate new insurgencies.[63]

The rebellion was eventually quelled by the so-called Great Peacemaker, Luis Alves de Lima e Silva, later to become the Marshal Duke de Caxias, the army's patron hero. Caxias (1803–80) represented well the army's old school. After receiving a cadet's rank while still a boy, he moved up quickly through the ranks by putting down regional rebellions in Maranhão, São Paulo, Minas Gerais, and Rio Grande do Sul. His achievements earned him titles of nobility and later a successful career as a Conservative senator who served as war minister and president of the emperor's Council of Ministers.

Caxias's feats were celebrated with equestrian statues, and writers secured his place as a patriotic hero in Brazil's official history, but the poor of Maranhão and other provinces preserved different memories of war and "nabbing time." Matthias Röhrig Assunção's oral history subjects illuminate how the popular memory of nabbing time in the 1800s has survived up to the present.[64] When major conflicts flared up, press gangs often targeted individuals like Marcolino Alves (cited at the head of this chapter). Inhabitants of isolated areas often lacked adequate protection. Maria Alves da Silva recalled her grandparents' stories of impressment during the Balaiada rebellion. She recounted how a poor household with three young men, one of whom held a National Guard post, negotiated with recruiters. When the agents arrived, they ordered the guardsman to work without wages for a landowner, and in return, none of the other lads would be pressed. Another interviewee explained that in his grandparents' time, free workers found sanctuary by grabbing hold of the wall that surrounded the house of a local landowner. According to the informant, the press gang did not dare touch those near the house because they respected the landowner.[65] Clearly, impressment reinforced the free poor's dependency on local notables, making some into literal hangers-on. Thus, impressment affected far more poor men than were actually forced into service.

Those who were adequately protected from peacetime impressment associated nabbing with wartime mobilization. One listed the campaigns that brought press gangs to his community: the Balaiada Rebellion (1838–41), the Paraguayan War (1864–70), and the Canudos Rebellion (1895–97).[66] Impressment periodically kept many rustics on the run, such as one interviewee's grandfather who was nicknamed "*cutia*" (a nimble cat-sized rodent with no tail) because the press gangs could never catch him. As imperial forces quelled regional challenges to the monarchy in the 1840s, Parliament tried to curb impressment abuses that could spark disputes. In 1846, it passed a law prohibiting impressment one month before and two months following an election to check electorally inspired dragooning.

As the regional rebellions subsided, lawmakers reorganized the army and the National Guard in 1850. Federalist policies had allowed provincial politicians to appoint or sack guard officers according to political rather than professional criteria, demoralizing its hierarchy.[67] Under the 1850 reform, appointments and dismissals of guard officers would require the imperial justice minister's approval. In addition, the guard's new charter no longer protected its members from imperial military service.

Authorities had long complained that even vagrants managed to obtain guard posts, thus undermining impressment. In 1844, Rio de Janeiro's police chief complained that "to get one recruit it was necessary to arrest 44 individuals [including] foreigners, married men, national guardsmen, artisans, and widowers with children."[68] In 1859, the army attempted to tap National Guardsmen for peacetime regular army service, but the guard's superior commander protested, "This measure while legal should only be implemented in cases of dire emergency. . . . there exists in this great country a great number of 'recruitable' men (*recrutáveis*) who, without demoralizing the National Guard or disrupting agriculture . . . should be recruited because they are vagrants. . . . When recruitment begins in any location there soon appears a great number of workers, everyone wants to become employed."[69] Efforts to incorporate guardsmen in regular peacetime army forces were abandoned.[70] Reforms did succeed, however, in diluting the guard's federalist character.

The 1850 army reform instituted seniority requirements for the promotion of officers. To earn cadet status one had to be eighteen years old, literate, and serve as a praça for two years, unless one had two years of education in a military prep school. One well-educated volunteer, whose cadet status was not recognized right away in 1860, described his foreboding when he and other praças were read the army's law code: "I listened, a little bit frightened, to . . . de Lippe's terrible articles of war, that pitiful list of firing squads and life imprisonment in shackles, but quickly I dispelled this impression with the conviction that I would survive and that all of these dark and draconian dispositions were not intended for me, but for those who had to be my subordinates, if not in rank, then at least in intelligence and instruction."[71] New rules required two years of service as a praça for military academy aspirants, and status-conscious potential cadets disliked being subject to the orders of NCOs of humble origins until they were recognized as cadets.[72] Lingering beliefs in "natural" social and racial hierarchies made it hard for mostly white officers to imagine themselves part of a leveled populace where men could expect equal treatment, at least according to army rank.

Other reforms enhanced officer education. Promotion became more strongly tied to education, talent, seniority, and service. Officers were routinely rotated to different regions to prevent the establishment of strong ties to local interests. By adhering more rigidly to a merit system, these reforms sought to stabilize the institution, making it less vulnerable to dissension and political intrigue. Officers became more dependent on their connections and performance *within* the army, making the career less attractive to elites. The high costs and limited enrollments of law and medical schools made military academy training an attractive free alternative sought out mostly by the sons of middle-income groups. Favoritism and corruption continued, but the 1850 reforms limited common abuses.[73]

In 1850, Brazil also began to enforce laws that prohibited the international slave trade. This promised the slow demise of slave labor because of the bonded population's low birth rates and Brazil's high manumission rates. For the time being, debates over abolition quieted down as the agroexport sector cast about to manage slavery's decline.

Reforms had little impact on the success of internal army recruitment, but the imperial military proved quite flexible in their efforts to secure manpower. In one instance, a Brazilian naval vessel in Liverpool recruited 20 Irish minors in October 1851, paying their guardians one pound, 16 shillings per head.[74] While such practices were piecemeal, they reflected the military's continuing recruitment difficulties, and the unshaken belief of many that Brazilians were not reliable or particularly good sailors or soldiers. The imperial government's skittishness about pressing large numbers of Brazilians and the belief in the superiority of northern European soldiers was confirmed by the mobilization for Brazil's war against Argentina's Juan Manuel de Rosas in 1851–52. Pedro II turned to Prussia for mercenaries for this campaign. Fortunately for Brazil, Rosas's support quickly evaporated, and Pedro was spared the necessity of sustaining a lengthy campaign with impressment.[75]

Embarrassed and frustrated by the abusive and unreliable methods used to man the ranks, one officer editorialized in 1854, "Every recruitment system that is not based on conscription establishes distinctions that all governments should carefully avoid because no one willingly subjects themselves to the tribute of blood [recruitment], in most cases spilled to protect the rich and powerful, precisely those who do not pay this tax. Among us, recruitment falls on the shoulders of the poor, christened with the epithet of vagrant. . . . Everybody knows that our soldiers only obtain their discharge after 19 to 20 years of service."[76] Praças' difficulties in obtaining timely discharges discouraged volunteers and it pushed some veterans who had legal rights to an honorable discharge to reenlist for the purpose of obtaining a reengagement bonus. The low status of soldiering allowed officials to ignore the legal rights of praças. For reformers, conscription seemed the only viable remedy for these ills that demoralized praça ranks. The lack of insurrection and foreign threats from the mid-1850s to the early 1860s put army mobilization problems on a political back burner. It took the Paraguayan War to revive these debates.

The history and norms of military recruitment in Brazil before the Paraguayan War illustrates the ways in which the process was linked to politics, patron-client relations, free-labor discipline, and conceptions of honor and order. Government decrees did not meaningfully alter the status of enlisted service or its relationship to patriarchal privilege, and the State reluctantly relied on coercive means to fill the ranks and to defend both family and national honor.

Chapter 2

Raising the "Pagan Rabble"

Wartime Impressment and the
Crisis of Traditional Recruitment,
1864–1870

Although conscription had been debated in Parliament before the Paraguayan War, it had never become law. For decades, the army's cadres defended the monarchy (in most instances) from internal and external threats. The mobilization required by the Paraguayan War, however, overtaxed the traditional recruitment system. To fill the ranks, the State adopted some modern methods but ultimately relied heavily on impressment. The scale of mobilization led authorities to violate the norms that previously limited it to the "unprotected." The wartime intrusion of public authority into private domains had never been as pervasive or sustained; it upset the balance of power between the realms of the house and the street. While this exertion of public authority was filtered through traditional channels of patronage, wartime mobilization eroded the ability of many patrons to protect themselves and their clients from State power. The conflicts over wartime impressment would move Parliament to pass recruitment reform after the war.

The Paraguayan War and Brazil's Mobilization 1864–1870

The Paraguayan War was the largest military conflict in South American history. Brazil mobilized more than four times as many troops as it had in any previous campaign, deploying some 110,000 men. This represented only 1.5 percent of Brazil's some nine million inhabitants; nevertheless the mobilization placed an incredible strain on social and political relations across the country.

Multilateral manipulation of Uruguay's internal politics sparked the conflict. Local opposition factions supported by Brazil and Argentina forced Paraguay's political allies in Uruguay from power in 1864. In retaliation, President Francisco Solano López of Paraguay launched raids on Brazil. The Triple Alliance (Brazil, Argentina, and Uruguay) then joined forces against Paraguay. The Brazilian army, however, bore the brunt of the campaign because instability in Uruguay and Argentina limited these governments' abilities to deploy men.[1]

Pedro II called on Brazil's free citizenry to volunteer to defend their national honor. In portraits, the emperor traded civilian garb for uniforms, and was styled the nation's "number one volunteer." Some willingly followed Pedro's example, but their numbers were too few.[2] The State soon had to convoke National Guardsmen and conduct large scale dragooning sweeps to fill the ranks. The inability to mobilize rapidly helped to turn what had been foreseen as a brief conflict into a five-year ordeal, twice as long as any of Brazil's other international campaigns. The Paraguayan front's often uncharted distances complicated deployment and supply. The lack of trained personnel, medicine, transportation, provisions, munitions, and wilderness skills plagued the war effort.

Despite Brazil's vastly larger population and greater wealth, the military lacked the railroads, munitions works, capital, and available manpower to respond quickly to the aggressions of tiny Paraguay.[3] The inept campaign made Brazilian officers keenly aware of their ill-preparedness. Mobilization difficulties made recruitment reform a paramount issue for many officers.

The army's mobilization categories in the table below require a succinct explanation. When the call to arms failed to attract enough volunteers, the government created special battalions, *Voluntários da Pátria* (Volunteers of the Fatherland; henceforth, Voluntários) in January 1865. This special corps offered higher pay and better enlistment and discharge bonuses. It also guaranteed an honorary discharge and a land grant at the end of hostilities with special pensions for disabled veterans and the dependents of fallen soldiers.[4] By creating a separate corps with special privileges and status, the government recognized and confirmed popular disdain for regular service. The Voluntários constituted the largest single category of forces, more than two out of five troops.[5] Their benefits borrowed from European and North American enlistment strategies. The promise of land

Amostra dos ultimos defensores da Patria que foram agarrados, enfardados, e euviados para o theatro da guerra, para defenderem ali a honra nacional!!!
Estamos aceados!!!

2. "Observe the latest defenders of the fatherland that were nabbed, put in uniform, and sent to the theater of war to defend there our national honor!!! We are elegant!!!" Confirming the low opinion of the reading public for regular soldiers, this cartoon points out the irony of sending men visibly without honor to defend Brazil's national honor. From *O Cabrião*, May 26, 1866, 77. *Courtesy of the Biblioteca Nacional, Rare Works Division. Photo by Gilson Ribeiro.*

grants to veterans constituted the first large-scale government promise to distribute land to native Brazilians of humble origins.

Two weeks after creating the Voluntários, the imperial ministry called up nearly 15,000 National Guardsmen. Initially, the government designated guardsmen to serve one year in imperial forces; however, when expectations for a brief campaign evaporated, most were retained until war's end. To encourage cooperation, the government extended the Voluntários' privileges to those guardsmen called into service. Even though many guardsmen failed to report for duty, the war secretary recorded the mobilization of 31,198 guardsmen to Paraguay.[6] By contrast, only 17,465 regular soldiers were recorded at the front. Regulars did not enjoy the more generous benefits promised to Voluntários; they were a disadvantaged minority at the front.[7] Furthermore, the service contracts of regular army volunteers required six years of service, and those recruited involuntarily faced a nine-year stint.

In November 1866, as reinforcement efforts languished, Pedro II or-

Table 1. Classification of Soldiers on the Paraguayan Front by Region

Regions	Voluntários da Pátria	National Guard	Volunteers & Recruits	Substitutes	Libertos	Total	%
NE	19,469	14,891	8,564	88	985	43,997	48.2
SE	13,335	7,344	7,028	606	2,555	30,868	33.8
S	1,909	4,947	689	100	397	8,042	8.8
CW	1,417	2,267	156	0	0	3,840	4.2
N	1,708	1,749	1,028	0	66	4,551	5.0
Total	37,838	31,198	17,465	794	4,003	91,298	100
%	41.4	34.2	19.1	0.9	4.4	100	

Source: Figures derived from RRMGu (1872), annexos.

dered the manumission of government-owned slaves willing to serve as soldiers. He urged masters and religious orders to manumit slaves for army service, and liberated funds to buy slaves at market prices. While some slaves chose to serve, many were sold or donated against their will. Venal masters took advantage of the opportunity to sell their most intractable bondsmen. In April 1867, owners in Rio enlisted 96 slaves: 28 were donated and the State purchased 68. One owner's name stood out because he patriotically donated ten slaves.[8] A Rio newspaper lampooned such "patriotism" by depicting a master with African features himself donating two slaves for the war. The master sarcastically addressed an Afro-Brazilian veteran who had lost an arm in the war: "You want to be decorated only because you lost an arm? Then what should I say, because I will lose no less than four."[9] These mobilization practices were far from the ideal of universal male conscription taking hold in Europe and North America, which contributed to increasingly strident militarist nationalism. Army data recorded 4,003 *libertos* or slaves manumitted for service, almost five percent of Brazil's forces.

Many freedmen soldiers had been government-owned slaves. Convents and individuals sold or donated another quarter, and owners presented another quarter as substitutes.[10] Some wealthier men hired free substitutes as replacements, or poor men themselves stood-in for a relative or friend. Slave and free substitutes were nearly equally popular methods of avoiding service, but both accounted for a small percentage of the overall mobilization.[11]

3. Parody of the trade in substitutes for service in the Paraguayan War. *O Cabrião* suggested that some prominent men contracted — here entrapped — poor men to serve as substitutes and then sold these substitutes to the highest bidders among national guardsmen designated for service at the front. These substitute auctions appeared similar to slave auctions for many contemporaries. From *O Cabrião*, November 18, 1866, 77. *Courtesy of the Biblioteca Nacional, Rare Works Division. Photo by Gilson Ribeiro.*

Perhaps the greatest difference between Brazil's mobilization for previous international campaigns and for the Paraguayan War lies in the latter's limited use of foreign mercenaries. Brazil conducted the most demanding military mobilization in its history, relying almost exclusively on its own population. Henceforth, the army no longer depended heavily on foreign mercenaries.

Women constituted an important mobilization category ignored by official data.[12] An 1865 cartoon "Liberty and Oppression" shows well-dressed Brazilian women (including nuns) signing on as Voluntários, juxtaposing them to bedraggled children, old men, and women being inspected by Paraguay's President López. The caption reads, "Brazil recruits warrioresses that will serve on the battle field as camp followers, inspire courage, reward acts of bravery, encourage the wounded, work in infirmaries, prepare cartridges, laugh at bullets, and scoff at canon blasts; . . . Lopes [*sic*] is recruiting children, old men and women as instruments of

A liberdade e a oppressão.

Em quanto o Brasil recruta guerreiras que, nos campos da batalha, vão servir de vivandeiras, estimular a coragem, recompensar os feitos de bravura, animar os feridos, percorrer as enfermarias, preparar cartuchos, rir da metralha e zombar dos canhões; rufando o tambor—

o Lopez está recrutando velhos, velhas e crianças, que emprega como instrumentos de guerra, sem receio de que se convertão em rezes destinadas aos matadouros.

4. "Liberty and Oppression: Brazil recruits warrioresses that will serve on the battlefield as camp followers, inspire courage, reward acts of bravery, encourage the wounded, work in infirmaries, prepare cartridges, laugh at bullets, and scoff at cannon blasts; . . . Lopes [*sic*] is recruiting children, old men, and women as instruments of war without caring that they will be lambs at the slaughter." Well-dressed Brazilian women (including nuns) sign on as Voluntários, juxtaposed with bedraggled children and old men and women being inspected by President Francisco Solano López of Paraguay. From *A Semana Illustrada,* September 3, 1865, 1972. *Courtesy of the Biblioteca Nacional, Rare Works Division. Photo by Gilson Ribeiro.*

war without caring that they will be lambs at the slaughter."[13] Here is yet another instance of Brazilian propagandists asserting their nation's superior civilization in terms of respect for female honor. Honorable Brazilian women play traditional female roles, whereas Paraguay's leader shows a lack of respect for families by forcing women and children to perform "men's" duties. Brazilian officials sought female "recruits," mostly the wives and consensual mates of praças. By having their wives accompany them to the front, perhaps some soldiers felt they could continue to provide their mates protection and preserve family honor. Women cooked and tended the wounded, and, contrary to the cartoon, they sometimes joined in the fighting. One officer noted, "The women who accompanied our column numbered 71, all but two marched on foot; almost all of them carried babies (*crianças de peito*). In a furious struggle with a Paraguayan soldier who tried to grab her child, one woman grabbed a sword from the ground and killed her assailant." These 71 women accompanied an invasion force of 1,680 soldiers. At the end of their retreat, 980 soldiers had died along with many "Indians, women, men, vendors, and peons" who accompanied the column. While they did not earn salaries, the women's passage was paid by the War Ministry, and they shared in the rations they prepared for the soldiers.[14]

It is difficult to estimate their numbers, but correspondence from Ceará indicates that great distances and cramped shipboard transportation did not deter women. The manifest of a force embarking for Paraguay from Fortaleza in April 1865 recorded 158 praças, 17 soldiers' wives (*mulheres de praças*), and 14 children (*filhos*).[15] Women on the front faced serious privations, and many conducted arduous marches with babies at their breasts. By September 1865, orders forbade the embarkation of the families of guardsmen and Voluntários. Ceará's governor responded, "I am aware that women who offer to march as praças in any force for the war theater should not be accepted."[16] The reference to women as praças suggests that officials expected them to pull their own weight in the field. It also implied a dubious association with the world of the "street" that belied the coded message about female honor noted in the cartoon "Liberty and Oppression." Costs and the priority to mobilize male praças prompted the army to halt female mobilization. If the one to ten ratio of women to praças in Ceará was a norm, however, then by September 1865 Brazilian camps already held a sizeable female contingent.

Who then were the men who protected these women and by extension Brazil's national honor? Were all men classed as guardsmen and Voluntários "volunteers?" While some did go to the front in a fit of patriotic fervor, most had to be pressured or coerced to cooperate with imperial directives. For instance, in 1867, Rio's police chief reported that of the 59 guardsmen he had remitted to the army, 17 presented themselves and 42 had been "captured."[17] Conservative war minister Barão de Muritiba admitted this fact in parliamentary debate at war's end:

> Muritiba — Impressment aided in the acquisition of volunteers; it was the weapon used to force the national guardsmen of some localities to promptly enlist under the decreed designation (cries of disagreement); this is the pure truth (cries of "here, here"). . . . Recall what was practiced in . . . Bahia, where individuals passed as volunteers . . . remitted under escort and in chains. . . . Pressed men [also] arrived from Minas Gerais with the denomination of "volunteers."
>
> Silveira Lobo — (Liberal) What great men Mr. Minister!
>
> Muritiba — I accepted them, and I believe I should have; they arrived with documents stating they were volunteers and had been advanced their bonuses.
>
> Silveira Lobo — It is proven that this nation is worthless!
>
> Muritiba — I am not trying to prove that this country is worthless; I am stating what in truth occurred. There was a great number of Volunteers of the Fatherland ("here, here"), but it is also irrefutable that a good many of them were obtained through coercive means.[18]

The authorities thus acknowledged what was secret to few: the government had dragooned many, if not most, Voluntários and designated guardsmen. While some volunteered and some initial public demonstrations of support for the campaign were forthcoming, a widening net of impressment sweeps disrupted cities and countryside, causing men to flee to the woods.[19] An 1867 cartoon showed the city full of wild beasts displaced by men hiding from recruitment in the wilderness.[20]

Only a month after the Voluntários decree, a Bahian recruitment agent despaired that even men with exemptions took to the wilderness out of fear of impressment. He advised Bahia's governor that "your excellency will only be able to enlist a greater number of volunteers through forced recruitment."[21] The irony of this statement captures well the abuse of the term volunteer. Impressment's pervasiveness is reflected by the common use of the term "recruitment" (*recrutamento*) as a synonym for impressment. Even the War Ministry categorized praças as "*voluntários*" (volunteers) or "*recrutados*" (dragooned).

As War Minister Muritiba indicated above, impressment served the State as a stick to goad reluctant guardsmen into reporting for duty. A guardsman's remarks in Minas Gerais accented this threat in April 1865, "Recruitment [impressment] is worse [than reporting for duty]; and it will be inevitable, if those [guardsmen] designated do not report; instead of one year [those pressed] will serve nine years as regular soldiers; and moreover they will be vilified as bad citizens."[22] The editorialist did not know that the one-year stint required of guardsmen would be extended for years, but many who did not report may have suspected the worst. The army's discharge record did little to inspire confidence. In urging his fellow militia men to report, the author stressed the unpleasant consequences of noncooperation over references to patriotism, manhood, or government benefits. The gender-ridicule common to mobilization efforts elsewhere seems curiously lacking in most Brazilian commentary. Securing cooperation for mobilizations, in any nation in any era, relies on fear of social stigma and credible legal action for noncompliance as much as social acceptance and public recognition for serving. A perusal of wartime cartoons and editorials indicates that much more space was dedicated to ridiculing soldiers (the unprotected poor) and recruitment profiteers than vilifying those who evaded press gangs, indicating widespread sympathy for impressment dodging.[23]

Recruitment offered many un- or underemployed men a new, if dangerous, job opportunity in press gangs. Locals sometimes ambushed press gangs, and undertook deadly prison breaks to free recruits. Others contracted poor men and then auctioned them off as substitutes to guardsmen called up for duty on the front. Conversely, some poor men scammed the army by profiting from enlistment bounties, only to desert soon afterwards.[24]

Most guardsmen had to be more than praised or cajoled to report for duty. The threat of a nine-year stint as a regular soldier for guardsmen who did not report for duty was certainly ominous. After all, guardsmen numbered among the protected, and being forced into the regular army signified being cast out into the ranks of the unprotected. Although many resented onerous and unremunerated peacetime guard duties that could remove a farmer from his fields for days or even weeks, they absolutely dreaded recruitment for regular army service. Some sympathetic and self-serving police delegates were accused of protecting local guardsmen called up for duty by hiding them on out-of-the-way farms where they performed agricultural labor.[25] Less privileged guardsmen had more to fear than a simple loss of social status. If they survived and secured a timely discharge, they would not likely return to their privileged positions as sharecroppers or the skilled jobs they had held. They faced being reduced to wage earners, which, according to Izabel Andrade Marson, "was for them a situation comparable to slavery." Nor could married troops who left their wives behind adequately protect their homes and family honor. As rancor mounted, officials belatedly took some steps in Rio to protect the honor and educate the children of widows of Voluntários. These youths were allotted funds for meals and kept in boarding schools. Still, as unfulfilled petitions document, the State's protection of families left behind, war widows, and honorably discharged veterans was woefully inadequate.[26]

A gap of culture, status, and education separated most commissioned officers from praças whether they were regulars, guardsmen, or Voluntários. Dionísio Cerqueira, a student at Rio's engineering school, volunteered as a regular before the Voluntário decree's promulgation. As he accompanied other recent enlistees, "all of the lowest levels of society," he reflected, "I then understood the scowl with which the Christian martyrs confronted the anger of the pagan rabble in the bloody arena of Flavius. It was the enthusiasm of faith."[27] The lack of such exceptional nationalist faith kept most "honorable" men from volunteering. Months later, the army recognized Dionísio as a cadet, protecting him from floggings and distancing him from the "pagan rabble."

Why were there so few regular soldiers if the threat of impressment was real? Most men pressed after January 1865 were accorded the consolation of Voluntário status.[28] War Minister Muritiba himself disclosed above that he accepted "volunteers" remitted in chains. With the solace of a Voluntário enlistment bonus, officials assuaged impressment's cruel injustice and perhaps dampened some inductees' resistance to their lot. The inclusion of pressed men in the Voluntários tarnished the corps' pretensions to a status above that of regulars.

As the war dragged on, criticisms of the emperor coalesced around

5. Woman: Hey, can't you see I am a woman?
Policeman: I don't want to know. A woman does not drive a wood cart. Come to the barracks and the inspections will prove your exemption.
Pipelet [observer on left]: Did you see that?!
Cabrião [observer on right]: What they should do is recruit the confounded carts that annoy us and break our eardrums.
Pipelet: Hilarious.
Impressment is obviously a danger to female honor here, as the policeman suggests that only an inspection of her naked body in the barracks would prove her exemption. "Honorable" poor women were forced to perform tasks normally performed by men during wartime, destabilizing gender stereotypes. The scene also suggests that some men crossdressed to avoid military impressment. From *O Cabrião*, December 2, 1866, 77. *Courtesy of the Biblioteca Nacional, Rare Works Division. Photo by Gilson Ribeiro.*

impressment. A Rio newspaper criticized plans for impressment sweeps in Minas Gerais, "This province's Police Chief confirmed what has been said everywhere . . . the government is firm in its intention to bring the people at bayonet point [into the army], even if [it] . . . results in the loss of hundreds of fathers . . . because this is what his imperial majesty's government wants."[29] Rather than taking issue with the reluctance of authorities in Minas to remit their share of recruits, the newspaper lambasted impressment as an imperial assault on honorable fathers of families.

The São Paulo periodical, *O Mosquito*, mocked impressment in "The Story of João Simplício Nabbed in the Wilderness of São Paulo." In this

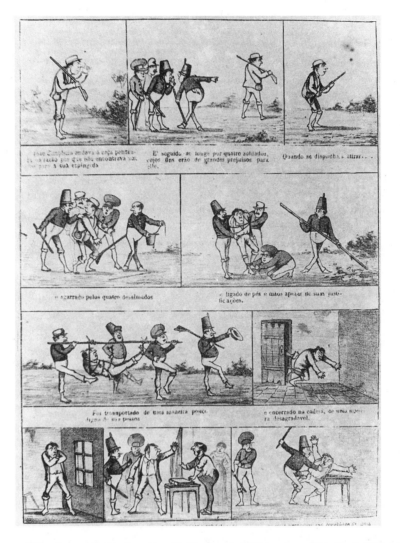

6. "The Story of João Simplício Nabbed in the Wilderness of São Paulo." In this cartoon, four soldiers nab hillbilly João, who is out hunting. The illustration depicts the press gang: a handful of men armed with firearms, clubs, and rope. *"Recrutas à pau e corda"* (club and rope recruits) became a derisive commonplace during the war. After subduing João, the soldiers bind and carry their prey to the police delegate, who tells him to take the soldier's oath to the flag. When João instead complains about the "abuse of his liberty," he is beaten and thrown into a cell. Later, he is transported to Rio where he and other "volunteers" await transshipment to Paraguay. Numerous cartoons and articles similarly satirized impressment. From *O Mosquito*, October 24, 1869, 5. *Courtesy of Biblioteca Nacional, Rare Works Division. Photo by Gilson Ribeiro.*

cartoon, four soldiers nab hillbilly João who is out hunting. The illustration depicts the press gang — a handful of men armed with firearms, clubs, and rope. "*Recrutas à pau e corda*" (club and rope recruits) became a derisive commonplace during the war. After subduing João, the soldiers bind and carry their prey to the police delegate, who tells João to take the soldier's oath to the flag. When instead, João complains about the "abuse of his liberty," he is beaten and thrown into a cell. Later he is transported to Rio where he and other "volunteers" await transhipment to Paraguay. Numerous cartoons and articles similarly satirized impressment.[30]

Impressment, however, was a dangerous business. In 1868, a retired army major who became a recruitment agent in Granito, Pernambuco, requested additional men and money to pay in advance to soldiers escorting captured recruits to the capital. He preferred to use troops from Recife who were free of local loyalties and better "respected." He added that within "the *patronato* system rooted in the interior there exists a prejudice founded on the principle known as family prestige, making any individual, even one without a social position . . . bold enough to oppose legal orders . . . [and they provide] protection to guardsmen called up for military service, dragoonees, and criminals who live among them." To prove the need for additional resources, he referred to an incident that occurred in the hamlet of Exu, where farmers eked out a living growing mostly manioc. When a press gang in Exu pursued a recruit who disappeared into the house of the "very poor" Antônio Geraldo de Carvalho, the rustic, arms in hand, refused to allow the patrol to search his house. To intimidate authorities further, Antônio and a band of armed men "insulted" legal authority by riding slowly past the police delegate's house, knowing he did not have the forces necessary to disarm them. Soon after, however, a relative came to assure the recruitment agent that Antônio would allow his house to be searched. He clarified that up to that date, they had resisted the actions of police authorities who had abused their powers by committing acts of vengeance. Still, the new agent warned, Exu "was like an independent nation where no one obeys anybody except for local rabble rousers, and where legal authorities are threatened with assassination daily."[31] As this case indicates, local toughs could complicate the effectiveness of impressment. Controlling recruiters themselves proved troublesome. In at least one case, unauthorized recruiters appeared in local communities hoping to profit from the troop trade.[32]

Alongside the club and rope recruits, the government resorted to calling up convicts. Men were recruited from prisons in Mato Grosso, Fernando de Noronha, and other sites. Wartime service seemed a more severe punishment than any prison stint, and, conveniently enough, prisoners did not have to be captured. Some convicts sentenced to life volunteered to serve in return for a pardon.[33] Authorities also proceeded to utilize recruitment to summarily dispense with law breakers. Take the case of the manumitted slave Braselino Antônio Dutervel Setubal. A local household head accused Antônio of molesting a boy under his protection and of infecting a number of young boys with syphilis. For this alleged offence he was remanded by Ceará's police chief to Rio as an army recruit. In a confidential letter, the police chief warned that legal efforts to retrieve Braselino were being made. Perhaps Braselino had posed as a freeman, and his owner was litigating for his return; or Braselino may have had a legal exemption as a freeman that his patron could document. In any case, the police chief asked the War Ministry to ignore such efforts, arguing that as a praça Braselino would "not only have his bad habits corrected, but it would also serve as an exemplary punishment for his bad behavior." It would be hard to find a more direct and concise association of army service, criminal punishment, and correctional practices. A reply from the adjutant general's office stated that it had ordered Braselino to be sent to Paraguay the next day.[34] Neither the police chief nor the War Ministry expressed concens about whether this alleged syphilitic child molester would make a good soldier or pose a health hazard to other troops or their families. The case illustrates the willingness of public authorities at the local and imperial level to conspire to ignore the legal rights of poor men and even, at times, their patrons.

At war's end, the war minister stressed impressment's ill-effects: "Impressment did occur on a large scale, the noble senator from Bahia pressed men, as his successors did to produce 'volunteers.' I affirm that this is the exact truth, as all of Brazil knows. The great means of the government could not enlist an adequate number of volunteers . . . it became necessary to manumit slaves, and resort to other methods which officers resented. These measures were prejudicial to the army, and they are still producing their ill fruits."[35] The war minister would not venture a more exact estimate than "large-scale" because, as he admitted, the records did not honestly report impressment.

The war minister specified one recruitment expedient he feared had set a dangerous precedent for discipline in the army: the manumission of slaves to fight. This policy drove slavocratic novelist and Conservative senator José Martiniano de Alencar to malign the emperor because it violated personal property rights. He claimed that Pedro II was the "soul of the war" and in 1867 called on Parliament to unilaterally withdraw. But the State did not force owners to sell or donate slaves, and the some 4,000 libertos incorporated into the army constituted less than one percent of Brazil's 1.5 million slaves.[36] While records may have been less than perfect, the necessity of accounting for funding to purchase slaves and the eagerness of men of means to have their donated bondsmen officially recognized militated against reckless record keeping. While there is some evidence of undercounting, it is unlikely that many more than 4,000 to 7,000 manumitted slaves served as army praças, much less than the 20,000 or 60,000 to 100,000 often cited.[37]

Recruitment corruption, be it in purchasing slaves at inflated prices or bribes paid to agents, angered many. As one newspaper denounced, "When public monies are squandered without compassion or piety, when protection and the patronage system distribute the state's patrimony, when one entrusts his friends with hundreds of *contos* under the pretext of working as an agent to enlist volunteers or buy slaves for the army, you take away the petty means of subsistence of the man who works his life away to preserve soldiers in the field."[38] Recruitment lent itself to the partisan spoils system, and critics often espoused classical liberal arguments of how armies squander productive resources.

Small numbers of bondsmen had been freed to fight before in Brazil, but the unrivaled scale of this slave mobilization is a telling barometer of the army's manpower crisis. Traditional recruitment had proven ponderous for a modern military campaign on a distant front. These inadequacies had serious implications for premises that underlie the Brazilian empire, but ultimately mobilization showed the lengths to which the State went to indulge its status and property-conscious citizenry. By law, owners had to consent to their slaves' sale, but agents sometimes whisked slave recruits to the front before legal claims could be processed.

In 1865, out-of-uniform recruitment agents nabbed Joaquim Soares do Bomfim in mountainous Minas Gerais. A runaway slave from the hilly coffee fields of Vassouras, Rio de Janeiro, since the early 1860s, Joaquim claimed to have followed the counsel of an agent who advised him to sign on as a volunteer rather than a "dragoonee." Joaquim posed as a free man and marched as a volunteer to the Paraguayan front rather than return to his life as a slave. He survived the calamitous expedition in Mato Grosso, returned home, and received his discharge. Subsequently, the son of Joaquim's owner kidnapped the veteran and demanded government compensation before releasing him.[39] Documents do not reveal the outcome of the heir's appeal, but Joaquim's case shows how some slaves could evade their masters by joining the army, and how agents sometimes encouraged "captured" recruits to sign on as "volunteers."

As slavery declined, the whites, blacks, and mestizos who composed the free poor became more uneasy about threats to their status. Wartime mobilization and then conscription threatened to blur measures of status among the free poor. In the antebellum South of the United States, slaveowners and poor whites defined themselves as "men of honor" against the stereotyped traits they attributed to slaves. They related ideals of southern honor and manhood to conceptions of what distinguished "white" men, poor and rich, from slaves and former slaves. In Brazil, slave stereotypes and African ethnicity provided markers of dishonor that many free people of color and whites used to confirm their superior status.[40] As slavery began to dwindle after the end of the international slave trade in 1850, however, this benchmark of status became less stable. This made impressment and the threat it posed to honorable manhood an even more important distinction of status for most members of the protected poor in the wake of the Paraguayan War.

In part, the State created different troop categories to segregate more honorable Brazilians from those considered less honorable: regular soldiers. On the front, however, guardsmen, freedmen, Voluntários, and regulars were integrated in reorganized front-line units. Necessity prevented the army from practicing more rigid forms of social segregation. There are even some indications that integration may have been a conscious strategy; Marshal Caxias, for instance, broke up the all-black Bahian volunteer unit known as the *zuavos bahianos*.[41] Still, social distinctions and prejudice often divided soldiers within regiments.

Predictably, integrating and controlling the mix of volunteers, ex-slaves, convicts, and pressed soldiers proved formidable. Partisan political intrigues weakened army cohesion and discipline. When Marshal Caxias took command of Brazilian forces in Paraguay in 1866, the experienced campaigner was determined to establish his authority. He removed officers he did not trust from key posts, reorganized battalions, and obtained the right to review and execute the sentences of military tribunals in situ.

The task of establishing discipline was an uphill battle complicated by grim frontline conditions. Many soldiers died from preventable diseases and treatable injuries.[42] Those who survived endured harsh discipline, grueling marches, and a frequent lack of food, potable water, clothing, munitions, and shelter. Conditions on the disastrous Mato Grosso expedition illustrate the extreme privations many suffered. The expedition had lost its mounts to disease during a two-year overland march through Brazil's interior to the northeastern corner of Paraguay. Even so, the commander foolishly proceeded to invade enemy territory on foot. Out of 1,680 Brazilian soldiers and officers who crossed the Paraguayan border, only 700 returned. Undersupplied and unable to fight effectively against a small Paraguayan cavalry unit, the Brazilians retreated and became lost.

One officer's memoir captured the harrowing experience of this ill-fated expedition. Besides the heart of palm for which they foraged (made dangerous by Paraguayan cavalry), there was only an exhausted bull left to eat:

A repulsive spectacle demonstrated how hunger had spread panic among our soldiers. . . . A circle began forming around it, each [soldier] waiting with anxiety for the blood to spill, some to catch it in some type of vessel and carry it away, others to drink immediately. . . . The butcher barely had time to cut the animal, it was almost necessary to rip the carcass' hind quarters from the soldiers' hands to take it to the place of distribution. The remains, the viscera, even the hide, all were divided right there and were soon devoured, hardly even cooked or boiled; repugnant food.[43]

This young officer's firsthand account of events used the devouring of uncooked meat and the imbibing of fresh blood to symbolize a descent into the cannibal's barbaric realm.

Unshod and famished, footsore soldiers were ordered to carry makeshift stretchers bearing comrades disabled by cholera. This close contact may have facilitated the spread of disease among the bearers and, in turn, augmented their labor as beasts of burden. At first, officers flogged with their sword flats soldiers who complained or resisted commands to bear the sick. Then, officers overheard some soldiers plotting: "Deserting into the woods, at least some of us will make it to safety, and if nothing else, we will cease to be the slaves of these tormenters [their officers]."[44] Even soldiers compared their condition to that of slaves in order to justify their desertion. Flight remained a principled response to injustice. Some bearers became so exhausted, footsore, and desperate after days of constant marching under the dead weight of the stretchers that they strangled or drowned their ill comrades when fording streams. At this point, it seems that officers began looking the other way. How else would this young officer have noted these horrific slayings in the memoir of the expedition? Finally, the commander relented and the ill soldiers were abandoned to suffer at the hands of the pursuing Paraguayan cavalry. Circumstances and poor leadership had driven these soldiers to desperate acts. Under such extreme conditions, it is remarkable that the troops remained as cooperative and mannerly as they did.

Difficult conditions drove many soldiers to seek salvation through desertion. One observer reported that seven to eight thousand allied deserters roamed Rio Grande do Sul and another three thousand wandered Uruguay.[45] The presence of the enemy, Indians, difficult terrain, bounty hunters, and other groups of deserters who turned to banditry made flight a perilous option.[46] Those captured faced the Count de Lippe's Code, which prescribed death for wartime desertion.

Army punishments harkened back to the public executions common to early modern royal justice.[47] One combatant chronicled the gruesome spectacle that accompanied the punishment of two Brazilian soldiers accused of attacking a superior officer. Both were sentenced to be struck with the flat of a sword until dead. After more than one thousand blows, the attending doctor declared that he could no longer detect their pulses. Then, in step to patriotic music, the battalions marched back to their encampment. Amazingly, the two soldiers survived the thrashing and two months later were reintegrated in the ranks, but others sentenced to death were not so fortunate.[48] Some recalcitrant soldiers were dispensed with less ceremoniously, and less serious infractions incurred beatings of less lethal intensity. One young officer noted that when discipline broke down, it was vital that soldiers be "immediately punished [flogged], which for the rabble is the symbol of legitimate authority."[49]

The most frequently judged military crimes in Paraguay indicate a preoccupation with attacks on superiors. Most telling were the twelve murders

Table 2. Crimes Most Frequently Judged by the Junta of Military Justice in
Paraguay, 1869.

Insubordination	17	Disrespecting a Superior (officer)	5
Wartime Desertion	14	Beating Soldiers	5
Murdering a Superior (officer)	12	Refusing Service w/Arms	5
Injuring a Comrade (praça)	7	Attempted Murder of a Superior (officer)	4
Theft of Money in Their Charge	7	Murder of a Civilian	4
Murdering a Comrade	6	Disobedience and Threats	4
Attempted Murder of a praça (Comrade)	6	Self-mutilation	3
Other Crimes	27	Total	126

Source: RRMGu (1870), annexos.

and four attempted murders against superiors. Officers had real reasons to
fear deadly reprisals from their troops. In the spirit of Frederick the Great's
maxim that enlisted men should fear their officers more than the enemy,
front-line military justice harshly countered resistance and the threat of
mutiny. Conversely, over the course of the war, five commissioned and
noncommissioned officers were judged for mistreating their soldiers. The
high command recognized that abusing corporal punishment could result
in the very disorder it sought to prevent. A balance between intimidation
and the bonds of patronage had to be struck, and for the most part, troops
and officers conducted an uneasy and unequal negotiation of discipline.
By emphasizing these divisive tensions, one should not lose sight that,
given the circumstances, the Brazilian forces demonstrated admirable cohesion overall.

The cases of two soldiers who appealed their convictions to the Council
of State reveal the dangers officers faced in inflicting corporal punishment.
Two Voluntários admitted that being subjected to or threatened with
corporal punishment caused them to assassinate their superior officers.
Private Manoel Luiz Pereira stated that he committed the crime in a state
of "temporary insanity" (*alucinação*) when his comrades told him that his
lieutenant intended to give him a few blows with a sword, a punishment
he considered infamous and one which he had "never suffered in eight
years as a soldier."[50] For some, the application of corporal punishment in
public, an act strongly associated with slavery, was too great an offense to
personal honor to be tolerated.

Discipline was not only maintained through punishment or the threat of castigation, but also through patronage and the group identities that characterize battle experiences. However, whether one was a volunteer, *liberto*, or a club and rope recruit, the attitude of the army's high command toward praças remained cavalier. Marshal Caxias voiced his deep-rooted traditionalism on the matter: "It has always been my opinion that . . . officers . . . be paid on time, but that praças should be paid three to four months behind schedule. Discipline profits from this practice and public coffers as well, because diseases and battles leave gaps in the ranks and thus, this final liquidation profits the treasury."[51] Caxias, the army's patron hero, gave little credence to the Frenchified rhetoric of the citizen-soldier. Public expenditures troubled him more than the difficult conditions soldiers confronted. The lowly social origins of most praças fostered the high command's disdain. By paying soldiers on time, some officers assumed that they only encouraged drinking and gambling. The benefits of regular pay for morale were not taken seriously by many. Instead, the disciplinary and training problems officers faced on the front convinced most of them that they needed a better class of recruits.

Wartime mobilization set the stage for political battles at home. Political dissension as a result of the emperor's war policies peaked in 1868 when he employed his *poder moderador* (moderating power) to dissolve his Liberal Council of State and nominate a Conservative cabinet. Pedro II's decision to dissolve Parliament stemmed in part from problems at the front. Marshal Caxias, also a Conservative senator, demanded that Pedro II dissolve the Liberal government so that he could consolidate his control over the army. He claimed that Liberal political intrigue, affecting promotions, funds, and the allotment of command positions, deterred him from effectively executing the campaign. He tendered a letter of resignation that accused the Liberal government of lacking patriotism. Fearing that Caxias's departure could break the morale of an unpopular war effort, Pedro II called for new elections.[52] Conservatives used their control of the Council of State to manipulate elections across Brazil, bringing cronies to power in the provinces. Part of their election strategy involved using the threat of impressment to intimidate and suppress Liberal supporters. A letter from the town of Ilha do Governador, Rio de Janeiro, accused the police delegate and justice of the peace of coercing voters to accept ballots supporting the Conservative party. It accused officials of threatening to imprison, prosecute, and subsequently impress voters if they refused to cast Conservative ballots. The letter went on to describe how the police delegate "clandestinely" stuffed the ballot box during a tumult inside the church polling place.[53] In fairness, both Conservative and Liberal incumbents used impressment to their political advantage, but the relative dominance of Conservative parliaments during the empire made Liberals more regular, if hypocritical, critics of dragooning.[54]

Outraged Liberals detailed recruitment abuses in Parliament. One cited a letter sent by a Conservative police delegate from the Serra de São Pedro, Ceará in 1868: "It is embarrassing to send only two recruits from such a populous district; it appears that these people know ahead of time [about impressment sweeps]. . . . you, sir, can be certain that I will continue to patrol [for recruits]. . . . [One of] the recruits [I am sending] knifed someone; I pardoned him because he said that if I absolved him he would serve as a recruit."[55] The senator specified that these cases of impressment violated the 1846 law prohibiting recruitment one month before and two months after elections.

The same senator presented a laundry list of abuses attested to in letters by local priests, judges, and officials from across Ceará. Recruiters surrounded a church in Sobral and, despite the priest's protests, nabbed two newlywed men when they set foot outside. Vengeful agents struck an elderly cowhand dead with a sword blow in Queixeramobim as he begged them to spare his son from impressment. The senator claimed that during the election period "bands" of unwilling recruits arrived in Fortaleza, where a warship waited to whisk inductees to the front. He added, "In every locality [of Ceará] there occurred . . . arbitrary arrests, *illegal searches of homes*, . . . beatings, injuries, and homicides. The legal officials disappeared, leaving only one ruling authority, the recruiter, there were general recruiters and partial recruiters, but anyone who said he was of the Conservative Party could make himself into a recruiter. If one had vengeance to take, he could request an armed squad saying he wanted to arrest John Doe, arriving at his enemy's home, he tried to make the arrest, there ensued a conflict and a murder."[56] His final remark, "This is common practice in Ceará . . . and unhappily it is common practice in the entire Empire," was heeded by cries of "*apoiado*" (hear, hear)!

These complaints illustrate the violent and overtly political nature of impressment. Wartime dragooning devastated poor families and the inviolability of their homes. While the testimony may have been inflated by partisan hyperbole, senators were not simply grinding a political ax. Impressment had long been a controversial issue linked to local and national political power, but wartime mobilization carried this dispute to new extremes.

Liberals answered Conservatives with sweeping reform proposals such as the gradual abolition of slavery. For radical Liberals, new proposals did not go far enough, and they formed the new Republican Party in 1870. The Republican platform pointedly decries violations of "individual freedom" when men are "subjected to arrest, to impressment, to the National Guard" and are thus "deprived the right of *habeas corpus*."[57] Wartime impressment shaped postwar partisanship.

Remembrances of War

The victorious Brazilian army's homecoming parade was far from triumphant. Rio's English- and French-language newspapers described it as an "unmitigated failure because the people of Rio were determined to manifest their opinion toward it by contemptuously abstaining from it." Reportedly only 200 of the 8,000 "respectable" citizens honored with invitations showed up — most who did were State officials and foreign consuls. In the end, the emperor ordered guards who held back the city's uninvited "rabble" to enter the "utter solitude" of the stands bringing a "simulacrum of popular life" to them. Foreign observers found the spectacle laughable, noting the dark skin tone of troops and the parade's rowdy and dusky spectators. Rio's cheeky French-language newspaper clucked that Pedro II was a poor organizer of solemn patriotic events but an excellent director of Carnival: a holiday when the poor of all races took to the streets for raucous merriment.[58]

Public resentment toward the war sprang from many sources. Some complained of the debt Brazil accumulated to fund the campaign. Others pointed to government corruption and the windfall profits made by crooked entrepreneurs who produced shoddy war goods — even the review stands built for the parade were so rickety that police inspectors ordered them reinforced.[59] Still others complained of the emperor's abuse of his political powers to wage an unpopular war. Though some dubbed veterans the "Saviors of Brazil," most privileged Brazilians likely found distasteful the idea of honoring the service of enlisted men with such lowly social and mostly nonwhite racial origins.[60] Authorities rarely made good

7. "La Fête du 10 Juillet ou le plus réussi des *zé Pereira Carnavalesco* présents, passés et futurs" (The 10th of July Celebration, or the most successful of Zé Pereira's Carnival events of the past, present, or future.) The caption describes the July 10th victory parade as a Zé Pereira (a carnival drum rhythm or group that plays this rhythm) Carnival event or a raucous street party unsuited to such a solemn and sober nationalistic rite. The cartoon portrays Prime Minister José Antônio Pimenta Bueno, the Marquês de São Vicente with a crown (many Carnival revelers dressed as kings), and a palmatório, an instrument used to punish slaves and underlings by striking them on the palms or soles. The cartoon and textual descriptions of events suggests that the Prime Minister, the Emperor, and other government authorities officiated a boisterous victory parade attended mostly by uninvited members of Rio's obstreperous dark-skinned "rabble." I thank Vitor Izecksohn for identifying the Marquês de São Vicente. *Ba Ta Clan*, July 16, 1870, 1. *Courtesy of the Biblioteca Nacional, Rare Works Division. Photo by Gilson Ribeiro.*

on the promised benefits of service, either. For most veterans, the State failed to provide a system of protection to replace that of private patronage. Just as in the 1870 parade, most affluent Brazilians preferred to ignore the services of veteran praças. As Eduardo Silva claims, most found it easier to emphasize the legacy of the club and rope recruits. Even the navy minister refused to pay for the freedom of a slave who ran away to join the war where he earned a commendation for bravery. The patriot languished in jail while the dispute went on for months.[61]

The Paraguayan War had been a period of national self-encounter for many, an experience that might have laid the basis for a broader sentiment of nationalism as it brought together Brazilians from different provinces, races, and classes on an unprecedented scale in a common struggle. One symptom of this self-encounter was the rise of regional literature, cheered by critics like Sílvio Romero who promoted the bard-priest Domingos Caldas Barbosa as a nationalist icon. The war also gave propagandists an antagonistic anvil against which to shape national identity and reflect on the "national race." Paraguay's Guarani Indian heritage permeated its predominantly mestizo population. Its agrarian economy, primarily oriented toward internal markets, was regulated by a unique system of state-owned and -financed farms controlled by Paraguay's president. Brazilian propaganda portrayed Paraguay's dictatorial political system, centrally directed economy, and indigenous racial composition as vastly inferior to Brazil's northern European–style constitutional monarchy, capitalist agro-export economy, and demographic base, which included a larger portion of European immigrants. In part, the war moved some to reject the Tupi-Guarani Indian as Brazil's traditional national symbol. Army officers, like the Visconde de Taunay, promoted instead the cult of the racially mixed hinterland pioneer, the *sertanejo,* as a substitute. Sertanejos played a vital role in the war, supplying men, material, and wilderness guides.

In 1875, a Republican newspaper criticized the use of a "naked [Tupi] Indian," wearing feathers and armed with a bow and arrows, to symbolize Brazil: "A savage in his primitive state represents Brazil, a nation that adopted the tribunals of civilization . . . having already raised arms — that is swords, firearms, and cannons — to civilize Paraguay, whose leader then was called chief and his people — a horde of barbarians." The editorial judged that in Brazil, a nation composed of many races, the Indian was not the predominant type. The harsh stereotypes of Indians — even those who were the army's allies — perpetuated by Brazilian officers were perhaps partly in retribution for Paraguayan propaganda that stereotyped Brazilian soldiers and officers as African "savages."[62] Racial and national identification were touchy issues on the front and at home.

For many leaders around the world, victory in warfare demonstrated a nation's superiority. Wars invited cross-cultural comparisons and a reassessment of status among nations. The American Civil War (1861–65) and the Franco-Prussian War (1870–71) lent new cachet to these comparisons. The Confederacy's defeat further isolated Brazil as one of the last bastions of slavery in the Americas, and it held uncomfortable implications for a slaveholding society's ability to conduct modern warfare. The Prussian army's victory over France made Germany's training and peacetime conscription system the new world standard.[63]

These international comparisons increasingly included references to race. Many nationalists viewed martial capacity in terms of bastardized Darwinian theory, which portrayed wars as competitive struggles among different national races for survival. In 1882, a Brazilian army periodical asserted that "[natural] laws are the same for individuals, races, and the vegetable and animal kingdom, the fundamental scientific formula of organic existence in the world [is] the struggle for life!"[64] Implicit to this analysis was a strengthening "scientific" association of national survival, race, and the nation in arms (the armed forces). In 1868, a senator argued that Poland and Greece's suffering showed that "dominion today . . . belongs exclusively to force."[65] Science rescued traditional beliefs in natural racial and social hierarchies. Moreover, some Europeans linked the genesis of organic nation-states to their citizenry's supposed "racial homogeneity." The army periodical cited above commented with envy on the Prussians' "admirable unity of race" to which it attributed their success, something Brazilian officers found lacking in their own population and soldiery. These theories vexed even the most fervent Brazilian nationalists because to take strong hold over a population, nationalism requires a certain imagined homogenization and leveling of citizens. Many feared that Brazil's racial, ethnic, and climatic heterogeneity could prevent it from becoming a united, modern, and ultimately "white" nation. Postbellum white nationalists advocated whitening Brazil's populace by inviting European and prohibiting African immigration. Senator Visconde de Taunay, a Paraguayan War veteran, became a leading advocate of European immigration.[66] By the 1910s, however, some conscription advocates would attack the fears of racial inferiority that dimmed brighter visions of Brazil's national destiny. Thus, the conscription dispute offers a unique vantage point from which to examine broader conflicts among interest groups and among competing ideas of race, manhood, and the nation in arms.

The Paraguayan War victory parade, however, demonstrated the sense of social distance that separated soldiers from more prosperous Brazilians. The war had not created a stronger sense among many sectors of the population that they belonged to a more homogenous and leveled citizenry. Indeed, it seems the opposite was true. Traditional concepts of honor, race, and status would continue to color the postwar debates on recruitment reform.

parg war further deepend the division in Brazils society

Chapter 3

The "Law of the Minotaur"?

Postwar Reformism and

the Recruitment Law,

1870–1874

Wartime mobilization's inefficiency and the political disputes it fomented politicized recruitment to an unparalleled extent and moved it to the heart of postwar legislative debates. Liberals backed a purely volunteer armed force while the incumbent Conservative government and most army officers promoted limited conscription. Advocates equated the draft with "scientific" military methods, "modern" bureaucratic practices, and "civilized" discipline. Parliament tempered this rhetoric by yielding on issues that appeared too radical to accommodate "Brazilian" values. The debate over conscription provides insight into how leaders interpreted and tailored their own versions of North Atlantic bureaucratic ideologies. As Nancy Leys Stepan underscored, "Historians give too little weight to the construction of intellectual and scientific traditions within Latin America or to the way these traditions shape the meaning given to ideas, as subjects of interest in their own right."[1] What is true of the adoption of European biological theory and method in Latin America is also applicable to military science.

Postwar Legislative Reformism and Conscription

New policies and reforms affecting slavery, electoral law, penal institutions, immigration, and church and state relations dominated the Brazilian Parliament's last two decades of existence. The 1874 Recruitment Law emerged amid a spate of postwar reformism. In 1869, Parliament began debating in earnest a recruitment reform law as Liberals and Conservatives embarked on a period of rancorous wrangling that contrasted markedly with the bipartisanship of the 1850s.

The mobilization of libertos presaged the most effective reform passed in the immediate postwar period: the 1871 Free Womb Law. This law freed all children born henceforth to slaves, limiting bondage to one last generation. It also stimulated debates on how to discipline a wage labor force and resolve Brazil's labor shortages. Representatives of the labor-hungry southeastern provinces mostly opposed abolition and lobbied for imperial sponsorship of European immigration. As stated earlier, they argued that hard-working Europeans would provide an efficacious example for the supposedly indolent Brazilian worker while "whitening" Brazil's racial mix.[2] Even so, central State subsidies to support European immigration would only be acted on after the empire's fall in 1889.

Liberals pushed for electoral reform throughout the 1870s, and in 1881, a Liberal Parliament approved the Election Reform Law. Hailed as a victory for democracy, the law actually diminished the electorate's size. New literacy restrictions and the burden of proving property requirements did little more than give greater weight to the voting power of urban areas without correcting the chronic fraud and violence that plagued elections.[3]

Meanwhile, politicians renewed penal reform efforts. Despite discussions of theory and methods, there was no sustained progress in adopting modern penal disciplinary regimes at the provincial or national level.[4] The overall failure of legislative reformism to bring about meaningful institutional change (with the important exception of the Free Womb Law) contributed to the empire's fall in 1889. The logic of patronage and privilege prevailed over liberal credos of equality before the law, despite baroque attempts to harbor the forms and dissipate the essence of these ideals. Universal male conscription, like universal male suffrage, conflicted with Brazil's social, gender, class, and racial hierarchies, which were shaped by Iberian tradition and by the legacy of slavery.[5]

The War Ministry pressured an obstructionist legislature to act swiftly on recruitment. In 1870, War Minister Muritiba argued that experience had revealed the inadequacy of traditional recruitment methods. He noted the army's perennial troop shortages, and warned that due to postwar discharges and "other well-known reasons," the army would continue to rely on impressment if volunteers ran short. Impressment did not keep

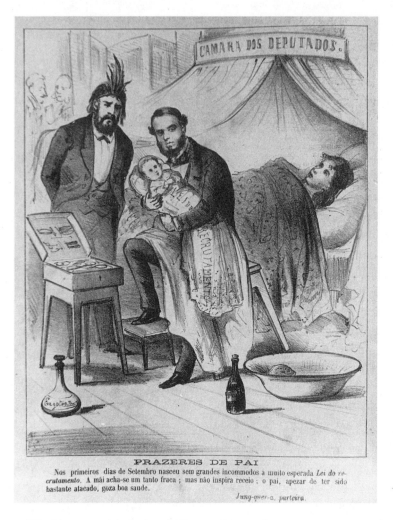

PRAZERES DE PAI

Nos primeiros dias de Setembro nasceu sem grandes incommodos a muito esperada *Lei do re-crutamento*. A mãi acha-se um tanto fraca ; mas não inspira receio ; o pai, apezar de ter sido bastante atacado, goza boa saude.

Jung-quer-a, parteira.

8. "The Pleasures of Fatherhood: The much awaited Recruitment Law was born without great discomfort. The mother finds herself a little weak, but it's nothing to worry about; the father, despite suffering numerous attacks, enjoys good health." Parodying the Recruitment Law's passage, this cartoon depicts War Minister Junqueira holding a newborn (the Recruitment Law), while its mother (the House of Deputies) lies enfeebled from giving birth. From *A Semana Illustrada*, September 13, 1874, 5744. *Courtesy of the Biblioteca Nacional, Rare Works Division. Photo by Gilson Ribeiro.*

pace with desertion, discharge, and disease, and thus the violence associated with dragooning continued to foment public outrage.[6]

To help break parliamentary gridlock and make the new conscription law more palatable to the public, the army promoted separate measures. First, Parliament abrogated corporal punishment in the army. Legally sanctioned floggings would be reserved for bondsmen, some convicts, and imperial sailors. This reform was hailed by Cândido da Fonseca Galvão, a black veteran of the Paraguayan War and an unofficial spokesperson for Rio's Little Africa district. Galvão emphasized that "free men are not slaves to be castigated" and held that beatings undermined the dignity of good citizens and soldiers.[7] Officially, the army adopted new punishments modeled after ideas of rehabilitation. Incorrigible troops would be sent to disciplinary detachments where officers would reward good behavior and apply nonviolent punishments. The abolition of corporal punishment in the army did have some impact on volunteers. A navy inspector explained that "individuals who pursue a military career prefer to enlist in the 20th Artillery Battalion in Corumbá [Mato Grosso], whose benefits are greater [than those offered by the navy] and where corporal punishment is prohibited."[8]

War Minister Junqueira argued that the abolition of flogging made possible yet another important leveling reform: the gradual elimination of cadet privileges. He argued that cadet status was predicated on a praça's legal susceptibility to physical punishment. "There are *praças* that enlist . . . supported by titles of nobility [cadets]; and if this reform ends corporal punishment, there is no reason for privileged ranks. Even more so because there is the recourse of enrolling in [the military academy]."[9] Cadet rank, based on ascribed status, protected the sons of army, navy, and national guard officers, nobles, law and medical school graduates, and higher level public servants from the blows of sword flats. The termination of cadet rank encouraged educated young men to enter the military academy, but those who already had cadet status continued to enjoy their privileges.

Reforms also curtailed another privilege of rank, the *camaradas*, or privates, assigned as personal servants for officers. The Recruitment Law specified that no soldier could be employed in the private service of officers. If the draft were to call up "honorable" free men, it could not assign them servile tasks. To discourage inequities further, volunteers and conscripts would be treated equally in terms of pay, status, and benefits. Reformers hoped to break down status barriers at the level of buck private. A semblance of social leveling was considered crucial to the initiation and socialization of tight-knit groups like platoons.[10]

The army also improved praça salaries, and promoted equality among praças of the same rank by eliminating pay differences.[11] The 1871 pay hikes did not make army wages competitive with similar jobs in the private sector, but they did make soldiering less onerous. Inflation soon ate away these increases, however, and soldiers would wait nearly twenty years for their next raise. In themselves, these reforms marked important advances, but Junqueira warned that all attempts to improve the army would be futile if a new recruitment system were not adopted, "The current recruitment system, beyond being vexatious and lending itself to abuses, is entirely unsatisfactory for obtaining the necessary personnel each year."[12]

As a final vote on the draft neared, one editorialist asserted that the Recruitment Law would be the only important legislation passed since 1872.[13] Another shamed Parliament, declaring that even in Russia, where "soldiers were little more than slaves," the government had adopted conscription.[14] They warned that "modern civilized" nations that strove to improve the living conditions of workers could not afford to forget the "patriotic class" of common soldiers.[15] For some, vanquishing Paraguay made manifest Brazil's regional superiority, but after the war, patterning important state institutions along North Atlantic European standards provided another scale by which to assess national "progress." One senator had the temerity to point out this irony when he dubbed the draft the "Law of Paraguay." In truth, Paraguay, sometimes called the "Prussia of South America," had a conscription system that facilitated its tenacious resistance to Brazil's invasion.[16] Most opinion leaders agreed that Brazil needed to reform recruitment—but which northern European model was most appropriate? The ensuing debate took on a uniquely Brazilian cast as it evoked an intriguing mix of traditional and modern reasoning.

The Recruitment Reform Debate

In his liberal assault against conscription, Senator José Thomás Nabuco de Araújo asserted, "If recruitment has a military aspect . . . it is a civilian institution because it is linked to almost all social problems."[17] Indeed, the conscription debate touched on myriad issues: slavery, labor, Church-State relations, penology, electoral fraud, and the family, among others. Differences between Conservatives and Liberals in terms of military policy cast doubts on the common assertion that the parties at that time were mere political affiliations or "labels" that differed little in terms of ideology and platform.[18] Most Conservatives supported the limited conscription plan in which a draft lottery would take place only when an inadequate number of volunteers and reengaging veterans presented themselves in a given year. Impressment would be outlawed. As "voluntary" enlistments usually accounted for less than half of an inadequate supply of troops, the law's authors anticipated that the draft would be required annually. The plan came closest in format to the French system, but the French had designed their draft largely in response to Prussian initiatives.[19] Men from eighteen to thirty years old would be enrolled in their local parish, providing a master list for the draft lottery. Politically, the plan was sagacious. Supporters could claim that the plan only resorted to a draft when there were too few volunteers, which made it harder for Liberals to criticize the project.

Many Liberals believed peacetime conscription to be the Trojan horse of tyranny. One labeled it a "Prussian monstrosity, the fifth essence of despotism . . . a means of enslaving the people to the caprices of their government officials."[20] A more lyrical orator dubbed the project "the law of the Minotaur," dooming the nation's youth to "immorality."[21] Liberals favored increasing sign-on bonuses and pay to attract volunteers. To pay for these increased costs, they favored reducing the army's size. Proconscription forces countered that the government could not afford to raise the wages and bonuses of praças and still maintain a force adequate for Brazil's defense. War Minister Muritiba contended that the nation required 16,000 praças (a reduction from 20,000), while Liberals proposed 12,000.[22]

Parliament annually fixed military troop strength, generating perennial battles over the army's size. Since troop strength rarely reached legally budgeted levels, Liberals felt it ludicrous to set higher quotas. Conservatives countered that diminishing the army's legal size would merely result in smaller, but still undermanned, battalions.[23] Both sides of the floor asserted that traditional recruitment had failed to produce adequate enlistment, but Conservatives lambasted Liberal contentions that a fully volunteer force could be raised. They argued that even when the state had doubled enlistment bonuses and increased troop pay during the war, it failed to attract enough volunteers.[24] To thwart Liberal criticism, Conservatives — even army war hero Marshal Caxias — further exposed the embarrassing fiction of the *Voluntários da Patria:*

> Silveira da Motta (Liberal) — I prefer the hiring of foreign mercenaries to recruitment in this country, because recruitment has been the principal arm of oppression (cries of "hear, hear") that all governments have used against their political adversaries.
>
> A Senator — And continues to be . . .
>
> Silveira da Motta — . . . tell me gentlemen . . . before 1864 did any of our generals believe it possible to raise an army of 50,000 volunteers in Brazil? No one.
>
> Caxias — Were all 50,000 volunteers?
>
> Silveira da Motta — I do not doubt that there were abuses . . . [25]

Both parties conceded that many Voluntários had been pressed, but both sides of the aisle interpreted impressment's shortcomings in a manner that justified their competing plans.

The Liberals wove another issue into the debate by urging a concurrent reform of election and recruitment laws. They argued that both Liberal and Conservative governments had wielded recruitment as an electoral weapon: "Recruitment is, no one can deny it, a political instrument, which parties use, both Greeks and Trojans, to . . . make the ballot boxes express a vote." This practice was nefarious because it "neutralized the influence of opinion."[26] In part, Liberals backed a voluntary system because they believed it would help eradicate electoral fraud. This policy dovetailed neatly with their efforts to legislate electoral reforms. Conservatives argued that the inclusion of a variety of parish authorities, including the parish priest, would prevent draft lottery fraud. One Liberal senator rebutted this view: "This military reform, is nothing but a Pandora's box, beyond violence it will bring fraud. . . . One could say, there is the justice of the peace to guarantee the lottery against the police delegate who violates it. But, sirs, who does not know that the justice of the peace is of the delegate's faction and his creature? One could say, there is the parish priest, but the priest [is one] against two, making use of the expression frequently employed by the Viscount of Abaeté, 'the parish priest looks, but he does not know how to see.' The draft lotteries will be as pure and sincere

as our elections."[27] For Liberals, justices of the peace, police, borough
inspectors, and priests could not provide sufficient checks on one another's authority to secure just elections, let alone an honest draft lottery.

One reason for doubting the probity of draft boards came out of the
ongoing conflict over the Religious Question, a Church-State dispute that
began in 1873 when the emperor had two bishops arrested and tried for
defying his authority. The requirement that Church officials sit on draft
boards disturbed Liberals and Republicans who favored the separation of
Church and State. One warned that the appointment would turn the
"local cleric into a public employee, make him hated, and expose him to
government persecution."[28] One moderate editorialist tried to strike a
middle ground on recruitment and elections: "Whatever reform is decreed, it is indispensable that recruitment ceases to be the weapon of
[incumbent] governments to gain votes and win elections. Whatever
project does not resolve this condition, is not worth making into law."[29]

Arguing that a volunteer system was a Liberal pipe dream, War Minister
Junqueira contended that draft boards would supplant personal fiat with a
just system where unbiased chance would select recruits. For him, the bill
provided "a voluntary system and equality in [exacting] the tribute of
blood. . . . The present system is bad because the manner in which the
government chooses recruits is arbitrary. The project substitutes expediency with chance: the draft lottery made . . . by local electoral officials
substitutes fraud with governmental discretion."[30] For Conservatives, reform offered the best hope of eliminating impressment's evils.

Still other objections to conscription included fears that it would disrupt Brazil's productive labor force. Conservative slavocrat José de Alencar
expressed fears that a draft would be used to call up slaves, but Junqueira
assured Parliament that in no instance would the project include bondsmen, "It is precisely to avoid arriving at the extreme where it becomes
necessary to manumit slaves and to free convicts from Fernando de Noronha [island] that it makes sense to adopt a law that enables the government to raise, during a war, the contingents required."[31] Thus, conscription, far from constituting a threat to slavery, was its best defense.

Liberals predicted that conscription would be more harmful to labor and
production than impressment. Senator Nabuco observed that "the number
of men you put under the flag is the number of laborers you remove from
the nation's production, weakening its strength." Moreover, the new re-

serve system penalized veterans: "Because of the risk that [reserves] will be called up for military service, they will not be employed by industry or agriculture."[32] Others went further, insisting that conscription undermined the family and stymied population growth. They cited France as an example of a nation that practiced conscription and whose population growth had slowed considerably after 1850.[33] Conscription threatened economic development, family formation, and, thereby, public order and morality.

Disputes over army recruitment's role in labor and security markets had pivotal regional and provincial dimensions. Gaps in troop contributions within and among provinces produced intense backbiting that is important to discuss briefly here because it shaped recruitment legislation. When the war minister conceded in 1870 that impressment would continue until a draft could be implemented, northeastern and *gaúcho* (Rio Grande do Sul natives) senators demanded that provincial troop quotas proportional to population be enforced. The war minister dutifully penned an imperial decree, but as in previous decades, the missive had little impact. The skewed recruitment distribution indicates an uneven web of patriarchal protection and cooperation with the central State explored more fully in chapter 6.

Minas Gerais was notorious for its failure to produce troops in both peace and wartime. In 1867, a Rio Grande do Sul newspaper cartoon bitterly commented on this injustice by portraying a typical scene in a Rio Grande household where a grief-stricken family holds a wake for a son fallen in battle. By contrast, the Minas household is shown filled with people dancing and celebrating a peaceful life.[34] Minas Gerais, thus, became an object of ridicule in the Senate. Angry senators showered verbal pot shots and thrust penned daggers at the honor of the nation's most populous province. Conservative Senator Figueira de Mello brandished his frustration with Minas Gerais with an amendment: "The contingents [to be drafted] for the army [will] be distributed among the provinces according to their free Brazilian-born population . . . because it is understood that neither foreigners nor slaves ought to pay the tribute of blood. . . . The senator for Minas was wrong . . . when he said that this amendment . . . was dictated by hate for his province. He also said . . . that this amendment was born of the suspicion harbored by this speaker in relation to Minas. I must admit that there was justice in this declaration because the actions of Minas when discussing contingents for the army make me certain that she [Minas] will make a valiant effort to proceed as she has in the past." Figueira de Mello then presented evidence that Minas Gerais contributed an unjustly small number of recruits.[35]

Despite his venom, Figueira de Mello failed to gain enough support for his amendment, whose main thrust was to base draft quotas on the 1872 census. Junqueira did not favor the rider because he thought the 1872 census inaccurate. Instead, he favored basing draft quotas on draft enrollment lists. This decision was ingenuous, and it obstructed conscription's implementation for decades.[36]

The Politics of Exemptions

Exemptions elucidate how Brazil's complex social hierarchies limited the scope of "universal" male conscription. Paraguayan War mobilization revealed the State's attempts to indulge and to manipulate its status-conscious citizenry. Because wartime impressment violated venerable norms regulating recruitment, the issue of exemptions took on added importance for the system of patriarchal and political "protection." According to one Liberal senator, "The army's generals agree that recruitment methods are deplorable and . . . fill the army with the dregs of the populace. They say that Liberals should be the most interested in a recruitment law, because when pressed they cannot find protectors."[37] He added that he would not vote for the law because it would not end politically motivated recruitment, a cornerstone of the coronel system of protection.

Significantly, the new law appeared poised to dismantle another important pillar of patriarchal protection. It no longer admitted marriage as an exemption, but it did make provisions for certain families: men who lived with, fed, and supported an "honest" sister, single or widowed; an only son who lived in the company of his mother, single or widowed, or a decrepit father; and widowers raising a legitimate or natural child.[38] The implementing legislation of 1875 specified that marriage and other exemptions that had applied to military service would be honored only for the first year of the draft. An imperial decision confirmed that "married citizens should not be included in the first draft, except those who volunteer or those legally separated from their wives and who do not provide [their spouses] with protection."[39] Thus, although the law did protect families whose livelihood hinged on a single adult male, it threatened two-parent household economies and their "honorable" status after the first draft in 1875. The perception that recruitment degraded the status of "men and sons of families" (code words for honorable males) could not be changed by decree over night. The law's indifference to family honor would inspire passionate public resistance.

Many Liberals and some Conservatives criticized other exemptions that betrayed the principle of universal male conscription. They proposed amendments to eliminate substitution and pecuniary exemptions: "It is clear that the project ought to pass, but . . . all that the project lost in barbarity it gained in foolishness; it is without coherence, without order, without system. For those countries that want to raise large forces there is a system based on the equality of the tribute of blood *inapplicable in Brazil but rational*. I do not understand why the noble war minister tells the senate that he wants to raise the army's moral level while defending measures that make the army a receptacle of vice and immorality, admitting substitution for money and of man for man."[40] This statement reveals the clash between traditional values and modern conceptions of civic duty. The senator recognized that the draft was a rational and fair way of raising an armed force, but it was "inapplicable" in honor-conscious and hierarchy-minded Brazil.

Conservatives blithely tried to drown out these criticisms by trumpeting the army's national integration ideology. They boasted that the draft would make all Brazilians (regardless of wealth, region, or birth) accountable for the tribute of blood, bringing all classes and regions of Brazilian society together under a uniform and equitable system of discipline. For Junqueira, draft "enrollment involves all classes of society, and luck will draw from each class a few individuals."[41] The law, however, continued to provide a patchwork of exemptions undermining its social leveling and integrating potential. The law required all males aged eighteen to thirty to register for the draft. In peacetime, however, fishermen, merchant marines, managers of manufactories, railway and steamship machinists, employees of "important" factories, a cowboy with more than fifty head of cattle, the owner, manager, or representative of a farm or rural business with more than ten employees, and the cashiers of commercial houses worth more than 10$000 milréis were exempt from the draft.[42] Of course, policemen, priests, seminarians, and graduates or students of medical or law faculties were exempt even in wartime. If anything, the law promised only to level strata of the protected and unprotected free poor.

While substitution and exemptions protected many, the Conservatives resisted extending exemptions to secondary students (outside the small number of students in Rio's public Pedro II and Lyceu schools), fearing a rash of false matriculations. In the meantime, to allay some public fears of leveling, Junqueira hinted at various points that illiterate enlistees would be preferred over literate ones.[43] The privileged wanted assurance that they could free their dependents from army service, preferably without payment. Army leaders had reluctantly accepted pecuniary exemptions; but by holding the line on student exemptions, officers could console themselves with the idea that prosperous Brazilians would have to contribute to the national treasury to escape the call-up.

Largely oblivious to the free poor's concerns with honor, Junqueira avowed the army and the draft's role in educating and disciplining citizens. To lend punch to his assertion, the war minister referred to General Moltke, the mastermind of Prussia's victory in the Franco-Prussian War: "Germany owed its recent great victory to what is referred to as the master school . . . to the army's morality and discipline; and without it . . . our nation's education will not be completed." The opposition retorted that Moltke referred to a "nation organized militarily, and under exceptional circumstances."[44] In truth, Brazil did not face the kind of military threats that Germany did, so how could Conservatives justify a draft lottery? Once again, Junqueira fell back on the army's integration ideology: "We say that presently military forces do not perfectly represent the country . . . everyone knows that recruitment is exercised in great part over the infamous strata of society, and so the army taken from this strata to some degree has to reflect its image though there exist honorable exceptions. The project . . . wants to raise the level, drawing men from all social strata, that represent perfectly the nation. It is in this sense that we say: we *will nationalize the army* . . . but the project does not *denationalize* [the ranks] by admitting in her breast some foreigners; with this we do not take away from its Brazilian character."[45]

Junqueira's analysis reveals that important elements of European military ideology and conceptions of national identity achieved greater closure after the Paraguayan War. For Junqueira, the ideals of the "nation in arms," where the army embodies a nation's masculine virtue, required a draft. Not only would the army no longer resort to hiring foreign mercenaries, but European immigrants and their sons would be exempted from the draft. The legislation's authors realized that foreign consuls would object to the inclusion of their citizens on draft rolls, and "whitening" advocates argued that a draft would scare off European newcomers if they were not exempted. The project allowed immigrants to volunteer—with the knowledge that few would. Junqueira dissimulated that the army intentionally excluded foreigners from draft rolls to preserve the military's "Brazilian" character and to "nationalize" the army.

Optimists suggested that the barracks could provide basic instruction to troops, making the army the largest institution for public education. While Junqueira's rhetoric appealed to the army's role in developing and sustaining the body politic, he cautioned: "The army will *not* be the school of instruction . . . but it is a school of punctuality and discipline." He did not think it possible to turn the barracks into literacy camps, but he did believe in the efficacy of instilling industrial attitudes toward time, work, appearance, and leisure.[46] Regimental schools would be experimented with, but they met with little success.

While some depicted the barracks as patriotic schoolhouses, others still described them as jails. Even Junqueira admitted that coercion would be necessary to enforce the draft, "Is it possible to for us to have an army composed exclusively of volunteers? . . . It is said with reason, that man-hunts . . . have reduced the army to a penitentiary that should be proscribed as soon as possible. . . . We have had to press men, if not in the cities, then in the countryside . . . such men will not have the motivations of *honor* [emphasis added] necessary to voluntarily report to the call for a draft."[47] Another senator similarly affirmed that most citizens lacked the "honor" to obey the law. The irony is that honor for most poor Brazilians meant protection from impersonal state power. The low regard of some leaders for the honor of humble citizens and soldiers made talk of recruitment or electoral reform a sophism. Still, Junqueira feebly defended the army's honor, "I will not allow you to say that the sons of families among us will be perverted by becoming part of the army, [an institution] that should always be a stimulus to morality and should be the image of a society."[48] Even as the war minister championed the army as a moralizing, disciplinary institution, he qualified his defense of it to justify reform of the recruitment process. Junqueira warned Liberals not to "instill fear of the army in the population, [causing] citizens to avoid serving."[49]

The opposition challenged Conservative assertions that the project law would bar criminals from army service. One senator noted that the letter of the law prohibited only those sentenced to "galés" (the galleys), a sentence usually reserved for slave convicts that since 1867 was being phased out.[50] It is difficult to tell if the bill's authors wanted to keep the draft rolls open to ex-convicts. While both camps used the imagery of the prison to describe the army, one clouded the issue by arguing that the depiction of soldiers as "criminals" was embroidered. Senator Barão de Jaguaribe, a Conservative, argued that "despite the fact that many believe that the army should be a type of correctional facility where police defendants and dangerous men are collected by means of recruitment, it does not always happen that way. . . . Those individuals who are distinguished as vagrants, shiftless, and without an occupation are ordinarily very industrious and agile, while the most active [criminals] procure protectors."[51] Perhaps Jaguaribe's analysis came closer to the mark by implying that police stereotyped most victims of impressment as "criminal" to justify their induction. He went on to defend the common Brazilian and revealed how his argument was linked to exemptions in the project law: "The great majority of the nation is made up of people less favored by fortune but scrupulously honest; it is this great mass that will have to supply the army [with men] because . . . [they] do not have the resources to substitute themselves or pay for a pecuniary exemption, while vagrants, these men fertile with resources are bound to have protectors." Apparently, conscription would continue to encourage the same criminal entrepreneurship that impressment inspired. Therefore, pecuniary exemptions helped to filter criminals out of the ranks, and the "scrupulously honest" poor would naturally end up serving. The logic of universal military service underwent a unique contortion here.[52]

While some castigated Conservatives for granting exemptions that favored the wealthy, Liberal senator Nabuco contradicted claims that a draft interfered with an individual's right to choose. Instead, he praised impressment's virtues for the poor: "The pressure [of impressment] does not fall on the shoulders of men useful to industry; it falls on vagrants and vagabonds. Now, is it inconvenient to exercise influence, and even corruption, to give a means of making a living to a vagrant? Is not this better than sacrificing industry, taking away useful laborers? I do not want the army to be composed of criminals and perverts. . . . There is nothing incorrect [however] . . . in forcing a man that has no means of making a living, who could lose himself in idleness, to adopt a profession in the army."[53] Nabuco's cavalier stance toward impressment and poor citizens' rights rivaled that of Conservative Marshal Caxias. As far as the less fortunate were concerned, corruption and influence peddling could be winked at, because by disciplining the free poor workforce and putting idle men to serviceable use, it increased export "production," the ultimate check on lofty liberal ideals of free choice.[54]

Junqueira belittled these "benefits" of impressment by stressing its violence. During the debate, Junquiera reported that Captain José Ribeiro da Silva Laranja had been assassinated by men resisting a press gang he led in Espírito Santo. The war minister repeatedly raised this incident, asking senators, "Is it worth conserving the actual state of recruitment?"[55] Another senator added that "squads surprise the incautious on the street and on the roads, day and night, hiding in ambush, leading in many cases to resistance and assassination. One reads stories of many murders . . . [many] have their origins in the act of recruitment."[56]

Senator Nabuco launched a counterattack by portraying the barracks as schools of delinquency. Discharged veterans were "accustomed to life in the barracks, [they] do not return to work nor to the countryside, they stay in the cities, becoming not producers but consumers. . . . The senate knows that a recruitment law with poorly considered dispositions can distort the vocations, customs, and habits of a people." Another senator backed up Nabuco: "After receiving his discharge, the soldier is unsuited to other vocations. . . . The project will diminish public wealth, free labor, and the population, and is contrary to the great principle of national defense."[57] Even though the draft would draw at most 4,000 men annually, Liberals contended that conscription would impose an untenable labor drain. Junqueira dismissed these objections, "Taking a draft from ten million inhabitants, and inducting four or five thousand individuals per year, I cannot understand how one can say that the project will take the flower of the population for armed service."[58]

Another Liberal senator changed tack, noting that in Germany, "everyone serves a short term of service [3 years], here a few serve a long time."[59] Junqueira answered this query: "If we reduce the years which the army volunteer serves to less than six . . . [then] just when the soldier is in circumstances to give his best service, he will get his discharge, because in this system discharge is invariable and obligatory. Presently discharges are not awarded with all exactness to those who have completed their terms because recruitment is insufficient . . . we are obliged to retain many soldiers who have already completed their contracts."[60] For Junqueira, a soldier's training and useful employment demanded six years of active duty. This may have been due to the technology of the day. In Brazil, as in France in the early 1870s, the standard weapon for most troops — muzzle-loaded guns — were difficult to handle. Companies of soldiers trained for years to learn how to load and fire strategic volleys with muzzle-loaded weapons. The Prussian army found it imperative to develop and to mass-produce a breech-loading rifle (the needle gun) to make a three-year service stint viable. Since the Brazilian army depended on muzzle-loaded guns until the mid-1890s, this likely encouraged officers to favor longer service contracts.[61]

Yet another Liberal objection questioned using a unified draft to supply men to the navy, which had not yet eliminated flogging and servile camarada duties. Junqueira rebutted that France had a similar system and added that the navy's apprentice school system limited its need for draftees. The perpetuation of flogging in the navy reveals that attempts to secure the dignity of enlisted service were piecemeal — a fact that would come back to haunt the State.[62]

The 1874 Recruitment Law passed by a small margin over Liberal objections and the protests of Conservative slavocrat Senator José de Alencar. While no imminent foreign or internal threat forced the State to allocate funds to military preparedness, penal reform, or social policy, the State possessed few institutional alternatives to impressment for disciplining "unprotected" poor men. Draft lotteries, like penitentiaries, were expensive innovations of industrial discipline that challenged Brazilian values. As one Liberal senator warned, the Recruitment Law needed to be "accompanied by complementary measures." Such measures were a long time in coming.

The Paraguayan War exposed the weaknesses of impressment, but in the end, Brazil still won the war. Wartime impressment and slavery's decline made the free poor more conscious of the fragility of their status. Although some questioned the legality and morality of press-ganging, the army's inadequate wartime performance and the perceived need to improve defense in deference to "civilized" Continental models seem to have been Parliament's main motivations in passing recruitment reform.[63] In pre-Enlightenment empires "criminals" often formed the bulk of the most powerful State institution responsible for managing public violence. Military reforms in the 1800s attempted to alter this dynamic, but to put legislation into action meant overcoming a variety of cultural, political, and institutional barriers. Attempts to implement limited conscription in the last years of the empire would throw light on the height and breadth of those obstructions.

Chapter 4

Whipping a Dead Letter

The 1874 Recruitment Law

under the Empire,

1874–1889

Ladislao Feliz de Oliveira, a "scrivener of the peace" for the Porto Real do Colégio parish, walked to the parish church north of Salvador, Bahia, on Thursday, July 1, 1875. Ladislao's stride may have been more sprightly than usual that winter morning as he looked forward to a holiday the next day honoring the province of Bahia's Independence Day. Then again, considering the task at hand, his gait may have been furtive. Ladislao was on his way to post an unpopular edict convoking young men to enroll for the draft. Suddenly, he was intercepted by an angry crowd of three hundred men and women armed with guns, daggers, kitchen knives, scythes, clubs, and machetes. After shredding the scrivener's handiwork, the group descended on the home of the justice of the peace, demanding at knifepoint his copy of the draft regulations. The justice acquiesced to the demands on the condition that they return the regulations after reading them. According to the justice, the "mob" immediately tore up the regulations, shouted "knavish" insults, and vowed to make a similar visit on August 1 when enrollment boards were scheduled to meet.[1]

This incident would dampen Bahia's Independence Day festivities and reflected rising tensions that resulted in several days of unrest in the provincial capital, Salvador. Similar actions occurred in numerous locations across Brazil from 1874 until the empire's fall in 1889. The Recruitment Law had been an important postwar victory for the army's modernization platform, but it proved to be a pyrrhic one. Relatively little attention has been given to the foot dragging and popular protests that obstructed the 1874 Recruitment Law's execution.[2] Longstanding interpretations have explained the frustration of army reforms in terms of the plantocracy's fears that a strong national army could threaten their autonomy over local affairs.[3] More recent studies emphasize the "honorable" working poor's resistance to conscription.[4] An analysis of the protests that foiled the draft's execution show these acts to be part of a larger struggle over the geography of honor that linked traditions of urban and rural protest.[5] At the same time, administrative problems and legal battles shaped the various struggles over conscription at both the national and local levels.

Military Conscription: A Hard Sell

The Recruitment Law's passage provoked a jubilant response from War Minister Junqueira. He praised Parliament and anticipated impressment's "abolition," but warned that it would continue until the new system was in place.[6] The language used to describe these reforms resembled that of abolitionists, and it emphasized the view that impressment, like slavery, was a barbaric anachronism. The injustice of impressment, however, would continue long after slavery's complete abolition in 1888.

Conscription's opponents had been outmaneuvered. Even so, one moderate Liberal editorialist applauded the law: "Brazil took one more step into the community of civilized nations. We give our cordial congratulations to the army. The nobility of the uniform . . . maintained by the heroic efforts of our soldiers, amid truly little dignified conditions, is finally recognized publicly. Brazilian civilization and its material and intellectual progress no longer permit the disrespect of this class that fought for national honor. Praise . . . to Junqueira . . . [who] produced a law that passes with all of its prestige and moral force."[7] This editorialist praised both parties for producing a law that promised to bring respect to the army and, thereby, Brazil. The Recruitment Law supplanted the victory parades denied most returning Paraguayan War veterans as "public" recognition of their wartime sacrifices.

Others gave more qualified praise. Republicans, ever careful to garner the army officer corps' favor, praised the law's passage, but lamented that exemptions favored the wealthy. Some blamed Conservatives for abandoning the ideal of universal conscription, a principle near the heart of Republicans who revered the French Revolution.[8] Still others predicted disaster. One Liberal senator who voted against the law delivered a prophetic caveat. He "deplore[d] that the country does not have the clear knowledge it should of Parliament's deliberations. The people have not made demonstrations against the project under discussion because they do not know its dispositions."[9] Indeed, news of the Recruitment Law's passage spread quickly and dissent ensued.

In nations around the world, advertising smoothed the transition from traditional to modern recruitment methods.[10] In Brazil, the Recruitment Law had an ominous public relations problem, and the State had few effective means of reaching the illiterate majority (about 85 percent of the 1890 population). Since the term "recruitment" itself implied impressment, how then could officials convince citizens that the infelicitously named "Recruitment Law" advanced justice? This reveals the political elite's distance and relative indifference to the fears of the largely disenfranchised poor. Impressment during the Paraguayan War eroded faith in the barriers that had protected less-privileged men from impressment. Loose talk of "recruitment" fueled anxieties across the nation.[11]

State propaganda for the law depended mainly on the Conservative, military, and government press. These organs reached only a small portion of educated Brazilians and preached mostly to the converted. Even within the means available, there is little evidence of orchestrated efforts to garner wider public support. The State could not rely on the clergy's persuasive powers because of the ongoing "Religious Question," the Church-State controversy over the emperor's 1873 arrest of two ultramontane bishops.

Conversely, conscription's enemies had a comparatively easy time stirring up discontent against the law.[12] Most Brazilians relied on word of mouth for information, and those who opposed the draft openly aired their opinions in markets, bars, masses, and festivals: nodes in the tangled webs of oral communication networks. Embarrassed Conservative officials attributed protests against the law to ignorance and the willingness of irresponsible Liberals and priests to incite the credulous. But, even if most Brazilians had a clear grasp of the new law's principles, they could convincingly point to a tradition of government disregard for the terms of service contracts. They did not require coaching from the better educated to draw this conclusion. Even those who had verifiable exemptions fled from press gangs. They preferred to avoid a stint in a recruit depository while the uncertain wheels of bureaucracy turned slowly. Those who sought to undermine conscription did not have to explain abstract reform measures, but could appeal to an abiding tradition of popular resentment and resistance to impressment. Soon enough this tradition surfaced.

In late November 1874, several weeks of disturbances swept the interior of Pernambuco and Paraíba as citizens smashed newly standardized metric weights and balances, looting and damaging property, and destroying municipal records. Authorities attributed the Quebra Quilos (kilo breaking) Revolt to public anxiety and ire over the metric system's adoption, new taxes, the Religious Question, and the Recruitment Law's passage.[13] As the furor calmed, army, national guard, and state police forces moved in and created further turmoil as they set about dragooning the "instigators." Officials eventually pardoned more prosperous land owners for their involvement, and quietly exiled a number of implicated foreign-born priests. The revolt heightened the anticlerical and xenophobic views of many officers. One remembered in 1878 that "six years ago, the bishops of Pernambuco and Pará opposed the State's decrees [the Religious Question] . . . a religious conflagration was ready to ignite the ire of fanaticism . . . when false clergymen . . . in Paraíba . . . incited the people to rebel against the adoption of the [metric] system of weights and measures . . . What did the government order? They resolved that the warrior's sword should cut down the bishop's crosier of evil priests."[14] Officers, however, directed most of their ire at poor freemen with impressment dragnets that nabbed a number of poor "fathers" of family (code phrase for honorable married men). In April 1875, Paraíba's governor requested that the war minister discharge sixteen married men inducted in the Vila de Ingá. The local priest sent their marriage certificates, and officials honored their exemptions after the men had languished for months in stockades as far south as Rio.[15]

Senator Francisco Octaviano called attention to overzealous impressment that did not allow honorable men time to prove their exemptions. He read a firsthand report suffused with the ideology of the house: "The madness of the Quebra Quilos Revolt did not produce robberies, deaths, nor disrespect the propriety of the *home and family*. Disgracefully, the same cannot be said of government troops. Recruitment is performed in a deranged manner . . . because it affects *fathers and men of work*" (emphasis added).[16] The protesters, according to this observer, had respected the propriety of families and the sanctity of homes, but imperial troops had not. Press-gangs meted out beatings and strapped recruits in moist leather vests that shrank as they dried, rubbing their victims' skin raw and constricting breathing. Some died before they could don a uniform.[17] Reports of such abuse did not inspire public confidence that the Recruitment Law would bring justice.

Joan E. Meznar has highlighted the Recruitment Law's role in piquing the anxieties that motivated the revolt. Registration of any sort generated resistance because many common folk feared it to be an underhanded plot to reenslave the free poor. An 1851 attempt at civil registration in Paraíba had to be shelved when the free poor led vociferous protests, alleging it would be used to re-enslave free individuals. Some participants in the Quebra Quilos Revolt dubbed the Recruitment Law "the law of captivity," claiming that it "turned citizens into slaves."[18] It is difficult to tell if protesters truly believed they would be literally "enslaved," or if they borrowed from the polemics of Liberal leaders. In any case, vulnerability to impersonal public authority was equated with a status uncomfortably close to slavery. Common understandings of the draft lottery's procedures must have been distressing, perhaps even more so if clearly explained. To be selected in a public lottery for army service may have seemed comparable to being auctioned off at the open slave market or to drawing lots among law-abiding citizens (those who would cooperate with draft registration) to see whose relative should serve a jail term. Impressment marked the distance between the protected and the unprotected, and as the protestors' language indicates, this distinction took on heightened importance as slavery declined.

The Quebra Quilos Revolt channeled public fears piqued by the 1874 Recruitment Law. Most subsequent antidraft disturbances would focus resistance on the enrollment process. A second wave of protests broke out when officials began to order scriveners of the peace such as Ladislao Feliz de Oliveira — whose story opened this chapter — to tack up edicts ordering men to enroll for the draft.

Registration and Remonstration

When registration boards convoked parishioners to sign up for the draft in August 1875, citizens exhibited a variety of reactions. In some parishes young men dutifully enrolled while in others draft boards encountered riotous protest. Most men kept their distance until they believed it was safe to go about their normal activities. In 1877, War Minister Caxias acknowledged that enrollment disturbances had occurred in Minas Gerais, São Paulo, Pernambuco, Paraíba, Espírito Santo, Ceará, Rio Grande do Norte, Alagoas, Rio de Janeiro, and Bahia. Typically, angry protesters, frequently led by women, stormed draft registration boards, threatened officials, and destroyed enrollment lists. Caxias echoed the arrogant analysis of provincial authorities who blamed "the people's complete ignorance of the new law's liberal principles which makes the burden of military service fall equally on the shoulders of the population's general mass."[19]

A brief analysis of the events described at the head of this chapter provide some clues about popular actions. The description was based on a report by the local justice of the peace. He named the most vociferous protesters, indicating that they were local residents. That participants intercepted the scrivener on his way to post an enrollment edict reveals that they possessed a modicum of organization and some sort of intelligence network. It is unlikely that such a large armed crowd would gather spontaneously. Antidraft forces now had the luxury of plotting their strategy, whereas impressment had favored press gangs with the tactical advantage of surprise. By destroying official notices and the materials necessary to conduct enrollment, opponents debilitated conscription's effectiveness and legitimacy. By intimidating board members and potential registrants, the protestors employed strategies similar to a more venerable Brazilian political tradition.

The disruption of enrollment boards reveals a modus operandi similar to election fixing. For instance, Mato Grosso's governor complained in 1884, "The election was proceeding in the local church when two unknown men snatched the books and papers from the table and destroyed them, afterwards running to hide themselves in the nearby wilderness." The Liberal governor grumbled that a "well-known Conservative" army lieutenant who headed a local detachment assigned to guard the church, had done nothing to stop the intruders.[20] These venerable tactics served draft resisters well. The Recruitment Law required that draft registration lists, rather than the 1872 census, serve as the statistical basis for the draft lottery. Without a representative cross section of young men on the rolls, it became difficult for authorities to claim that a national lottery could be conducted fairly. Enrollment difficulties proved to be the law's Achilles heel.

Meanwhile, the conflict over enrollment edicts in the scrivener Ladislao's parish spilled over into Bahia's Independence Day. During the traditional parade in Salvador, praças of the army's 18th Infantry Battalion, holding public dignitaries and an effigy of the emperor, marched toward a review stand. The 18th's line of approach forced back the ranks of the Lyceu Imperial de Artes e Ofícios's Patriotic Militia Battalion. According to press accounts, when the militia men pushed forward to retake their former position, a melee broke out due to the army praças' "condemnable savagery." Such an affront, intentional or not, required redress for the sake of corporate honor. Tensions were probably heightened by the differing social status of the combatants: the lumpen (army praças) versus the labor aristocracy (artisan battalion). The 18th allegedly charged the patriotic battalion with their bayonets. Officers and men of the 18th, police, and ordenança units joined the fray. The artisans warded off their foes, rallying around their banner and "defending it with valor." Amid this "horrible confusion," the 18th's commander, Lieutenant Colonel Frias Vilar, reportedly "did nothing" to restrain his men.[21]

The press blamed the army for the conflict, but determining fault for a riot is often illusory. Fears of draft registration probably made the patriotic battalion and others quicker to vent their frustrations. It is even conceivable that such a conflict could have been planned to discredit registration efforts. In any case, Salvador's public blamed the army, and specifically Lieutenant Colonel Frias Vilar, for the disorders. A month before draft boards were scheduled to first meet, the army became the focus of the city's popular animosity.

The next morning, agitated groups huddled in the streets grumbling that the lieutenant colonel should be brought to justice. Rumors spread that Frias Vilar was being transported to prison for his actions during the riot, and crowds scoured the streets in search of vengeance. They discovered Frias Vilar and began to stone him. Frias Vilar fled, but he was soon found, severely beaten, and narrowly escaped death.[22] Unrest continued, and observers reported that in the districts of Salomé and Igreja Nova inhabitants did not intend to give their sons' names to draft boards, and they threatened officials and armed themselves. Officials pleaded for a mounted force to patrol dangerous areas to prevent further disorder.[23]

Bahia's Conservative governor berated the Liberal press for inciting resistance to draft registration. Despite enhanced security measures taken in early August 1875, isolated incidents disrupted the work of several Bahian draft boards. In the Vila de Camamu and Santa Anna do Catu, armed men and women stormed churches where enrollment boards met; they shredded documents and broke benches and tables. Other boards rescheduled enrollment, calling on the governor to provide twenty praças or more for security.[24]

While similar disruptions occurred in scattered parishes throughout Brazil, the intensity of resistance varied. The Quebra Quilos Revolt and the Bahian Independence Day melee were exceptional. In Ceará, the governor reported disturbances of "little consequence": "Some women, mothers, wives, daughters, and sisters terrified by the new Recruitment Law whose rigorous design seemed too excessive in their eyes, naturally protective of those connected to them by the ties of family and consensual union, invaded the locations where enrollment boards functioned in Tamboril, União, Santa Quiteria, and Acarape. . . . They ripped apart [enrollment] records . . . retreating afterwards to their houses without committing any other act of violence. . . . This act, practiced by persons of a sex which in all ways exceeds that of men in dedication and tolerance, beyond being singularly exceptional, did not constitute more than an exaggerated demonstration of family affection, provoked by fears and fed by ignorance. . . . The incidents do not deserve more than passing mention."[25] The chauvinistic report reveals why women were particularly effective operatives in draft resistance. Male officials were unwilling to admit that these acts of female vandalism posed a serious threat to public order. What honorable man would use force on "women of family" whose physical and rational faculties were assumed to be far inferior to those of men? That these women acted in public in large numbers may have protected them from the potential "dishonor" of taking to the streets and challenging authorities individually. Sensible authorities avoided taking strong-arm actions against groups of female protestors, aware that such acts could unleash popular fury.[26]

According to this report, women's gender predisposed them to an "exaggerated" but admirable preoccupation with family welfare. Their actions refute the idea that the public sphere was exclusively male, and they indicate that competing conceptions of proper womanhood were as prevalent as conceptions of manhood. Certainly women throughout Latin America often participated vigorously in public protests. In this case, the protesters feared that the draft would split up their families. Drafting a male family member into a low-paying, minimum six-year contract posed severe hardships for modest households. Families might be forced to uproot themselves from established networks of mutual communal support to accompany draftees to garrison towns. Honorable status and economic security were usually closely correlated, especially for poor families.[27] The poor also sensed, probably correctly, that moral arguments would sway their social superiors more effectively than laments about economic privation.

For Ceará officials, women's vandalism was no more than misguided virtue, better left unpunished. These women targeted documents, and no violence or further disorders were reported. Clearly this analysis was self-serving. Local leaders were probably glad for any excuse to suspend the exercise of a disruptive, unpopular measure. The incident also shows the ambiguities that could transform formulaic ideas of gender and the geography of honor. By taking to public squares to defend their homes and families from the draft, these women domesticated the street and claimed it as an appropriate sphere for feminine militancy. Even the police noted the protesters' etiquette in "returning home" after the protest. By acting to protect their men, the women reversed stereotypical gender roles.

Male vandalism invited violent resistance from officials. In some parishes, male protestors suffered injury, punitive impressment, or death. A district judge in the tobacco growing town of Cachoeira, Bahia, granted three writs of habeas corpus to men dragooned in late 1875, but the provincial government would not remit them because "they had no exemption" and were "trouble makers and without a licit means of making a living. . . . They had already been sworn in for active service and had cooperated with draft disturbances . . . on the occasion of draft enrollment." Cachoeira's justice of the peace had halted registration when the men in question directed insults and threats at him. Female protesters certainly ran risks, but they could not be pressed.[28]

In the cotton fields of Paraíba and Pernambuco, where only months earlier the Quebra Quilos Revolt had unleashed pent-up anxieties over the Recruitment Law, there were few enrollment disturbances. Pernambuco's governor reported: "Predictably the work of enrollment boards has been slow and difficult. . . . In Leopoldina, where a board was attacked . . . one of the aggressors was killed. . . . In Itambé, the enrollment books which had been completed and stored in the church, were discovered destroyed, the author of this act is unknown. . . . Rumors that circulated about grave disorders occurring when enrollment boards met have proven false."[29] The governor credited the relative calm to the efforts of parish authorities who explained the law's purpose and justness. Mention of local officials stumping for registration is rare. The governor claimed that they dispelled "suspicions" that the new system "would impose new and greater personal sacrifices" on common people.[30] The Quebra Quilos Revolt moved officials to take special precautions to promote enrollment.

Resistance in the coffee state of São Paulo rocked the rural parishes of Franca, Santo Antônio, Santa Rita, Carmo, Rijania, São Simão, Socorro, and Rio Verde. Bands of armed assistants invaded registration boards, destroying enrollment lists. The police chief reported: "Board members, who could only count on the insignificant help of a few local [police] detachments, could not resist these rioters, and for this reason, we do not have to lament deaths or injuries. . . . The seditious movement was caused by elements from outside this province."[31] It is strange to hear a police chief expressing relief that no violence occurred because there were not enough officers to enforce the law.

Minas Gerais, famous for its mines and dairy products and infamous for producing few recruits, played host to predictably stiff resistance to registration. In 1876, the governor lamented that enrollment had produced the majority of public disorders. The new law had been "difficult to execute" and the "people [were] violently opposed it." They arrived fully armed to disrupt and destroy paperwork in several localities. As an example, he gave the experience of Ponta Nova, where some sixty women destroyed enrollment lists.[32]

Some parishes did not carry out orders to draw up draft lists, but many conducted the process without incident. In Rio Grande do Sul, the governor beamed, "The excessive intelligence and spirit of order of this province's sons were honorably revealed by the unaltered tranquility that prevailed during the entire military registration process. Much different from what occurred in other provinces."[33] Still, the number of men enrolled in Rio Grande do Sul and elsewhere were few.

While many parishes cooperated, the disturbances that marked enrollment emboldened the law's opponents to propose its repeal in September

1875. War Minister Junqueira found himself saddled with an old debate. A Liberal senator for Minas Gerais attributed the impressment abuses that followed the Quebra Quilos Revolt to the Recruitment Law, and introduced a bill to scuttle the law. Junqueira repudiated these charges, "The noble senator . . . begins by stating that he knew that numerous disturbances would erupt, and he proposes the suspension of the law as he proposed the suspension of the law establishing the metric system three years ago. . . . The noble Senator also referred to the disturbances in Paraíba [the Quebra Quilos Revolt], attempting . . . to procure arguments against the law. . . . If only now [the province] is attempting enrollment for this law's execution . . . how can one say that men with exemptions, old men, married men, and others were pressed because of this law? The truth is that a draft lottery never occurred. . . . Among us there are some provinces that until today have not distinguished themselves in producing recruits, but this is not a question of conscription nor of the limited draft lottery system, or any other; it is a question of recruitment in any form; [these provinces simply] do not want to produce recruits."[34] Universal male conscription and universal weights and measures, both serviceable to nation building, produced popular protests and high-level political opposition. Junqueira cleverly discredited the senator's argument by claiming that Minas Gerais was opposed to any kind of recruitment.[35] He also denied that the Recruitment Law had sparked the Quebra Quilos Revolt. Indeed, impressment, not the draft, was to blame for abuses, but, the war minister's statement did not acknowledge that in part the protest anticipated the Recruitment Law's enforcement.

Conservatives credited Liberals with fomenting disorders. The viscount Rio Branco argued that enrollment disruptions "should be attributed to individuals who desire to gain from these disturbances." Junqueira was a bit more even handed, stating with accuracy that "never in any country when this question has been raised have the people not protested, because the tribute of blood is the most costly to pay." While antidraft protests were to be expected, Junqueira asserted that he "consider[ed] the limited draft lottery law, a true letter of liberty (*carta de alforria*) for the Brazilian citizen. . . . It is a law instituted in favor of the poor man; . . . this law does not subject him to impressment by the arbitrary powers of the police chief, his deputies, the military recruitment agent, the neighborhood inspector, or the cop on the beat."[36] Once again, proponents of conscription borrowed abolitionist rhetoric, "manumitting" the citizen from abuses of public authority.

Conservatives blocked Liberal attempts to kill the legislation, but they did make some concessions to increase protections from the draft. Parliament approved the creation of insurance companies to protect men from conscription. Even in small provincial capitals newspapers began carrying advertisements for these companies.[37] Draft insurance made it possible for men of more modest means to insure themselves for the 400$000 milréis (approximately US $220) necessary for pecuniary exemption. This law confirmed the general perception that the draft would target the honorable poor, and through it Parliament further watered down the already diluted ideal of universal male conscription.

Even before these measures were in place, others planned to undermine the leveling potential of the draft for profit. The president of Rio's city council Lieutenant Colonel Antônio Barroso Pereira recused himself from serving on a draft board in 1875 after a local judge convoked him because of a conflict of interest. He claimed to have government approval to organize a company "whose purpose is to provide substitutes for those enlisted for service."[38] Apparently, some planned to gain by selling substitutes to affluent draftees, a practice that had been lucrative during the Paraguayan War.

Anyone who bought draft insurance or invested in selling substitutes wasted their money. The phrase "all attempts to enforce the 1874 Recruitment Law met with little success" became common in Minas Gerais's reports in the 1880s. When other unpopular local and federal measures were passed, enrollment boards became lightning rods for public discontent. According to an official, in northern Minas Gerais in 1880, during attempts "to execute the laws regarding civil and military registration . . . no less than one thousand men armed themselves in the Paulistas, Turvo, and Vermelho districts. . . . This revolt began with a priest's declaration about civil registration and the District Judge's order to Justices of the Peace to proceed with military registration, this coincided with the promulgation of a new tax for municipal schools. On New Year's Day, 300 armed persons met in Turvo, running roughshod through the streets, shooting guns, they went to the Justice of the Peace's office and burned all documents regarding military enlistment."[39] Draft boards became a rally-ing cry for civil resistance to other unpopular measures.

Resistance to draft registration peaked in 1875, but it continued to occur through much of the country as the federal government pressured provincial presidents to carry out enrollment. For instance, in 1884, the board of Conceição de Alagoas in Minas Gerais was attacked by "a group of fifty women using disguises, [who] suddenly entered and completely destroyed the paperwork." The justice of the peace despaired that "in this parish it is impossible to conduct military registration, this is the fourth time it has been attempted and we are always interrupted by women."[40] One would think that after three previous attacks, the local draft board would have taken appropriate precautions. Even disguised, the women who undertook such carnavalesque attacks were probably recognizable to the board. One can almost imagine officials informing the assailants when to show up, but the justice complained that the board had been working for three days when the attack occurred. Officials themselves resented these extra duties, and they did not relish facing popular reprisals.

Beyond scattered disturbances, serious administrative difficulties under-mined enrollment. The regulations governing the enrollment and execu-tion of the lottery were confusing. Precious time and momentum was lost answering questions on procedural matters and rounding up board mem-bers. In an incredible legislative oversight, even finding the required per-sonnel to form the draft board proved difficult.[41] Also, the law made no provision for augmenting the pay or reducing parish officials' duties as an incentive. Passive draft resisters simply boycotted the registration process. By 1877, a total of 104,485 eligible citizens had registered for the draft nationwide. This was only about 10 percent of the men aged twenty to thirty counted in the 1872 census. Negligent parish officials were threat-ened with fines for not conducting enrollment, but few fines were assessed and fewer collected.[42] Caxias lamented that the State lacked the data neces-sary to conduct the lottery even though the law had provisions for execut-ing it before registration was fully completed.[43] Where active resistance did not occur, officials bemoaned the exhaustive efforts necessary to com-plete enrollment. Bahia's governor griped, "I have constantly employed all efforts and many times the repressive means with which the law empowers me. The increasing number of parishes in the province [numbering 172], the distance of many of them from the capital, the difficulties and slowness of communications in such an extensive territory, and the repugnance some have inculcated in the population for this beneficial law that will establish the desired equality in the distribution of the onerous tribute of blood [thwarted registration efforts]."[44]

Many men who did register claimed exemptions to the draft. In the hardscrabble farming town of Apiai, São Paulo, 87 men between the ages of eighteen and thirty were registered. Of these, only thirteen made no claim to exemption.[45]

Immigrants relied on their consulates to protect them and their Brazilian-born sons from enrollment. In 1884, Espírito Santo's governor complained that a local draft board insisted on enrolling the sons of Dutch and German fathers. The war minister circulated an Imperial Resolution of March 1876 that exempted the sons of foreigners from enlistment. Even though they were born in Brazil they were not liable to registration or impressment as long as they were enrolled with the appropriate foreign consulate.[46] Few foreigners signed on for army enlisted service, unlike the U.S. army during this period. The Brazilian free poor justly resented the protection and advantages afforded to immigrants. This made the army a very "Brazilian" institution, more easily given over to nativist sentiments.

Active registration resistance was scattered, but effective. Minas Gerais (with more than 1.6 million male inhabitants in 1890) reported in 1886 that only 3,716 men from ages eighteen to thirty had been registered. Of these, 2,976 were eligible for peacetime service, 202 for wartime service, and 538 were exempt. The president admitted that "draft boards have ceased to function for the most part, some for lack of a sworn-in delegate . . . and others for lack of state police to protect them from the customary aggressions of ruffians. . . . After fourteen years of enrollment, the difficulties with its realization continue. . . . Only after some adjustments to the law and the adoption of simple methods for its execution will it be possible to arrive at the results desired."[47] Similarly, Ceará's governor advised in 1881, "It did not seem useful to initiate [draft] enrollment to me because it would coincide with the nomination of special electors, [in addition, draft registration] seemed unnecessary to me given the excessive number of volunteers that have presented themselves to enlist destined to serve in the south."[48] Five years later the same governor adjusted his defense, "Not withstanding [my] reiterated recommendations . . . military enrollment has not been carried out with desirable regularity . . . because of the light regard given to this task by the majority of the responsible authorities."[49] Even in Rio Grande do Sul, registration continued without incident, but some parishes became lax in remitting lists. The province's most populous city, Porto Alegre, registered only 270 men in 1880.[50] Local officials' gusto for enrollment evaporated, while some opponents had converted foiling registration into an annual sporting event. Meanwhile, impressment persisted through the empire's twilight. In January 1889, Republican journalist Raul Pompéia observed that Rio's population was squeezed by the twin plagues of military impressment and yellow fever.[51]

The Military Question and the Empire's Demise

The government's ineffectual attempts to implement the Recruitment Law contributed to a variety of grievances that destabilized civil-military relations. The underlying sources of conflict between army officers and imperial politicians were rooted in the heightened ambitions and changing ideology of the former. Since the Paraguayan War, army officers felt they had earned the right to exercise greater influence in national affairs.[52] The war had encouraged the absorption of European military theory, and officers increasingly strove to emulate the organization, ideology, and esprit de corps of Europe's model armies: Germany and France. These superpowers had demonstrated the potency of land-based militarism in forging a national identity and promoting economic, political, and cultural unification. Similarly, Brazilian officers and their allies began to emphasize the army's role in galvanizing national unity.

More than any other national institution, the army incorporated men of different social classes and races from across the country. This quality enhanced the quasi-mystical link between army and nation enshrined in the European concept of the nation in arms. The army's triumph in Paraguay differed from its primary missions in the 1800s: quelling domestic rebellions. As a result, officers began to portray the army as the linchpin of national unity and to lay the ideological foundation for the slogan "the Army — agent of national integration."[53] As Colonel Benjamin Constant Botelho de Magalhães, the military academy's positivist mentor, observed in 1890, the soldier is the "embodiment of national honor."[54]

The early exponents of the army's "integration" ideology studied at the military academy in Rio, perhaps Brazil's most influential institution of higher education in the late 1800s.[55] It produced and employed some of the nation's most authoritative scholars and became an intellectual redoubt of the period's most prevalent school of political and philosophical thought: positivism. Inspired by Auguste Comte, positivists possessed an almost mystical faith in science, mathematics, and technology's ability to unify and modernize a nation. Far from monolithic, positivism appealed to Brazil's civilians and officers. It exhibited a variety of schools of thought, ranging from orthodox positivist churches to eclectic heterodoxy — some positivists favored conscription, others doggedly opposed it.

Army officers' more modest social origins accentuated their resentments of the civilian political elite's arrogance. Military academy graduates thought highly of their "scientific" education, and came to consider themselves the intellectual and patriotic superiors of civilian and religious leaders. Novelist Lima Barreto parodied officer hubris by depicting an army colonel's touchy reaction to the suggestion by a subordinate that he did not know something: "He was offended three times over: in his individual honor, in the honor of his caste [the army], and in the academic establishment he attended, the Military Academy at Praia Vermelha, the top scientific establishment in the world."[56] Civilian elites often unceremoniously snubbed officers' political and social aspirations. Officers returned this disdain by referring to politicians as *casacas* (frock coats). Most casacas studied law or medicine at one of Brazil's four facilities of higher education, largely elitist preserves due to the high costs of attendance. Conversely, if a candidate passed the military academy's qualification exams, he was paid to attend.

By the late 1870s, army officers had grown restive with casaca neglect. As one veteran officer wrote, "The army at that time [the early 1860s] was disrespected, this disrespect was suspended to a limited extent during the Paraguayan War, but it was greatly aggravated after the war."[57] Budget and troop cuts, slow rates of promotion, and the government's lack of resolve in enforcing the Recruitment Law made officers extremely thin-skinned. They interpreted criticisms of the army as assaults on "military honor" that could result in lethal reprisals. One incident involved the assassination of a mulatto editor of a humorous tabloid. In 1883, a group of cavalry officers led by Colonel Moreira César (famous for his botched attack on Canudos in 1897), killed the editor because of his satirical remarks about the army. Moreira César's punishment was a transfer to the crocodile-filled wetlands of Mato Grosso.[58] Civil-military tensions were heightened by a series of showdowns known as the Military Question. The "question" centered on an officer's right to criticize government leaders. Since the 1850s, army regulations required officers to get approval from the war minister (usually a casaca) before publishing material. The Liberal Parliament that came to power in 1878 reiterated these decrees.

Brazil's leading authority on European armies, an outspoken abolitionist, and an avid conscription advocate, Colonel Antônio de Sena Madureira, became the central protagonist in a dispute over censorship in 1886. The colonel defied the war minister's authority, claiming that officers had the right to defend military "honor" in the press. His acerbic pen inspired brother officers to contest casaca censorship. The government arrested the recalcitrant colonel and other officers despite the Supreme Military Council's ruling that officers, like civilians, had a right to freedom of expression.[59]

As a result, army officers formed the Military Club in June 1887. At the urging of the club's first president, Marshal Deodoro da Fonseca, the State retracted Sena Madureira's official reprimand. The Military Club then exercised its newfound lobbying voice to exhort the crown not to employ army troops to chase down runaway slaves in October 1887. While army officers subsequently claimed that this epistle constituted a brash abolitionist stance, it dovetailed more precisely with the army's efforts to withdraw from what it considered police work. Deodoro reasoned that "the army is for wars of loyalty in the defense of the throne and the fatherland; for other tasks that require armed force, there is the police."[60]

The Military Club would form a nucleus of army opposition that overthrew the monarchy on November 15, 1889. While it gave officers a new sense of corporate solidarity, the commissioned ranks remained deeply divided along generational, educational, and political lines of cleavage. The most salient division arose between the majority of officers who had no formal military education, the *tarimbeiros* (barrack bunks), and the younger generation of military academy graduates, the *doutores*. The hubris and idealism of doutores raised tarimbeiro hackles when they criticized their superiors. Doutores' world view, steeped in positivism and republicanism, contrasted with that of the more conservative tarimbeiros, but they shared a unifying distaste for casacas.

Postwar reformism went too far for some but not far enough for others. The Military Question alienated many army officers from the imperial monarchy; the Religious Question, the clergy; the abolition of slavery, the landholding aristocracy; and the lack of urban representation and services, the expanding middle sector. The ideological germs of positivism and republicanism thrived in the empire's ailing body politic. Strains of republican positivism succeeded in turning army doutores against the monarchy. Broadly speaking, the army coup that overthrew Pedro II marked a victory of Republicans over monarchists, officers over casacas, and, within the officer corps, doutores over tarimbeiros. Doutores would take positions of great influence in the republican government, leading the new cult of republican positivist nationalism.[61]

The 1874 Recruitment Law met with active and passive resistance because it threatened the status and livelihood of "respectable" poor families. The poor played the decisive role in foiling the draft's execution. Common Brazilians and their more influential supporters subscribed to ideology of the "house" and to patriarchal privilege as moral and rhetorical wedges against conscription. The State's inability to execute a draft was emblematic of the post-bellum wave of legislative reform that ultimately failed to resolve contradictions in the imperial order. Many Republicans, civilian and military, had long favored the 1874 Recruitment Law. By supporting this and other army objectives, they had wooed many army doutores to their cause.[62] The Liberal and Conservative parties would be swept away by the republic, but political divisions over conscription remained. Brazilian republicanism eventually developed several factions, some conducive and others resistant to conscription. The officers who dominated the new government breathed new life into the Recruitment Law. These very efforts, however, resuscitated traditional antidraft strategies and inspired new efforts to whip the dead letter of 1874.

Chapter 5

"And One Calls This Misery a Republic?"

The 1874 Recruitment Law

under the Early Republic,

1889–1905

Prussia outstripped conscription, which was always attended with varying degrees of hardships, but invariably pressed heavily upon the lower classes, by a system of universal service, the leading idea being to distribute the military burden equally among all classes. — Baron Colmar Von der Goltz, *The Nation in Arms,* 1883

Now, as Von der Goltz sees it, any military organization must reflect something of the national temperament. On the one hand, there are the hard-and-fast Prussian tactics, in which a mechanical precision of fire is everything; and on the other hand, there are the nervous tactics of the Latin, with all the stress on a knightly intrepid sword play. — Euclydes da Cunha, *Os Sertões,* 1902

The new army will not be a prison, it will not be a chamber of tortures, it will not be a branch office of a Dantesque inferno. — Deputy Alcindo Guanabara, House of Deputies, 1907

The conscription controversy provides a unique lens through which to analyze the transition from empire to republic. It reveals a shadow area of republican rule. Law now prohibited impressment and official statistics did not record the press gang sweeps that marked the early republic. It also clarifies a shift from older ideals of patriarchal privilege and family honor to new concepts of the hygienic conjugal family.[1] Active draft resistance shifted from towns to cities as the urban working class became primary targets of conscription and nation building.

Republican propaganda proclaimed the new regime a step forward for equality and progress, but what did this mean for Brazilian praças? The citations above provide some clues about the paradoxes that the ideal of universal military service, so intriguing to the leadership of Brazil's armed forces, posed for Brazilian society. The German nation had been forged around the Prussian army's "blood and iron," and its highest ranks remained largely an aristocratic preserve. Civilian doctors, lawyers, politicians, and businessmen sought military titles to garner the status of Europe's most respected army.[2] Conversely, when Brazil's army-dominated government granted civilian ministers the honorary rank of brigadier in 1890, Finance Minister Rui Barbosa de Oliveira expressed embarrassment. He wanted to refuse this "honor," but accepted it for political reasons. The French minister, present at the ceremony, found it humorous because it was difficult to seriously congratulate the ministers for this accolade.[3] For members of the civilian political elite, such as Rui, the honor of an army rank was dubious. Army officers, however, signed documents with titles inflated with irony: "Citizen Doctor General" (*Cidadão Doutor General*). These titles asserted the leveling ideology of republicanism while latching onto the legitimizing title of the traditional political elite: *doutor.*

In Germany, universal service incorporated an impressive spectrum of social classes by 1900. Broadly speaking, enlisted service was well regarded as an honorable citizen's duty. Prussian military traditions evolved from unique antecedents, most saliently, defense requirements that levied a ponderous portion of its human and economic resources. Brazil's defense needs did not require a similar investment. The privileged could turn their attention to other matters without fear of losing their property and power to hostile invaders.

Brazil's best-selling 1902 nationalist treatise, *Os Sertões* by Euclydes da Cunha narrated the army's campaign (1896–97) against the millenarian followers of Antônio Conselheiro in the dusty backlands town of Canudos, Bahia. Da Cunha cited Germany's Marshal Von der Goltz to lend authority to his assertion that Brazil's army reflected its "national temperament." A military academy graduate, da Cunha reaffirmed the increasingly common association between a nation's armed forces and the national "race." In his view, the "hot-tempered" Latin soldier broke lines in battle, seeking one-on-one combat, but if he lost sight of his officers, a praça would beat a disorderly retreat.[4] Da Cunha emphasized the "Latin" race over the many descendants of Africans and Indians in the ranks. The "mechanical precision" of Prussian tactics were anathema to the Brazilian soldier's "knightly" bravado. Likewise, I would argue, the ideal of universal service was an execration to Brazil's traditional social and racial hierarchies.

Deputy Alcindo Guanabara, who presented a new conscription bill in 1906, indicated that enlisted service was still trying to extricate itself from the images of punishment, bondage, and even hell. If the army reflected Brazil's national temperament, the metaphors were still painful despite the efforts of sincere nationalists to embellish them. In *Os Sertões*, da Cunha imputed classic barbaric traits to retreating soldiers who happened onto a goat, "these unhappy heroes, ragged, filthy, repulsive-looking, could be seen squatting about their bonfires, tearing the half-cooked flesh as the flickering light from the coals glowed on their faces, like a band of famished cannibals at a barbarous repast."[5] This Dionysian feeding frenzy on "uncooked" meat echoed those of Visconde de Tuanay's *A retirada da Laguna* (1871) and reveals the continuing ambivalence with which army-educated authors regarded praças.

The republic did away with noble titles but not traditional conceptions of privilege. Most of the wealthy viewed laborers and praças as dependent underlings rather than fellow citizens. Few privileged Brazilians had military training, whereas many Germans and Japanese with aristocratic backgrounds performed military service. By 1900, Germany and Japan had negotiated an arranged marriage between universal service, industrialization, and a stratified aristocratic yet bourgeois social hierarchy. In Brazil, this coupling might be more accurately described as an ongoing series of attempted shotgun weddings. An imperfect marriage between conceptions of status and conscription did not occur without conflicts, threats, coaxing, compromises, appeals to honor, and a tacit recognition that some of the vows would not be carried out with complete fidelity. The emergence of new ideologies, trends, and political alliances reoriented the debate.

Republican Politics and Military Service

The coup coalition that deposed the Bragança dynasty and promulgated the republic did not mobilize broad-based support, but the lack of an organized opposition gave the regime a brief honeymoon. More radical

Republican officers convinced Marshal Deodoro da Fonseca, the Military Club's president, to lead a coup, ostensibly to unseat Parliament's Ministry Council. Once consummated, Deodoro reluctantly agreed to inaugurate a republic. A fragile alliance between officers (doutores and tarimbeiros), historic Republicans and "eleventh-hour" Republicans supported the 1889 coup and created the federalist 1891 Constitution.

The adoption of a federal system aimed to correct problems associated with the empire. The imperial Constitution made no provisions for reapportionment of representation based on population growth. Provinces like São Paulo that grew rapidly during the 1800s resented their relative lack of political clout. Moreover, Paulistas felt aggrieved because imperial revenues were based almost exclusively on import and export taxes. Only a fraction of the revenues levied on São Paulo's lucrative coffee exports were reinvested there. Not surprisingly, São Paulo became a Republican stronghold. The 1891 Constitution, however, turned the tables, placing coffee interests in a position of political ascendance. The new charter allowed states to write constitutions, to create military police forces, and to levy taxes on exports. Given the highly uneven distribution of Brazil's populace and export wealth, these policies shifted the locus of power southward, favoring the provinces of São Paulo, Minas Gerais, Rio Grande do Sul, and Rio de Janeiro. The northeastern states, whose sugar plantocracy had enjoyed great influence under the empire, resented their declining influence and revenues. The autonomy of state governments was far from absolute, but wealthy states were better able to ward off federal intervention. Regional tensions shaped not only the republic's economic policies, but also reignited disputes over recruitment disparities.[6]

After approving the Constitution, army officers pressured reluctant federal delegates to elect Marshal Deodoro as president. He won by a slim margin over São Paulo's civilian candidate, Prudente de Morais. From the get go, Deodoro's relations with Congress were tense. He regarded the criticisms of politicians and their hesitant support of his election as personal insults. In November 1891, he declared martial law and dissolved Congress, alleging that monarchist plots threatened to topple the republic. A political impasse ensued as politicians and officers challenged Deodoro's actions. An embittered Deodoro was soon forced to step down, and his younger Vice President Marshal Floriano Peixoto assumed the duties but not the title of president.

The shaky army-dominated government promoted conscription as it reorganized the fledgling republic's defense. In the short run, it resorted to ad hoc measures to enhance security. In 1890, it required National Guard units to muster weekly. Since the guard's 1873 reform, law required guardsmen to muster once a year, but even this was done infrequently.[7] As a result, the guard's rolls swelled during the late empire and early republic as men sought protection from army service in a post that required few duties in ordinary circumstances. One senator joked in 1896, "When the conscription law is put into effect . . . there will not be anyone to participate in the lottery because the national guard is growing at an alarming rate."[8]

Guardsmen, particularly those involved in nascent labor movements, resented the renewal of militia obligations. The newspaper, *O Echo Popular,* spoke mainly for State workers in Rio — artisans in the army and naval arsenals, mint workers, railroad employees, and typesetters. State laborers became an important part of the *Jacobinos* (jacobins) faction, the radical Republican wing.

Urban workers' organizations were united in their opposition to exploitation, particularly oppressive National Guard duties and military recruitment, but they were splintered by ideologies, leadership, ethnicity, and occupations. Various socialist organizations formed and almost as quickly dissolved during the early 1900s. Socialist leaders like Vicente de Souza favored the expansion of the franchise to better defend workers' interests. Some anarchists believed that the strike was the only valid weapon workers possessed to combat the capitalist class, but most favored a more moderate stance that included unionization and the electoral process. Eventually, some of these groups fused, forming Anarcho-Syndicalist unions that, like their European counterparts, tended to preach against nationalism; instead, they promoted a cosmopolitan worker's movement based on class identity. Union members tended to be in more highly skilled and better-paying manual labor occupations. Most Brazilian workers, however, did not join unions.

Floriano won over an important part of the labor movement by creating government jobs. Many public workers became staunch *florianistas,* but most opposed augmented guard service and were dead set against conscription.[9] In 1889, a Porto Alegre labor newspaper's first edition included among its editorial priorities, "*O Operário* (the laborer) will save workers from the clutches of recruitment."[10] The editors viewed both impressment and the draft as adverse to workers' rights and economic growth. Still not all labor groups opposed conscription. A Socialist party project in Rio Grande do Sul called for obligatory military service — with physical incapacity as the only exemption — on the condition that the period of required military service be reduced.[11]

O Echo Popular reprinted in 1890 essays by the former Liberal Bahian senator Rui Barbosa who had long advocated terminating the National Guard. Rui pointed out that France had abolished the institution "after verifying that it always served every kind of tyranny." For Rui, the guard "only exists to perturb the economy of the proletariat classes that compose its lower ranks," while guard officers, "political chiefs and bureaucrats," who enjoy "wearing ridiculous and pompous uniforms, . . . do not perform their duties but oppress the honest worker." The worker, Barbosa concluded, "finds himself threatened with jail if he does not show up for duty, [and guard] exercises are held on Sundays set aside for rest amid the comfort of family and home which he is deprived of during the week." The lack of recruitment data makes it hard to say how often guardsmen were pressed into the regular army for failure to fulfill guard obligations, but fear of this fate inspired vehement labor opposition.

Many Brazilian Republicans cherished the ideal of the citizen-soldier made popular by the French Revolution. In revolutionary France, however, it had been the National Guard that best embodied the citizen-soldier ideal, whereas most Brazilian Republicans felt the army was the institutional expression of the popular will. Colonel Lauro Sodré, a leader in Rio's labor movement, imagined the alliance between the army and the common people as a historic compact, "In our history there is not a single page that records a victory of liberty over arrogance in which the army did not stand at the people's side, rising up to defend their rights; the army is the people themselves, it is the association of the people united by the ties of discipline."[12] While enamored of the French Revolution, Jacobinos found the guard a threatening vestige of monarchy and idealized instead the army as the *povo fardado* (the people in uniform). In 1891, Jacobino Deputy Colonel Alexândre José Barbosa Lima unsuccessfully proposed the guard's abrogation in Congress.[13]

O Echo Popular stressed that the guard deprived workers of their family life: "We are certain that our brother workers and the proletarian classes that are going to be sacrificed in a holocaust for the vanity of . . . ridiculous officers, will not have difficulty comprehending the abysm that awaits them. . . . How many tears will their mothers and wives have to cry every time that despotism carries them to jail and from there to the ranks of the army because they were absent on the days consecrated for rest."[14] Laborers resentment of guard duty paled in comparison to their fears of regular army service. While some Jacobinos claimed the army embodied the popular will, most ironically feared becoming part of it. For many laborers, protecting family honor outweighed their concerns with national honor. Workers criticized the Recruitment Law, which made no provisions to exempt married men, in the terms of house and street. As a labor editorialist wrote in 1892, "The domestic home, this sanctuary of the family, will always be sacred for us." An impassioned letter to the director of public works from a municipal coachman in Rio complained of being "recruited" by the National Guard in 1890. He requested that the director convince his commander to release him from guard duty to attend to his family and orphans at his charge. The director responded that this request was beyond his authority.[15]

O Echo Popular stated that the onus of the guard's "restoration" fell unjustly on workers' shoulders, "The ministries proclaim daily that fifty to one hundred men have been enlisted, when the truth is that with great financial sacrifice and threats, commanders only manage to scrape together a few dozen ragamuffins, who do not have anything to wear. . . . The employees of the commercial houses exempt themselves from guard duty. . . . Fathers, who do not want their sons to lose their place in commerce, pay the *pataqueiros* (cheap actors), men who do not have a livelihood other than by performing the [guard] duty of others."[16] The pataqueiros further weakened the guard's patrician pretensions, and it temporarily became a less secure and more demanding haven from army service. The inequities of guard duty offended honorable workers, but they were even more upset that the penalty for not fulfilling guard duties was impressment.

O Echo Popular puzzled over the motives for the guard's mobilization in 1890, "The people made use of the army against the monarchy because it was a necessity." Now, the National Guard, a militia that "served the monarchy" appeared to be a means of opposing the army. The editorialist advised workers to refuse to fulfill their National Guard duty, "What does the government intend to do? Oblige us to serve by means of army or police troops? Will army troops do this?"[17] A follow-up article was more explicit, "The national guard is hostile to the army and the laboring classes, let us consider whether or not the guard is too onerous for the nation."[18] Some labor leaders portrayed the guard as at best a useless monarchist vestige and at worst a threat to the republic. Labor saw renewed guard service as a threat to their interests in 1890, but armed conflicts soon changed the tenor of the debate. While many workers in Rio supported the army-dominated Republican regime and many praised the army as the "people in uniform," the Jacobinos' labor wing did not want to perform guard duty, much less serve as regular army praças.

As protests mounted against the government's renewal of guard duty, army leaders hoped to resolve their manpower needs by pushing for a draft. To motivate local officials, the Republican government decreed in 1890 that it would conduct impressment only in those districts that failed to conduct draft enrollment. Despite this threat, the war minister admitted in 1891 that registration had failed to provide an adequate base from which to conduct a lottery. Moreover, volunteers were in shorter supply because Republican policy abolished enlistment bonuses. Since the 1891 Constitution prohibited impressment, he urged immediate action to resolve the army's manpower problems.[19] The government's inability to implement the 1874 Recruitment Law shows that much more than the firm backing of a majority in the central government was necessary to execute conscription.

The 1891 Constitution incorporated the 1874 Recruitment Law, but aspects of this imperial law violated the republic's federalist system. Added motivation to adapt the law to federalist principles came on January 19, 1892, when army sergeant Silvino Honório de Macedo led a barracks putsch intended to restore Marshal Deodoro to power. Sergeant Silvino's Revolt emerged from the conspiratorial air that swept over a military still bitterly divided by Deodoro's fall. Apparently, Silvino was privy to conspiracies hatched by high-ranking officers in the army and navy who supported Deodoro.

On January 19, 1892, Silvino and his band of rebels subdued the officers who ran the prison fortress of Santa Cruz at the mouth of Guanabara Bay near Rio. This Pernambucan sergeant then convinced or coerced the fort's soldiers and civil and military prisoners to join the revolt. Floriano acted swiftly to quash the mutineers. He claimed the revolt was an international monarchist plot thickening the conspiratorial fog first whipped up by Deodoro. With some difficulty, Floriano's troops defeated the rebels. Despite investigations that indicated Silvino had contacts with high-ranking officers, Floriano brought few officers to trial. He even pardoned Silvino in recognition of his courage.[20]

Eleven days after the revolt's outbreak, a decree adapting the 1874 Recruitment Law to federalist guidelines passed. A follow-up measure required states to supply a portion of recruits commensurate to their representation in Congress.[21] Meanwhile, insubordination arose in the frontier states of Mato Grosso and Amazonas when governors refused to recognize Floriano's order for military governors there to step down because of their support of Deodoro. With officers plotting against him, Floriano was anxious to legitimize the draft. The splits in the military hierarchy panicked officers. A general sent to assume the governorship of Mato Grosso reported, "The garrison of this state has revolted. . . . [These rebels are] sons of the petty politics that unfortunately has invaded even our class. . . . The complete dissolution of our army is evident."[22] While the Iron Marshal prevailed in Amazonas and Mato Grosso, new revolts again threatened army unity.

The most serious armed challenge to Floriano's regime came when war broke out in Rio Grande do Sul. The Federalist War (1893–95) is best grasped as a conflict between rival political blocs within that state. Floriano backed Júlio de Castilhos, a historic Republican, over those of Silveira Martins, the state's former Liberal party boss. About one third of the army was garrisoned in Rio Grande do Sul, and most soldiers there were natives of this southernmost state. When the conflict began, officers and troops fought on both sides, crippling army strength and fracturing the brittle integrity of its command chain.[23]

This crisis redoubled when tensions between the army and navy erupted in rebellion on the eve of Brazil's Independence Day in September 1893. Led by high-ranking naval officers who believed that their branch of service had been ignored and mistreated by the army-dominated government, the Armada Revolt (1893–94) spread panic through the nation's capital. Some leaders of this revolt had monarchist sympathies, but most participants only sought to defend their corporation's interests. Rebel forces commandeered the navy's vessels and occupied outlying areas near the capital, paralyzing port traffic. Foreign consuls declared their intention to protect the property of their nationals from rebel bombardment, and United States navy cruisers placed themselves between the rebel fleet and the capital to protect Floriano.[24] Rebels and florianistas skirmished for six months, and Floriano responded with executions, mass incarcerations, censorship, deportations, and of course, stepped-up impressment. One of the victims of Floriano's firing squads for his participation in the Armada Revolt was the unrepentant conspirator Sergeant Silvino. Florianista officers and civilian Jacobinos were promoted rapidly to high posts within the army and State administration. Unable to engage the army in a decisive battle, the Armada Revolt's remaining leaders fled in February 1894.

Without the support of São Paulo's treasury and to a lesser extent its growing military police forces, Floriano's government might have collapsed. The coffee barons who dominated São Paulo's politics built up their state's military police forces to employ them as a bargaining chip with Floriano. With this leverage, they pressured him to respect scheduled elections in 1894, insuring the selection of Prudente de Morais as the first civilian president. São Paulo's political leaders grasped the importance of state police forces as a check on the federal army's power. Other prosperous states would follow their example.[25] By 1895, the army had gained the upper hand, and Prudente negotiated an end to the Federalist War, offering generous amnesty terms to rebel army personnel.

The rapid succession of revolts did not allow time for draft registration. Censorship and a lack of army documentation make it difficult to quantify impressment, but qualitative sources indicate that recruitment followed familiar patterns. To defend itself, the government pressed soldiers, even though the 1891 Constitution expressly forbade it. Novelist Lima Barreto depicted a middle-aged Afro-Brazilian farmhand's reaction to the outbreak of the Armada Revolt. Even though he lived far from Rio, he explained to his employer why he would not return to work, "There is a revolt in the capital, and they say that they will be recruiting, I am headed for the wilderness." Taking to the hills in times of upheaval continued to be a survival strategy for underprotected rural and urban laborers. Barreto also depicted a popular troubadour who failed to escape the clutches of a press gang in Rio's bustling outskirts. The bard protested his capture and implored an officer he knew for his release, the officer refused, describing the songster as a "recalcitrant volunteer, a patriotic rebel."[26] Instead of releasing him, the commander awarded the composer a corporal's rank, and he grudgingly agreed to serve when they returned his guitar.

An 1893 cartoon in a Rio periodical shows policemen chasing down men in the streets and is accompanied by the caption, "Recruitment has inspired fear in many people." The next panel depicts the police chief with a broom sweeping men into a cell, "The police affirm that it is only a clean up of the capital." In the final illustration, a well-dressed man is taken in hand by policemen, "But to take this clean up to the point that you want to recruit a distinguished police delegate, that is a good one!"[27] Rebellions led to new rounds of impressment, and press gangs were not always discriminating. Sometimes officials fell prey to their own agents. For expediency's sake, Republicans shelved plans for a draft.

With the return of civilian government in 1894, the most salient issue defining Republican factions was whether one sought to augment or minimize the army's role in politics. The latter faction tended to favor federalism or states' rights. Army officers themselves split between those who favored political activism and those who preferred to focus on professional matters. These camps were far from impermeable and defections from one to the other were not infrequent, but these divisions shaped the legal battles over conscription.

In August 1896, debates on the Recruitment Law hinged on the issue of states' rights. The 1892 reform of the Recruitment Law ambiguously stated that the "federal army would be formed from contingents supplied by the states." It did not specify who would select the authorities to form draft boards. Some believed that district army commanders should be empowered to nominate boards because they allegedly were "above the petty interests of parish politics, offering better guarantees of justice than local authorities." Groups that would come to be called "antimilitarists" contended that such a measure violated states' rights; only governors had the right to form draft boards.[28]

A senator for São Paulo reasoned that "the federal government does not have the ability to create authorities in ample numbers to send to each locality in the nation. These military commissions would . . . [also] run the risk of encountering opposition from local populations."[29] Others added invective to this assertion: "The population will be turned over to the good will of sergeants who would lead detachments into the interior to conduct recruitment. . . . It would be dangerous for civil authorities

S. Sebastião, sendo prevenido, em tempo, de semelhantes resoluç
e, em vista do seu nome não lhe offerecer bastantes garantias, re
dar as de Villa-Piogo, afim de n

O recrutamento tem sido o espantalho de muita gente
e continúa a dar sorte.

Affirmam que se trata apenas
de uma limpeza na Capital... 9b

9c

9a–c. "Recruitment has been the terror of many people, and it continues to bring luck. They [authorities] affirm that it is only a clean up of the capital [Rio's chief of police is depicted with the broom]. But taking this clean up to the point of wanting to recruit a distinguished police delegate . . . that is really a good one!" Recruitment sweeps continued in the early republic despite being prohibited by law. These sweeps sometimes caught prominent men, in this case, a police delegate. From *A Revista Illustrada,* March 1893, 4–5. *Courtesy of the Biblioteca Nacional, Rare Works Division. Photo by Gilson Ribeiro.*

because the conflicts would be numerous."[30] The image of "lowly" sergeants, mere *praças*, rather than civil authorities conducting recruitment was calculated to shock the sensibilities of civilians who had grown weary and wary of the army's political power. As empire-era Liberals had, antimilitarists portrayed conscription as a euphemism for continued impressment. By affirming the right of states to control recruitment, these politicians hoped to void conscription on constitutional grounds. If the late empire served as a guide, there was little chance that state, let alone local officials, could be counted on to conduct conscription. A new mobilization crisis, however, soon brought this dispute to a head.

In November 1896, the followers of lay religious leader Antônio Conselheiro repulsed an attack by one hundred Bahian military policemen sent to arrest him, triggering what the army called the Canudos War (1896–97). Interestingly, Conselheiro's religious peregrinations first gained him renown in the Northeast's interior in 1874, precisely when the Recruitment Law first sparked unrest there.[31] In 1893, he founded a millenarian community in Canudos, an isolated backland village in the dry mountains of northern Bahia. The devout sought to build a city removed from the corrupt and secular republican world to await God's second coming. Despite its isolated location, Canudos quickly became Bahia's second most populous city, a magnet for mostly poor northeasterners seeking spiritual guidance and security in uncertain times.

Canudos's rapid growth worried local leaders jealous of Conselheiro's expanding influence, while Republicans in coastal capitals found his promonarchist rhetoric threatening. The backlands prophet preached against a number of the State-building laws enacted by the new Republican regime: civil marriage, civil registration, civil administration of cemeteries, the separation of Church and State, and the new system of taxation. The increasing impressment that resulted from the Armada Revolt and the civil war in Rio Grande do Sul squeezed Bahia and the surrounding states just as Antônio founded his holy community. Many who relocated to Canudos were perhaps inspired as much by fear of mounting press-gang sweeps as by religious fervor. Canudos and other religious settlements founded in the 1890s became viable alternative communities to citizens pressured by drought, political instability, new taxes, economic hardship, and war.[32]

The second army force of some 1,800 troops sent to Canudos under the command of the Republican hero General Moreira César met emphatic defeat in March 1897. The rout spread panic through coastal urban centers as levies of troops were rounded up to quash Canudos. Rumors flew. How could rustic backlanders defeat federal troops? Republicans turned to their conspiratorial tradition and depicted Canudos as a front for an international monarchist plot. Some Jacobinos volunteered to defend the republic in its time of need.[33] Even so, most additional troops were pressed. In Rio, Jacobinos took to the streets persecuting suspected monarchists. Amid this uproar, the government declared martial law. In July, a little-noticed special amendment to the annual budget fixing troop strength gave district military commanders the power to appoint and direct draft boards. Given the circumstances, there was no time to conduct draft enrollment, but the measure revealed the central government's resolve to conduct conscription to defend itself. The government's shaky legitimacy amplified problems in mobilizing the 12,000 men necessary to besiege Canudos. The army suffered some five thousand casualties (many of whom probably deserted) before it razed Canudos in October 1897.

The public greeted Canudos veterans in Rio with unusual patriotic fanfare, but their moment of glory was tarnished when a Jacobino soldier tried to murder President Prudente de Morais on the review stand. He succeeded only in killing the war minister, who defended the president. Jacobinos hoped the murder would topple the civilian government, which they believed had "prostituted" the republic. They longed for a leader like Floriano to establish a republic untainted by the "backward" influences of rural oligarchies. The plan backfired; instead, Jacobinos discredited themselves at a crucial juncture, but they would continue to scheme.[34]

Just as the Paraguayan War led to a reassessment of race and nation, so did the Canudos War. Da Cunha's *Os Sertões* attempted to square social Darwinism (which took a dim view of the racial miscegenation so characteristic of Brazil) with nationalist formulas that prized a nation's unique folk culture. He concluded that the conflict did not have its origins in an international monarchist plot; rather, it boiled down to a race war between the more European society of Brazil's coast and the mixed-race population of Brazil's dry hinterlands. That the revolt was fought by sertanejos, the frontiersmen that many Republicans had charged with symbolic nationalist significance after the Paraguayan War, made da Cunha's conclusion even more disturbing. Though rife with contradictions, da

Cunha expressed doubts about Brazil's racial, ethnic, and climatic hetero-geneity for national destiny. His analysis suggested that Brazil's diversity could prevent it from becoming a modern, unified, and ultimately "white" nation. To prevent Brazil's national dismemberment and to save it from the dustbin of history, da Cunha advocated integrating the hinterland populations into the "national life."[35]

With the election of a second civilian president in 1898, a new balance of political power took shape, the "politics of the governors." Republican federalism decentralized government bureaucracy and party structures. The empire's national-level Liberal and Conservative parties were swept aside, and most attempts to establish a Republican party with a national political projection faltered. Political parties came to be primarily state-based. The system fortified the hand of rural coronéis who came to control state party structures. Coronéis delivered a large majority of votes to their state party chiefs in return for control over local affairs. Likewise, state delegations to the federal Congress were expected to support the president in return for state autonomy. These political compromises heightened sensitivity to federal power exercised in the states.[36]

As this new political configuration took shape, Congress reconsidered the Recruitment Law in 1899. One senator reiterated the federalist para-dox posed by the law: "The 1874 law cannot be executed in this regime, even though it was altered in 1892," because the federal government does not have the constitutional authority to nominate draft boards and to require state officials to cooperate with them.[37] Politicians who feared militarism wanted to maintain local civilian control over draft enrollment, a process still vitally linked to electoral politics and penal justice. Conscrip-tion's proponents countered that only federal control over the registration process could guarantee the just implementation of a draft. They de-manded that draft board members who failed in their duty be "fined, imprisoned, and removed from office."[38] The issue involved a struggle between civilian and military, federal and state preeminence.

"And One Calls This Misery a Republic?"

This phrase figured last in the prolix headline "The Draft, Recruitment, The Abolition of Habeas Corpus, The Navy Minister's Hubris, Coercive Labor."[39] The article presented a labor perspective on Brazil's first draft lottery in late December 1903. Beginning in 1902, Brazil again experienced problems mobilizing forces to a distant front. Border disputes with Bolivia and Peru required the army and navy to deploy men to the far western territories of Acre and Mato Grosso. This show of force helped bring Bolivian recognition of Brazil's claims to Acre's rubber-rich forests. As a treaty neared final approval, the navy minister approved a draft lottery in Fortaleza, the principal port and capital of Ceará. In need of men with nautical skills, he conducted a draft lottery among seamen and stevedores registered with Fortaleza's port authority.

Fortaleza's mariners organized a strike to protest the draft, and the Rio labor newspaper *A Nação* followed these events, stressing the navy's history of treating sailors abusively.[40] The navy minister defended his actions citing the special recruitment decree issued during the 1897 Canudos War. *A Nação* argued that the minister's "illegal" draft involved deceit tantamount to impressment.[41] Ceará's state police attempted to escort the draftees to disembark, but striking protesters and their family members obstructed their path. Police fired upon and charged the crowd, killing four and injuring thirty-six civilians. Draft resistance gained a new and highly publicized group of martyrs.

The Rio magazine *A Larva* reported that "the police, in the most perverse and hypocritical manner, injured Ceará's people as they claimed their rights! The strike against the naval draft lottery in Ceará made the generous blood of its people . . . run through the streets of Fortaleza! . . . The minister wants to enlist, cost what it may, the men necessary to fill vacancies in the ranks, but the methods employed are bleak."[42] *A Larva*'s cover depicts police goose-stepping over the Constitution set atop prostrate men, women, and children in pools of blood. A black police soldier grimaces and shouts, "Believe or die!" He points his bayonet at the chest of a defiant white mariner. This depiction, unlike most previous depictions of recruitment, was not a humorous cartoon, rather it aired a new sensitivity to recruitment abuses, if not to racial stereotypes.

Lieutenant-Colonel Lauro Sodré led a protest against the navy minister's actions. A Jacobino, positivist, florianista, and labor advocate, Sodré had served as Pará's governor under Floriano's regime and later lost a dark-horse presidential electoral bid in 1898. During the latter campaign, he solidified ties to cadets at his alma mater, the military academy, and to Rio labor groups who later helped to elect Sodré as a senator for Rio. Sodré

10. "Harsh Law," a magazine cover, illustrates the Fortaleza Draft Massacre, which cost the lives of stevedores and their families who protested the draft for the navy held in their city based on the captain of the port's matriculations of dockworkers and seamen. The illustration shows military police troops from Ceará marching over the constitution and crushing the draft lottery protesters underfoot. They hold forth pictures of their political boss, Governor Acioli, as they threaten a European-looking stevedore. From *A Larva*, January 8, 1904, 28. *Courtesy of Biblioteca Nacional, Periodicals Division. Photo by Claudio de Carvalho Xavier.*

questioned the legitimacy of the 1897 decree, claiming it was unsuited to peacetime because it had been passed under martial law. He added that "it is not possible to have a draft lottery without previous enrollment," and that it was "absurd to conduct a lottery based only on the matriculation of port authorities."[43]

Others, however, defended the draft's legality, "Conducting enrollment in a state or in part of a state is not an illegality capable of annulling all registration, military conscription can be made partially or totally." The navy minister's supporters berated Lauro Sodré for removing the question from the "serene stage of public administration" to "popular meetings, the streets, and agitations." He concluded that it was not possible to construct a "strong Republic with the liberal instincts of the multitude."[44] This view reflected the elitist attitudes belittled in the headline "And One Calls This Misery a Republic!" Despite efforts to defend the draft in Fortaleza, it was an unimpeachable setback for the 1874 Recruitment Law. It became clear that only new legislation could generate the momentum to execute a draft. Meanwhile, new support for and opposition to the draft would come from a seemingly alien set of government initiatives: obligatory public health measures.

Obligatory vaccination and universal conscription may seem to have little in common, but for many, both violated traditional boundaries between public and private rights. Labor unions, Jacobinos, orthodox positivists, monarchist elements, and even influential mainstream politicians like Senators José Gomes Pinheiro Machado and Rui Barbosa would join forces to oppose the 1904 Obligatory Vaccine Law and the 1908 Obligatory Military Service Law. In 1904, public hygiene laws appeared poised to empower officials to regulate new aspects of private life, space, and the body.[45]

Lauro Sodré formed the League Against Obligatory Vaccination (*Liga Contra a Vacinação Obrigatória*). The 1904 (smallpox) Vaccine Revolt would be the last hurrah for Jacobino street actions. Rio was the epicenter of rioting against the Vaccine Law, but less spectacular protests occurred elsewhere. Opposition to the Vaccine Law rested on scientific, cultural, and moral grounds, but as José Murilo de Carvalho convincingly argues, the most inflammatory objections for workers were those that stressed the home's inviolability.[46]

The Vaccine Law's opponents pointed out that it undermined other

TRES MINUTOS DE VERDADE

Argollo :—Sentinella ! Isso não são modos de estar no
seu posto. Fique firme !
Soldado :—Ah ! Sr. marechal ! não posso... Vim do
Amazonas e ainda estou neste estado !
—Oh ! Então aquillo por lá é tão ruim ? Não é isso o
que me informam os generaes...
—Com perdão de V. Ex., mas neste ponto, a verdade
está commigo. Antes não estivesse...
—Na sua opinião, então...
—Na minha opinião, sr. marechal, aquillo por lá é um
matadouro obrigatorio, trinta mil vezes peior que a vac-
cina...

11. "Three Minutes of Truth" depicts a sick soldier returning from Acre.

Argollo: Sentinella! This is no way to man your post. Stand up straight!

Private: Ah, marshal sir, I can't . . . I returned from the Amazonas and I am still in this
state.

Argollo: Oh! But is it so bad over there? That is not what my generals inform me . . .

Private: I beg your pardon, sir, but on this count I am right. If you have not been
there . . .

Argollo: In your opinion, then . . .

Private: In my opinion, sir, Amazonas is an obligatory slaughterhouse thirty times
worse than the smallpox vaccine.

Illustrating the fear of service in the insalubrious region of Acre during border disputes with Bolivia in the early 1900s, this cartoon compares the danger presented
by the 1904 Obligatory Vaccine Law to those in enlisted military service in the
Amazon region. From *Malho*, November 12, 1904, 25. *Courtesy of Biblioteca Nacional, Periodicals Division. Photo by Claudio de Carvalho Xavier.*

State efforts to bolster poor families. Republicans took special care to foster public order by enhancing the protection of poor women's honor, giving judicial priority to enforcement of deflowering laws. Female victims or more commonly their male protectors brought cases against men accused of seducing (not raping) "honest" virgins age sixteen to twenty-one with false promises of marriage. If convicted, the seducer had to marry his victim or serve a jail term. Enforcing seduction laws reflected elite concerns for securing public order by stricter regulation of the lower classes' bodies and sexuality. Reformers hoped to foment the formation of more stable working-class families, reducing illegitimate births, mendicancy, and criminality among the very population that supplied the army with much of its men.[47]

Positivist intellectuals lent scientific legitimacy to the venerable concept of the home's inviolability. The vice director of Brazil's orthodox Positivist church, Raimundo Teixeira Mendes, wrote tracts criticizing obligatory hygiene, military service, and public education measures. He argued that the "proletariat's incorporation into modern society means reorganizing the proletarian family, to the end that wives, the elderly, and the young are sustained by the mass of healthy men. Then hospitals, asylums, kindergartens, and primary schools will disappear because the happiness of the proletarian home will extinguish lust, prostitution, misery, alcoholism, and disease."[48] By helping the poor family and defending its honor, Teixeira Mendes felt the State could do without many costly modern institutions. To better achieve this paradise, a worker's party in Rio Grande do Sul called for obligatory marriage for men by age thirty and women by age twenty-five.[49]

To many, the vaccine and recruitment laws threatened the values that seduction laws were intended to fortify. Unlike previous public health laws that had already condemned a great deal of Rio's working-class housing for sanitary reasons, the Vaccine Law was thought to give male officials the right to enter private homes and handle females. Among others, labor leader Vicente de Souza gave voice to this fear in a street rally against the Vaccine Law, dubbing it "the Violation of the Home Law." According to Vicente, when the household head returned home from work, he could not "affirm that the honor of his family was unblemished because a stranger had legally penetrated his home . . . and brutalized his daughters' and wife's bodies [with injections]. He added, "The immoral woman gives herself to whoever wants her, but the virgin, the wife, and daughter will have to bare their arms and shoulders to vaccine agents." Teixeira Mendes believed that the Vaccine Law neither respected "propriety nor feminine delicacy! . . . Positivist science and morality are decidedly against obligatory vaccination." In Congress, the physician mayor of Rio Barata Ribeiro declared that the Vaccine Law revoked the citizen's "guarantee of the home and the tranquility of his family."[50]

Leaders of the November 10 protest used the rhetoric of honor to incite a crowd of some five thousand. The rally boiled over into several days of rioting in Rio. Rioters cursed the police, but shouted *vivas* to army units they met, hoping that Jacobino elements within the army would join in the revolt. Some 300 military academy cadets attempted to march on the presidential palace, but the fast action of their school's commandant, General Hermes Rodrigues da Fonseca (the nephew of former president Deodoro), prevented them from realizing their objective. This act earned Hermes the trust of antimilitarist politicians. After days of unrest in which rioters destroyed street cars, gas lights, and other symbols of urban reform, calm was finally restored.[51]

Police and army units moved through the poor sections of Rio, supposedly arresting the riot's instigators. Hundreds were summarily exiled to the Amazon, including some military academy cadets.[52] Despite the riots, the Vaccine Law was eventually implemented. Deaths from yellow fever and smallpox dropped precipitously in Rio. These improvements helped smooth the way for future obligatory health policies.[53] Henceforth, reformers would adopt the language of social hygiene, the family, and science to promote the draft.

New Models of Manhood, Race, and Militarism

Meanwhile, international trends glamorized martial arts and exploits, suggesting a new military model of masculinity. In 1905, Japan's defeat of Russia exposed the myth of European invincibility. Brazil's war minister noted that Europeans now respected the Japanese on the basis of their military prowess, and urged Brazilians to learn from their example.[54] In 1908, Boer War hero Baden Powell founded the Boy Scouts in England and it quickly spread to nations across the world. The Boy Scouts made practicing military skills and nationalist ritual part of leisure culture for the sons of Brazil's urban middle and upper classes. By 1917, São Paulo required scouting instruction for boys in all its public schools.[55]

Robust men-of-action, such as Theodore Roosevelt, became admired international figures. Teddy's legendary Rough Riders and the Charge of San Juan Hill formed an integral part of his charismatic mystique. Roosevelt's 1913 Amazon expedition with Brazil's most famous hinterland explorer and ambassador to unpacified Indian tribes, General Cândido Rondon, inspired admiration for these paragons of masculine virtue.[56] The public servant, patriot, frontiersman, explorer, sportsman, statesman, humanitarian, and warrior became an archetype of Belle Époque manhood. Brazilian army officers like Rondon were the public figures who best conformed to this new male role model. To emulate them, the fathers and sons of even notable families joined gun clubs (*linhas de tiro*) and Boy Scout troops, where they drilled, wore uniforms, learned new skills, and performed patriotic rituals. As in Germany and Switzerland in the 1800s, gun clubs became important organizations in organizing public patriotic ritual in Brazil.[57] Sporting clubs such as the Young Men's Christian Association, crew teams, and soccer clubs also became increasingly popular. These activities were praised as hygienic alternatives to the bar and brothel for youths. Draft advocates tapped into the militarist and sporting craze to mobilize support for a draft lottery.

Proponents enlisted new scientific ideas to support conscription. Eugenics, a branch of hereditary science concerned with the rational management of human genetic traits, made inroads among Brazilian scientists. Influenced by neo-Lamarckian precepts of evolution prevalent among French and Italian eugenists, Brazilian physicians and politicians began to support aggressive State action to improve Brazil's "race." Many Brazilian eugenists supported a draft as a vehicle for improving the personal hygiene and health of the "national race."[58]

These trends slowly began to alter perceptions of military service. Instead of representing an emasculating punishment, enlisted service began to be more closely identified with masculine civic duty. Continuing reforms of the conditions of service helped to recast enlisted service as acceptable to honorable poor families. Eugenists' calls for expanded government action to improve the race supplanted positivism which had called for protecting the patriarchal privilege of the home. Army officers, many public health officials, and their political allies embraced eugenics to argue against those who supported states' rights. These trends laid an ideological foundation from which draft advocates remolded notions of the proper relationship between the house and the street, family and national honor.

Before continuing a narration of the battle over conscription, it is essential to examine how recruitment functioned in the absence of a draft. A thematic approach is best suited to this analysis, which examines trends in praça recruitment, service, social origins, and work over a broad period of time. Only with a clearer understanding of these issues is it possible to perceive how attitudes toward enlisted military service began to change in the early 1900s.

II

SOLDIERS, THEIR LIVES, AND

THE ARMY'S INSTITUTIONAL ROLES,

1850–1916

Chapter 6

The Troop Trade and the Army

as a Protopenal Institution in the Age of

Impressment, 1850–1916

The chapters of this section change pace by moving away from a narrative approach to examine army enlisted service in the age of impressment. They analyze broad periods of time to understand how army enlisted recruitment and service functioned over the course of more than a half-century. The chronological scope of each varies somewhat according to evidence available, but they generally consider the period from 1850 to 1916. It is difficult to fathom the entrenched bureaucratic and popular resistance to the draft without a fuller examination of recruitment in relation to the army's institutional roles. Changes in the terms and conditions of enlisted service and discipline in the ranks illuminate why resistance to conscription began to wane in the early 1900s.

Politicians debating recruitment flamboyantly referred to it as the "tribute of blood," even though few soldiers were injured or killed in battle. While clashes over conscription's implementation continued, impressment proceeded apace. This chapter examines the patterns of army recruitment as well as the army's role in Brazil's fledgling penal justice system. The analysis makes an important distinction between traditional disciplining methods (such as beatings, executions, intimidation, simple incarceration, military impressment) and more modern ones (conscription, surveillance, education, social segregation, the use of uniforms, hard labor in prison, coordinated exercises, and so on). A closer examination of impressment patterns reveals the collateral costs conscription incurred for other institutions linked to the State's disciplining capacity. These trends also elucidate a broader process whereby the State gradually moved away from disciplining the "unprotected" by incorporating them into its institutions.

Exacting the Tribute of Blood

Geography, climate, strategic concerns, politics, and economics shaped the distribution of volunteers and those pressed into the troop trade. The term "troop trade" is used to emphasize that soldiers are laborers that practice a trade. Scholars seldom examine soldiers under the rubric of laborers, and seldom do they compare the coerced labor performed by many soldiers to other coercive labor forms like slavery, indentured servitude, serfdom, and debt peonage (although Brazilians in the 1800s often did). James Scott's theoretical analysis of popular resistance in caste societies often mentions in passing military impressment and conscription as a labor tax exacted from underclasses, but few scholars specifically focus on these topics.[1] Soldiers are often depicted as the State's minor henchmen who often oppress more sympathetic victims of State coercion: ethnic and racial minorities, slaves, ritual organizations, labor unions, and women, among other groups. In Brazil (and many other nations in the 1800s), soldiers were also direct "victims" of State coercion. Political and theoretical antipathy led scholars to portray soldiers as pawns of the State or the capitalist class. Though "agents" of the State, troops still had agency. Politicians and even officers fretted over praça loyalty and feared their potential for rebellion.

Both liberal and Marxist traditions tend to see soldiers as outside the all-important sphere of production. Few consider the security costs that both trade and production require. The term "troop trade" emphasizes that the barriers separating those who exercised State-legitimated force as soldiers and those who passively or aggressively resisted the State were quite porous.

Furthermore, the army took on volunteer and coerced workers more readily in some localities than others. As chapter 1 shows, the troop trade was a type of internal penal transportation system for strategically relocating a small but notable portion of "dangerous" men. By these means, officials in some areas "traded" the security risk represented by criminal or idle men to those hungry for garrison laborers. Finally, the troop trade flowed southward from Brazil's northeast, paralleling the coerced migration route of the internal slave trade after the State actively interdicted international sales of bondspersons in 1850.

Even though impressment directly touched few among the unprotected poor, scholars of Latin America — as did contemporaries of the period — frequently refer to impressment as the most feared form of "social control" in the 1800s.[2] Contemporaries, however, more often noted the disruptions and partisan disputes surrounding impressment. By outlining the broad contours of the troop trade, this section seeks to show how and why the tribute of blood was exacted so unevenly. The trends discussed below are interpretations of data organized into tables in appendix B.[3]

As noted earlier, politicians from Rio Grande do Sul and the Northeast singled out Minas Gerais, home to one in five Brazilians, as the least cooperative province in contributing troops. Data confirms this perception of Minas, but then again, all southeastern provinces outside the capital district of Rio contributed comparatively few troops [appendix B.5, B.6, and B.7]. The Southeast was the only region that did not produce a proportion of troops equal to or greater than its share of male population. In explaining why his government had not inducted the number of recruits required by annual quotas in 1876 [appendix B.2], Minas Gerais' governor claimed that while there were many men suitable for impressment in his province (*recrutáveis*), he did not have the police, army, or National Guard troops necessary to "capture" recruits and escort them to distant army garrisons. In short, he argued that because the army stationed few troops in Minas, impressment was a heavier burden for his province.[4]

Population was a poor predictor of the number of troops each province produced. If one compares recruitment to the geographic distribution of troops, however, one finds some evidence to support the claims of Minas' governor. Troop distribution illuminates the army's strategic and political priorities. The army stationed a large number of troops along Brazil's southern and western frontiers to police the border, deter invasion by Argentina, and support units that still occupied vanquished Paraguay in the 1870s. The larger part of army forces were based in the imperial and provincial capitals where they maintained internal security, performed police duties, and protected government property. The densest concentration of troop population occurred in and around the capital district of Rio (Côrte) where about a third of army forces garrisoned. The Côrte contributed the third largest contingent of soldiers in Brazil from 1870 to 1882, producing alone two thirds of the southeastern region's recruits. Even so, the army had to transfer more than half of the troops required to man the capital's regiments from outside the Southeast [appendix B.3, B.4, and B.7].

Roughly another third of the army's forces bivouacked in the scattered outposts of Rio Grande do Sul, the province with the vanguard position in troop contribution. Rio Grande do Sul's share of the tribute of blood increased from 11.9 percent in the 1850s to 17.5 percent in the 1870s. By the 1880s, Rio Grande do Sul paid a rate of military labor tribute four times greater than the province's 1872 portion of national male population. Even though the South came to produce nearly one fifth of all recruits, it still required large numbers of soldiers from other regions to man its frontier outposts [appendix B.3, B.4, and B.7].

If one looks only at the cases of the Côrte and Rio Grande do Sul, one might agree with the governor of Minas Gerais whose pyramid logic implied that it takes local garrisons of army troops to capture and incorporate new recruits. The Northeast, however, which supplied nearly half of all the nation's troops, did not conform to this pattern [appendix B.1]. The Northeast's garrison size fluctuated more than other regions, but typically held from one fifth to one fourth of army forces. This region provided approximately half of the army's manpower, but officers transferred more than half of the men inducted there to other regions. Northeast garrisons were engorged at times because battalions held excess recruits (referred to as *agregados*) many of whom would eventually be moved southward.[5]

The troop trade's main currents flowed southward from the northeast to Rio, the hub of the troop trade, mostly on public transporation. Northeastern commanders had the privilege of selecting the healthiest and best-behaved recruits, washing their hands of troublesome men by transferring them. Qualitative and quantitative data indicates that this pattern continued into the early 1900s. As General Dermeval Peixoto observed:

> At times there was a scarcity of volunteers in the regiments of the [nation's] capital. [Then] the *levas* (pressed recruits) from the north[east] arrived. . . . The volunteer and *leva* were, at the beginning of the 1900s, the same rustic men, the *sertanejo bronco* (rude backlander), the unhappy fellow countrymen who failed, but who attempted to remake himself, many times as a refugee, in the army's ranks. . . . It was a degrading spectacle. . . . The *levas* brought bands of disheartened and sad Brazilians; the majority raga-

muffins enfeebled at an early age by the first struggles for life in the back-lands and in the areas surrounding the coastal cities of Bahia, Alagoas, Sergipe, and others more to the north. . . . They walked in procession through the streets between the docks and the army's headquarters where they stooped waiting to be picked by the adjutants of depleted battalions. Deserters and vagabonds appeared among the *levas*.[6]

Officers in Rio picked over recruits in public in scenes that resembled a slave market. Excess troops, particularly those with disciplinary problems, were transferred to Rio Grande do Sul or even farther to the western forts of Mato Grosso. In 1873, a commander in Mato Grosso complained that most of his men had been transferred there as punishment for their poor disciplinary records.[7]

Hard times and drought led many northeast backlanders to seek better fortune in and around the region's coastal cities.[8] Inexpensive coastal ship-ping made it feasible to transfer northeasterners (whether inductee or volunteer) from a relatively central area to depleted regiments in other regions. Authorities in landlocked Minas Gerais and the interiors of São Paulo and Rio de Janeiro found recruitment far more inconvenient and costly. Mountainous terrain, the lack of navigable rivers, and the absence of well-articulated railroads raised the costs and complicated the logistics of impressment in these provinces. A small escort could rapidly and se-curely transfer a large number of pressed men in a ship's hold. A similar overland expedition could require a larger escort force, prolonged travel, and less security.

Most men were recruited in larger urban centers, but many of those dragooned in cities had migrated from rural areas, as Dermeval Peixoto stated above. War Minister Junqueira had stressed in 1874 the need to balance urban and rural recruitment: "Presently manhunts in the streets provoke complaints and uproars; by the project [law], the government will no longer only look for recruits in the cities; it will, with the enroll-ment of all parishes, recruit farmers and men of rural commerce." In 1859, Rio de Janeiro's provincial police reported delivering 71 army recruits, only one of whom volunteered. In the provincial capital of Niteroi, 31 recruits were apprehended, but small municipalities from across the prov-ince also delivered recruits: Capivary 3, Parahyba do Sul 5, São Fidelis 3, São João da Barra 4, Valença 2, Barra Mansa 2, and so on. Clearly, urban centers produced more recruits, but smaller towns in Rio de Janeiro, from the mountainous rainforests around Resende to the sugarcane fields of Campos, supplied inductees.[9]

The Southeast's low recruitment levels may also have reflected the region's relatively dynamic economic growth. Better employment opportunities, higher wages, and more fertile land to squat on made volunteering for the army's poor pay and Spartan conditions less attractive. Moreover, southeastern authorities probably sought to limit recruitment as much as possible because it tended to cause violent disturbances, disrupt agricultural production, and (before 1888) weaken the increasingly fragile discipline of slave labor (by 1872 two thirds of all slaves in Brazil resided in the Southeast). European immigrants, an increasingly important source of labor on coffee plantations by the 1880s, were particularly sensitive to the threat of impressment. Brazilian authorities guaranteed immunity from military service to immigrants and their sons. Impressment sweeps that nabbed immigrants could potentially complicate foreign affairs and undermine a vital labor source.[10]

Recruitment patterns may also have been a rough barometer of intra-elite political conflict in different areas. Some planters insisted that the presence of impressment gangs encouraged the free poor to seek out jobs on plantations to secure protection from recruitment.[11] But others, such as engineer André Pinto Rebouças, a mulatto who served a stint as an officer during the Paraguayan War, criticized in a major treatise on agricultural reform both National Guard service and military impressment as detriments to the organization and productivity of agricultural labor and immigration: "Just the word recruitment [army impressment]: [makes] fathers abandon sons and daughters, husbands abandon wives, sons abandon mothers, farmers abandon their crops."[12] Even an 1874 report from the Conservative minister of agriculture, Visconde de Rio Branco, included complaints that in frontier areas of Rio Grande do Sul onerous National Guard duties and army impressment induced many poor Brazilians to flee to Argentina crippling agriculture in Uruguaiana.[13] Likewise, political bosses often accused their political rivals of using impressment to harass their clients or infringe on their authority over their labor force.[14] While some [probably those who were incumbents in local politics and their confederates] believed impressment an ally in securing a steady work force, others insisted it disrupted agricultural industry.

The number of men actively serving in the army were modest when compared to Brazil's population. Thus, the army did not represent a significant drain on the Brazilian labor market despite planters' complaints to the contrary. A senator for Ceará voiced this overstated fear in 1896, "We are a nation that needs laborers for agriculture and we should not divert labor to our army."[15] While impressment tapped a small number of men, manhunts in themselves could potentially dislocate many more men than those actually dragooned. Adult and adolescent males fled or fought when police, army, or National Guard troops came near. They feared being victims of impressment, extortion, or other abuses.[16] If press gangs passed through during crucial periods such as harvesting, planting, or elections, they could imperil a land owner's economic well-being and his political ambitions. Labor shortages and planters' fears that recruitment would disrupt labor relations and production likely induced leaders of the politically and economically powerful provinces of the Southeast to minimize impressment sweeps. The leaders of this powerful, labor-hungry region had little interest in enforcing a Recruitment Law that would force them to pay their fair share of the tribute of blood.

Volunteers and the Dragooned

As noted earlier, recruit categories for the Paraguayan War (1865–69) did not accurately measure impressment because many pressed men were officially incorporated as "volunteers." Therefore, it is better to compare recruitment during the more peaceful pre- and postwar years to discern long term trends. From 1850 to 1862, army data showed that three of five recruits had been pressed into service. From 1870 to 1882, data records a marked increase in voluntarism; only one in three troops are officially recorded as dragooned [appendix B.8]. While voluntarism increased through the early 1900s, it is important to observe how army practices and official categories often masked coercion.

Hard economic times in the postwar period for the Northeast's principal export crop, sugar, coupled with the climatic disasters in the Northeast's dry interior, where cattle ranching, goat herding, and subsistence agriculture predominated, pushed poor men to volunteer. The Great Drought of 1877–79 sent thousands of parched refugees fleeing from the Northeast's interior to Brazil's humid coasts where many without employment prospects volunteered to serve in the army. As Gerald Michael Greenfield and Durval Muniz de Albuquerque Jr. argue, periodic droughts spurred a gradual reimagining of Brazil's regions that divided the "North" into two distinct areas by the 1920s: the North (the Amazonian states of Pará and Amazonas) and the Northeast (the drought-prone coastal states from Maranhão southward to Bahia).[17] Data shows that patterns of enlisted recruitment distinguished the Northeast from other regions [appendix B.1, B.3]. When André Rebouças griped about fear of army impressment in a treatise on agriculture, he explicitly outlined the region that would come to be designated as the Northeast: "Have you traveled through the interior? Ask the sons of the interior of Maranhão, Piauí, Ceará, Pernambuco, Alagoas, and Bahia what recruitment [impressment] is? . . . All flee to grottos, to the thickest forests, to the most inaccessible mountain peaks! And then begins a real manhunt with dogs and rifles, as in the old days before Charles Sumner, Harriet Beecher Stowe, and Abraham Lincoln, when one hunted runaway slaves in the Mississippi swamps!"[18] Army impressment and its association with servile labor was already strongly identified with Brazil's Northeast by the early 1870s before the Great Drought of 1877. But most men recruited in the Northeast were not hunted down in the interior as Rebouças suggests. Officials nabbed most sertanejos when they fled to coastal areas and cities to escape drought.

Drought and army recruitment worked in tandem to develop an image of the Northeast characterized by poverty, malnutrition, exploitation, and a lack of education. On Christmas Eve, 1877, Ceará's governor dispatched a letter to the war minister: "Recently large numbers of individuals have presented themselves to enlist voluntarily. . . . It so happens that daily more than sixty civilians volunteer for army service, due to lack of resources . . . because of the horrible drought. . . . It is estimated that 60,000 unfortunate people have migrated to the coast, and among them are single men, fit for military service, who would prefer to serve in their [native] province [of Ceará]."[19] The governor requested special permission to recruit more troops, above and beyond quota levels, essentially as a disaster relief measure.[20] Securing the recruitment of drought victims was one creative way of trying to provide relief without tapping provincial coffers, particularly in the hardest hit provinces of Ceará and Paraíba. The War Ministry had officially suspended recruitment in September 1877, but it granted the governor's special request to accept refugee volunteers. However, War Minister Caxias cautioned that the "government could later transfer them [the recruits] to the most useful location for military service."[21] These recruits hoped to serve close to home, but for northeastern troops transfer to distant garrisons was a likelihood.

While some volunteered to escape disaster, many found it difficult to escape their new army careers. Because the army continued to deny praças timely discharges, some soldiers reenlisted to receive a reengagement bonus, knowing they would spend years in the ranks awaiting an honorable discharge in any case. As one observer stressed, this constituted a "forced reenlistment" within a troop category that accounted for approximately one in ten recruits.[22]

Even the category "volunteer" included many who were coerced into service. For instance, the army integrated scores of military apprentices (mostly orphans and juvenile delinquents) into regular army units as "volunteers," whether they wanted to do so or not. As shown in chapter 2, crafty recruitment agents convinced some men they apprehended that it was better to sign on as a volunteer in order to earn an enlistment bonus that, under the empire, pressed men did not receive.[23] When the Liberal party took power over Parliament in 1878, these historic opponents of the 1874 Recruitment law, set out to replace Conservative recruitment agents. They also invented new categories to describe recruits. Under the first years of Liberal rule, the number of men recorded as pressed almost disappeared. While such a result is possible given the large number of volunteers during the Great Drought, it seems unlikely that impressment would decline so quickly. An 1883 editorial in a Conservative Ceará newspaper claimed that the Liberal party's new recruitment categories were impressment under a new guise: "The time will come when our incautious countrymen cease to be swindled by the group of paid recruitment agents nominated recently. It could be that the impotence of [their] seductions is at this time being backed up with ostensible and disguised violence, in this case, it is necessary to neutralize this practice by requesting habeas corpus [for inductees] from the judicial power."[24]

Unfortunately, documentation does not allow us to estimate precisely how many men listed as "volunteers" or reengaging veterans were actually coerced into signing on. But inferring from both qualitative and quantitative sources, it seems likely that closer to one in two enlistees from 1870 to 1883 had been coerced into service, as opposed to the one in three recorded in official statistics.

Efforts to uncover aggregate recruitment data after 1883 proved unfruitful. Although no official reason surfaced for discontinuing the publication of these figures, it is likely that national defense concerns and the controversies of recruitment itself led the government to withhold such data.

Praça records show that illegal impressment continued under the republic and that northeasterners continued to predominate in the ranks.[25] Under Brazil's republic (1889–1930), the cynical abuse of the term "volunteer" became even more extreme. The republic's 1891 Constitution expressly outlawed impressment and eliminated the volunteer's enlistment bonus. Even though army officers dominated the early republican government, they proved unable to implement conscription despite renewed efforts to enforce the law. Instead, the government continued to rely on impressment to fill its ranks.

By the early 1900s, shorter minimum-service contracts and more timely discharges made army service seem less onerous and risky to potential volunteers. The war minister's 1914 report to Congress revealed the rising tide of volunteers when it griped that Brazil's draft laws were flawed because they stipulated that conscription could take place only when too few volunteers presented themselves. The war minister then ironically celebrated that "in the last few years the numbers of volunteers have happily diminished" making it necessary to institute the draft.[26] This trend implies that attitudes toward enlisted service were gradually changing.

From 1850 to 1916, economic, social, political, and strategic needs shaped recruitment patterns. Striving to keep its labor costs low, recruitment efforts centered in areas where army compounds were nearby or where the army itself had enough active-duty soldiers to conduct impressment: the Côrte and Rio Grande do Sul being the most prominent examples. The army focused its other recruitment efforts in the Northeast, where economic decline and climatic disasters pushed migrants toward coastal cities. The consequent concentration of un- and underemployed men in areas easily accessible to cheap transportation made the Northeast the largest producer of recruits. In turn, northeastern authorities depended on the army to absorb, watch over, and put to work potential or proven delinquents.

Provincial authorities across Brazil viewed the power to name recruitment agents as vital to their ability to defend themselves from political rivals, to punish or threaten trouble-making clients, and to manage potentially dangerous men. It is only natural that northeastern senators grumbled that the local "legal" authorities were superceded by the rule of "recruiters," particularly if they were "outsiders." As long as the local authorities controlled the flow of recruitment, they seldom called attention to the system's injustices. To the contrary, they praised their own moderation. As Pernambuco's governor reported in 1876 that with "the old system of recruitment still in effect . . . [my administration] has proceeded to conduct this function with moderation, I have granted all properly proven legal exemptions."[27] Brazil's underdeveloped penal system led administrators to depend on the army as an institution of penal justice, but it also served as a poor relief measure in drought-stricken Ceará and Paraíba. When speaking of São Paulo, Rio de Janeiro (province), and Minas Gerais, however, one has to restrict assertions of army recruitment as an instrument of social control. Even in core areas of recruitment, the numbers of men pressed were relatively few. Regional recruitment imbalances shaped the significance of the army's role in social control from area to area: a factor unrecognized in existing scholarly literature on social control.[28]

The long-standing interpretation that the plantocracy politically and financially choked army reformism in the 1800s to protect their local autonomy finds much support in the evidence examined here. It is also true that the "honorable" working poor risked open confrontation with authorities to protect their male family members from military service.[29] The web of social relations threatened by recruitment reform presented here is more complex than previously formulated. By examining recruitment as a specialized tribute labor system, the competing regional interests, geographic conditions, and specific events that undermined conscription's implementation become more intelligible.

Conscription carried with it incalculable hidden administrative costs in terms of State-sponsored social control for the Northeast, the federal capital district, and Rio Grande do Sul. These areas depended more heavily on the army for policing duties, for the administration of prisons and orphanages, and to absorb and to attempt to control "dangerous" men. Conscription would have required an augmentation of police forces and available prison capacity to maintain the status quo of penal justice in areas with higher rates of recruitment. The more equitable distribution of recruitment, as outlined in the 1874 reform, entailed time-consuming and costly transportation and bureaucratic rigor. Even assuming that those who were selected in a draft lottery would cooperate, regional logistics would have presented staggering complexities for the creation of a viable reserve force. A draft lottery presumed a high degree of public compliance motivated by a palpable anxiety of ridicule and punishment for noncompliance. To operate effectively it also required infrastructure, communications, and a bureaucratic capacity lacking in most of Brazil in the late 1800s. Given these conditions, mobilizing a reserve force in an emergency would have been so cumbersome as to have been almost futile. Orders from Rio often took weeks or more to arrive in frontier areas before better-integrated telegraph systems were installed in the early 1900s.

Only after the first draft in 1916 did the Southeast slowly begin to pay a more equitable share of the tribute of blood. And even then, the army began to draft men who lived in closer proximity to garrisons in order to lower transportation costs and facilitate the mobilization of reserves in a national emergency.[30] Still, geography, infrastructure, and troop deployment only partly explain why the 1874 Recruitment Law ended up in a dead-letter bin. The army began to make a number of important changes in its institutional roles that slowly changed public opinion about enlisted service. The next section examines the army's efforts to extricate itself from its role as the linchpin of Brazil's penal justice system.

The Army as a Protopenal Institution

The Brazilian army's size, its share of national budgets, and its preeminent role in the management of government-legitimated violence made it the primary institutional bridge between the State and the "criminal" underworld in the late 1800s. The State did not fashion the army to perform this function, but it proved convenient given circumstances, precedent, and the government's limited institutional capacities. Police and judicial officials, responding to perceived threats to civic order, summarily remanded thousands of Brazilian-born free men to serve minimum stints of six years in the barracks. Army orphanages inducted hundreds of street children. Authorities confined many civilian convicts, considered too dangerous for peacetime military service, in army-administered prisons, penal colonies, and stockades. Brazil did not have a national police force like Mexico's Rurales, but army soldiers commonly performed police duties across the country.[31] The army's largely unrecognized centrality to Brazil's criminal justice system meant that reforming its recruitment, training, and function altered important aspects of the State's bureaucratic management of public discipline. This section will interpret statistical data in appendix C on the weight of the army in Brazil's penal justice system compared to other public institutions.[32]

It is instructive to start with an example of everyday police work and the danger of migrating, even short distances, for poor men to areas where they were not known. In 1874, the police delegate of the hardscrabble farming town of Botucatá, São Paulo, imprisoned João Nepomoceno de Almeida Nobre as a recruit. But before going to the trouble of sending João on to the army, the delegate inquired about the recruit's reputation and exemption status with his hometown police delegate in Porto Feliz. The latter delegate replied that he did not know João, but after making inquiries, he came up with five reasons why João should not be dragooned. João lived with and "protected" his mother, an honest widow, and his sister whose husband had abandoned her. He was a carpenter who practiced his trade, and his brother had died in the Paraguay War. João was "well-mannered" and had migrated to Botucatá in search of work to sustain his family. The delegate released João highlighting the importance of an honorable reputation with one's neighbors to the free poor's security.

The Botucatá delegate mentioned that he had been informed that João was disorderly and that he had kidnapped and deflowered (*raptado*) a young woman of Porto Feliz whom he later abandoned.[33] Such dishonorable acts clearly merited impressment. In this manner, police delegates across the nation acted to protect family honor and public order. Even in São Paulo, where recruitment levels were notoriously low, police relied on impressment, rather than the courts, to punish suspected nonhomicidal wrongdoers. Another man dragooned in the coffee town of Valença, Rio de Janeiro, in 1859 confirmed the impression that authorities only pressed disorderly, immoral, and violent men. He appealed his impressment by stating that he had always lived "meekly and peacefully" in his town.[34]

Authorities admitted that there existed far more disorderly men than were ever pressed into the army. Many men like João Nepomoceno, however, were held until their exemption status could be confirmed. Undoubtedly, this caused many to proceed with greater trepidation toward authorities who were not afraid (based on suspicion) to trample on their rights as free men to come and go.

But not everyone who was pressed would ultimately serve. In 1875, Pernambuco's governor noted that from November 1872 to December 1874, only 529 of 1,003 men sent to the recruit depository were enlisted.[35] Of the 398 men sent to the same recruit depository in 1874: 232 were enlisted, 108 were liberated after proving or paying for legal exemption, 29 were rejected for physical incapacity, 2 died, 1 deserted, and 26 remained in the facility. Still, impressment nabbed a relatively small number (roughly 1,000 annually) of Brazil's population of some nine million in 1872. It is only when one considers the capacity of other public institutions of social control that the magnitude of the army's role in Brazil's penal justice system and the relative weakness of State institutions becomes apparent. In part, the lack of intensive wars to fight led Brazil's colonial armed forces and militias to perform other functions.[36] The army's function as a jailor and a police force constituted a more consistent part of its job than its transcendent duty to guard Brazil from enemy invasions and to train men to fight conventional wars.

To gauge the army's role in police work and criminal justice, it is necessary to examine briefly the civil penal system. In the colonial era, army fortresses and stockades formed an essential part of Brazil's civil prison system. Brazil's 1830 Penal Code called for the construction of civil prisons suitable to apply Walter Crofton's Irish System for reforming criminals.[37] It introduced "prison with hard labor," a sentence to be carried out within prison walls, entailing the construction of new correctional prisons. The 1824 Constitution required provincial governments to plan, fund, and build their own prisons, but over the course of the 1800s, only four out of twenty provinces (São Paulo, Bahia, Rio Grande do Sul, and Pernambuco) and the imperial capital district (Côrte) constructed new prisons conforming in some respects to Jeremy Bentham's panopticon design.[38] Under ideal conditions, these prisons added capacity for some 1,300 correctional convicts.

The construction of modern prisons stalled under the early republic with some notable exceptions, such as the founding of Brazil's first juvenile prison in 1902 in the prosperous state of São Paulo and the expansion of some older facilities. Overcrowding, stingy budgets, and the lack of qualified administrators and personnel undermined the ability of these new facilities to apply the essence of modern rehabilitative discipline: work regimes, cellular isolation, rigorous surveillance, and segregation by gender, age, and severity of crime.[39] Atrocious conditions in new correctional prisons were topped by more traditional jails. A second tier of traditional prisons and ad hoc jails (mostly private properties rented by municipalities) warehoused convicts. For the most part, traditional prisons had no work regimes and they often lacked basic sanitation and security.[40]

The data presented in appendix C.1 gives a ballpark sense of the limited capacity of civil prisons. While far from comprehensive, these figures are a preliminary attempt to measure the size of Brazil's prison population. The numbers for São Paulo in 1886 (977) and Minas Gerais in 1910 (2,180) are particularly instructive because they include the greater part of the jail population throughout their jurisdiction. The large figures for these populous and wealthy states must be balanced against smaller, less prosperous ones like Alagoas, which in 1923 logged a total of 180 prisoners. State and local governments resented the burdensome costs of supporting "idle" prisoners and the even higher costs of running prisons with work regimes.[41] Prison populations naturally fluctuated, but even though the data is patchy, it seems reasonable to assert that Brazil's civil prisons in the late 1800s held no more than 10,000 individuals at any one time under normal circumstances: a tiny proportion of Brazil's 14.3 million inhabitants estimated in the 1890 census. The actual figures for civil prison inmates may have been lower, but even if there were 20,000, it would not substantially alter my argument.

Most prison inmates were sentenced for homicide. From 1855 to 1923, Bahia's penitentiary accepted 5,039 convicts; of those, 3,012 were convicted of homicide, compared to only 800 for crimes against property. Bahian convicts entering the penitentiary averaged a little more than 74 per year. As late as 1923, a recorded 261 of Bahia's 351 penitentiary inmates were held for homicide. A 1923 survey of the populations in eight major state prisons reveals that about 70 percent were convicted of murder. This stands in stark contrast to industrializing nations like England that exported thousands of convicts for crimes against property to Australia before constructing modern penitentiaries in the mid-1800s.[42]

Civil jails, clogged with hardened convicts, had limited capacity for lesser offenders. Since there was little expansion of prisons from 1870 to 1916, rising arrest rates meant that civil prisons were little more than dangerous revolving doors that turned with increasing speed for those accused of less serious crimes.[43]

Even though impressment could relieve pressures on crowded jails, local officials often frustrated the efforts of state and imperial officials to dragoon. As one police delegate in the rural town of Barreiros, Pernambuco, emphasized in 1874: "One cannot effect anyone's imprisonment, even [those] suspected [to be] deserters or [those usually destined] for [military] impressment, because the local district attorney will act to free the prisoner, which the local judge will sanction leading to fines and court costs that triple normal [recruiting] costs. Under these conditions, I do not know how one can do police work."[44] For this delegate, the disruption of cost-effective impressment and the apprehension of deserters unjustly impeded everyday police work. It also shows how police depended on the cooperation of local authorities to carry out their duties.

Enlisted army service worked as a partial escape valve for overburdened civil prisons by incorporating offenders and the "criminally" idle. Judges did not transfer men suspected of homicide or other crimes they deemed worthy of trials. It is difficult to estimate precisely how many men pressed into military service had committed criminal acts. Since there were no trials, the police delegates' assertions were the only evidence of transgressions (even in the cases of suspected horse thieves and "sodomites").[45] Appalling conditions in Brazil's civil prison system may have given some officials pause before trying and sentencing a man for what they considered a lesser offense. Impressment diminished court costs and eased pressures to build expensive new prisons. Local officials thus shifted the costs of social control and "rehabilitation" to the central State. In turn, the army's manpower needs obliged it to take on tough cases.

Compared to prison conditions, army service probably offered better chances of "reforming" offenders. In 1872, War Minister Rio Branco noted the general repugnance most Brazilians demonstrated for army service at the same time as he lauded its important social mission: "The army has saved many individuals from dangerous idleness, living lives useless to society. In military institutions [the idle] encounter severe vigilance and prompt correction of wrongs, reforming their habits while instructing and preparing them to be better citizens." The use of dishonorable men to enforce the law tended to undermine its credibility and legitimacy in the eyes of the poor and the privileged alike. Hence, the Brazilian phrase, "For my friends, anything; for my enemies, the law."

Officers had to negotiate an uneasy discipline with reluctant troops, regarded by much of the public with fear and disdain.[46] Some officers took more of an interest in shaping their troops' characters than others, but except for the police forces, the army certainly offered a more consistent disciplinary regime than other public institutions. Troops wore uniforms, performed group exercises, and were required by their officers to perform work—an element regarded as central to moral rehabilitation and physical and mental health by theorists from Jeremy Bentham to Karl Marx.

The small percentage of Brazilians who actively served in the military might make it appear deceptively insignificant. In peacetime, only about 2,000 men (volunteers and dragoonees) entered the army's ranks in a given year. As the war minister complained in 1912, only 1.1 per thousand inhabitants of Brazil actively served in the armed forces, compared to 2.2 per thousand in Mexico, 4.6 in Japan, 8.7 in Germany, and 13.5 in France.[47] The Brazilian army's institutional reach through recruitment was shallow compared to continental Europe where powerful rivals pressured one another to expend vast resources on defense. However, when compared to Brazil's civilian penal system, the importance of the army's role in criminal justice and policing becomes readily apparent. Peacetime praça ranks typically numbered between twelve and sixteen thousand men. As impressment accounted for about half of these enlistments, then the army incorporated between six and nine thousand individuals who were considered "criminal."[48]

Not surprisingly, discipline in the ranks was undermined by impressment. As a war minister noted as late as 1914, integrating recruits a few at a time, year-round hampered the ability of officers to train men according to "consecrated methods."[49] Discipline was further impaired by the policing duties army troops routinely performed. In 1871, the war minister urged that army service be restricted to garrison duty, warning that this could only succeed "if [provincial] police forces stopped depending on the assistance of army troops," a practice "prejudicial to military discipline."[50] Despite the pleas of the high command, provincial governments continued to rely on local army troops as police auxiliaries. In fact, after the 1873 reform of the National Guard largely deactivated that force, the army appears to have been required to perform more police duties than before.[51] In the small town of Iguarassu, Pernambuco (where once-prosperous small-holders were squeezed by falling cotton prices after the American Civil War), the police delegate complained in 1874 that the guard's deactivation had "weakened the principle of authority in a frightening manner."[52]

Army troops seem to have taken up the institutional slack in police work around the country. In 1885, a circular letter from the war minister complained that "north[eastern] states, which lack [adequate] police forces, use army praças for police detachments." This common procedure could separate troops from their garrisons and officers for extended periods of time. In 1875, Maranhão's governor ordered a local army commander to station his regiment in the troubled town of Caxias: "The presence of a respected force . . . will restore tranquility of spirit to Caxias' good citizens, so shaken by the fear of disorder. . . . The police force currently present in Caxias will withdraw when your force arrives, the requisition of praças for patrol work will be directed to you. . . . I recommend that you help the police with its recruitment duties, exemptions will be respected with the utmost scruples, you should not remit any recruits to the capital without honoring the time allowed to each one to prove his exemption." While establishing order, this army battalion was also encouraged to carry out another traditional police function: chasing down their future comrades.[53]

As improvements occurred in the terms and conditions of army enlisted service in the early 1900s, officers bristled at suggestions that their troops perform duties that smacked of police work.[54] In 1913, the war minister drew attention to a few scattered units in Amazonas and Acre that were being used by local prefects to perform "police functions," duties "alien to those required of the army in the 1891 Constitution." The war minister requested that all such isolated units be fused with larger battalions where soldiers would receive proper training. It would appear that elsewhere the army had succeeded in preventing state and local officials from consistently diverting army troops for police duties.[55] Most troops now spent more active hours training in and around their garrisons. Still, discipline and training often remained slack, especially in frontier garrisons.[56]

As the army withdrew from everyday policing duties, it also sought to escape its role in the administration of civilian convicts. Forts and army arsenals provided prison space for some of the nation's most dangerous military, civilian, and slave convicts.[57] Liberal reformers had hoped to reduce the civil justice system's reliance on military facilities to confine convicts by requiring provinces to build penitentiaries. However, the foundation of an army-administered penal colony on the island of Fernando de Noronha in the 1830s expanded the army's role in Brazil's penal system [appendix C.2].

This penal alternative, about 290 miles off of Pernambuco's coast, followed Portuguese precedents of exiling criminals to colonize unsettled frontiers. For Brazilian jurists, however, much of its inspiration and validity sprang from the penal transportation systems of England and France.[58] By the 1860s, though smaller in scale than Europe's penal colonies, Fernando de Noronha's civil prison population was more than four times greater than the largest of Brazil's provincial prisons and greater than all of the new correctional penitentiaries combined.

Military tribunals remitted only about one-fifth of the island's inmates, the remainder came from overflowing civil jails. Authorities attributed the rapid growth of the civilian convict population to the lack of penitentiaries capable of adequately administering the sentence of "prison with hard labor." Convict slaves, freemen, and soldiers, some accompanied by their wives and children, formed the island's penal population.

During the Paraguayan War, the island's penal population fell brusquely because the government dragooned a few hundred convicts to fight at the front (some of whom petitioned to enlist in return for pardons).[59] Nevertheless, by the late 1870s, a continuing stream of convicts had restored this population to antebellum levels. As in civil prisons, inmates convicted of homicide predominated. Among the convicts on the island in 1880, 1,050 civil prisoners had been sentenced for murder; 130 for larceny; 24 for counterfeiting; and the crimes of more than eighty prisoners were unknown. More than 700 had been sentenced to perpetual imprisonment; the rest served temporary sentences, except for 13 who should have been executed and 24 whose sentences were unknown.[60]

The War Ministry usually accepted only those convicts with a sentence of six years or more to Fernando de Nornoha because of transportation costs. Thus, the island held the most hardened of provincial inmates. In 1876, of 1,260 civilian prisoners, 963 originated from northeastern provinces, 215 from the Southeast, 60 from the South, 22 from the North, and none from the Central West.[61] Again, the weight of the army's role in managing criminals varied among regions and provinces, but even so, the penal colony wove most provincial prison systems into a national penal network. Its regulation was reformed in 1877, but the noted jurist Evaristo de Morais observed, "Even after the justice minister assumed responsibility for Fernando de Noronha's maintenance the army continued to administer it."[62]

In the 1890s, the Republican government's federalist policies led to the closing of what had become Brazil's central prison. Fernando de Noronha reverted to Pernambuco's domain, and all inmates from other states and the military apparently had been removed by 1900. The closing of Fernando de Noronha as a national prison in 1896 represented a sizeable reduction in civil prison capacity, placing even more pressures on overcrowded provincial jails. While some civilian convicts were still held in military fortresses and stockades, the army's administration of permanent and predominantly civilian prisons drew to a temporary close.[63] Acting as a jailor for civilian criminals was just as inconsistent with the army's modernizing goals as was police work and the impressment of "criminals" into the army's ranks. Meanwhile, a similar process of expansion and contraction characterized the army's role in managing "dangerous" juveniles.

Army apprentice schools got their start in the early 1800s when Dom João VI ordered Rio's army arsenal to take on abandoned children as apprentices; Parliament regularized their status in 1831.[64] Similar schools later spread to army arsenals in Rio Grande do Sul, Bahia, Pernambuco, Mato Grosso, and Pará. The lack of men trained in the use and maintenance of artillery for the Paraguayan War led to the founding of Rio's artillery apprentice school in 1865. In 1876, infantry apprentice schools opened in Minas Gerais and Goiás. At its peak, the apprentice school system handled nearly 1,200 boys from age ten to eighteen, annually producing scores of trained "volunteers" for undermanned regiments.[65]

Unsatisfied with the quantity and quality of troops, the army high command hedged its bets on the success of the 1874 Recruitment Law. It expanded its investment in the education of wayward boys to secure cheap labor and guarantee a future generation of more highly skilled soldiers. If an artisan apprentice demonstrated aptitude he could be graduated to the status of "army laborer" at age sixteen. Regulations obligated elected apprentices to serve the arsenal for a minimum of ten years. Those who had not demonstrated ability would serve as "volunteers" in regular army units for the standard six years of service as did boys serving in artillery and infantry apprentice schools when they reached nineteen years of age.

Some artillery and infantry apprentices who demonstrated capacity and discipline were transferred to active duty with a NCO's rank, and a handful climbed from apprentice schools to the army's system of higher education, the gateway to a commissioned officer's rank.[66] While some willingly sent their sons to serve in army apprentice schools, the police and *juizes de orphãos* (judges' orphans' judge) enrolled most boys. The provincial police of Rio de Janeiro reported sending 49 minors to the army's artillery apprentice school in 1875. At the end of the Paraguayan War, a large group of Paraguayan orphans were incorporated into the artillery apprentice school, temporarily swelling its ranks [appendix C.3].[67]

Army apprentice schools shared a picaresque reputation with naval apprentice schools, whose rough company and dour discipline become folkloric.[68] It remains a commonplace for parents to threaten to enroll their children in a navy apprentice school when they misbehave. Navy Ministry mail reveals that the apprentices of Rio's army and navy arsenals included some of the city's most notorious *capoeiras,* who terrified the public and frustrated the police. *Capoeira* refers to the uniquely Afro-Brazilian martial art, music, and dance form, and to the individuals who practiced it. It requires great strength, timing, grace, and flexibility to execute acrobatic leaps, kicks, and head butts, but most whites viewed it as an embarrassing vestige of African savagery. Police repressed the mere practice of capoeira on the streets, in part to give urban centers a more European veneer for foreign visitors. Some capoeiras were members of urban gangs that armed themselves with easy-to-conceal razors and conducted deadly street rumbles. They became an integral part of urban political life in the late empire by forming part of the informal security forces that protected polling places for powerful patrons. A Conservative senator denied that it had been easy to punish these gang members with impressment by stating that "in this city there exists a class of individuals, against which the authorities fight and who possess a thousand means of escape, I refer to capoeiras." Another senator added, "The good [capoeira] artist is sure to find someone who will give him money to exempt himself [from military service]." But these claims contradict the complaints of Rio's police who attested that there was little he could do to punish recidivist capoeiras who were army veterans, National Guardsmen, arsenal employees, or active duty praças.[69]

Correspondence between Rio's police chief and the Navy Ministry recorded several cases of apprentices illegally remitted for active military service because of capoeira.[70] In one such instance in September 1876, the slave mother of Pedro Nicolau Liberal requested that her son be returned from active navy duty because he was only fifteen years old. Rio's police chief claimed that Nicolau, armed with a razor, had been involved in a capoeira street fight. Despite his age, the chief convinced the naval minister to punish Nicolau by enrolling him for active duty and shipping him out of Rio. Nicolau's mother explained that her son worked "assiduously" at the arsenal to buy his mother's freedom and never involved himself in capoeira. Nicolau's mother, probably with the assistance of her owner, had her son's baptismal certificate certified and notarized. After a few months at sea, the navy returned Nicolau to police authorities for normal judicial processing.[71] Others who did not have family or patrons in a position to protect them were probably not so lucky as Nicolau.

Correspondence from the previous year indicates that the transfer of underage apprentices like Nicolau formed part of a clandestine effort to break up gangs composed of "army praças and army and navy arsenal workers."[72] On June 1, 1876, a navy arsenal worker was killed by a "Portuguese" in a capoeira rumble. At the scene, the police arrested three members of the "gang of navy arsenal workers."[73] In response, Rio's police chief sent a confidential request to the Naval Ministry: "Authorities cannot always find a means for any legal action [against capoeiras] as they . . . disperse before police forces arrive, I judge it my duty to suggest to your excellency [Naval Minister] that these turbulent *maltas,* many of them navy arsenal workers, [be] transferred to active duty . . . and sent away from Rio. . . . I add that the [army] War Minister, at my request, agreed to transfer his arsenal workers, when they are imprisoned for practicing capoeira. . . . This will reduce the repetition of such events."[74] The chiefs of the army and navy agreed to transfer troublesome arsenal workers and apprentices for regular service. These actions demonstrate the willingness of the high command to sidestep the law to reinforce public order. Only those who could activate a patronage network to file costly petitions could protect their rights. The incorporation of troublesome youths in the apprentice schools was a double-edged sword for the army, navy, and police who attempted to work in concert to control these young men. Ironically, their military status as apprentices afforded these capoeiras some protection from arbitrary police procedures.[75] Military apprentice schools, to the dismay of authorities, had been partly subverted into capoeira schools that propagated values and practices that military discipline was intended to suppress. Regular service and transfer loomed as punishment for bad behavior.

Army apprentice schools initially expanded in the early 1890s, but then the government began to close them. A consolidation of army arsenals in 1896 closed half of the artisan apprentice schools, and by 1901 those remaining appear to have been shut down [appendix C.3]. The apprentice schools fell victim to the army's restructuring, budgetary constraints, and plans to modernize education. The army began to fund more *colégios* intended to prepare boys with better educational backgrounds for careers as commissioned officers. By shutting down apprentice schools, the army reduced the State's institutional capacity to deal with abandoned and delinquent boys (although navy apprentice schools continued at a reduced capacity).[76] The army's modernizing ambitions and desire to improve the image of enlisted service were inconsistent with the duties of being the nation's largest institution for wayward boys, policing, and civil prison administration.

The Republican State's greater propensity to abandon public offenders in uninhabited frontier regions was likely a symptom of this institutional transition. As Miguel Calmon noted, "Since the beginning of the Republic, deportations were always made to the extreme North. . . . Marshal Floriano Peixoto's government decreed the internal exile (*desterro*) of various persons of public notoriety to Cucuhy and Tabatinga. After the Vaccine Revolt (1904) . . . deportations to [the state of] Amazonas were made *larga manu*."[77] Similar deportations followed the Canudos Rebellion (1896–97), the Chibata Revolt (1910), and the Tenente Revolts (1922; 1924–27). Police exploited these deportations to round up their local nemeses and ship them off with rebels and rioters.[78] This type of unregulated ostracism had occurred under the empire but not on this scale.

Earlier in the 1800s, the foot soldiers of insurgent forces had frequently been transferred to other regions and integrated into the army there. Under the Republic, this practice became less common but did not disappear completely. During the insurgencies of the 1890s, Private Isaac Noberto de Carmo's record showed that he had been imprisoned by the state police of Rio de Janeiro as a "rebel." He was transferred to the federal capital where he was imprisoned for five months, being afterwards, "by whose orders it is unknown," enlisted in the army's 10th Infantry Battalion. Army reforms, however, slowly began to cut off this penal destination for rebel troops.[79]

Conclusions

Theorists from Max Weber to Michel Foucault, E. P. Thompson, and Benedict Anderson have emphasized the roles of bureaucratic public institutions (penitentiaries, schools, armies, navies, orphanages, police forces, asylums, and administrative bodies, among others) in disciplining individuals for participation in nationalist societies. Others, such as Eugen Weber, have focused more specifically on the significant role national militaries played in introducing citizens, particularly rural inhabitants, to nationalist ritual and doctrine.[80] Less attention has been given to how different public institutions evolved in relation to one another. The question of institutional fit is particularly useful when comparing how one of the largest agro-export economies in the world selected and adapted North Atlantic bureaucratic practices. Developing nations like Brazil lacked the funds to reform the entire panoply of modern institutions simultaneously. Difficult choices had to be made between competing agendas supported by constituents with differing degrees of political power. The levels of capitalist development, while they cannot reliably predict the timing of institutional reforms, certainly shaped outcomes. Accordingly, among nations and regions of similar development levels, there are likely to be significant patterns in the struggle to modernize State institutions.

The army's attempt to rationalize its training, recruitment, and function directly impinged on Brazil's police, prison, orphanage, and judicial systems. The weight of this transition varied among provinces and regions, but no other set of reforms, save those abolishing slavery, could compare to the scale of its impact on institutions of social discipline and the lives of the poor. Halting efforts to modernize a variety of state institutions occurred in the late 1800s. Those who held power in Brazil could have selected to give greater emphasis to modernizing prisons, police, educational, or orphanage institutions before reforming the army. In some instances, these institutions did receive the attention of reformers, but the primacy of national defense and the political influence of army officers and their allies ultimately made military reform a higher priority of the central government.

The army's retreat from its once prominent position in penal justice and everyday police work indicate that caution and qualification needs to be used when generalizing about the State's increasing role in "disciplining" the free wage labor force. Other public institutions were pressured to supplant the army's former duties. The republic's federalist system shifted the brunt of police problems to state governments, and some were in a better position than others to make this transition. Prosperous São Paulo and Minas Gerais did not press many of their "dangerous" citizens for army service in the late 1800s, and because they possessed small army garrisons, they did not depend heavily on the army as a police auxiliary. Conversely, Rio Grande do Sul, the Côrte, and the Northeast had comparatively high rates of impressment and a greater dependence on the army to perform police duties, guard civilian convicts, and harbor abandoned children. For these areas, army reforms had a more profound impact on the web of public institutions liable for social control. Could the banditry that swept the Northeast's backlands in the early 1900s be related to this shrinking capacity? This largely overlooked factor needs to be taken into consideration when comparing regional experiences. In future, researchers must look more intensively beyond the State for answers as to how immigrants, former slaves, employers, and political bosses negotiated the transition from a slave to a wage labor market.

The growth of militarized state police forces in the Old Republic has correctly been read as a response to rising crime rates, the decline of slavery, increasing migration and immigration, and dizzying urbanization. In addition, one must add the army's withdrawal from everyday police work. Army modernization and specialization itself sped the growth of state police forces.[81] Many officers rightly viewed growing state police forces as a threat to their reform efforts, "The same politicians that in their states organize these armies [of state police] try to weaken and retard the improvement of the federal army . . . police armies are organized to counterpoise the federal army!"[82] Still, intimidation and temporary incarceration were in most instances the best these police forces could muster to counter less serious crimes for lack of alternative institutional capacity.

In 1880, if one conservatively adds the number of men pressed into the army and apprentice schools to those guarded by troops in stockades and penal colonies, the army directly handled some eight to twelve thousand men and adolescents considered "criminal." While a fuller survey of the nation's prison population awaits further research, the evidence indicates that the army alone dealt with a large portion of the civil criminal population, perhaps equal to or greater than the civil prison system. Republican military reforms slowly closed off this significant institutional destination for non-homicidal criminals and reduced the credible threat of such penalties. Most states did little to expand penal institutions as their populations grew and Army reforms shut down a vital part of the system's institutional capacity to deal with "dangerous" men and boys.

These changes indicate that more traditional patriarchal strategies of social control (including paramilitary security forces or forces not constituted under State auspices) probably played a more important role than the "State" in the transition from slave to wage labor in Brazil.[83] If one equates the army's modernization with progress, as many Brazilian leaders often did, then one has to question exactly how this progress enhanced the State's ability to "discipline" its citizens. Under the republic, the results were very uneven. Rather than rely on blanket assertions that the State increased its role in disciplining the work force as slavery declined, one should distinguish between strata of the poor. Analysis should also consider the reach and the linkages between public disciplining institutions in different regions and the strategies they pursued. In many areas, army reform in the late 1890s significantly reduced the State's institutional capacity to discipline the unprotected poor: precisely when a peacetime post-abolition order was being negotiated.

The army's centrality to penal justice in Brazil and many other nations was a crippling impediment to military reformism. In much of Europe and the United States the growth of penitentiaries, reformatories, poor houses, schools, penal colonies, and orphanages enabled their armies to make a smoother transition from impressment to conscription. In continental Europe, the need to mobilize effective militaries to deter the threat of invasion by powerful neighbors facilitated conscription's adoption.

Conversely, in Latin America, politicians were not so pressured to invest in armed forces to protect their property from foreign incursions. Thus, in industrializing Europe, the rise of conscription, emigration, fears of foreign invasion, and the growth of modern reform institutions and penal colonies were complementary processes in the development of social "discipline" and nationalist sentiments. In Brazil, the draft would push the growth of other modern institutions to replace the army's previous function as a protopenal institution, but the expansion of prisons, orphanages, and schools did not keep pace with the demands created by the reduction in the State's capacity to deal with less serious offenders because of army reforms. The reach of these institutions never extended to as large a proportion of the populace as they did in Europe, North America, and Japan. This crude comparison is made here to suggest the utility of examining the sequencing and depth of institutional reform to unfold a more rigorous comparative history of State building. But, how disciplined were Brazilian soldiers in the age of impressment? The next two chapters examine who soldiers were, how they lived, and the nature of discipline in the army.

Chapter 7

Brazilian Soldiers and

Enlisted Service in the Age

of Impressment, 1870–1916

The broad patterns of recruitment and the army's changing role as a public institution of social control does not reveal exactly who soldiers were and what they did beyond police work or guarding convicts. A collective biography of praças and a thumbnail sketch of the texture of their lives and labor reveals that, by the early 1900s, alterations in the terms and service that praças performed brought about changes in recruitment patterns. Slowly, these shifts began to distance praça duties and status from those linked to slavery, penal servitude, and the coarse realm of the street.

Brazil's Praças

So far, the profile of Brazilian praças has perhaps unfairly reproduced an image of bedraggled unfortunates, as outsiders often portrayed them. Most of the remarks in this section are based on a survey of 315 career files found in military police inquiries from 1896. The survey privileges those tried by the army legal system, and its representativeness has to be viewed with some caution. Still, these documents reveal surprising diversity in soldiers' backgrounds and characteristics.[1]

Career records begin with a soldier's rank and number. This was the new impersonal bureaucratic identity of recruits. In a practical sense, it avoided confusion among numerous João(s), José(s), da Silva(s), and dos Santos(es) (common names). Like prison inmates, authorities assigned soldiers numbers, breaking down individual identity to facilitate complex group activities. Officers, by contrast, adopted more personalized noms de guerre rather than digits.

Records then listed a soldier's name and those of his parents, giving the reader a vital handle on his social status. Even in an institution that preached meritocracy, birth status and race influenced the assessment of one's quality in a society that valued family honor and in which many pinned their hopes for national destiny to the "whitening" project. Thirteen of 315 defendants could not name either parent, but most could name their fathers, and if not, then their mothers. The lack of a surname suggests that a soldier was an ex-slave. A black private from São Paulo "Fortunato, the son of Adão" was convicted for his third desertion in 1896, and he received a six-year sentence. Republican records do not indicate whether or not a recruit was pressed, but it is plausible that Fortunato had been dragooned. Slavery's abolition eight years earlier must have seemed a cruel mirage for the unfortunate Fortunato. Even soldiers with surnames could have been ex-bondsmen because many slaves obtain "family" names before their letter of liberty.[2]

Some ex-slaves entered the army as boys. The 1871 Free Womb Law made provisions for owners who did not want to raise their slaves' sons after age eight. Rio's police chief presented a judge the following petition, "the minor, Leão, whose services Dona Matilda Rita de Nascimento relinquishes usufruct, so that [Leão] be presented and integrated into a Company of Apprentices in one of the Arsenals of the Corte." The file contains Leao's letters of liberty and alludes to compliance with the Free Womb Law. Leão would be required to work as an apprentice until age seventeen. Afterward, he would either serve ten years as an arsenal laborer or complete a regular service contract as an army "volunteer."[3] Clearly, the "liberty" Leão's mistress granted was limited.

Not all praça defendants had humble backgrounds. Several were sons of army officers, and one father held the title of *doutor*.[4] A "black" deserter from Pernambuco, Private Antônio Ferreira da Silva claimed to be the son of Bishop Ferreira da Silva.[5] José Peixoto, the legitimate son of President Floriano Peixoto (1891–94), also appears in trial transcripts in 1896. After his father's death in 1895, José was dismissed from the military academy, a hot bed of Jacobino conspiracy. His graduation would have assured José a commissioned rank, but regulations required those dismissed from the academy to serve out a contract as a praça. José then received an unenviable posting at the prison-fortress of Santa Cruz. At age nineteen, with three years of army service, José was charged with desertion. He denied the charge and produced evidence to support his case. His court-martial found him guilty, but the Suprema Tribunal Militar absolved him.[6] Whether or not José was persecuted by his father's political enemies, his example confirms that if the army was a place of social mobility, it had elevators moving in both directions, even for prominent citizens. Academy students who did not apply themselves or who involved themselves in sedition could serve as praças.[7]

In the army records, a soldier's parentage was followed by his birth date and place of birth. The ledgers record only the province or foreign nation of birth, which makes it hard to discern urban versus rural origins. The survey indicates that immigrants and their sons continued to dodge impressment because only four praças were foreign-born (Paraguay and Portugal) and few had non-Iberian surnames.

The ages of praças varied between sixteen and fifty-eight years—the average age being a little over twenty-four. Two-thirds of the sample were between age eighteen and twenty-six. Slightly more than one in ten were married men. Some enlisted as married men, but a few married after enlisting. The low percentage of married men seems consistent with the traditional taboos that protected them from impressment.

Four out of five of the 178 praças whose records indicated occupations had no specialized skills (*sem ofício*). Those with skills included eight stone masons; five carpenters; three shoe makers; two tailors, musicians, blacksmiths, and furniture makers; and one scrivener, painter, caulker, cowboy, gunsmith, machinist, tanner, cigarette roller, and coachman. Many "without skills" were or had been rural laborers. Most of the skilled laborers listed probably worked in the casual urban labor market where economic downturns and subsequent unemployment could make them indistinguishable from the unprotected poor.

By the 1890s, records included detailed descriptions of praças' physical traits—a practice not extended to officers. Before photography was an affordable technology for identification, detailed written descriptions were the best substitute. Praça depictions bear a resemblance to those published in newspapers before abolition describing runaway slaves. They included height, hair (color and texture), eyes, nose, lips, skin color, and other distinguishing marks like scars and tatoos. As many studies have shown, racial categorization in Brazil is mostly in the eyes of the beholder.[8] Caution must be used in evaluating these categories, but they do offer a rough gauge of racial composition. I assume that skin tone constituted an evaluation of the sum total of features and culture that placed an individual in a racial category for scribes who recorded these preconceived groupings. Unlike census returns, army records were intended to make it easy to identify deserters.

Army records use four major categories for skin color — *branca* (white), *morena* (light brown), *parda* (dark brown), *preta* (black) — and three less common groupings — *fula* (dark black color of people originating from Guine), *indiática* (Indian); and *cabocla* (usually a mixture of Indian and white, it also suggested hinterland origins). If one collapses these categories into white, mixed race (*parda* and *morena*), black (including *fula*), and Indian (*indiática* and *cabocla*) about 20 percent of the soldiers were white, 25 percent black, two percent Indian, and more than 50 percent of mixed-race. In Brazil's 1890 census, the population was 44 percent white, 41 percent mestizo, and 15 percent black.[9] Thus, blacks and mestizos were overrepresented while whites were underrepresented. The racial composition of praças reflected Brazil's venerable racial hierarchy. Still, one of five praças was white, which reveals that "whiteness" did not assure protection from impressment. It is plausible that army justice dealt more leniently with lighter-skinned soldiers, and if so, they might be slightly underrepresented in this sample.

Approximately one in three praças were listed as literate, about twice the rate of the general population in 1890. It is likely that the ability to sign one's name was taken as literacy by army scriveners because some men whose records listed them as literate claimed they could not read copies of their court testimony.[10] In this restricted survey, rank and literacy confirm the racial hierarchy found in larger Brazilian society. Race provided a rough measure of access to education, and illiteracy limited the ability of nonwhites to rise above a private's rank. It is also credible that literacy "whitened" a recruit's racial categorization. By contrast, officers' records did not mention race, probably because they were presumed to be white, but qualitative sources show that many junior officers were nonwhite.[11]

The survey of praças reveals that the typical soldier was of mixed race, unskilled, illiterate, and unmarried. Most lacked the skills needed for a modern military where increasingly complex machinery, weaponry, and communication skills required a basic education. The presence of volunteers and pressed men of low status made it difficult for reformers to

Table 3. STM Defendants by Race, Literacy, and Rank

Color	Literate*			Rank				
	#	Yes	No	Priv.	Corp.	Serg.	Ensign	Officer
Branca (White)	43	26	17	37	0	3	3	0
Morena (Light brown)	33	11	22	30	2	1	0	0
Parda (Dark brown)	66	24	42	65	1	0	0	0
Preta (Black)	47	6	41	47	0	0	0	0
Fula (Dark Black)	4	1	3	4	0	0	0	0
Indiática (Indigenous)	4	0	4	4	0	0	0	0
Cabocla (Mix of Indian and white)	3	0	3	3	0	0	0	0
Subtotal	201	68	132	190	3	4	3	0
Missing	115	38	70	93	3	2	13	4
Total	315	106	202	283	6	6	16	4
%	100	34	66	90	2	2	5	1

Source: Based on a survey of records in the ANR, Suprema Tribunal Militar, Inquéritos da Polícia Militar (1896).
*In seven cases, literacy could not be determined.

convince the honorable poor that army enlisted service was "respectable." The working conditions and treatment of praças made enlisted service even more unappealing.

Everyday Life in the Barracks

Before dawn across Brazil, bugles awoke soldiers for morning roll calls, a practice not dissimilar to the assembly of slaves on large plantations or at mines.[12] Soldiers housed in barracks arose and scurried to ready themselves, and those who lived off-base made their way to their regiments. They knew that tardiness or improper dress could result in disciplinary action. Some arrived puffy-eyed with hangovers, others weary from performing a night watch, and still others, better rested, may have looked forward to their duties. As they stood in formation, awaiting their numbers to be called, some may have pondered what the day would bring, or what awaited them upon discharge. This section depicts some of the expectations, frustrations, tragedies, and triumphs of praças. The difficulties a soldier faced were in many ways similar to those facing other poor Brazilians whom most soldiers interacted with on a daily basis, but the rhythms of their work days were marked by different rules and the bugle rather than church bells. The analysis here is in no way an exhaustive account of soldiers' lives in the age of impressment, but an effort to illustrate some salient aspects of them.

Ostensibly, praças lived under national laws and regulations, but their living conditions, work, and leisure defy sweeping generalizations. Army facilities varied greatly. Conditions in urban centers where barracks had long stood differed from frontier regions where often there existed only very primitive structures, if any at all. Some lived walled in fortress ramparts and others in private homes or buildings alongside civilians in surrounding communities. Where conditions permitted, officers, NCOs, and some trusted privates enjoyed separate off-base quarters. These men lived in residences provided by the army, but more often they rented or owned their own homes. Most lived near their bases, giving some boroughs and towns a distinct army flavor.[13] At Tamandaré Fort in Pernambuco, officers built homes 150 yards (*braços*) from the garrison's walls where they grew large gardens. In 1865, the commander ordered that the homes and garden plots be moved six hundred yards back to prevent them from hindering the fort's defenses.[14]

Army regulations required praças to get their commander's permission to live off base. This enhanced their ability to reward trusted soldiers with manly freedoms and privileges. As one officer recalled, "To live off base was the desire of every soldier, old or new; this meant receiving in cash the value of one's room and board . . . married soldiers and NCOs . . . and some reenlisting soldiers with good comportment enjoyed this privilege. The clause 'return to the barracks' always accompanied any punishment of those who lived off base." Private Jacintho Franco de Godoy, for instance, was ordered in 1895 to "return to the barracks" because his commander learned that he no longer lived with his wife. Officers could grant off-base privileges as an incentive for good behavior, much as masters rewarded trusted slaves with the right to a private abode and access to provision grounds.[15] To marry and to establish a family household were badges of status desired by many praças. But others preferred simply to live with consensual lovers (*amazias*). Indeed, many of Brazil's poor lived together based on a promise to marry at a future date. Marriage fees and in many areas the lack of clergy made waiting for an official ceremony untenable for many poor Brazilians. Men and women who made such promises were expected to uphold them, and abandonment by either spouse could spark social censure and, for men, lead to impressment.[16]

Officers and praças often lived in close proximity and developed close ties. In Maceió, Alagoas Lieutenant Alfredo Baptista Jardineiro befriended the teenage daughter of a corporal in his company. Witnesses stated that the officer treated the girl as "if she were part of his family," and she accompanied him while he directed garrison duties. Tragically, the Lieutenant was convicted of raping the corporal's daughter. Citing the dishonor visited on his family, the corporal requested an immediate transfer.[17] Sometimes soldiers lived in closer contact with their officers than they may have liked. Relationships between officers and praças were not usually this degrading, but as one civilian complained in 1910, "In the barracks there is the absurd custom of making soldiers the personal servants of officers."[18] Despite new regulations, many praças still worked as camaradas (servants) cleaning the homes or tending to the gardens, laundry, and livestock of officers.

As in civilian society, praças sought out patrons, and officers, in turn, cultivated clients to protect their interests. An incredulous medical examiner asked a recent graduate of the Sergeant's School in the 1920s, "My boy, who is your *pistolão* ("big shot" or officer patron)?" When the NCO replied that he did not have one, the doctor responded that "in all my years in the army I have never seen such a young first sergeant."[19] This comment reveals how important patron-client relations between officers and praças had been in the age of impressment and how they began to change after conscription was implemented in 1916.

In more developed compounds, separate latrines, cantinas, and stockade cells existed for officers, NCOs, and privates. Privates were generally forbidden to enter these areas without permission. Thus, social space reinforced hierarchy by preventing what officers called "social pollutions." As in caste societies, army hierarchies generally affirm that familiarity can breed contempt and weaken respect for authority and privilege. Like slaves and humble peons, army subordinates were admonished to show deference by not looking into the eyes of superiors and ceding the right of way. The out-ranked also manifested submission by saluting, confirming acceptance of hierarchical authority. One praça was sentenced to twenty-five days in solitary with reduced rations for failing to notice and salute a captain of his battalion while traveling on a suburban train.[20]

Uniforms (not always available and not always uniform) distinguished rank, but other nuances of status were also visible. Officers, NCOs, and privates could be distinguished by facial hair. Praças were not permitted to use sideburns, this was the mark of an officer. According to one observer, sergeants imitated officers who were aficionados of the goatee, whereas, corporals and privates were typified by a simple moustache or a cleanly shaven face. Most praças used dull cotton uniforms cinched at the waist with a belt and simple leather boots. Boots provided a hint of respectability as slaves were denied the right to wear shoes, but the uniforms themselves were not appropriate to the colder climates of southern Brazil. Some praças expressed their individuality with tatoos; a practice most officers associated with barbarism.[21] These differences between ranks reflected the cultural and social gulf that separated the common soldier from his officers. For many praças, the differences in race, culture, and class were compounded by regional diversity. Most southerners and southeasterners looked down on northeasterners, but most northeasterners took pride in their home state and region, and many officers shared their northeastern origins and pride of place.[22]

The conditions and type of work performed by praças varied greatly over time and place. Perhaps the most bleak peacetime task required of soldiers was the telegraph service, which, from the 1860s to the early 1900s, strung up lines across Brazil. Soldiers sent to telegraph crews in the Amazon lived in camps and braved tropical diseases, relentless pests, and sometimes hostile Indians. Private Ignácio Fabber griped in 1904 that he had deserted the telegraph gangs because when he failed to meet his quota for digging post holes, he was flogged. The officer defending Ignacio justified his desertion based on his white complexion, which was supposedly unsuited to such arduous work in a steamy clime. The racist defense, however, did not win Ignacio's acquittal.[23] The vile conditions and savage treatment soldiers faced on telegraph gangs were akin to indentured servitude.

By way of a counterintuitive contrast, soldiers and civilians sentenced to hard labor at prison on Fernando de Noronha's penal colony lived under a much less exacting work regime than their law-abiding counterparts. In 1879, inspectors of this island penal colony were appalled to find that most convicts concluded their hard labor at midday, working between 4.5 to six hours per day. To inspectors this seemed like a vacation rather than punishment because law-abiding slaves, soldiers, and common laborers regularly worked ten to fourteen hours per day. Moreover, since 1871 Pernambuco's governor forbade the flogging of prisoners, a penalty still legally applied to slaves and sailors. One inspector noted a common expression used on this beautiful tropical island, "On Fernando [de Noronha] the prisoner comes to party." Organized into platoon-like work gangs, most convicts tended fields or herds but others worked in a cobbler's shop. Smaller groups worked as musicians, scriveners, or domestics (*camaradas*) for army officers, NCOs, and in one case, for another convict. A convict could build or buy his own residence, although some four hundred "wretched" prisoners slept in a crowded barracks-like structure. The state also allowed married convicts to bring their wives and children rather than leaving them "unprotected" on the continent where officials feared honest mothers might be forced into prostitution. Brazilian law attempted to accommodate patriarchal privileges and responsibilities even for its most hardened criminals, which demonstrates the powerful influence of conceptions of honor. Married convicts enjoyed the privilege of living with their family, and most could attend dance associations and even a theater company for diversion. Army and even slave convicts had more liberty than most regular soldiers on the continent. Despite the dangerous company, a stint as an army prison guard or as a convict on Fernando de Noronha was less onerous than regular service elsewhere.[24]

Most soldiers performed tasks commonly associated with army life: guard duty, never-ending paperwork, and the cleaning and maintenance of arms and facilities. Others performed police duties or worked alongside State-owned slaves at the army's gunpowder works and iron furnaces. The minister of agriculture requested army troops to help with all kinds of public works from railroads to telegraph lines. The minister of justice sometimes called on army troops to maintain public order in immigrant colonies or to quell slave rebellions.[25] Still other praças worked preparing food, cared for the sick in army infirmaries, or tended horses in cavalry units. "Artisan" soldiers worked out of arsenals as masons, plumbers, carpenters, gunsmiths, smiths, metal workers, tanners, and tailors. They provided the army with needed skills to supply and to maintain troops, equipment, and facilities. When one considers the wide range of activities in which enlisted men were engaged, the term "troop trade" takes on fuller meaning. Army troops produced goods as well as services. The army used a wide array of labor forms in the 1870s: slaves, convicts, the dragooned, orphans, volunteers, and wage earners.

In urban centers, company musicians practiced daily and enlivened patriotic and religious festivals with the popular marches of the day. The brassy music of Recife's Carnival season, *frevo* (distinct from the Afro-Brazilian drum rhythms of Rio's Carnival), evolved from military marches. The army trained many musicians, and soldier musicians in Recife made time to participate in civilian life and flavored its regional culture.

The duty that a soldier performed also reflected status. When an army patrol broke down the drunken Sergeant Ernesto Carlos Schmidt's door in Rio Grande do Sul and dragged him into the street, the officer of the rounds belittled him, "[You] are not worth the worst bugler in the 28th Battalion's band."[26] Officers and most praças deplored the status of buglers as "boylike." Mostly white officers routinely chose black soldiers as buglers. As one recalled, "I never saw a white bugler." The prince of Rio's Little Africa, Dom Obá II, once grumbled about racism, asking whether blacks and browns were suited only to be "buglers and soldiers."[27] To be tagged a "bugler" likely bore a racial barb for Sergeant Schmidt.

Because regiments were often undermanned, work for those who remained in the garrison multiplied. As Ceará's governor observed in 1881, "Because of the great number of discharges . . . [the 15th Infantry Battalion] bears the inconvenient if not prejudicial duty of servicing the Capital's garrison always [performing] double duties for six, eight, or more days. . . . The new Commander has not once had the chance to inspect his troops, or perform exercises, [this] hampers discipline and instruction."[28] Double duties required a soldier to be on duty for sixteen to twenty hours daily. No wonder discharges were grudgingly granted to troops.

Instruction in the arts of war, given these demands, was almost uniformly weak. Officers lacked the resources to adequately train and control men who were often coerced to perform public service. Commenting on the early 1900s, General Estevão Leitão de Carvalho recalled, "Units had no program of instruction of any kind: an instructor directed, from a distance, the recruit's training, which was entrusted to the disciplined or truculent care of a sergeant or even a corporal; when they were considered 'ready' . . . they began to live the life of a soldier."[29] The backgrounds of most praças offered little preparation for military training and service modeled on Continental armies which many Brazilian officers desired to imitate. Exercises were limited mostly to pay day and the day before it. The lack of uniform training regulations further complicated what little effective training existed. As one officer noted, the military academy in Porto Alegre still used cavalry instructions issued by the Portuguese, whereas officers who studied cavalry at the military academy in Rio used a different set of instructions.[30] In 1900, a soldier with two years of service reported that he had only seen a shooting exercise and that even those troops had fired blanks. Instruction in the interior suffered even more from a routine shortage of officer staffing.[31] The development of more uniform training would only come after 1916.

Inefficiencies also typified the army's purchase and upkeep of material. The army stocked a variety of small arms and cannons, which complicated training, not to mention the storage and distribution of appropriate ammunition. As one officer recalled, frontier garrisons in the 1920s did not have munitions for exercises. Even the army's horses had it bad; many perished during the winters of Brazil's south because of a lack of shoeing in the damp temperate climate and rocky terrain.[32]

The bureaucratic requirements of punishment hindered military readiness. As a junior officer noted in 1878, penmanship was mightier than swordsmanship for career advancement: "It is natural that a man who enlists supposes that he will learn to handle a weapon, learn platoon field exercises, . . . and finally be instructed on how to be a man of war, but unhappily this is not what occurs. If he never rises to the rank of corporal he will never learn platoon exercises well, will never see brigade exercises unless in combat, and finally, he will never be a perfect soldier; but if he rises to the post of forriel [lance corporal] his fate changes . . . he is condemned to be inseparable from paper work; he will write a lot. . . . He will forget about the army but in compensation will live writing. . . . It is not unusual to hear said in the barracks: John Doe is a good Captain, he has hand writing like a printing press, but Tom Doe is not meant for soldiering, his lettering is illegible."[33] Literacy and penmanship could earn a private quick promotion to the NCO ranks.

For all praças' work, whether in security, bureaucracy, or production, the government was a very unsympathetic employer. In 1908, a corporal from Rio Grande do Sul described hardships praças endured because of lack of pay: "The praças of this garrison have for four long months struggled with all sorts of suffering . . . poor *fathers of family*, poor starving mothers, have grown desperate because of their inability to attend the cries and tears of their poor children who beg for bread due to the lack of payment of our salaries. . . . Who is the unhappy child that shamefully approaches a house with tears in his eyes and [whose] tremulous voice begs for a scrap of food for his sick mother? . . . Not one officer helped us. . . . The limited credit that I had in local stores was cut, whether for the vender's lack of confidence or for his complete lack of sympathy" (emphasis added).[34] These "privations" could lead to conflicts with merchants, further demeaning the image of soldiers in the public mind. On April 27, 1895, for instance, one private in Belem, Pará, spent fifteen days in the stockade for provoking a civilian owner of a kiosk that refused to sell him goods on credit.[35]

While peacetime privations for praças could be intolerable, wartime conditions were often desperate, particularly when duty took troops far away from supply lines. In the bone-dry, scrub forest of the Canudos front, troops often lacked food and were almost always thirsty. One NCO became so hungry that he drank foul-smelling grease used to lubricate cannons. He and his men had to drink water from a puddle in a deep depression into which several enemy corpses had fallen. The gritty saffron-colored water was almost too putrid to stomach.[36] Private Octaviano Corrêa de Miranda deserted in 1915 from the front of the Contestado Rebellion in the pine forests of western Paraná. He walked all the way to Rio to complain personally to the war minister about the lack of pay (ten months overdue) and food.[37] Clearly, these were adversities that soldiers sometimes faced in war, but the lack of an adequate quartermaster corps unnecessarily redoubled their suffering and undercut the effectiveness and morale of army troops.

A soldier's diet was often as poor as his pay. As one officer held, "Rations are so stingy that they seem a sad alms that you throw to an indigent so he will not die of hunger."[38] He noted that this led to illness and filled ill-equipped infirmaries. In the 1860s, regulations allocated soldiers a 0.907 liter ration of manioc flour (the staple starch of Brazil's poor) per day in Salvador, Bahia, the same ration distributed to slaves employed by the public granary and prisoners of municipal jails. Once again law established uniform equivalences between slaves, convicts, and soldiers. Other staple rations would include beans, rice, jerked beef, and sometimes salted cod, occasionally supplemented by fruits and vegetables from regimental gardens. The quality of much of the food was quite low, but then again so was that consumed by most poor Brazilians.[39] A young girl's diary from Minas Gerais recorded the complaints of a woman who prepared beans for soldiers in the 1890s. She insisted troops had become "stuck up; if I waited until I found black beans without weevils [in the market] I would never eat; and now soldiers are wanting the impossible!"[40] While soldiers ate poorly (wretchedly in some cases) so did most Brazilians who had to stomach weevils and spoilage. Soldiers at least had the security of being fed, in most instances, according to guidelines. Even outlays of wine and *cachaça* (fiery sugarcane brandy) were regulated by army directives, "16 centiliters of wine per soldier on Sundays and one dose of one twentieth of a liter of cachaça on days of exercises and marches."[41]

While soldiers were more patient with lack of pay, withholding proper rations could incite insubordination more quickly. Regulations forbade soldiers to refuse their meals from the regiment mess. In Bagé, Rio Grande do Sul, soldiers refused to eat their breakfast because there was no bread in 1908. The commander then ordered them to eat, but the troops instead threatened to revolt and march to the city. Two privates were arrested and tried for sedition for their parts in this protest.[42] Corruption often further impoverished the soldiers' simple diet, inviting protests and unruliness. Complaints about graft in the army supply system were common. In the late empire, an agent for the soldiers' mess was elected from the junior officer ranks. Even though the post involved mounds of paperwork and brought no additional pay, officers vied for election. In many cases, suppliers worked in collusion with agents to defraud the soldiers' mess.[43]

Many volunteers and dragoonees strove to ameliorate the conditions of service by rising to the NCO ranks. NCO posts required basic literacy because they had to read and transmit the orders posted each day by officers delegating duties for each company. Some illiterate soldiers did become NCOs but their numbers were few, and some ambitious, hardworking, and brave NCOs managed to vault themselves into the commissioned ranks. Battlefield promotions provided one means of catapulting institutional barriers which normally separated the careers of officers from praças.[44] The most secure route of advancement, however, was through the army's educational system.

As noted previously, a small number of apprentices gained access to officer education. The School of Artillery Apprentices annually sent its top three graduating students to the army's preparatory school, a stepping stone to the military academy.[45] Most apprentices entered the army and remained praças, but it was theoretically possible for an orphan to become an army officer. Entrance examinations and the fulfillment of service requirements regulated admission to the military academy. Most cadets received their secondary education at the army's preparatory schools in Rio, Rio Grande do Sul, or Ceará. Some diligent soldiers from humble backgrounds took advantage of free education provided in off-duty hours at the army preparatory school in Rio, but dividing attention between school and full-time duties prevented all but the most exceptional and dedicated soldiers from succeeding. Age limits also diminished the possibilities for older soldiers to take advantage of the army's higher education.[46] Privates and NCOs outside of Rio had little or no access to these educational perks. Although the possibilities were limited, the army probably offered a few humble men a better shot at social mobility through education and meritorious service than almost any other institution save the Catholic Church.[47]

An NCO's pay was low compared to wages for similar work in the civilian sector, but he enjoyed greater job security and his housing, food, and clothing were subsidized by the army.[48] As noted in chapter 1, the army required candidates for the military academy to serve two years as praças before becoming eligible for entrance exams, unless they had attended a military high school. Many famous Brazilians held briefly the rank of praça in their youth: the Visconde de Taunay, Getúlio Vargas, Dermeval Peixoto, Joaquim and Juarez Távora. Some went on to become generals, but others truncated military careers for politics. Privileged praças could usually find loopholes to escape the ranks. Getúlio Vargas eventually managed to obtain a false medical statement to secure his discharge, but not before he had served with his unit in the insalubrious frontier of Mato Grosso during the Acre crisis in 1902. As Robert M. Levine observes, "The experience marked him—he was disillusioned, although in later years he said that living under difficult conditions had taught him how to judge others."[49] Vargas would be the first major political leader whose military service had been completed at the rank of a praça.

While praças often used the language of patriotism, it is difficult to assess how deeply ingrained these sentiments were and how closely soldiers identified themselves with their institution. Conflicts between army, police, National Guard troops, and immigrant groups indicate that praças often took insults to comrades or their corporation seriously enough to brawl. In 1908, police and army officers requested that actions be taken to end provocations between the 24th Infantry Battalion and 3rd Battalion of National Guard Infantry, whose headquarters were nearby one another. Police and army officers complained of constant provocations between the troops of these battalions. It added that both guardsmen and army troops included many "hooligans" who showed open contempt for police authority. The war minister requested the justice minister who administered the guard to "consider the urgent necessity of transferring guardsman R. D. Manoel to any other location" because of his instigation of fights. In 1915, Corporal Joaquim Victoriano was tried for leading a praça revolt in Fortaleza with the intent of attacking the police who had beaten several of his comrades. Street fighting between police, National Guardsmen, army soldiers, and immigrants indicate at least a strong loyalty to comrades common to the psychology of military units and the nativist bent of many army praças.[50]

How army praças understood and related to nationalist and militarist ideologies is difficult to plumb. One finds only fleeting references to these matters in documentation. It is hard to tell how much care officers took in instilling these ideas, and still more difficult to know how seriously praças took them. Obviously, individual responses to corporate ideology varied. One might look at the messages officers sent through disciplinary actions in relation to patriotic and religious events. For example, Sebastião Francelino's record shows that he was, "imprisoned on April 4, 1895, for being intoxicated . . . asking his company sergeant for his supper and faulting in proper respect toward him. [He] was released on April 13 in observance of the passion and death of Our Father Jesus Christ."[51] Despite the anticlerical, positivist views of many Republican officers, they still provided clemency in deference to Good Friday. Indeed, army justice granted early releases for disciplinary sentences on a variety of religious and patriotic holidays: the day of the Americas' discovery, All Souls' Day, the anniversary of Marshal Floriano Peixoto's death, the Republic's tenth anniversary, and the first anniversary of the Canudos Campaign.[52] But, beyond engendering reverence for holidays, there may also have been a practical need to empty the stockades on these occasions as commanders needed troops to parade or to provide security for events.

Clemency seems an odd way to inculcate a sense of national or religious culture among troops. But through one means or another, soldiers partook of this culture and developed their own sense of identification. In an 1897 prison letter from Santa Cruz Fort, Private Francisco dos Santos III pleaded with the war minister to commute the rest of his sentence. He beseeched the goodness of the war minister's heart and the "soul of *Senhor* Marshal Floriano Peixoto."[53] Francisco articulated his vision of army and nation through an appeal to the soul of a dead army hero to win favor and to show a sense of institutional solidarity.

Respect for nationalist rituals was often lax even among officers. One young officer noted that his superiors often laughed or made indecorous remarks during the raising and lowering of the flag in the early 1900s. On his own, this officer collected money to buy a new flag to replace the battalion's tattered banner.[54]

Few veteran praças expressed their sense of national pride in relation to enlisted service as fervently as the Afro-Brazilian who styled himself Prince Dom Obá II. Dom Obá, an NCO discharged from service after the Paraguayan War with an honorary commissioned rank, proudly wore his uniform to public audiences with the emperor and other dignitaries. Many white Brazilians and foreign dignitaries believed Dom Obá to be an embarrassing eccentric because he festooned his uniform with an African turban complete with plume and was reputedly a sot. Dom Obá had volunteered to fight, and in published editorials, he expressed great pride in his military service to the nation and the emperor. Many Brazilian praças also interpreted their service to the nation in sophisticated ways that converged and diverged with Dom Obá's views. That many poor and enslaved black and browns in Rio respected and even paid obeisance to Dom Obá indicate that the views he expressed and the posture he struck in terms of nationalism and loyalty to the emperor were popular ones. In any case, the documentary basis for an analysis of popular nationalism in the age of impressment among Brazil's regular soldiers is difficult to mine in a systematic way. The actions, pleas, complaints, and plots of many praças show they were familiar with leveling nationalist rhetoric and had an alternative sense of their own rights as citizens and patriots. They often vindicated their motivation to take great personal risks as a selfless defense of their family, their political party, their state or province, their Brazil, and prominent officer and political patrons. Local, national, patriarchal, and personal linkages and identities often existed side by side, not only in the minds of praças, but also in the minds of officers and oligarchs.[55] Politicians and officers often pointedly sought to discredit praça protests as lacking political consciousness, indicating an attempt to suffocate alternative nationalist visions.

Brazil's two most popular military historians of the era spawned few heroic role models for praças. Both Alfredo d'Escragnolle Taunay and Euclydes da Cunha portrayed army praças in an ambivalent fashion.[56] The latter described the Brazilian soldier as "a terrible but heroic blackguard." Da Cunha depicted one heroic praça in *Os Sertões* who refused to join a nightmarish retreat in 1896 during the Canudos campaign: "There was the legend of Corporal Roque, not quite so thrilling a one, but one nonetheless which made a deep impression on the public mind. A humble private who in a rare burst of courage had become another being, his heroism served to mark the culmination point of the battle. He was Moreira César's orderly; and, when the troops fled and his commander's body was left lying alongside the road, he alone had remained with it, loyal soldier that he was, guarding the venerated remains, which had been abandoned by the army. On his knees by his commander's corpse, he had fought there until his last cartridge was gone, being finally struck down, giving his life for a dead man." Roque is not praised for his initiative in battle or his willingness to die for his nation, but for his loyalty to his superior. "Not so thrilling" a story because as the public began to plan civic celebrations of Roque's heroism, he showed up alive. Da Cunha chortled, "Unfortunate enough not to have died—he [Roque] cut short the immortality that was being thrust upon him." The praça as a conscientious patriotic war hero simply did not get good billing in the military history of the age of impressment. Similarly, Brazilian naturalist novelists yielded no analog to Stephen Crane's classic *Red Badge of Courage*.[57]

While the annals of military history and literature made little room for inspiring praça role models, officers often sought the aid of clerics to moralize the "pagan rabble." Under the empire, war ministers routinely complained that the army's staff of chaplains was inadequate to minister to soldiers who required moral and spiritual guidance to improve discipline. The low pay offered to chaplains and the prospect of working with praças attracted few clerics. The anticlerical attitudes of many Republican officers and the antipathy of Church hierarchy for a positivist-inspired government that separated Church and State put efforts to proselytize to soldiers on a back burner in the 1890s. Only with the nationalist revivalism of the 1920s and 1930s would there be a reapproachment between the army and the Catholic Church. Clearly, many soldiers sought out religious fulfill-ment on their own, whether in the Catholic Church, popular religious festivals, Afro-Brazilian spiritist rituals, spiritism, or even the Positivist Church.

As military police inquiries show, soldiers often found rest and relaxa-tion in brothels, taverns, simple coffee houses, and the homes of comrades who lived off base, as well as street festivals, markets, circuses, and other public celebrations. Many shared public life, work, and romance with slaves and the free poor alike.[58] Their testimony, explored more fully in the next chapter, recounted tales of encounters, parties, dances, and conflicts at these locales. Republican reformers claimed to have demonstrated greater tolerance for female prostitutes in the vicinity of barracks in an effort to curb sodomy. These efforts reflected common assumptions that men needed to realize themselves sexually to be physically and psychologi-cally healthy.[59] Thus, as noted in the Introduction, the bordello and the barracks not only shared a parallel association with dishonorable social space, but a special and useful connection in the eyes of authorities for social control, especially the protection of the daughters of honorable families from the lust of male loners.

Both work and leisure allowed soldiers to interact with women that they might court. Soldiers often married into the families of comrades, but they also married and found lovers among laundresses, vendors, and domestic servants (some of whom were slaves). Since soldiers had to have present-able uniforms, they often developed close ties to women who cleaned clothes, either because they washed their own clothes alongside laun-dresses or employed women to clean their clothes.[60] Some privates and NCOs stretched their slim wages to realize the pain and pleasures of father-hood and the honor of heading a family.

While some praças managed to attain a modicum of conventional re-spectability by heading a household, marrying, and nurturing children, the larger public image of soldiering as a dishonorable form of servitude proved difficult to dislodge. The prejudice against praças overlapped with broader social hierarchies as the comment of one Germanophile officer reveals. In 1916, he criticized citizens who thought that "the fatherland that we all enjoy should only be defended by the poor, the unprotected, and the black. . . . since birth they have always heard that the uniform is a punishment and that a soldier is a bum."[61] The officer carefully singles out blackness to suggest that only poor and unprotected "whites" served as praças.

It is little wonder that members of the lighter-skinned middle sectors and elite often expressed disdain and a stricken sense of social violation when praças exerted their legal authority over them as representatives of State power. The governor of Amazonas expressed this ire in 1912 by reference to the house and street: "They awaited me on the street, a painful and humiliating surprise. About forty army and police praças commanded by a sergeant impeded me from entering my own house (you see sir what a violence they committed!) . . . taking me afterwards like a vulgar criminal to the police station. I, governor, colonel of the National Guard, among praças like any other malefactor."[62] Regulations did require that an officer be arrested by someone of equivalent rank, and when this privilege was not respected, officers demonstrated revulsion. As late as the 1950s, General Henrique Lott refused to wear his uniform because he said it had been sullied by the army. "I made it known to officers of my rank my repulsion at the flagrant disrespect for military legal procedures in relation to my arrest, including the disrespect for a common right of citizens — the inviolability of one's home at night — and even more so because an officer of a rank much inferior to mine made my arrest." Though this response comes from a more contemporary period it reflects the lingering sense of social hierarchy that infused the civilian and the military mind and the right of a citizen to the inviolability of one's home at night.[63]

If praças often failed to command the respect of more privileged civilians, it is not hard to imagine that veterans invited little regard. Following the careers of praças after their discharge is difficult, but anecdotal evidence reveals the paths taken by some. As noted earlier, many believed that soldiers were unsuited to other professions after spending years in the ranks, and this perception hindered their search for work. Others who had acquired skills working in the army arsenal or as scriveners had a better chance of finding higher-paying and more secure jobs in businesses or in the public sector. By law, veterans were to be preferred when competing for public sector jobs. But before competing for public jobs, veterans had to obtain a discharge. As Ceará's governor noted in 1871, "The troops that

12. "Scenes of Recruitment: Military recruitment agents prefer to press men whose qualities and comportment should become respectable. Meanwhile, the city of Rio is full of grifters and capoeiras [practitioners of the Afro-Brazilian martial art and sometimes gang members]. In some cases, it is good to be a vagabond." Impressment continued after the Paraguayan War, but this commentary suggests that it did little to repress capoeiras and generally combat crime. From *O Mosquito,* January 20, 1872, 8. *Courtesy Biblioteca Nacional, Rare Works Division. Photo by Gilson Ribeiro.*

exist in this province do not exceed 78, almost all of them from the extinct 26th Battalion of *Voluntários da Pátria.* . . . Relics of this heroic corp . . . continue to serve."[64] Many of these veterans would wait years for legal discharges that Voluntário contracts promised to grant at war's end.

One option many veteran praças lucky enough to be discharged favored was work in expanding provincial military police forces. The police delegate of São João dos Campos, São Paulo, praised the services of a furriel whom he nominated for the post of second sergeant. He described him as a dedicated officer and proud army veteran of the Paraguayan War. Some former comrades became adversaries in the street battles between police and outlaws. As noted earlier, some praças joined capoeira gangs that often participated in criminal activity or provided informal paramilitary protection services. Others became members of outlaw communities. In the outskirts of the isolated frontier town of Cuiabá, Mato Grosso, an army deserter from Pernambuco became the commander of a feared *quilombo* (runaway slave community) whose activities unnerved local ranchers and authorities in the 1860s.[65]

After the Paraguayan War, reports of criminal veteran gangs appeared. In Salvador, officials called the war minister's attention in 1876 to members of the company of Invalids of the Fatherland (units that sheltered disabled veterans) who caused "immoral" disturbances: "Veteran and disabled praças constantly wander about the city committing robberies and gambling in a debauched state." The local commander reported to the war minister: "I could mention many other incidents . . . practiced by discharged praças of disbanded units of *Voluntarios da Pátria,* large numbers of whom wander through the streets watched over only by the police and not by the Company of Invalids, . . . I believe that I have always punished . . . those under my command blamed by the newspapers and the police, but without a doubt this problem . . . can only be solved by gathering up all the discharged veterans into a regiment and subordinating them to the barracks [where] they would remain unable to leave and to loiter about the city, troubling authorities, and bringing unfounded recriminations on those who take great care in maintaining discipline and public tranquility." Needless to say, officials did not take such costly steps to confine all veterans in barracks to protect the public; indeed, some were expelled. The colorful Prince Dom Obá II, who had been injured at the Paraguayan front, was discharged from this very same Bahian Invalids' regiment for insubordination and intemperance before he migrated to Rio in the 1870s.[66]

A news story from Rio told the sordid tale of Manoel José dos Santos who had deserted from the Count d'Eu's Company of Army Apprentices in 1869. Manoel had subsequently served as a policeman in Rio's Urban Guard, but because of his bad conduct as a cop, he was sent to serve in the army as punishment. But Manoel managed to secure an exemption from army service by presenting false documents. The editorialist suggested that a man versed in these criminal skills deserved a "rigorous punishment."[67] Ironically, it was probably impressment. Manoel and the cases of other deserters reveal the facility with which some were able to hide from authorities within the very forces of order. As Thomas Holloway perceptively put it, "The social division between the forces of order and disorder were more like a permeable membrane than a solid barrier."[68]

An 1874 Rio newspaper associated veterans with the world of vagabonds and *malandros* (grifters). It listed individuals wanted by the police because they were "known" vagabonds. It included the veteran army praças "Antônio Capitão" (captain Antônio) and João Bonifácio, vulgarly called "Voluntário" (volunteer); their mocking nicknames allude to their army service.[69] Another newspaper report on the movement in Recife's prison in 1874 recorded twenty-four murderers, two robbers, three counterfeiters, twelve muggers, ten recruits, and three deserters.[70] These common associations reconfirmed the sordid perceptions of soldiers and veterans.

Some veterans did become vagabonds. Many thronged with mendicants in church entrances, and some sought refuge in overcrowded poor houses.[71] The unique Brazilian term for an urban slum, *favela*, derived from the makeshift community built on Providence Hill near the War Ministry in Rio by veterans of the Canudos campaign who awaited their mustering out pay. This association of squalor and enlisted army service must have pained and amused many men who had camped near Mount Favela at Canudos. Praças thus indelibly marked Brazil's urban landscape and vocabulary with their architecture and ironic word play.[72]

As John Schulz remarked on Voluntário benefits: "To the government's disgrace, as stacks of petitions in the Arquivo Nacional attest, many widows, orphans, and cripples did not receive their pensions."[73] In 1914, Brazil's war minister reported that out of the more than 69,000 men whose mobilization status for the Paraguayan War qualified them to receive the benefits of the Voluntários da Pátria decree, only 3,648 had been indemnified.[74] Of these, 1,332 were privates; 1,477, NCOs; and 839, commissioned officers. The case of the veteran musician Raymundo Alves da Silva was typical of many. On presenting his paperwork, the veteran was informed that the provincial legislature had not yet allocated money to survey lands designated for veterans in Rio de Janeiro.[75] Because military colonies were often situated in distant, unfavorable sites, most title-holding veterans preferred to sell their lots to speculators for a fraction of their worth. But only veterans with an influential patron and some luck could enjoy even this fraction of promised compensations. Even as Congress debated conscription anew in 1907, the issue of untendered veteran land grants was still a topic of shameful debate. The Jacobino politician and former army officer Lauro Sodré criticized new legislation that would finally guarantee a pension to veterans (thirty-seven years after the conflict). Sodré wanted the measure to include families who lost their primary breadwinner in war. He observed that this legislation had been under debate for decades, and reminded Congress that the republic had to undertake obligations long ignored during the empire.[76]

Some disabled Paraguayan War veterans were accepted into the "Invalids of the Fatherland" regiments. Rio's invalid asylum came to be symbolically housed not far from the city's garbage dump, on the island of Bom Jesus in Guanabara Bay. On the fiftieth anniversary of Brazil's victory, a journalist scorned the care of aged Paraguayan War veterans at Bom Jesus, whose pensions and meals were so miserly that most had to beg or to work on the mainland to sustain themselves and their families. Even after this exposé, little changed. Indeed, the government forced debilitated veterans out of their lodgings on Bom Jesus in 1925 to make space for political prisoners from more privileged backgrounds.[77] Clearly, new laws had done little to better the lives of most impaired veterans and their families.

If praças could not count on receiving promised pensions, they could be more certain that if they died in invalid asylums or on duty, the army would provide a pauper's grave.[78] Minas Gerais' governor grumbled that it was necessary to spend 14$000 milréis (approximately $5.25 at that time) on a praça's funeral when the army only allowed 5$500 milréis ($2.06) in 1872. By comparison, a Bahian regiment paid 100$000 milréis ($37.52) to bury a retired general who died in poverty in 1875. A decent burial was considered an important marker of status for the free poor. Many early labor and religious brotherhoods first organized to guarantee this final dignity to members.[79] This knowledge may have comforted some as they settled in at night to the sound of taps, the very tune that might be played at their funeral. But even in death, most soldiers' grave markers did not recognize their national service. These were tombs of truly unknown soldiers.

Life was tough for army praças, but they were better off than their comrades in the navy. Few volunteered to be a sailor because they were more likely to die than to receive a discharge.[80] From 1836 to 1884, the navy registered 3,019 deaths: 2,695 by disease; 255 by accident; 66 in combat; and 3 by execution. By 1884, a mere 152 seamen praças had had the salty grit to hold on long enough to earn a navy pension, and only 87 disabled seamen were allowed to join the Asylum of Navy Invalids. Only 2,012 sailors completed their contracts, compared to 1,617 sailors discharged for physical incapacity. Finally, 133 were dishonorably discharged for serious crimes, and 329 proved a legal exemption from service.[81] Disease discouraged army and navy enlistments and motivated desertions. Piecemeal statistics from the army's Medical Corps give a rough idea of annual mortality rates. In 1871, 190 deaths were reported in the army's central hospital in Rio. In 1873 and 1874 army hospitals from around the country recorded 513 and 497 deaths. These figures did not include all states where the army had garrisons, so they underestimate total army mortality rates. Unfortunately, the data does not indicate how many of those who died were active-duty praças, but it is possible that as many as two hundred praças died in any given year. Militaries are efficient conduits of disease, and the Brazilian army was no exception, but it was not nearly as deadly as naval service. Consciously or not, this knowledge influenced officials to place darker-skinned men and boys in the navy. As one observer of the early 1900s quipped, "The navy was all black," except for their white officers.[82]

The army lost further manpower through discharges. Of the 740 discharges granted in 1871, officials granted only 180 for fulfilling terms of service, while 560 were issued for "incapacity." The ill, the mutilated, and the unhinged moved to the front of discharge waiting lists.[83] The army's annual manpower turnover through discharge, mortality, desertion, and violent crime probably amounted to some 2,000 men, or from 10 to 20 percent of the army's peacetime enlisted forces in a given year. This is not to mention the losses in training and labor from men held in stockades or recovering from injury or illness in infirmaries.

Between enlistment and desertion, discharge, or death, enlisted men could experience a variety of hardships, but despite limited opportunities, most managed to squeeze pleasures from life in a uniform and some managed to better their lot. The abuse of contracts, untendered benefits, long work hours, low pay, and hazardous conditions, however, made soldiering an unattractive career. By the early 1900s, betterments in the terms and conditions of service encouraged more poor men to volunteer. Still, even improved conditions left much to be desired, and those who volunteered continued to be seen as undesirables. Although impressment diminished in the early 1900s, enlisted service continued to be associated with criminality and marginality. Honorable families feared that their sons might serve alongside dangerous men. Soldiers who involved themselves in disturbances and crime confirmed these associations. The next chapter examines crime and punishment in the barracks to explore further the nature of enlisted life.

Chapter 8

Days of *Cachaça*, Sodomy, and the Lash

Army Crime and Punishment in the Age of

Impressment, 1870–1916

Save for a few honorable exceptions, the calm and impartiality that should be observed, whether for punishments or rewards, is very uncommon among us, it depends on the good or bad humor of commanders. . . . [Our lax discipline resulted from] the Jesuit influence on Brazilian education, the army's original formation with criminals sent from Portugal, and the excrescence which is given the name "regulations" made by Count de Lippe. . . . The delay in the execution of penalties . . . makes punishment seem a consequence of being a soldier and not of committing a crime; beyond this, soldiers become [adepts at] vice in the stockades, their emotions numbed, and the inaction to which they are obligatorily subject degenerates them. —Amordius, *O Alvorada,* 1878

The worse the discipline in an army is, the more despotic a form it assumes. —Baron Von der Goltz, *The Nation in Arms,* 1906

As the army's role shifted and the nature of enlisted service changed, officers attempted to modify disciplinary strategies and to prevent crime in the ranks. The social distances that separated officers and praças attenuated the commitment of the former to new methods. Some officers, like the one cited above, found the Jesuits and Count de Lippe convenient non-Brazilian scapegoats for castigations they hungered to change. In an army that relied on impressment, discipline was often lax, crime rates high, and punishments harsh. Officers urged soldiers to be both violent and calm, masculine, yet passive and obedient. These sometimes contradictory directives created tensions within and among praças that could undermine the overarching ideal of discipline.

Conceptions of masculine honor could further enfeeble attempts to cultivate discipline and esprit de corps. As researchers have noted, manliness in societies of honor demands an audience. Manhood is tested and competence exhibited in public; if not, a man can suffer from gender ridicule.[1] Such proof sometimes came at the expense of a comrade's honor, encouraging confrontations detrimental to military discipline. Clearly, some individuals are less concerned with the opinions and jeers of their peers, and understandings of proper manly behavior varied with circumstances, region, groups, and individuals. Nevertheless, men often made sense of or at least rationalized their behavior in terms of a broadly shared language of honor. This language, expressed verbally and physically, could be interpreted and acted upon in a variety of ways. The contradictions between some "traditional" ideas of honor and modern military discipline forced reformers to address conceptions of masculinity.

Other incongruities in army culture and rhetoric complicated discipline. Draft advocates lauded army service's ability to stir a leveling sense of patriotism, but modern militaries preserve an authoritarian chain of command, and in the eyes of military law officers are a privileged class with legal rights akin to those enjoyed by ancien regime nobility and clergy. The maintenance of hierarchy and the sense of social distance between ranks in the Brazilian army in the age of impressment made punishment a central part of barracks life through the early 1900s. As an officer observed, "The main activity in the regiments was the *expediente;* it was the time dedicated to administrative work of a disciplinary character."[2] Many resented the tedious bureaucracy of punishment that in 1877 recorded 2,500 praça incarcerations for crimes and infractions.[3] Praça scriveners and officers spent hours each day on disciplinary paperwork. Others guarded those punished for infractions or convicted of crimes. Disciplinary records reveal much about everyday life as well as the tensions and solidarities that shaped change and continuity in the army and Brazilian society in the age of impressment. Over the years, improvements in praça discipline and decreasing crime rates in the military would recuperate the army's public image and make it easier for the public to accept a draft in 1916.

Army Law and Practice: Brazil's *Foro Militar*

A truly Brazilian system of military justice began in 1808 when Dom João VI organized a high military court in Rio, the *Conselho Suprema Militar de Justiça* (Supreme Military Council of Justice, hereafter CSMJ). The CSMJ regulated military justice by reviewing decisions reached by local courts-martial to provide some uniformity to a hodgepodge of regulations. Army law included the 1710 Code, Count de Lippe's 1763 Code, the Ordinances of 1805, and the 1830 Imperial Criminal Code.[4] Once a citizen became a soldier he was subject to a separate legal system: the *Foro Militar*. The Brazilian Foro was not as comprehensive as the *Fuero Militar* of Spanish America,[5] but it did separate soldiers from the jurisdiction of civilian courts in most instances.

Count de Lippe's 1763 Code remained the basis of army law until 1899. For reformers, it embodied all the characteristics of a barbaric legal system because it did not comply with modern precepts that punishment should fit the crime.[6] Repeated calls for a new army legal code went unanswered, and judicial amelioration was piecemeal and jarring. After the army abolished flogging, Pernambuco's police chief attributed "acts of insubordination and incredibly ferocious crimes" among army praças to this 1874 reform. He felt, however, that these were only temporary problems that new disciplinary methods would soon resolve.[7] After 1874, new regulations specified that soldiers who repeatedly committed infractions be sent to disciplinary companies and separated from their regiments. Attempts were also made to adopt barracks schools as a means of fostering literacy and discipline. By the 1880s, both practices were largely discarded, and they had little effect on army crime rates (appendix A.1).

Traditional disciplining methods continued long after the law prohibited flogging. As an officer despaired in 1878: "The French . . . speak much of their soldiers' honor and despise degrading [corporal] punishments, and those that deserve them, after being punished, are discharged from the army. . . . Even Russia, subject and accustomed to the most atrocious despotism . . . has attempted to prevent debasement in its military punishments. Among us there is still much degrading castigation that should be eliminated . . . a punishment no less debasing is the brutal way that superiors [officers] give orders to their inferiors [NCOs] . . . yelling, mistreating, and gesticulating like true madmen . . . But these are the consequences of the old school, of the count de Lippe's system, vestiges of feudal discipline."[8] As the passage suggests, floggings persisted and soldiers were only expelled if they committed heinous felonies.

Only after the abolition of slavery and the transition from empire to the republic did more systematic army court reforms begin. In 1893, Marshal Floriano Peixoto's government abrogated the CSMJ and established the Suprema Tribunal Militar (STM). The STM was a more specialized body empowered to "establish precedents for cases not regulated by existing law" and "verify whether defendants had committed a crime under the military courts' jurisdiction."[9]

Republican reforms did little to change the authoritarian mettle of military justice, but they did lay out clearer procedures. If the evidence indicated a crime, commanders formed a court-martial of seven officers. Commanders of garrisons, forts, arsenals, ships, and expeditionary forces had legal jurisdiction over their troops. Thus, most defendants faced courts-martial at their home base.[10] Defendants under age twenty-one were assigned a *tutor* (an officer) to represent them.

During the trial, defendants could pose questions to the prosecution's witnesses through the court's presiding officer and call their own witnesses. Praça defendants rarely mounted a defense; most had no reply when asked if they had a defense. For good reasons, many may have believed it more prudent to acquiesce and to hope for clemency, since procedures gave officers great influence over a trial's outcome. In 1896, army statistics showed that the STM had more than an 80 percent conviction rate (appendix A.5). If commanders formed a court-martial, it was likely to convict, unlike Brazil's civil courts.[11] The court voted on a majority basis to decide a case, and if it determined guilt, it awarded a sentence. All decisions were then forwarded to the CSMJ and after 1893 to the STM in Rio for review.

While the CSMJ had only three judges, the STM was composed of fifteen nominated by the president. The army carried the preponderate weight in the court with eight judges, four for the navy, and three civilian magistrates. Vice President Floriano Peixoto packed the new court with his supporters. Control over the military court made it easier to purge or to lean on foes within the armed forces while maintaining a facade of judicial impartiality. While most STM defendants were army praças, it also reviewed cases for the navy, militia forces, and the capital district's police forces (appendix A.4). Marshal Peixoto, like the Duke of Caxias before him at the Paraguayan front, grasped the value of mastering the military's legal apparatus to consolidate his authority. These reforms are given scant attention in explaining Floriano's consolidation of power. The subsequent expansion of military court jurisdiction in times of political instability reveals the need for further research on the institutional instruments of military rule.

The CSMJ and STM passed final judgment on all cases; they could alter or approve a court-martial sentence based solely on transcripts. The army's adoption of the navy's criminal code in 1899 improved the uniformity of sentencing,[12] but military justice continued to function on a variety of overlapping and often confusing levels.

Disciplinary Infractions

At the unit level, a disciplinary committee assessed punishments for non-criminal infractions. Disciplinary actions appear as laconic entries in a soldier's record, and officers used records to temper or to intensify punishments. Officers had substantial prerogatives in the determination of what constituted a criminal or a disciplinary offense. Intoxication, an unsightly uniform, causing public disorders, missing roll calls, failing to recognize and salute a superior, or harassing poor civilians were all "minor" offenses that were likely to earn a praça extra guard duty during their day of leave, confinement to the barracks, or extra cleaning duties — practices common to modern army life around the world.

Before 1874, officers could legally employ a wide array of tortures, including beatings with tree saplings, the flat of a sword, or *palmatórios*. After 1874, punishments such as incarceration combined with exhausting exercises could be prescribed. The *marche marche* forced a soldier to march back and forth at an accelerated pace for two hours burdened with a backpack laden with clay tiles. Incarceration was often accompanied by orders that rations be reduced or restricted to bread and water. Thus, a soldier's body could still be publicly tormented with overexertion and by withholding proper nutrition.

Sanitary conditions in army prisons were infamous; two cases presented to the STM in 1896 were closed because the defendants died while awaiting a court decision. Regulations stipulated that soldiers weakened by isolation in dark cells and an inadequate diet undergo a perfunctory medical exam daily, but such formalities were not always followed.[13] The security of stockades, like small town civilian jails, were often precarious. In Manaus, the bustling rubber port near the confluence that forms the Amazon river, *Anspeçada* João Correa de Araujo explained in 1908 that the battalion's stockade was "a room whose door opened from both the inside and out." The sergeants who imprisoned him did not lock the door. Later on, João began to feel hungry, and he left the cell to buy something to eat, as it was "customary for prisoners of that cell to do."[14]

Commanders determined the severity of punishment for an offense and, if there was one, the victim's status. José Francisco Cardoso's record proves this latitude: "On May 29, 1894, [José] was imprisoned for twenty-five days for having forced himself on a woman [*uma mulher*] for libidinous ends and attempting afterwards to steal her money." Later that year, "On December 31, [José] was imprisoned for twenty days in a cell for having missed the day's final roll call. While on guard duty, he had become intoxicated. It was necessary for the officer of the day to send for a stretcher to carry him back to the compound."[15] The rape and attempted theft from "a woman" is given nearly the same penalty as the victimless crime of an imprudent sentinel's New Year's Eve drinking spree. The civil courts in São Paulo routinely sentenced those found guilty of rape from one to five years.[16] "Honest" women could expect protection from authorities, but women of questionable virtue were vulnerable. For example, Private João Claudio de Santa Anna was "imprisoned for six days on August 24, 1894, for having shown disrespect for a family lady [*uma senhora de família*]."[17] There were obviously different rules at work for a "woman" and a "married family woman." The senhora's complaint resulted in a punishment of comparable severity to a poor woman's rape. Marriage and class worked as reinforcing badges of honor that offered "respectable" women greater status. Sandra Lauderdale-Graham relates the pithy comeback used by a senhora to disqualify the protests of another woman in a street quarrel: "Who are you to argue with me? I am a married woman."[18]

Military justice could be rather lax in terms of soldiers' indiscretions, sexual or otherwise, when victims were of low status and without prominent patrons. Army troops and police sometimes instigated disturbances and, in some cases, were detained in their barracks during holidays to preserve order. Poor civilians were rightly perturbed that some serious offenses committed by soldiers received relatively light punishments.[19]

Fears that soldiers would cause disruptions were not unfounded. On March 4, 1891, a commander punished José Maria da Silva with eight days of imprisonment at reduced rations for wandering Rio's streets armed with a baton randomly beating civilians. After this incident, José's discipline improved, and he was promoted to the rank of *anspeçada* in August 1891. Four days later, the anspeçada was "definitively" stripped of his rank and jailed for ten days for beating a sergeant who upset José by ordering him to form part of a cleaning crew.[20] The events described here are nearly identical to a number of cases where much more severe penalties were assessed for the crime of physical assault and "lack of respect." Why were Antônio and José spared this fate? Perhaps, in their commanders' opinion, the injuries inflicted were not severe. Or, maybe Antônio was protected by a pistolão (an officer patron). The records indicate the power officers had in drawing the line between disciplinary infractions and crimes.

In 1896, more than 90 percent of the 315 STM defendants surveyed were privates — the same rank as approximately 80 percent of all army personnel (appendix A.4). Officers depended heavily on the opinions of NCOs when investigating crimes among privates. As General Dermeval Peixoto reminisced, "What they [*Cabos do dia* (corporals of the day)] said to the sergeant about anything that occurred in the praças' barracks would be believed."[21] Officers were less likely to take legal action against NCOs because they could strip them of rank without resorting to an inquiry. As Narcizo Coelho Vianna's record stated, he was "definitively stripped of the rank of corporal on April 10, 1900, for . . . the vice of inebriation."[22] NCOs had a tough job managing and motivating praças who did not desire to serve, and some turned to the bottle to blot out the travails of everyday stress.

Stratification between the ranks was codified. For infractions, officers could only be punished by admonition, reprehension, or simple or rigorous imprisonment for eight days.[23] Sergeants were exempted from corporal punishment although they were liable to others, including double duty, confinement to quarters for up to thirty days, salary deductions, and temporary or indefinite loss of rank. On February 2, 1889, First-Sergeant Alfredo Baptista Jardineiro was reprimanded for the "indiscipline" of signing a collective manifestation for the release of an officer being held for "criminal acts." Army headquarters suspended Alfredo's rank for thirty days.[24] In addition to these punishments, corporals and privates were subject to reductions in rations and pay, as well as exhausting physical exercises. Private Brigido Justiano d'Olivera was imprisoned for eight days with "rations of water, bread, and cachaça for the first four days," because armed with a revolver and in a state of intoxication, he provoked disorder in the sleepy streets of the western river port of Corumbá, Mato Grosso, in 1901.[25] While denied meals, Brigido received a dose of chachaça likely considered a necessity for warmth in winter months.

If disciplinary punishments could be harsh and arbitrary, courts-martial were even more feared. Reformers had long decried the lethargy and treachery of military justice. As one groused in 1879: "The present methods are beyond being prejudicial for those accused of crimes, not only because their salaries are reduced, but also because of the time it takes from the initiation of an investigation until its conclusion. . . . Supposing that an officer is submitted to a court-martial in Pará, how many months will a prisoner be victimized because he finds himself so distant from Rio? At the minimum, one year, and this is if everything proceeds according to the established laws, that is, when the members of the court-martial do not divert themselves . . . and continue to work [on the trial] every day. . . . Almost always, the officers nominated to . . . the court-martial, are time and again distracted by other responsibilities, even leaving the garrison to perform police work, head detachments, etc."[26] The officer argued that those who formed a court-martial should not be selected by commanders, but by lottery, as juries were in civil courts, to prevent rigging decisions. This would prevent commanders from persecuting subordinate officers. While officers complained that the army's justice system could be used to persecute them and their families, it was much more often used to prosecute praças. While a criminal investigation dragged on, a private did not receive his wages at all, endangering the precarious finances of praças with families. One army publication noted that married soldiers awaiting trial or hospitalized received no pay, sometimes forcing their wives to practice prostitution to feed hungry children.[27] While there was likely hyperbole in these allegations, they indicate the fear that even officers had of courts-martial.

Commanders tended to call for inquiries only when a crime was serious, impossible to ignore, or when a commander was personally motivated to pursue lengthy legal action. In most instances, they preferred shorter-term punishments.[28] From the commander's perspective, inquiries represented a real loss of unit labor in battalions that were frequently short on manpower, especially the officers needed to man courts-martial.[29] General Dermeval Peixoto described a commander's prerogatives in the early 1900s: "It was up to the commander's discretion, some more and some less sensitive, in determining whether the weight of severe punishments should be attenuated or exacerbated according to the infraction. . . . There was no difference, in practice, between what was punishment and what was castigation. . . . [Predictably] at the end of the [punishment] detail there was no exultation of duty."[30]

The vagaries of army justice and the offences committed by praças in public made army service appear a repellent and dangerous occupation to most civilians. Praça violence bred popular fears of soldiers and resentments toward the army. But, as soldiers ceased to perform routine police functions in the 1900s, popular animosity seems to have turned more and more to growing state police forces.[31] To gain greater public confidence and respect, the army sought to prevent crime in the ranks and improve troop discipline in and around the barracks.

1896: A Year in the Life of Army Crime and Punishment

The survey of 1896 courts-martial cases of 315 soldiers are examined below. Illustrative examples are also drawn from other military police inquiries canvassed for subsequent years up to 1916 when the army court-martial document run in the National Archive ends. These cases allow for an analysis of army justice in practice and they illuminate otherwise obscured aspects of everyday barracks life. The readers should keep in mind that the vast majority of these soldiers were tried for desertion.

Praça defendants in 1896 had service records that ranged from a few weeks to thirty-eight years. On average, four years elapsed between enlistment and trial proceedings, but almost one-third had served less than a year and one half. For example, Private José dos Santos, aged fifty, had served only one year when he deserted from the town of Cachoeira, Rio Grande do Sul. José, a married man, faced a charge of "desertion in wartime," and his court-martial sentenced him to death. The STM subsequently commuted the sentence to six years of prison at hard labor.[32] The army's willingness to take on a man of such advanced age illustrates how periodic demand for recruits outweighed selectivity.

More than three-quarters of courts-martial were for desertion. It accounted for almost all offenses classified as "crimes against military honor and duty" — the one category that dwarfs all the others (appendix A.3). Praças perpetrated nearly all of the crimes against military honor and duty with the exception of a few charges against officers for drunkenness, misconduct, and dereliction of duty. The second largest category of charges, those against the republic's internal security, were dominated by trials for insubordination, the most democratic crime in terms of rank. Violent crimes form the third largest category, and the remaining groups include libidinous behavior, petty thievery, and graft.

Desertion required commanders to report and to publicize the crime to maximize the chances for capturing the fugitive, therefore, it could not be dealt with by disciplinary committees, unlike other potential crimes. Desertion's pervasiveness makes it a logical point of departure to begin an examination of crime and punishment in the barracks.

No problem more clearly illustrates the army's manpower and discipline problems than desertion. From 1870 to 1916, the STM reviewed 17,723 desertion cases, an average of 377 per year (appendix A.1). Desertion disrupted recruitment and training, and it undermined propaganda that attempted to associate army service with nationalism and honorable duty.[33] To stem desertion, the evidence indicated that the army would have to resolve the root motivations for going AWOL: stingy and tardy pay, low esteem, abuse of praça contracts, brutal punishments, poor food and living conditions, and inadequate health care.

Desertion rates fluctuated. The conflict-ridden 1890s witnessed a dramatic increase in desertion trials (appendix A.1). These figures have to be treated with some caution, however, because from 1891 to 1898 statistics do not separate army from navy, National Guard, and federal police desertions. After 1908 (when minimum service contracts dropped to two years), desertion convictions dip, failing to rise above the annual average of 377 desertion trials from 1870 to 1916. This decrease in desertion occurred despite mobilizations to combat the Contestado Rebellion (1912–16) in western Paraná.

Most soldiers offered no defense for their desertion, but those who testified gave a variety of reasons. The most common complaint was fear of corporal punishment. Private Sebastião Gregório do Macedo claimed that he deserted his battalion in Rio in April 1900 because his sergeant severely castigated him. Sebastião fled to live in Niteroi, a city across the bay from Rio. Four years later, police in Niteroi caught Sebastião in a police impressment dragnet and delivered him for army service in the somber prison-fortress of Santa Cruz on the tight-lipped mouth of Guanabara Bay. As soon as he could obtain leave, Sebastião returned to his original battalion and reported himself as a deserter. Sebastião probably decided to serve out a new contract in the more pleasant locale of Rio's residential borough of São Cristóvão, rather than guard some of the nation's most perilous convicts in Santa Cruz.[34] Options were limited, but privates like Sebastião could manipulate army justice for their own ends to ameliorate service conditions.

Others echoed similar complaints of physical abuse. In 1904, Manoel Pereira Nunes claimed that he had been severely "corporally punished" by his commander when late for roll call. When running late on another occasion, he feared a similar castigation, so he deserted. José Thimoteo dos Santos testified that he had deserted on two previous occasions, but he was pardoned because he was captured in periods of amnesty. While José had deserted on these first two occasions because he "wanted to," his third desertion had been motivated by his sergeant's "persecutions." Austerlino Elias de Aguiar testified that he decided to desert because he was vexed by the constant insults and blows that an NCO directed against him. Eduardo José Ramos deserted because he was always feuding with comrades. Manoel Basílio da Silva fled because his mother threatened to go to the barracks to convince his commander to punish him. The apprentice bugler Naderio de Roza deserted because the adjutant sergeant of buglers whipped him and always required that he perform personal services (camarada duties).[35]

As testimony indicates, the venerable practice of floggings proved difficult to extirpate. In 1908, Private Francisco da Silva Segundo testified that after he was beaten with a sword flat, he turned to address his tormentor: "Thank you very much lieutenant sir, you flogged me for no reason, and I who so pleased your children." The lieutenant then threw himself at Francisco, delivering additional blows. Attempting to escape, Francisco grabbed hold of a captain standing by, but even then the beating continued. Francisco was placed in the stockade, but he cried out, asking to be taken to the infirmary. In response, a guard told him that "Lieutenant Nascimento said that your hospital is a beating with a sword."[36] This brutality illustrates the ties of familiarity that bound together soldiers and officers; these ties could unravel and subject a soldier to an officer's rage. Officers of the court-martial did not comment on the illegal flogging.

Soldiers disdained illegal floggings and sometimes acted collectively to prevent them. A squad on maneuvers in Rio Grande do Sul in 1909 attacked an officer who ordered them to stand in formation to witness the flogging of an insubordinate private. Five praças broke ranks to prevent the beating and a fracas ensued. These praças were then tried for mutiny, which reveals the danger of this kind of open defiance, even though the act they disrupted was illegal.[37]

In wartime, officers apparently applied illegal floggings even more liberally. One veteran of the Canudos campaign (1896–97), chronicled the "bath of blows" two cowardly praças received from their lieutenant's sword when they hid themselves while their comrades fought bravely. The two became the company's laughing stock and soon deserted. They later presented themselves to their battalion in Pernambuco when the army declared an amnesty for deserters after the war.[38] Private José Bernardo de Salles also deserted from Canudos because while out foraging for food, he had become lost. He did not return to his battalion the next day for fear that he would be flogged for his absence.[39]

Other cases demonstrate that despite the prohibition of servile camarada duty (the use of privates as personal attendants) officers disregarded this directive.[40] In 1879, officers complained that the government's termination of the officers' supplement for domestic servants was tantamount to reestablishing camarada duty: "It seems incredible that in the 1800s a Liberal government unanimously proposes to enslave the national soldier. . . . Obliging one to serve as a servant or slave cannot possess any other connotation if we speak clear Portuguese. . . . There existed the infamous corporal punishments, that terrorized and subjugated the soldier, [he served] with repugnance. . . . Unhappily officers understood [then] that a soldier's condition was that of a slave . . . but . . . with the new methods of correction, it is already impossible to proceed in this manner. We believe that it has been proven that we will not have camaradas, unless . . . [to] immortalize the "liberalism" of your excellencies . . . [you] reestablish corporal punishment in the army!"[41] The reform of corporal punishments and camarada duties had not taken strong hold, inducing many to flee from service to escape injustice. Floggings and camarada duty approximated the servile status of slaves.

Other soldiers claimed financial reasons for deserting. Private João Martins da Costa confessed that he deserted because he earned "too little, and being responsible for sustaining his family," he elected to desert to procure more profitable work.[42] Similarly, First-Sergeant João da Silva Porto deserted after faithfully serving for ten years. He resolved to "leave military life to find a better future in the civilian world that would assure his subsistence."[43] Antônio de Mello Albuquerque began his military career when the police of Recife sent him to serve in the navy's apprentice school in 1890. When he became an active duty cabinboy and married, Antônio found his salary of 7$200 milréis inadequate to sustain his family who lived in "near misery." Antônio deserted to earn a better living. He worked shoveling coal for businesses in Salvador, Bahia, but Antônio's luck ran short. In 1896, he was pressed to serve in the army, and he fought in the Canudos campaign. Upon returning to Salvador, Antônio turned himself over to navy officials as a deserter.[44] Harsh conditions at Canudos, where troops often lacked food and water, may have convinced Antônio of the advantages of a sailor's life.

Private Jorge dos Santos gave the most unusual reason for desertion. He claimed to owe more than 100$000 milréis to the government. The army charged soldiers for equipment and uniforms in their possession that were lost, stolen, or damaged. For some reason, perhaps a delicate state of health, Jorge feared that he would not be permitted to reenlist, so he decided to desert to "prolong his permanence in the army."[45] Some soldiers like Jorge seemed happy enough to stay in the ranks; ironically, Jorge deserted to avoid the uncertainties of civilian life.

Some deserters would not suffer separation from their family or the place they desired to live. Marcelino José dos Santos testified that when his commander ordered him to transfer to the South, a cold region by Brazilian standards, it was "against his every desire." He decided to desert to avoid the transfer. Others deserted when they were unable to obtain transfer to their home states.[46]

Those who had faithfully completed their term of service sometimes deserted in protest or desperation. In 1877, a junior officer highlighted this injustice:

When a soldier is not discharged soon after completing his contract, he who does not have the courage to wait four, five, or six years deserts. . . . If he is not captured and is happy [as a deserter], he certainly will not advise anyone to enlist; however, if captured, he serves a sentence and loses all the credit for the time he had served. He can be nothing other than a bad soldier. . . . Enlistment is a contract between the soldier and the government . . . when one of the parties fails to fulfill its responsibilities, the contract is null and void . . . a soldier is not made in a day, and the state desires to keep [experienced] praças as long as possible; but this desire has a limit, [and it is] not only age, but one should also consider that soldiers should not be authorized to serve too much time because it hinders their ability to find civilian work, making them unemployable and prejudicial to society . . . It is easy to prove that the government's lack of good faith harms those already enlisted and deters civilians [from enlisting]. In March 1877, it was ordered that discharges be given to those who had completed their contracts in 1870! . . . Commanders should be empowered to discharge soldiers . . . any commander who . . . fails to grant [a merited] discharge . . . should be held responsible before a tribunal . . . Only in this way will we attract volunteers.[47]

The editorialist emphasized the irony of punishing deserters. Even War Minister Rio Branco noted this injustice in 1872: "There are at least a thousand praças who deserve a discharge. . . . Discharges for conclusion of contract falls only to those soldiers who besides their services in the last campaign have exceeded their time of service by many years." Rio Branco went on to clarify that he could not grant discharges to those who deserved them because recruitment produced few troops.[48] As long as the army remained a protopenal institution, the army would continue to depend on men who served against their will.

A number of cases illustrate this problem for army discipline. Private José Nogueira da Silva testified that he went AWOL when his battalion was ordered to march to the Canudos front. Since José had already completed his contract, he believed it unjust for the government to send him to war.[49] Similarly, Private Narcizo Coelho Viana eloquently justified his desertion in 1900 in patriotic terms: "Having served for the six years required by law, I requested on diverse occasions my discharge. . . . Two long years passed while I waited . . . anxious to return to "civilian life" as was my right solemnly affirmed by the military institutions of my fatherland. . . . Would it be just . . . to enslave a man who freely sought out his fatherland and served it in the institution dedicated to preserving it? Obscure in my post as a soldier . . . I invoked the law dozens of times and the only response I received was silence."[50] Here is an instance in which a soldier used his own ideas of patriotic duty to defy army authority. Taking matters into his own hands, Sergeant José Aggripino de Oliveira forged his own discharge in 1896. For this act, he was sentenced to twenty-five days solitary confinement and definitively demoted to a private's rank.[51]

The STM began to recognize that soldiers who had completed their contracts had some justification for deserting. In 1904, Corporal José Zeferino da Hora was absolved of desertion by the STM because it was "very clear from his record that the defendant was constrained for four years . . . after completing his time of service."[52] Others who deserted after completing their contracts, however, were not so lucky, but in the 1900s, the army began to grant more timely discharges as the duration of minimum service contracts diminished.[53]

No single attribute or condition (location, geographic origin, race, literacy, and so on) indicated a strong proclivity toward desertion. Though some regions, garrisons, and commanders offered better conditions and treatment than others, none of these factors could overcome the root problems of desertion. One exception was that praças had a greater propensity toward serial desertion when located in frontier regions. The career of Private Antônio Pereira de Oliveira is instructive. Antônio was born in Rio, the son of unknown parents (*paes incognitos*). An illiterate mulatto without a skilled trade, Antônio estimated that he was twenty-one or twenty-two at the time of his trial. His record shows that he "volunteered" in 1890 when he must have been fifteen or sixteen years old. Antônio had a poor disciplinary record, and this was probably why he was transferred to the western frontier town of Cuiabá, Mato Grosso. In only five years of service Antônio deserted eight times. In all but the last instance, he returned to his battalion during a period of amnesty for deserters. Unluckily, Antônio was captured in a period when no amnesty was in place after his eighth desertion. The STM overlooked his former pardons, and punished him with a six year jail term, far stiffer than the standard six-month sentence for a first desertion.[54]

Perhaps the lack of men to replace a deserter and the dearth of officers to conduct tedious inquiries in frontier garrisons made officers quicker to forgive and forget. In 1874, Mato Grosso's governor pleaded that numerous Paraguayan War deserters captured in his province be pardoned: "Many did not understand the responsibility that weighed upon them when they abandoned their regiments. . . . It is difficult to prosecute them because their records have not been found in their unit's archives. . . . some have been placed at liberty because of the absolute impossibility of organizing their prosecution. Others find themselves imprisoned as deserters because of irregularities in unit records."[55]

Army reports recorded only the number of deserters tried without noting how many successfully escaped to civilian life. The navy kept more complete records, and a brief digression helps to place dissertation in perspective. From 1836 to 1884, the navy enlisted 14,435 men and experienced 6,568 desertions, averaging 137 desertions per year. Over half (3,529) of these deserters either chose to return to the navy or were captured. This desertion rate is high given that the navy ranks grew from 37 men in 1836 to 1,094 in 1850 and to 3,074 by 1884. In some years, the navy lost more than 10 percent of its men to desertion.[56]

As noted earlier, Brazilians feared a Jack Tar's life more than a soldier's. In part this was because one in five sailors died on active duty, and very few died in battle. Lethal sanitary conditions inspired desertion. In 1900, sailor Manoel da Costa Ribeiro claimed that he deserted the navy to escape death because an outbreak of beriberi on his ship was "killing everyone on board."[57] Navy desertion in STM statistics underestimated total rates because navy officers could legally use summary corporal punishments for desertion rather than courts-martial. In 1887 for example, Sailor Martinho Elenterio dos Santos was punished with twenty-five *chibatas* (flogging) for first-time desertion.[58] Corporal punishments degraded and demoralized many sailors. As one elderly Afro-Brazilian sailor sardonically recalled, "The whippings and beatings I experienced [as a sailor] broke my spirit and made me comprehend what it is to be a Brazilian citizen."[59] Adolfo Caminha, a former navy officer, portrayed a black sailor in his 1896 novel *Bom Crioulo* (literally "good nigger") who muses, "A sailor and a

Table 4. Navy Praça, Enlistments, 1836–1884

Volunteers	330	Substitute	83
Dragooned	6,271	From other corps	244
Reenlistments	124	Libertos	307
Navy Apprentice Schools	7,076	Total	14,435

Source: ANR, GIFI, 12.1 Repartição do Ajudante General, Mappa estatístico do Corpo de Imperiaes Marinheiros do ano de 1836 a Dezembro 1884, by Secretary João da Cruz Rangel, ca. 5C–486, fo. 488 (folhas not in order).

black slave, in the long run they come down to the same thing."[60] No wonder mostly white authorities tended to place men and youths of darker pigmentation in the navy rather than the army.

If navy desertion statistics are a reliable indicator, for every soldier captured after deserting another succeeded in eluding authorities. Inferring from navy statistics, a doubling of STM trials for army deserters would yield a conservative estimate of all desertions. This would yield 35,446 army desertions from 1870 to 1916, an annual average of some 754 desertions. If praça ranks averaged approximately 15,000 troops over this period, then the army lost about 5 percent of its men annually to desertion.

Even if a deserter had better than even odds of escaping detection, he could not be free of anxiety as a civilian. Police, recruiters, and soldiers kept their eyes peeled for them. A familiarity with deserters' haunts and habits could yield a profit. The deserter Antônio Borges Enrique's record shows that a soldier from his battalion made his capture and received a reward of 8$000 milréis.[61] While such a policy helped the army recover more men, it is doubtful that these men and their comrade-captors remained friendly and cohesive brothers in arms.

The prospects of escaping capture were bright enough to make desertion an attractive option. The army could not afford to spend the time to capture and process numerous deserters and still hope to modernize enlisted service. To make up for this heavy turnover, the army had to regularly replenish the ranks with impressment and deny discharges to those who completed their contracts.[62] There was little officers or the military justice system could do to prevent desertion under prevailing conditions. Army law sought to encourage wayward soldiers to return by giving more lenient sentences to those who returned voluntarily. Those who returned of their own free will were sentenced to two months of prison for a first desertion as opposed to six for those captured. The high court's periodic attempts to offer clemency for deserters who returned voluntarily was not very enticing. Of a total of 401 desertions (including cases of serial deserters), in only sixty-seven, or less than one in five, cases did a praça return voluntarily. For the STM, however, it did not matter if a soldier returned of his own free will or was captured in a period of amnesty. Both were pardoned. In 1896, more than one-third of the desertion trials resulted in amnesty (appendix A.5). By 1900, the army abandoned this periodic desertion amnesty policy, opting instead for shorter minimum service contracts.

Amnesty often made little difference to the soldiers in question. While it removed the crime from the deserter's record, he often spent months in the stockade awaiting pardon from the STM. Even those duly convicted often spent more time in the stockade than their sentence required because of the long wait for STM decisions in distant regiments. In 1880, the war minister advised that "deserters not be forced to serve more prison time than their crime merits."[63]

While officers bitterly complained about desertion, they proved uncreative in finding ways to stem it. In lieu of higher pay and improved conditions, they hoped that a draft lottery would recruit a better class of men. Unable to obtain these objectives, some proposed that desertion could be reduced if the army recruited men locally to serve in "fixed" garrisons that would not place great distances between the soldier and his kith and kin. The army maintained eight "fixed" infantry units in eight different provinces in 1870. In 1872, however, the war minister rejected suggestions that the creation of fixed regiments would ease the "burden of military service on families." He insisted that the attractiveness of deserting diminished in regions whose inhabitants and topography were unfamiliar to troops.[64] Desertion rates show that both fixed regiments and transfers did little to deter soldiers from going AWOL.

The army proved unable to ameliorate the conditions that resulted in high desertion rates, much less secure more thoroughgoing discipline, until conscription was implemented in 1916. Violent crime reveals why some deserted, and shows the tenacity of traditional ideas of masculine honor that often undermined discipline.

Violent Crime *dangerous*

Despite legal protections, violence and the threat of it permeated army life, making soldiering an unpleasant and dangerous occupation. From 1870 to 1916 the STM reviewed 887 homicide cases and 2,155 cases of malicious wounding, or an average of 19 murders and 46 dangerous assaults per year (appendix A.1). This average outpaced the criminal statistics of most provinces though it is widely recognized that provincial police and the public underreported crime.[65] Likewise, many army crimes were unreported or treated as disciplinary infractions.

In the 315 trial transcripts surveyed from 1896, thirteen acts or threats of violence were committed with knives (mostly *navalhas* or razors); five with revolvers or pistols; three with bare hands; two with rifles; one with a club; and one with a saber. In most instances soldiers used weapons that were not standard issue. Commanders were careful to lock up fire arms when soldiers were off duty, which was when most violent crimes occurred. The prevalent use of navalhas suggests that many praças took the precaution of walking about armed for purposes of self-defense. Easy to conceal navalhas were the preferred weapon of capoeiras. Thus, simple disputes among troops could quickly escalate into deadly fights. When Private Francisco Soares de Lima attempted to snatch a watermelon bought by his comrade Private Manoel João da Silva, Manoel pulled out a knife from his belt and gravely injured Francisco. Francisco subsequently died from the wound, and Manoel served a ten-year prison term.[66]

Circumstances moved some praças to commit acts of violence upon themselves. In 1896, Private Pedro Antônio de Barros of Maranhão attempted suicide after twelve years of service by cutting his throat with a razor. Pedro had served two sentences of one year and six months for injuring comrades, perhaps precipitating his transfer to Rio Grande do Sul. The private claimed that he cut himself because he feared the punishment his sergeant was going to "inflict" on him because "in a state of intoxication, he had abandoned his post and gone to the house of a prostitute." Pedro received a six-month sentence for leaving his post, and afterward, he would be among the few praças expelled from the army—not for his crime, but because he had sliced his vocal cords making himself unfit for duty.[67] Less tragically, an intoxicated Corporal Antônio Francisco Maciel tried to kill himself with a rifle in his quarters after an ensign had stripped him of his rank. He was absolved because attempted suicide was "not a crime" under the army's code.[68]

Most violence occurred in and around army compounds between privates. Five out of eighteen violent offenses, where location could be determined, took place in the barracks, making them the single most dangerous location. Other prominent locations included army compound premises, the street, and to a somewhat lesser extent taverns, cafés, camps, and the stockades themselves. The army expelled men convicted of murder, such as Private Manoel Francisco da Cruz who was "condemned by Jury for the crime of murder" after having deserted. The army discharged him and returned him to civil authorities for incarceration.[69]

Most violent crimes were rationalized in terms of offenses to honor. Anspeçada Antônio Pereira's case illustrates both the cooperation and conflicts in praça life and how ideals of honor shaped an important part of the culture of violence. Antônio admitted to stabbing to death both his wife and a comrade after discovering them having sexual relations in his home in Corumbá, Mato Grosso. An illiterate mulatto from Ceará, Antônio was thirty-three years old when Ensign João Lopes Ribeiro provided the following written defense of the private's actions:

> Antônio Pereira is a son of the North, he is one of these meridional organisms, essentially nervous, passionate and warm, vibrant and languorous, loyal and dignified, impulsive and ardent, that the sun of Ceará customarily impels to the Amazon region in search of work . . . for the progress and glory of his fatherland. Antônio is a sertanejo. He was born and raised . . . in accord with honor and dignity. . . . The sertanejo's simple and good soul is as . . . uncluttered as a summer day. His family is an indestructible social molecule. . . . Our poor soldiers, our modest comrades, resigned and stoic . . . often suffer because military service does not always allow them the necessary leisure to prepare their rations. It was then that Antônio opened the doors [of his house] to other companions, and his wife became the cook for all. . . . The woman, this eternal social victim, [was] once again the bauble sacrificed to the caprices of male egoism . . . the honor of that home received from the household head's friend, the most lethal of blows!"[70]

The ensign's flowery (not to mention chauvinistic and racist) defense invoked the language of house and street to emphasize how this praça's honor had been violated. He portrays Antônio as a simple sertanejo, and his use of scientific metaphors echoes those found in Euclydes da Cunha's *Os Sertões* published only two years earlier. According to the ensign, northeasterners like Antônio, who formed the bulk of the soldiery, were modest men who valued family honor above all, although they were naturally (biologically) given over to extreme emotions.

Antônio had trusted his comrades and allowed them to enter his home, the vessel of family honor. Antônio's wife prepared the uncooked rations of her husband and other comrades who lived off base and apparently did not have wives or family. Such an arrangement was probably not uncommon in battalions across Brazil. But, Antônio had been treacherously betrayed. The ensign's defense included hearsay that even officers had visited Antônio's humble house to enjoy intimate relations with his wife who was described as a "semi-clandestine prostitute of whoever desired her." Whether true or not, Antônio had become the laughing stock of his battalion: the *corno* or cuckold. By opening his doors to comrades, Antônio left himself susceptible to both real and speculative assaults on his honor.

These appeals to honor were intended to pique the sensibilities of court-martial officers. One officer described the attitudes toward honor among students at the Colégio Militar in Rio in the 1920s: "A man could not admit that one's sister be the object of the same pleasure that he sought from another's sister, and cuckolded husbands were victims of ridicule that no one accepted for themselves or their family, naturally, and one could only save himself from this ridicule by killing the woman. Separation of a couple . . . was always assumed to be linked to the inability of the husband to perform his sexual duties. . . . The military education that the Colégio Militar provided demanded the elevation of the cult of machismo and sought to elevate to the maximum perfection these prejudiced tendencies that were naturally refined and practiced."[71] It seems clear from Antônio's case that a similar set of ethics preoccupied praças who murdered unfaithful partners. While Antônio had stabbed his comrade once, he had gored his wife repeatedly. Clearly she was the object of his dishonor that had to be completely repudiated.

For the ensign, some of the blame lay with Antônio's wife, but principally the ensign argued that her seducer, by his betrayal, had "armed Antônio with a dagger and dug the grave of Antônio's wife." The ensign lauded Antônio's revenge, "Praised be the dagger that wounds, praised be the blade that rips apart so much putridness, so much pus!"[72] Following the language of da Cunha, the ensign explained that Antônio's revenge was as natural as molecular chemistry. The ensign cleverly presented the violation of Antônio's honor and home in an attempt to pique the moral outrage of the jury over the transgression of these building blocks of social order and dignity. Despite the ensign's efforts, the court-martial convicted the anspeçada to a ten-year sentence. Antônio served six years before he was relieved of the rest of his sentence.

Why did officers not recognize Antônio's "sacred" right to avenge his honor? Civilian juries much more readily dismissed similar charges on these grounds. Perhaps because Antônio was not officially married to his mate, his claim to be defending family honor was foiled. Or maybe many officers did not believe that most praças had honor to lose. But it is more likely that officers, concerned about discipline, hoped to deter crimes that were justified by the logic of honor.[73]

Jealousy could provoke deadly conflicts among praças. Private Joaquim Ferreira claimed a drunken comrade entered a house where he was resting with his lover (*amazia*) and another woman. He claimed that his comrade insulted him by trying to seduce his lover and threatened him stating, "Of the two, one, your life or your woman (*china*)." Joaquim left the room, grabbed a revolver, and shot his comrade twice.[74] While rivalries over women could generate deadly conflicts among praças, same-sex liaisons also preoccupied reformers who hoped to improve barracks discipline and the image of enlisted service.

Combating Sodomy on the Land and on the Sea

Many officers came to identify same-sex intimacy with jealousies that could undermine discipline just as they did illicit heterosexual affairs with married women. Reformers believed more and more that modern military discipline required the regulation of sexuality to maintain respect for authority, unit cohesion, and public health. Aspects of modern military discipline were at odds with prevalent ideas of honor and sexuality that invited violent retribution for transgressions or slights.[75] To implement a draft, reformers would come to realize that the sexually segregated world of the barracks had to be made into a social space that was not associated with sexual danger.

As noted in the Introduction, medical literature affirmed the barracks' unsavory renown for sexual "deviance." Some officials felt them an appropriate destination for those who practiced "repugnant vices." Pernambuco's police chief wrote in 1874 that he had sent three men to the army because they "continually caused disturbances" and were "known to practice sodomy." The honorary brigadier general, politician, and entrepreneur José Vieira Couto de Magalhães wrote fondly in his secret diary of same-sex erotic encounters with soldiers, Indians, and slaves.[76]

Literature confirmed the association of soldiering and same-sex liaisons. Former navy officer-turned-novelist Adolfo Caminha depicted a romance between a muscle-bound black sailor and a blond-haired blue-eyed cabin boy in his 1895 novel, *Bom Crioulo*. The sexual subordination of a white adolescent by a black man, who escaped slavery only to be pressed into the navy, shocked the values of literate Brazilian society, which generally placed white males on top socially and sexually. But it complemented bigoted medical assertions that Africans and Indians brought sodomy to the *bagaceira* (the sugar plantation's lax moral environment) and "contaminated" the Portuguese with this "perversion."[77] Bom Crioulo was a perfect physical specimen, hard working, tolerant, unselfish, and philanthropic; in most respects, he was a eugenic Brazilian Billy Budd.[78] He was the ultimate hygienic citizen, except when he drank too much or was flogged, which made him unpredictable and violent. As the black sailor carried on his affair with Aleixo, he grew thin and weaker. Caminha suggests his "unnatural" desires undermined his physical and psychological health. Bom Crioulo viciously slays his lover when he learns that the youth has betrayed him by sustaining a "manly" heterosexual affair with a female Portuguese prostitute.

Caminha's racy novel condemned same-sex desire as an "illness." When acted upon, it had serious consequences for health, sanity, and national destiny. A zealous Republican and abolitionist, Caminha disparages Brazil's heritage of monarchy, aristocracy, impressment, slavery, and flogging. He implies that they are the root causes of Bom Crioulo's sexual "pathology" and Brazil's national malaise. A heady mix of sexuality, race, masculinity, politics, and nation are mobilized to rebuke the old regime and praise the republic's "scientific" efforts to correct vestiges of the empire's supposedly corrupt social, sexual, and political order.[79] As if responding to Caminha's novel, one doctor reported efforts to combat sodomy in 1906. He stated that during the empire the "degrading vice of sodomy" was common in the army, and held that by tolerating female prostitution near bases, enlightened republicans had almost eradicated pederasty in the ranks.[80]

Caminha's sympathetic portrayal of Bom Crioulo as a black "victim" of a "pathological disease" led many in Rio's literary circles to ostracize him. Perhaps some of Caminha's sympathy for Bom Crioulo came from his own bitter ordeal with affairs of honor. He had to forswear his navy career when he refused to break off an affair with the wife of an army officer. Thus, not all disputes of honor ended in violence, but there often was a high price to pay. Two years after *Bom Crioulo*'s publication, an embittered Caminha died of tuberculosis, virtually a pauper at age twenty-nine.

How common same-sex relationships were in the military is hard to know, but court-martial records reveal they were not infrequent. In the year after *Bom Crioulo*'s publication, drunken and belligerent Horácio Veloso accosted and offered Private João Estácio five réis "to serve him as a woman" or to act as the passive partner in anal sex. João hotly replied that he was "not a young boy [*gury*] nor a woman to serve such ends." When Horácio continued to taunt João, a fight ensued that cost Horácio his life and João eight years in an army prison.[81] The exchange reveals the violence that insults to masculine honor could unleash, and the common belief that women and children were sexually passive while men were sexual actors. This created a gender hierarchy in which the "penetrator" dominated the penetrated; the passive partner attained an emasculated femininity or, at best, an attenuated masculinity as a "boy." Shame rested with the passive partner because active partners often boasted of illicit sexual conquests as proof of virility. Not everyone (including praças) viewed sexuality in this way, but it was a prevalent perception, and remains salient in Latin America.[82]

Caminha challenged this idea by imposing a shameful, unhygienic, and unmanly homosexual identity on both active and passive partners. However, by defining same-sex desire as a pathological illness rather than proof of manly dominance by the active partner, he reinforced the idea that a male's sexual desire required a release that if denied or misdirected could result in physiological and psychological degeneration. Most Brazilians expressed their concept of sex between men in terms of honor. They were neither homosexuals nor heterosexuals per se. The "offense" stemmed from an immoral act rather than from an abstract identity shaped by a sexual preference for one's own gender. The term homosexual only became commonly used in the mid-1900s. Until then, officials referred to intercourse between two males as "sodomy, pederasty, libidinousness, sexual inversion, and immoral acts," as they did in Brazilian army documents.[83]

In practice, the army suppressed same-sex couplings at various levels. Manoel Cardoso do Nascimento was jailed for six days for having beaten "a woman" in August 1900. In October, he was held in isolation for eight days for trying to practice immoral acts in a group cell of the stockade with a comrade.[84] The practice of homosexual acts received a sterner censure than beating a lower-class woman. Similarly, Antônio Moreira Ignacio was imprisoned for fifteen days without supper for having abandoned his sentinel post guarding the company arms in December 1891. He was found on top of the fort's gate practicing immoral acts with a comrade.[85] These acts did not result in full-blown trials, but were handled as infractions, indicating that these couplings were not uncommon. Even though most officers disapproved of these encounters, they were not unexpected.

These disciplinary actions to repress same-sex sexuality were mild when one considers that the army's 1899 penal code defined coercive homosexual aggression as a crime punishable by sentences of one to four years. By contrast, Count de Lippe's 1763 Code made no specific mention of "sodomy."[86] Even though the army began to define same-sex rape as a distinct crime, it rarely prosecuted soldiers on the charge and the law did not specifically define sex between consenting adult males as a crime.

Most officers and men were aware of a partially submerged world of same-sex relations. The unwanted sexual advances of comrades, however, could lead to violence because passivity was considered feminine or boyish submission, an insult to manly status. The mere mention of being a passive sodomite could spark deadly fights. Private João Francisco d'Almeida claimed that Private Aristides de Souza mistreated him by knocking his hat off and then stating that "all *Alagoanos* [natives of Alagoas such as João] served as women." João replied that not all Alagoans were and then clobbered Aristides in the face with a piece of wood breaking his teeth.[87] In 1916, Manoel Martins dos Santos claimed he was minding his own business on his battalion's patio when Benedicto José Rodrigues without justification "struck him in the face" with the following words in front of other praças, "You changed sexes because you served as a woman for a civilian." In response, Manoel stabbed his "inhuman and gratuitous" detractor to death.[88] A court-martial sentenced Manoel to ten years in prison despite his claims of defense of honor.

Even if most Brazilians regarded soldiers as "dishonorable," enlisted men did not see themselves in that light. Most rationalized their actions in the language of honor when defending themselves, their women, and their homes from violation. The "macho" culture promoted by the army pressured soldiers to prove periodically their prowess and dominance. Proof of virility often came at the expense of a comrade's honor. This code of ethics sanctioned confrontations inimical to modern military discipline. Reformers like Caminha sought to portray both the active and passive partners of same sex couplings as shameful, unhygienic, and unmanly. If the Brazilian case is indicative, it could be that the Prussian-inspired military reformism and the great military mobilizations of the 1900s were an important channel of a significant cross-cultural restructuring of sexual identity. This is to suggest that homosexual identities in Brazil during the 1900s were created through a simultaneous process of the imposition of categories by outsiders and through redefinitions of self by communities of men who preferred their own gender for sexual and romantic relationships. Traditional ideas of passive (female) versus active (male) roles continue to exist side by side with new, more companionate and egalitarian hetero- and homosexual identities and ideals.[89]

Reformers strove to modify the barracks' image as a place of sexual danger. If the sons of honorable families were to be called on to serve the nation, they needed to feel that the barracks was an honorable and secure masculine social space. Sexuality, venereal disease, public health, and fears of racial degeneration and heterogeneity shaped ongoing conflicts over army recruitment and discipline.

While many privates deserted or committed crimes, most did not find themselves before a court-martial. Reforms in army disciplinary practices were not effective in terminating flogging nor did they have a measurable effect on army crime rates. Still, the army established a more disciplined and slightly less violent environment by the early 1900s. The problems that plagued the army's relations to Brazil's larger labor market could not be resolved by the reform of disciplinary practices alone. The army had to reduce the number of men who had criminal backgrounds in the barracks and to expel those who committed crimes. Better discipline, conditions, pay, and shorter contracts would improve the barracks' image. Only with a draft could officers implement the modern training methods that had proven more effective in disciplining men for war and peace in other nations. Rescuing the barracks from an association with "perversion," danger, criminality, servility, and disease was essential in order to recast enlisted service as an honorable masculine duty rather than an emasculating punishment.

III

IMPLEMENTING CONSCRIPTION

AND REORIENTING THE ARMY'S ROLE,

1906–1945

Chapter 9

"Tightening Screw"

or "Admirable Filter"?

The 1908 Obligatory Military Service Law,

1906–1916

Armed with a fuller understanding of how recruitment and the army's role in larger society functioned, it is fruitful to return to a narrative approach to analyze the forces that led to the draft's implementation and enforcement from 1906 to 1945. By withdrawing from its role as Brazil's central penal institution by the early 1900s and improving the terms and conditions of service, the army began to breach important barriers that thwarted wider support for conscription. This chapter examines the reformulation of draft legislation and the forces that coalesced to insure its execution.

Edgar Carone and Frank D. McCann pioneered investigations of the political movements that promoted Brazil's first draft lottery in 1916. Carone concludes that the bourgeoisie sought to use the military as a hedge against the hegemony of rural oligarchies and to inculcate bourgeois values among the lower classes. McCann examines the army officer corps' alliances and ideology in greater detail. He argues that, as in the United States and France, conscription occurred when the urban middle class joined forces with the officer corps to demand it. Though their definitions of the civilian groups behind conscription differ slightly,[1] McCann and Carone correctly pinpoint the crucial alliance between officers and reform-minded members of privileged urban groups, the government and reformers could not impose this law without garnering greater popular cooperation.

An examination of how privileged urban men succeeded in building a consensus broad enough to allow for the realization of a draft lottery in December 1916 requires deeper analysis. This chapter expands the field of analysis to the dialogue, latent and manifest, between reformers and the "honorable" poor over conscription. To make a draft possible, the army would have to significantly modify public attitudes about soldiering. Efforts to alter perceptions of "honorable" manhood and its relationship to national honor proved essential to the execution of a draft and other "progressive" reforms. The international military arms and organizational races that pitted nations against one another in a struggle for supremacy in an age of unabashed imperialism provided a driving political and ideological impetus for army modernization.

"Hermes' Law"

The energetic, monocle-wearing, and chain-smoking Marshal Hermes Rodrigues da Fonseca became war minister in 1906, in part as a reward for his suppression of an attempted uprising by cadets under his command during the 1904 Vaccine Revolt. Hermes was the moving spirit behind army modernization; he became so closely identified with military reform that the 1908 Obligatory Military Service Law was commonly referred to as "Hermes' Law." As a commander, Hermes had distinguished himself by his rigorous standards of barracks hygiene, the emphasis he placed on field exercises, and his initial determination to steer clear of political conspiracy. Crowds in Rio marveled at the novelty of Hermes' battalions who could march smartly in tight formations.[2] An ardent Prussophile, Hermes sent his most promising junior officers to Germany to train with Europe's crack land-based force. When they returned, they became bold conscription advocates and a political force in their own right known as Young Turks (a comparison to the officers who overthrew the Turkish State in 1908 and modeled their nation along the lines of Western nationalist and militarist ideologies). The Young Turks began publishing their views in a new army professional journal, *A Defeza Nacional,* in 1913.[3]

Conscription's political front men took greater care to package their bill. They renamed their legislation the "Obligatory Military Service Law," wisely expunging the loaded term "recruitment." A group of young federal Deputies favored by President Affonso Pena, the so-called "Kindergarten," provided the nucleus of support for the new draft law. Led by Deputy Alcindo Guanabara the Kindergarten went on the attack in Congress in 1906:

Alcindo Guanabara — Some misleadingly claim that in the moment of danger, volunteers will rise from the cobblestones, as in the time of Paraguay. Cincinato Braga — In those days they said, *"Deus é grande mas o mato é maior"* (God is great but the wilderness is bigger).

Alcindo Guanabara — After forty years, we still see that regiments, spread through the provinces are incomplete, deficient, much below budgeted limits.[4]

Kindergarten politicians pushed for conscription amid a spate of patriotic fanfare. The following month, the Escola Normal (teacher's school) of São Paulo held its first flag ceremony. Patriotic solemnities quickly spread to other urban centers, involving military officers, intellectuals, students, and ordinary citizens. In Fortaleza, Ceará, a patriotic ceremony in May 1907 inspired a journalist: "On few occasions has this land witnessed spontaneous manifestations of such great significance, of such a popular character, as the reception given the 9th Infantry Battalion yesterday. . . . He who lives in Fortaleza is familiar with the people's indifference for such events, had to note the greatness of the popular spirit . . . united in a communion of ideas . . . such a great multitude hurriedly and jovially marched to receive the proud soldiers of the national army. No political issue divided them there. People of all classes together . . . characterized the manifestation."[5] Only four years after the naval draft tragedy that convulsed Fortaleza's port (chapter 5), army troops were treated to an unusual patriotic banquet. Capitalizing on the new fascination with nationalist ritual in urban centers across Brazil, Congress approved a national Flag Day in November 1908. The rhetorical ties between military service and patriotism were being drawn tighter.

Hermes heightened public interest in military service by conducting the first large-scale field exercises in 1906 near Rio. Maneuvers became an annual event, and soon other battalions around the country began holding similar exercises. The press glamorized the maneuvers, firing the imaginations of adventurous young men. That same year, privileged *Cariocas* formed Swiss-style gun clubs (*linhas de tiro*) to practice marksmanship and military drills. Hermes encouraged the tiro clubs, supplying ammunition and grounds for their activities. Some tiro members participated in army field exercises as "maneuvers volunteers."[6] This domestic patriotic ferment was reinforced by international trends.

The International Military Organizational Race

The new push to modernize recruitment did not occur in a vacuum. International events both justified and spurred reformers' efforts to execute a draft. The protection of personal and national status and honor were crucial issues in the debate over conscription's benefits and costs. Peacetime military preparation unleashed an international "organizational race" just as critical as ongoing and more thoroughly studied arms races. Advocates portrayed peacetime conscription as a practical necessity and a mark of modernity. They believed a draft would help Brazil compete in an era when militarist rhetoric pitted nation against nation in what some depicted as a Darwinian struggle for survival.

One "Kindergarten" deputy emphasized the tactical advantages of conscription while attacking venerable liberal arguments that a draft would retard Brazil's economic growth: "All the nations that conduct draft registration for obligatory military service normally enroll 5 to 8 percent of the population capable of bearing arms . . . with [Brazil's] population of 25,000,000 . . . we could, in the first survey, enroll 1,250,000, and after those with exemptions are excluded there would remain 800,000 or 500,000. What are five, ten, fifteen thousand men taken from this total? It is an insignificant contingent that will not harm the development of our economic forces."[7] *O Estado de São Paulo* echoed this analysis, "[It is essential that all] able-bodied citizens pass through the active ranks making it a school and a nucleus for reserves." It declared that the National Guard was an ineffective reserve because it is an institution "ridiculously incapacitated by electoral coronelismo." The reporter pointed out that in 1905 Japanese reserves — with only three years training — had defeated Russian soldiers with more than five years in the barracks. Russia practiced conscription, but it required long terms of service, enfeebling its reserve force's effectiveness.[8]

Alcindo Guaunabara presented a table to Congress to illustrate just where Brazil stood in the international organizational race. It stressed the preponderance of conscription among the world's most advanced armies: Germany, France, Italy, Spain, and even Portugal. Perhaps more worrisome, many of Brazil's hemispheric rivals had adopted conscription: Peru, Bolivia, Chile, and, most disturbingly, Argentina. Deputy Wenceslau Escobar gave voice to this fear when he related his experience in Argentina where the citizens of Corrientes cooperated with the draft and received conscripts with music and "vivas" at train stations.[9]

The eclectic table included several entries that appear calculated to associate the lack of peacetime conscription with "backwardness." In particular, African and American nations with sizeable African-descended populations stand out. Haiti, Congo (a Belgian colony), Venezuela, the Dominican Republic, Panama, and Liberia were counterbalanced only by Abyssinia. The inclusion of these nations was probably calculated to pique the fears of politicians sensitive to perceptions of Brazil's supposedly inferior racial stock.

The table implies that economically developed nations that did not practice conscription were exceptional. England, the United States, Australia, Holland, and Canada's reluctance to adopt peacetime conscription originated in their strong liberal traditions and comparatively light land-based defense needs.[10] The British had the best navy in the world, but their army was second rate by comparison. The United States had militarily dominated its western territories by the 1880s, and faced no real land-based military threat. Henceforth, the United States put greater stress on naval development. Brazil's 1891 Constitution had been modeled after the United States charter, but as the war minister observed when the army endured mobilization troubles in 1903, "Without a national draft lottery, adopted by all the nations whose organization we take as models . . . we will continue to struggle with serious difficulties filling gaps in the ranks."[11] Most officers did not consider the United States or England viable models for Brazil's army.

Brazil's primary imperialistic concerns focused on matters that dovetailed with the army's "national integration" ideology. The army had traditionally been engaged in frontier settlement to secure Brazil's vast hinterlands. General Cândido Rondon became synonymous with frontier exploration. In 1910, he would help to found Brazil's Indian Protection Society intended to minimize the shock of contact between natives and "civilization." The army concerned itself with hinterland colonization because Brazil bordered every South American nation, save Ecuador and Chile. It successfully settled boundary disputes with nearly all of its neighbors in the late 1800s and early 1900s on the basis of occupation (*uti posseditus*).

Deputy Guanabara's chart sold peacetime conscription as an essential measure for Brazil's defense and development in an increasingly threatening global environment. The opposition balked at such comparisons, "We cannot compare ourselves with Prussia, France, or even Italy, [nations] overflowing with population, and where . . . militarization of the nation is an economic factor, it is a means of distracting the immense populations of these societies that perturb their nations' peace and tranquility. . . . Is not this the only onus that a poor enlistee suffers?"[12] This deputy voiced liberal suspicions of conscription as a sinister tool of social control, distracting and oppressing Europe's "masses." One senator flatly stated that conscription lottery would be unjust. "The rich do not need defending my friend, the rich, have money to avoid enlistment. . . . Be frank, let us speak the truth . . . enlistment will weigh on men who do not have a position in society."[13]

Republican leaders split between those who worried a draft would encourage military interference in politics, and those who believed it would refocus officer attention on professional matters. Antimilitarists tended to support states' rights guaranteed in the 1891 Constitution, while proconscription forces favored stronger central government. Conscription's most radical opponents, the Jacobinos were still regrouping after their involvement in the 1904 Vaccine Revolt made them to appear extremists in the eyes of many.[14] But powerful opponents like Senators Pinheiro Machado and Rui Barbosa continued to militate against a draft.

Conscription's opponents were unable to convince enough of their peers that a draft was a tool of despotic oppression. Instead, they relied more heavily on the issue of states' rights to cloud the bill's legality. While the law's opposition recognized the federal government's right to require states to produce recruit quotas, they insisted that only the states could determine how troops would be selected. One deputy raised the banner of states' rights alongside that of voting rights, "The project is unconstitutional because those drafted and those serving as reserves cannot be called anything other than praças, the Constitution proscribes their voting rights. . . . I [also] judge it unconstitutional because it violates . . . the Constitution by authorizing federal intervention in the states to conduct enrollment and the draft."[15] It seems ironic that those interested in depoliticizing the army would protest a reservist's loss of voting rights. The fact that only 2 or 3 percent of Brazil's population voted during the Old Republic (1889–1930) makes the objection seem even more spurious.[16] But, impressment was an electoral weapon, and many feared the draft's potential influence on the ballot.

As shown in chapter 6, improved conditions and shorter minimum service contracts attracted more volunteers. Alcindo Guanabara cited Pierre Baudin's *L'Armee Moderne* to support this policy, "For about twenty five years . . . all the peoples of Europe have endeavored, by all possible means, to reduce military duties, and most importantly, the duration of service that each citizen should serve."[17] Shorter contracts lessened the burden of duty, helped to change public attitudes toward enlisted service, and sped the creation of reserve forces. After serving two years, Brazilian soldiers who did not voluntarily reenlist passed onto a reserve list for the next seven years, according to the 1908 law. The army's acquisition of easy-to-load-and-fire Mauser rifles, beginning in the 1890s, made it possible tactically to train an effective reserve infantry.

According to the 1908 law, a married man would no longer be permitted to volunteer as a private, but he would be liable to the draft. Volunteers had to present letters of good conduct from local authorities to qualify. Attempts to improve the quality and restrict the numbers of volunteers were intended to make a draft lottery necessary to fill the ranks. The 1908 law reiterated the constitutional "abolition" of impressment. Brazil's listless bureaucracy made enforcing these requirements difficult, but the State made efforts to shore up troop respectability.[18]

Alcindo Guanabara submitted data on military exemptions in Austria-Hungary, Spain, Argentina, Germany, France, Belgium, Italy, Peru, Russia, and Romania. Critics commented that Brazil's "law of 1892 . . . preserved most of the exemptions established in the 1874 law,"[19] and the new law voided many occupational exemptions. Public employees, those at work in commerce, and students now enjoyed no protection from the draft. Draft-age public employees, moreover, were required to register or risk losing their jobs. Nonetheless, personnel in key industries (such as rail, power, and telegraph) continued to be protected.[20]

A weakness of the 1908 law was that it only required a draft when volunteers failed to fulfill the army's manpower needs. By setting stricter limits on volunteers, reformers aimed to guarantee that a draft would be required annually. The new law also established more rigorous lower limits for recruits. Individuals condemned for "infamous crimes" with a sentence of two years or more and those deprived of their rights as citizens could not serve. Draftees sentenced to jail one or more times for less than three months would be accepted, but they would serve in the "federal territories or in frontier garrisons."[21] Opponents complained that this measure "restores the penalty of *desterro* (internal exile) even when martial law has not been decreed."[22] The links between penal transportation and recruitment remained prominent, but officers desired to alter enlisted service's association with criminality. When Rio's police chief requested that the army provide 250 carbine rifles and military instruction to students of the 15th of November Correctional School in 1908, the war ministry refused because only "superior and secondary" schools qualified for the program established by the new law.[23] Reformers hoped to leave memories of the notorious army apprentice schools behind.

The growing importance of military police forces in maintaining a balance of power between wealthy states and the federal government also emerged during the debate. An amendment to subordinate state police forces to the federal army as third-line reserve forces drew fire. One deputy quipped, "Police forces cannot be supplied to the army nor conduct exercises with them. . . . State [police] forces cannot, without expressly violating our regime's fundamental laws, be incorporated into federal forces. . . . It would transgress states' autonomy." Supporters of the amendment noted that the police forces of Rio Grande do Sul had already complied with this reform to no ill effect. The amendment to subordinate state police forces to the War Ministry was voted down by a four-to-one margin.[24] States would control their military police forces and governors were free to disagree about what constituted a national emergency.

After lengthy debate, however, "Hermes's Law" passed in May 1908. Later that year, Marshal Hermes's prestige and popularity surged when, at the personal invitation of Kaiser Wilhelm II, he made a pilgrimage to Berlin to observe German army exercises. This international recognition of Hermes stimulated public interest in the transcontinental cult of militarist nationalism.[25]

Despite the support generated for military reform, Hermes's Law did not immediately bring about conscription. Congress failed to allocate the funds and to put in place the coercive mechanisms necessary for the bureaucracy to begin the draft. As Senator Lauro Sodré observed years later, "the [republic's] great reforms . . . have occurred through the authorization given in budgetary laws."[26] Legislating conscription was more appealing than funding it. The new law remained a dead letter for eight years. Like its 1874 predecessor, the law suffered from powerful enemies, defects, and lack of popular support. While protesters no longer stormed draft boards, passive resistance to registration subverted the draft.

A few students from Brazil's most prestigious law school in São Paulo demonstrated their enthusiasm for the conscription law's passage by volunteering for regular service in 1908. Editorials proclaimed that the new legislation had assured Brazilians that their sons would no longer be subject to "degrading" punishments or placed in contact with immoral elements that had formerly composed the army. Some tried to lead by example, but this patriotic euphoria was short-lived. Few of their peers volunteered in the following years.[27]

Congress recognized the linhas de tiro (gun clubs) in 1909 with a decree that organized the *Confederação de Tiro Brasileiro*. The tiros formed a forceful lobbying group that pressured for the Obligatory Military Service Law's approval, but hypocritically they sought exemptions for their members. Young men who trained with the tiros for two years and participated in annual military field exercises as "maneuver volunteers" were awarded a reservist's card. Most army officers considered tiros a useful short-term measure to increase Brazil's reserve forces until the draft could be held. The government subsidized tiros, but members also paid dues, making the position less accessible to most poor Brazilians.[28]

The relationship between the tiros and the regular army reflected old status-conscious patterns perhaps best captured in a 1908 patriotic ceremony in Rio. A newly formed tiro battalion received a Brazilian flag from a Voluntário da Pátria. The Voluntários had been established during the Paraguayan War in an attempt to segregate men of "honorable" status from army regulars. Similarly, tiros allowed the "better sort" to imitate the fashionable military trends emanating from the North Atlantic at a safe distance from the regular soldiery.[29]

When the 1908 draft law passed, tiro units experienced explosive growth. But, when Congress failed to fund the law, enthusiasm for the tiros dissipated. In 1913, the war minister reported that the tiro confederation was in a phase of "patent decadence."[30] Two years later, he explained that most had disappeared because they had been manipulated by local politicians for electoral purposes and because the draft lottery had not been executed. He observed that the "majority" of tiro members participated "only to escape regular service," and accurately predicted that when the draft was instituted, the tiros would flourish once again.[31]

While tiros provided a new upscale escape hatch from regular service, others continued to seek protection through National Guard posts. In 1890, the Republican government had briefly called up guard units for weekly duty, but soon afterward, these units returned to inactivity. All but a few lacked equipment and effective organization. According to the 1908 law, the National Guard was subordinate to the War Ministry as a reserve force in wartime. To the army's dismay, the 1908 law did not wrench control over the guard's administration from the Justice Ministry in peacetime. The opposition objected, asking how the militia could serve as an institutional check on the army if it was subordinate?[32]

The Young Turks found this arrangement absurd. They used Justice Ministry figures to expose the preposterous size of the guard's ranks. In 1916, the Justice Ministry had registered 2,976 guard brigades with more than 239,176 officers. According to one Young Turk, this meant that 4,511,540 guardsmen were registered, eligible, and trained for peacetime duty and more than 10,000,000 for wartime, if regulations on the formation of brigades were followed. Brazil had an estimated population of only 30 million inhabitants in 1918. Theoretically, more than two-thirds of all Brazilian males were guardsmen.[33] Despite nearly perennial calls to reform the guard, no tangible measures were carried out. The institution became a caricature of itself, ridiculed by the Young Turks and the press. When the State finally abrogated the guard in 1918, few defended this engorged paper tiger.[34] Army reformers praised the elimination of this vestigial organ of monarchy.

Most men who were no longer protected from recruitment under the new law hoped that the draft would not take place and that, if it did, their connections could still curb the impersonal power of the State. Others took more activist stances by protesting and attempting to impede conscription legislation.

The "Tightening Screw"

Most people who participated in draft resistance were illiterate, and the interpretation of their actions requires a careful weighing of literate observers' descriptions. While the strategy of storming draft boards appears to have died with the empire, passive resistance continued. But noncooperation, that venerable Iberian tradition of "obeying but not complying," left few records behind. Some, however, found in the printing press new ways to reach a larger public.

Penny-press entrepreneurs in the early 1900s provide vivid insights into popular attitudes toward conscription and the nation.[35] One pioneer of *cordel* (handbill) literature, Leandro Gomes de Barros (1865–1918), was from the small northeast town of Pombal, Paraíba. Gomes may have witnessed the Quebra Quilos Revolt (partly inspired by the 1874 Recruitment Law) as a boy when it swept through this cotton growing region.[36] Gomes joined a venerable bardic tradition that traced its origins to the mulatto composer Domingos Caldas Barbosa and beyond.[37] Unlike most composers of the era, Gomes did not sing his verses in public nor partake in the improvisational poetic duels where quick-witted performers matched verses. Rather, he printed his ballads on handbills to be sold, and later to be read or sung by others.[38]

When legislative debate on conscription began, Leandro published "O Sorteio Militar" (The Draft Lottery) in 1906. His bet that this lyrical tirade against the draft would find a sympathetic audience and turn a profit is an indicator of continuing popular repugnance for army service.

O brasileiro se torce,	The Brazilian gets twisted,
Mais do que um parafuso,	More than a screw,
A seca aperta o norte,	Droughts choke the North,
No sul aperta o abuso,	In the South abuse is tightening,
O imposto bota na prensa,	Taxes put us in the vise,
O sorteio acocha o fuso.	And the draft lottery tightens the screw.[39]

For Leandro, conscription was yet another way the Republican government sought to tighten the screw for ordinary Brazilians. Like former draft protesters, he uses conscription as a lightning rod to focus attention on a variety of anxieties about high-handed State actions. He inveighs against the corruption that plagued the poor, describing how humble folk planned

to bribe local officials with pigs, burros, and other goods to protect themselves and their families from the draft.[40]

The lyricist plays relentlessly on the idea that the lottery would recruit
everyone — the insane, limbless, blind, retarded, elderly, priests; and even
the dead would be called up. Only those who held the title doutor (privileged graduates of law or medical faculties) would be spared. When asked
why he would recruit unfit troops, a fictional delegate answered, "If it falls
in the net, I call it a fish, and what comes out [of the net] goes in the cake."
Clearly, Leandro humorously tweaked popular fears of the indiscriminate
mixing of social strata, and therein lies the comic relief. Comedy and
humor is often based on incongruous situations where social statuses are
confused or reversed. Like the annual pre-Lenten celebration of *Carnaval*,
in which the poor often masquerade as rich or famous people, the draft
lottery would bring about a humorous confusion of social status. Instead
of the individuality of Carnival, however, the draft, more like an anti-
Carnival, would obscure status through impersonal, drab uniformity.[41]

Gomes goes on to examine the issue of masculine honor:

Zé Churumella já disse:	Zé Churumella has already declared:
O governo me sorteia,	If the government drafts me,
Eu pego minha mulher,	I will grab my wife,
Vou liquidal-a na peia,	Put her in horse fetters and kill her,
Fico livre do sorteio,	I will be free from the draft,
Morra embora na cadeia.	And instead I will die in jail.[42]

The hyperbole suggests that defending honor, even if it meant death in
jail, was preferable to the travails of barracks life. Zé's decision to kill his
wife was not humorous because it was an act of gratuitous misogyny,
rather the humor lay in a moral dilemma. The draft threatened to separate
man and wife, but honor dictated that a man protect his spouse. By killing
his wife, at least Zé had the peace of mind that his honor would remain
intact. Otherwise, why not commit some other horrid crime to exempt
himself?

A Ceará humorist with the pseudonym "Jack" mused on Hermes's Law
in a column that hinted at the geography of honor, "Eye on the Street."
"[T]he people, the press, Congress, the government, everyone thinks the
draft lottery is necessary and just," observed the wag. Even Jack, having
passed the age of eligibility, thought it was a good idea. Many were more

receptive to the patriotic ideal of conscription, but few were ready to see it applied to themselves or their kin. Jack also jokes about a haughty, rich, and handsome young man who had never married his fiancée because he was too busy running a fashionable clothing shop. When drafted, he hires a doctor to arrange an illness for him, but army physicians judge him to be fit. The young man has such bad luck that he draws service in Acre, on Brazil's insalubrious western frontier. He entrusts his business partner to protect his shop and his fiancée, but when he returns four years later, both of them are gone.[43]

The draft clearly threatened the ability to defend one's livelihood and to avoid being cuckolded. Jack composed a ditty (*modinha*) that stressed this threat, "He who has a wife or a mother-in-law has a powerful weapon, the draft lottery and volunteering, 'Do not irritate me or I will enlist in the army!' There is no ill-tempered loud-mouthed woman (*cascavel*) who will not quiet down upon hearing these words. The [draft] law is a good one, but it will be the terror of fiancées, wives, and mothers-in-law."[44] Here public duty looms as a humorous escape from the burdens of private patriarchal duties. Readers laughed at these exaggerated circumstances, but this black humor also tapped into deep-rooted fears. Instead of viewing enlisted service as the fulfillment of a citizen's manly virtues, most felt the draft imperiled their manhood.

Balladeers and humorists were not the only ones who anticipated public reaction to the draft. Olavo Bilac, a journalist and poet, wrote,

It is not difficult to predict the commotion the Obligatory Military Service Law will produce amid this population that has always been horrified by the pack and the gun. When the Paraguayan War broke out . . . recruitment, already euphemistically referred to as "volunteering," spread indescribable fear from the coast to the interior. Hicks left their villages in Rio de Janeiro, São Paulo, and Minas, to hide themselves in the trackless recesses of Mato Grosso and Goiás, penetrating virgin forests, driven by haste and the winds of terror, preferring to live with the ants, the jaguars, venomous snakes, and ferocious Indians rather than don a uniform and doff the volunteer's beret. Many never returned home. . . . The hillbilly's fear of the uniform is still the same today. On the day that the Obligatory Service Law is put into effect, it will cause the same panic and fear in our countryside that it did in 1865.[45]

These do not sound like the words of a man who would later become the draft's most inspired crusader, but his words confirm the views of Leandro Gomes de Barros. Both agreed that conscription would inspire fear in and disproportionately affect the poor.

The expected panic did not occur because the draft was not executed forthwith. Instead of storming boards of registration, rustics kept their distance, and most active draft resistance shifted to urban centers. Anarcho-syndicalists, orthodox positivists, monarchist elements, and antimilitarist politicians reinvigorated decades-old digs against peacetime conscription.[46] The Brazilian Anti-Militarist League (Liga Anti-Militarist Brasileira, LAMB) was formed by Rio's working-class organizations in 1907 to lobby against conscription.

In December 1907, *O Voz do Trabalhador,* an anarcho-syndicalist paper of the Confederação Operária Brasileira (Brazilian Workers Confederation), reported that five thousand workers had gathered in Rio's São Francisco square to protest conscription as Congress deliberated on the bill. Later some six hundred members of the Federação Operária (Worker's Federation) met to debate, and an idealistic young officer Lieutenant Gentil Falcão attended the meeting. After an open-floor debate began, Gentil rose and proclaimed conscription the only way to reform the army and require all citizens to serve their fatherland. A labor leader then asked Gentil to define "fatherland." The lieutenant responded that it was the "intimate relationship that links a people to the land in which they were born. This fatherland has the right to demand that its sons perform their duty to defend it." Labor leaders disagreed with Gentil, insisting that "the fatherland is the family, it is not a piece of land."[47] Angry workers' shouts frustrated Gentil's attempts to respond.

Subsequently, labor leaders criticized the draft and other State initiatives. One advised household heads to resist militarism in public schools that makes children believe that the "army and the fatherland are beneficial to workers" and other "canards."[48] Another added that "workers do not want to serve the fatherland, they want to live for their families, dignifying them through the honor that springs from their daily labor." Workers also accented the home's inviolability. As one laborer simply put it, "The home is the most sacred place of a society."[49]

Labor leaders joined forces with orthodox positivists and antimilitarist politicians to form the LAMB in 1907. They addressed their first manifesto

(handwritten margin note top: LAMB - against conscript)

specifically to mothers, who had been effective in undermining the draft in the past. It warned mothers that if their sons were drafted they would serve alongside criminals and be treated like "slaves." The manifesto urged mothers to teach their children to oppose the draft and to discourage them from imitating other children (perhaps Boy Scouts) who dressed up in uniforms and learned the skills of war.[50] The LAMB reiterated that the draft would undermine "honorable" families: "The law prohibits marriage of those who fall into the [draft's] clutches. The unlucky draftee will be celibate by force! Attending to natural necessities, natural for men, one can affirm that in order not to be mummified by the demands of desire, he will give himself over to pleasures of prostitution — it will be a tendency toward prostitution and consequently syphilis, ills that the military draft will unintentionally foment. At age thirty, debauched and syphilitic, the ex-soldier will then constitute a family."[51] A healthy man's supposedly uncontrollable sex drive would naturally force praças who were not permitted to marry to seek out prostitutes or, worse still, comrades to prevent a "mummification" of passion. Though the LAMB lost the legislative battle, it worked to stymy the law's execution. LAMB propaganda mixed class struggle and eugenics with vintage rhetoric that portrayed the barracks as a threat to the family, public morality, and the future of the "race."

(handwritten margin note: Induced fear thru vintage rhetoric)

The LAMB predicted that the draft would not level all classes, but only the lower classes. It urged eligible citizens not to cooperate with any kind of State enrollment or census because these lists could be used to compose draft rolls. Like its forerunner, the 1908 law required draft enrollment as the basis for the lottery.[52] The LAMB rejoiced at the results of renewed draft registration in 1909. Totals were even lower than those of the mid-1870s. Labor celebrated that less than 90,000 registered out of Brazil's 20,000,000 inhabitants. Minas Gerais, "the jewel of Brazil," lived up to its heritage of begrudging recruitment; it registered a mere 8,000 out of 4,000,000 citizens. The state and city of Rio de Janeiro enrolled 11,000; most were public employees who stood to lose their jobs for not complying. The LAMB chastised State workers who registered and only later grumbled when they found that the lottery's onus could fall unfairly on their shoulders. The results in all states were encouraging with one exception: São Paulo registered 60,000, two-thirds of the national total. The LAMB blamed the state's large foreign-born population for the result.[53]

Not all antimilitarist resistance was undertaken by labor. The lawyer

Joaquim da Silva Nogueira asked for an order of habeas corpus for his client Eduardo Lima in January 1908 before the Obligatory Service Law had been enacted. The advocate alleged that his client's constitutionally guaranteed liberties were threatened by the draft. The judge threw out the petition on the grounds that the threat in question was not yet implemented.[54] Labor, orthodox positivists, and members of the political and judicial elite who opposed militarism employed an arsenal of strategies to foil conscription. Adding to their direct efforts, new political events would soon distract the government from the conscription controversy.

Of Military Damnations and Salvations

In 1910, Marshal Hermes won the most controversial presidential election since the founding of the republic. His campaign fed conflicts between those who favored military involvement in politics and antimilitarists. Indeed, the candidate who opposed Hermes's candidacy, Bahian senator Rui Barbosa, chose the name *Partido Civilista* (Civilian Party) for his party. The congressional strongman, Pinheiro Machado, who (like Rui) had opposed the Obligatory Vaccine and new Military Service Laws, backed Hermes's candidacy. This partnership did not ultimately bode well for the draft.

The Republican party machines of Rio Grande do Sul, Minas Gerais, Pernambuco, and most other states supported Hermes's candidacy. Barbosa's Civilista party enjoyed the backing of São Paulo's Republicans (historically antimilitarist) and his home state, Bahia. Barbosa made the army's proper political role the central campaign issue. He conducted an unprecedented public speaking tour, and his platform specified that praças were in dire need of "schooling, moral education, and higher wages." He supported the "development of military and civic instruction in the armed forces . . . [conducted] with particular diligence among privates, whose intellectual and moral character constitute the base of all military organization in a civilized country."[55] While he spoke of improving the lot of praças, Barbosa cast suspicion on the motives of military officers. His platform was a rehash of classic liberal ideas, but his unusual campaign set the 1910 election apart. Republican party bosses in most states insured that the official tally favored Hermes.[56] Hermes's victory renewed hopes that a draft would be executed swiftly.

Days after Hermes took office, however, navy praças mutinied, demand-ing reasonable work hours, better pay and food, and a ban on flogging. The Anti-Flogging Revolt's leaders were black NCOs returning from train-ing in England where they learned to navigate recently purchased battle-ships. The navy had no vessels capable of matching these dreadnoughts, and a brief attack on the rebel ships was easily rebuffed. The mutineers controlled Guanabara Bay, and they threatened to bombard Rio if their demands were not met. The State's vulnerability to a few hundred "dark-skinned" praças was humiliating. Navy brass felt that the murder of two officers during the revolt set a dangerous precedent.[57]

The rebels' cause inspired public sympathy. Many felt shame for the "savage" punishments and deplorable conditions that sailors endured. The day after Deodoro's provisional junta took power in 1889, it had decreed flogging's abolition in the navy. But in 1890, he had reversed this decision, and Rui Barbosa himself, then Deodoro's finance minister, had signed the decree reinstating flogging for sailors. Two decades later, Barbosa negoti-ated a peaceful settlement to the Anti-Flogging Revolt. He was one of the few leaders who affirmed the justness of the rebels' demands. He praised their dignified restraint, "We extinguished slavery over the black race, but we maintain slavery over the white race among the fatherland's service-men."[58] Many of Barbosa's peers would have disputed his depiction of most sailors as "white." Cartoons caricatured the African descent of the mutineers and especially their leader Sergeant João Cândido.[59] Leaders grudgingly conceded the demands of swarthy rebels only when they real-ized they could not match them militarily.

The government guaranteed the rebels amnesty and promised to abolish flogging. Once the ships had been surrendered, however, rebels and sus-pected sympathizers were inhumanely packed into crowded army, navy, and civil jails. Some died soon after being incarcerated. Then the govern-ment began to renege on its amnesty agreement by introducing measures to discharge rebel praças. These actions sparked a second revolt that was encouraged by agents planted among the prisoners by the police. The second uprising brought a heavy-handed crackdown, sweeping amnesty aside. The revolt centered in the navy prison on the Ilha das Cobras adja-cent to Rio's port. More than one hundred poorly armed rebel sailors were killed by artillery bombardment even as many tried to surrender.[60]

Many rebels were shipped off in crowded vessels to the Amazon without due process. In 1911, the *Satélite* transported 105 ex-sailors, 44 prostitutes, 293 convicts from the House of Detention, and 50 army praças to the Amazon. Nine "bandits" were executed en route. One witness with the rural sanitation service attached to General Rondon's telegraph service in the Amazon described how an American company building the Madeira Railway refused to accept some 400 exiles as workers. Most ended up in Rondon's camp stringing telegraph lines or they were contracted out to local landowners as rubber tappers. While many admired Rondon's frontier exploits, his mission attracted few volunteers. The sanitation employee wrote Senator Rui Barbosa denouncing officers for allowing prisoners to be decimated by disease and for viciously beating them.[61]

The Anti-Flogging Revolt had important implications for conscription. Despite the rhetoric of reformers, the revolt demonstrated that "degrading" punishments continued in the armed forces. For Deputy Alcindo Guanabara and others, the *Satélite*'s voyage probably resembled a "Dantesque" military damnation to the Amazon's "green inferno." This episode fomented anew fears of a draft.

The Anti-Flogging Revolt was soon obscured by federal interventions known in state politics as "salvations." Those who backed the salvations claimed that they were demolishing corrupt rural bossism. In practice, they did little more than replace governors who refused to pledge support to Hermes with equally corrupt opposition factions. Varying degrees of intervention transpired in gubernatorial elections in ten states. In states with strong police forces, intervention was limited to army troop transfers or maneuvers. In Amazonas, Ceará, Pernambuco, and Bahia, however, federal intervention resulted in the unseating of ruling clans. In these states, opposition factions invariably selected an army officer to be their candidate. Hotly contested political campaigns were uncommon, and incumbents often regarded opposition candidates as insurgents. Political violence tended to pit state policemen against locally garrisoned federal troops. In Amazonas and Bahia, friction between army and state police led to the bombardment of state capitals by the former — something the Anti-Flogging rebels refrained from.[62]

These bitter battles politicized conscription. Enrollment efforts floundered as Hermes struggled to put out one political firestorm after another. Besides, his strongest congressional supporter, Senator Pinheiro Machado, opposed the draft; this compromised the president's ability to take decisive action. The "salvations" did little to undermine rural oligarchies; if anything, they strengthened factions who opposed the idea of active duty officers vying for political office. Oligarchs bided their time and reasserted their control after Hermes's mandate ended.[63] As coronéis restored their control, new developments refocused attention on the draft.

War, Millenarian Rebellion, Race, and "Science"

While the *salvações* had been a setback for conscription, new events and ideologies would facilitate the draft's execution. In the 1910s, influential groups of educated Brazilians, worried about Brazil's defense capacities, found new "scientific" reasons to support conscription. By attributing new significance to conscription, intellectuals, officers, and politicians would galvanize a political coalition with the strength to implement the draft.

World War I demonstrated the awesome power of modern war machines and made military preparedness appear a transcendent issue of national survival. Belgium proved that neutrality and diplomacy could be a poor defense against military might. Imperial powers unmasked presumptions about European civility by violating the sovereignty of weaker nations, not only abroad, but in Europe itself. As one Brazilian officer addressing the Military Club put it, "The European War is eloquently demonstrating to us what the destiny of weak peoples will be."[64]

Fears of European imperialism were heightened by a millenarian movement known as the Contestado Revolt. Miguel Lucena Boaventura, the movement's leader, was a wandering lay holy man who had deserted from Paraná's military police force. Like Antônio Conselheiro, the mystic leader of Canudos (1893–97), Boaventura preached against the republic and favored monarchy. He died in 1912, but his faithful regrouped and expanded the flock in a remote holy city amid the thick pines of Paraná. Most followers were Brazilian-born poor displaced by land speculation after the construction of a major railway linking the region to the metropolises of Rio and São Paulo. In December 1913, army troops sent to disperse the "fanatics" were repulsed. By 1915, the army had deployed 7,000 soldiers, nearly half of the army's forces to the region. A scorched earth and siege operation took almost a year to wear down rebel resistance.[65]

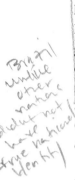

The Contestado Revolt recalled the Canudos Rebellion of the 1890s and the disturbing analysis of Euclydes da Cunha's 1902 nationalist treatise *Os sertões*. Da Cunha expressed what the army's national integration ideologues had long feared—that these rebellions boiled down to a race war. Brazilians remained divided by region, ideology, race, climate, class, language, and culture. Worse, the Contestado Revolt ensued as Brazilians read daily about European soldiers who supposedly died for national honor. It revealed that many Brazilians still did not identify with the nation-state. Some, swayed by social Darwinism and da Cunha's *Os sertões*, took the Contestado Revolt as a sign that Brazil's racial and climatic heterogeneity could deter it from becoming a modern, united, and "white" nation.

Before World War I, in an attempt to "whiten" and consolidate the "national race," the State subsidized mostly European immigration and prohibited the entry of "racially undesirable" peoples from Africa and China. Army-educated nationalists were strong proponents of immigration as a policy to enhance Brazil's economic and racial development.[66] Ironically, during World War I, isolated German, Japanese, Italian, and Polish immigrant colonies (where few bothered to learn Portuguese) seemed a surprising threat to national unity. Many feared that these colonies could become beachheads of foreign domination. When Brazil declared war in 1917, the campaign against the "German peril" escalated, including violence against German and Teuto-Brazilian property, a ban on German-language publications, the temporary closing of some German schools, and restrictions on German-owned businesses.[67]

Meanwhile reformers in urban centers saw a threat to national security in the strikes led by mostly anarcho-syndicalist labor unions. These fears were exacerbated in 1915 when a coup plot was uncovered among labor militants, firemen, police, and army sergeants. These groups opposed the Young Turks who had learned in Germany to place a premium on sergeants' training. Thus, they drafted measures to reform sergeant training that would cut short the careers of many active duty NCOs. Deputy Maurício de Lacerda, a stalwart of Rio's labor movement, unsuccessfully argued the sergeants' case in Congress. According to one report, if the sergeants' plot had succeeded, the first to be killed would have been the "*germanistas*" (Young Turks).[68] In December 1915, the army stifled this coup plot and implicated some 100 army sergeants in Rio. As a result of inquiries and reforms, many of these sergeants were forced to retire. Some disgruntled NCOs began to organize a second plot, but police snoops uncovered the conspiracy on April 6, 1916. The plot involved Deputy Maurício de Lacerda, journalist Agripino Nazareth, ex-navy sergeant Dias Martins (a leader of the Anti-Flogging Revolt), labor activists, and active duty NCOs in Rio's police, army, navy, and fire department.[69] The sergeants and their allies sought not only to protect their careers, but they also hoped to institute social and political reforms, including a secret ballot. Many military academy cadets sympathized with the sergeants' movement, and one historian has argued that the Tenente (lieutenant) Revolts of the 1920s drew much of their program from the Sergeants' Revolt.[70] Reformers took this plot and increasing labor unrest as confirmations of the need to reorganize army service and indoctrinate the ranks and the populace with a unifying nationalism. As one journalist put it, "Obligatory military service is, in effect, an excellent way of disciplining the people, teaching them to obey."[71]

Studies and surveys by public health specialists made Brazilians more aware than ever of their population's poor health. The image of Brazil as an immense hospital was forwarded by hygienists like Drs. Miguel Pereira, Belisário Penna, and Carlos Chagas. Most Brazilian health officials followed neo-Lamarckian genetic theory. They argued that by improving public sanitation, education, and physical fitness, the State promoted "race improvement." Eugenist-backed State interventionism supplanted the less intrusive policies of positivists who defended the ideology of the house and opposed obligatory State measures.[72]

In this climate, a draft became the most practical and vigorous State measure to improve defense while instructing a broader cross-section of Brazil's ethnically and racially diverse lower classes in hygiene, physical fitness, discipline, the Portuguese language, and national identity. Draft advocates apparently struck a chord with urban middle and upper classes by arguing that a draft could transform the poor and ameliorate problems that haunted visions of Brazil's national destiny. The renowned poet Olavo Bilac both symbolized and facilitated the conversion of Brazil's urban middle and upper classes to the cause of conscription.

Olavo Bilac (1865–1918): The "Admirable Filter" and the House

The drive to implement conscription in the past had lacked adequate support from organizations outside of the halls of Congress. While tiros (civilian gun clubs) had backed the draft since 1906 and continued to do so, they made few coordinated efforts to lobby Congress. An impassioned orator, Olavo Bilac filled this leadership vacuum. He emerged as a civilian missionary for conscription, which he argued was essential for national survival and renewal. As Bilac and his allies realized they faced an uphill battle to implement a draft, they began to pay more attention than they had in the past to the sensibilities of the poor in order to promote conscription.

Bilac's most important predecessor, Lieutenant Gentil Falcão began to respond to labor's persuasive appeals. Falcão had been directly confronted by the arguments of disgruntled anarcho-syndicalists in 1908. In 1910, he toured Minas Gerais delivering public speeches and publishing editorials in favor of conscription. Later in 1923, he would publish *A defesa nacional ou o regulamento do sorteio em linguagem popular* (national defense or draft regulations in popular language). Falcão, a pioneer of army public relations, became convinced that reformers had to make the draft intelligible and acceptable to the respectable poor. Significantly, he and others began to talk about the army in explicitly familial terms to domesticate the barracks. For Falcão, the army would "make Brazilians into brothers serving their common mother: the nation." Officers would treat their conscripted "brothers in arms" with affection, and the barracks would no longer be the refuge of the social reprobates. Humiliating punishments and tasks had been eliminated. The new soldier would be an auxiliary rather than his officers' servant, much less a slave.[73] The stigma of servile labor and corporal punishment preoccupied workers in a society that had only abolished slavery two decades earlier and that had recently witnessed the Anti-Flogging Revolt. Bilac would amplify and popularize Falcão's message.

Olavo Bilac's father had already departed to the Paraguay War when he was born in Rio in 1865, but Olavo himself would never serve in the army. An avid republican patriot, he penned a famous official hymn to the Brazilian flag. He had opposed the draft in part because he had been persecuted by President Floriano Peixoto's regime, but he soon became the draft's most charismatic convert in the 1910s.[74] Like the mystic leaders of the millenarian Canudos and Contestado communities, Bilac became a wandering lay missionary in 1915. But he did not preach to the poor in remote rural sites, nor encourage citizens to eschew the secular republican creed, nor to form holy communities apart from Brazil's coastal society to prepare for God's second coming. Instead, the poet traveled to major urban centers where he preached to the wealthy and educated and extolled the cult of republican nationalism. He stressed the need to integrate and educate Brazil's citizens with a unifying sense of national identity, and the urgency of preparing to ward off a potential second coming by European conquerors. For Bilac the "nation is the great magic, the inviolable taboo that should be blindly adored, without being touched."[75] And woe be unto the "moral monsters" who doubted this creed because to "deny the fatherland is to deny all social and moral life."[76]

Like Falcão, Bilac mercilessly assailed the idea that conscription was pernicious to home and family. For the bachelor poet, "The fatherland is a thread that links the family and humanity. To deny one is to deny the others. He who does not conceive the ideal of fatherland cannot conceive of the idea of a home, nor human solidarity. Without a fatherland, and therefore, without a family, without a society, man annuls himself."[77] The sanctity of one's home could only be defended with a clear understanding of a citizen's duty to his nation. To have citizens it was imperative to teach all the "hygiene of the body and the soul, primary civic and military instruction."[78] Thus, hygienic measures, like the Obligatory Vaccine and Military Service Laws, far from attacks on family honor, were the best means of protecting it. The rhetoric of physical, social, and spiritual hygiene justified the penetration of public power into formerly sacrosanct areas of private domain.

Other less famous draft advocates refuted perceptions that enlisted service implied sexual "deviance." A 1916 tract ridiculed the common prejudice against sexually segregated institutions: "How is one to have an idea of fatherland if he does not have a home or a family?! Everyone disparages the honest celibacy of the priest and the soldier. . . . For the miserable life they lead, if they are not sexually deviant, they are [assumed to be] eunuchs."[79] Propagandists began to address the specific prejudices that shrouded the barracks in a sinister fog of social castration and sexual perversion. Internationally, conscription was creating new types of homosociability that had to be given social sanction and brought into harmony with nationalist rhetoric that idealized the heterosexual nuclear family.

Bilac himself did not harp on this note, perhaps because it was widely rumored that this bachelor patriot preferred young men as passive sexual partners.[80]

Reformers took pains to praise the "celebate" young men who would serve their nation like stoic priests. They explained how the draft and army discipline would serve to fortify family values, community solidarity, the work ethic, and masculine virtue. Previous attempts to implement conscription had not been accompanied by a persistent attempt to sell it to the public and recast soldiering's image. Unlike the mobilization for World War I in the United States, where draft dodgers were subject to gender ridicule that labeled them emasculated "slackers," in Brazil, propagandists had to convince the public that army service was manly.[81]

Through their newspapers, some labor leaders returned Bilac's fire and brimstone, mixing hygienic and pagan metaphors evocative of the biblical Moloch: "Young men do not be fooled by . . . the cult that surrounds the blood-drinking idol that is called the fatherland. . . . The fatherland is a kind of virus that contaminates your brains and brings you to the insane extreme of exterminating your peers. . . . Old [German General] Moltke said that peace was prejudicial to humanity. The poet Bilac is being paid by the high command to affirm this Moltkean monstrosity in golden phrases."[82] Drawing inspiration from internationally famous pacifists like the French socialist Gustave Hervé, labor leaders protested conscription. Still, most of the labor press preached to the choir. Meanwhile, the mainstream media gave generous coverage to Bilac's speeches and patriotic events.

For Bilac, the first step in nationalist revival involved executing the draft, "In Europe, today, when the war opens wide gaps in the ranks of combatants, governments call up fresh army reserves, phalanxes of adolescents, the dazzling reserves of a nation's Spring."[83] The draft's tactical benefits were secondary, however, "What is universal military service? It is the complete triumph of democracy; the leveling of social classes; the school of order, discipline, and cohesion; the laboratory of self dignity and patriotism. . . . The cities are full of unshod vagrants and ragamuffins . . . uncouth animals, only human in appearance and depravity. For these dregs of society, the barracks would be a salvation. The barracks are an *admirable filter* in which men cleanse and purify themselves: they emerge conscientious and dignified Brazilians — these wretches without conscience, without dignity, without a country who constitute the amorphous mass of our multitude"[84] (emphasis added). Bilac implores youth to support conscription to break down class barriers to develop that "imagined" leveling and homogenization that allows nationalist sentiment to flourish. For Bilac the "admirable filter" would play a key role in making uneducated urbanites into citizens. Conversely, he felt that the draft would cure the elite's "parvenu" egotism, avarice, and indifference.[85] The draft would bring all classes, races, and regions together and fulfill the prophecy of the army's national integration ideology. One might render Bilac's view of the "new" armed forces as a kind of institutional liver for Brazil's body politic that would recycle, purify, and homogenize the nation's mixed blood through the "admirable filter" of the army. It would distill an ennobling and unifying sense of patriotic identity to be carried throughout Brazil's vast territorial extremities by reservists.

Bilac also pondered the crossroads between personal and national honor. While Brazil was without a "perfected collective patriotism," its citizens happily did possess "personal honor, an individual patriotism." Invasion by a foreign aggressor "despite all its evils" could work as a "formidable force for national integration."[86] Conscription's supporters noted that even the socialist Gustave Hervé had turned his back on pacifism and embraced war mobilization after Germany invaded France.[87]

Bilac draws connections between personal honor and the need to bind this sentiment to national honor. This transition was necessary to prevent what the poet feared most: "the possibility of [national] dismemberment terrifies me . . . this immense territory populated by twenty-five million people who are not connected by intense ties of support and agreement for the same ideal, through their civic education, through military cohesion; ridiculous conflicts over frontiers within our fatherland, exploited by rhetoric, envenomed by fanaticism, giving rise to fratricidal wars."[88] Here Bilac refers to the struggle to quell the Contestado Revolt (1912–16). To prevent national disintegration, the "cultivated classes" who have "education, thought, and conscience" have to bring classes and regions together through this bold project. Nationalist fanaticism had to replace divisive religious, racial, class, and regional identities that he blamed for fomenting labor unrest and the recent Anti-Flogging, Sergeants', and Contestado Rebellions.

Bilac draped conscription in the "scientific" language of hygiene and racial "regeneration."[89] He had some success in selling conscription as a masculine eugenic motor for improving the health, hygiene, intelligence, discipline, genes, and sense of national identity among a broader cross-section of Brazil's diverse lower classes.[90] He stressed that "generalized military service" was "obligatory primary education; obligatory civic education; obligatory decency, obligatory hygiene, obligatory muscular and psychic regeneration."[91]

The grim lessons of World War I made recruitment reform seem a transcendent issue of national survival. If Brazil hoped to mobilize an army capable of warding off powerful potential European aggressors (let alone its regional rival, Argentina, which had adopted conscription in 1901), it had to take stock of and develop its human resources. Since most poor Brazilians did not attend schools, the draft became a way of socializing a larger portion of them. The Young Turks had emphasized the hygienic benefits of military training even before Bilac popularized these ideas. In 1914 a lieutenant wrote, "The barracks are today a civic and military school where moral education cultivates the sentiments and hygiene benefits from the development of the muscles by the rational practice of gymnastics and by the intense preparation of men for appropriate military tasks."[92]

In 1915, Bilac was named president of a patriotic society formed to promote the views he so passionately espoused, the National Defense League (*Liga de Defesa Nacional,* LDN). The LDN received political and financial support from educated urbanites, army officers, health officials, and politicians. Bilac used his position as a bully pulpit to stress the need to disseminate the Portuguese language in isolated immigrant communities of Japanese, Germans, Poles, and Italians, where parents raised their children in Old World languages. Bilac made a special effort to address youth. He promoted scouting as training for future citizen soldiers. "The boy scout . . . learns to shoot, hike, run, jump, swim, mount a horse, fight, defend himself, and handle arms; he maintains constant care of his body and soul; and avoids the practice of all vices." Concerns that youngsters of all classes were poorly physically prepared and lacked basic skills reveal heightened concerns with public health and education for the sake of national defense. For Bilac "scouting, above being patriotism, is principally a school of honor." Again he ruminates on the "sacred abstraction"

of individual and national honor to stress that scouting and enlisted service were honorable masculine duties.[93]

For one reporter, Bilac's appeals to youth inspired a new mood:

[The military] represents the living incarnation of the national ideal. The
enthusiastic movement that one now observes in support of the armed
forces . . . originates principally with our young people . . . the enthusiasm
with which youths respond to the appeal made to their patriotism and the
alacrity with which they enlist themselves to receive instruction in the
army. . . . In the army an intellectual effervescence and feverish professional
activity make the moment ripe to try, for the first time, to equip Brazil with
the defensive resources without which we will be at the mercy of strong
peoples. . . . Today we find ourselves granting the armed forces a function
only they can fulfill as the regulating and moderating element of national
life.[94]

The military's national integration ideology and the idea of the "nation in
arms" were making new inroads among civilian leaders of opinion.[95]

As momentum built for conscription in 1915, one officer reflected on
why the draft had been so arduous to implement. He drew a direct connection to the 1904 Vaccine Revolt and the ideology of the house, "Military service of a compulsory character for all citizens is really an exotic
plant among us because it comes from other more prudent peoples and
never became part of Brazil's institutions. How could it be well received by
a society in which men live only for themselves? . . . Natives of Rio were
also hostile to collective hygiene, which hardly demanded anything from
the individual, *beyond not permitting one to defile the place where one lives,* all
of us remember the extreme public reaction against the prophylactic measures for small pox." This Young Turk lamented Brazilians' sensitivity to
what they perceived as public encroachment on the private sphere. The
LAMB retaliated by criticizing officers for lumping "those who combat the
draft lottery with those who combated the obligatory Vaccine [Law]."[96]

Fortuitous political breakthroughs accompanied the enthusiasm for
the LDN's unique lobbying and favorable press.[97] Senator Rui Barbosa's
Anglo- and Francophilia moved him to pressure the government to declare war on Germany very early in the conflict. His enthusiasm for this
political objective led this staunch antimilitarist politician to soften his

stance against conscription.[98] In addition, the congressional puppetmaster Pinheiro Machado was using all of his political leverage to manipulate the seating of federal deputies when an assassin brought an untimely halt to his machinations in September 1915. His death led to a breakdown of his Conservative Republican party (PRC), an interregional coalition of mostly rural coronéis who opposed a strong federal army. The 1915 draft debate included recriminations about the "egoistic" opposition of coronéis and the PRC. As one political foe put it, "With the advent of obligatory military service, the embryos of Pinheiro Machado if they are gestating will be fatally aborted." Another answered his own question in a veiled insult to Pinheiro Machado, "Can a *caudilho* maintain his tyranny with a national army that is not mercenary? No!"[99]

Draft opposition now rested mainly with labor unions and a few isolated intellectuals like Alberto Torres. One of the first Brazilian critics of biological determinism, Torres called conscription "the old panacea of the authoritarian spirit."[100] While dissent threatened to undermine conscription, the voices of opposition were drowned out by the clamorous gong of nationalist oratory. The mostly foreign-born labor leadership was an easy mark for xenophobic nationalists, who now depicted the draft's opponents as foreign extremists.[101]

Even the popular lyricist Leandro Gomes de Barros, who reprinted his 1906 song protesting the draft in 1916, changed his tune in 1917 when German U-boats sank four Brazilian freighters. Brazil declared war on Germany, and Gomes published a handbill of patriotic songs, "Echos da Pátria" (echoes of the fatherland). Gomes called on common Brazilians to volunteer to "defend our fatherland, honor, name, and national symbols."[102] He did not explicitly advocate conscription, but he did state, "The Brazilian army is very well disciplined, and a man's free will allows him to exercise his sacred right to give his life for the fatherland."[103] Faced with foreign aggression, this poet depicted enlisted service as a sacred duty.

Others joined the patriotic chorus. The son of a famous Paraguayan War commander, Fernando Luis Osorio Filho, penned *O espírito das armas brasileiras* (1918) to explain Brazil's patriotic history and its role in World War I to youth. It urged young men to join scouting and tiros and to enroll for the draft.[104] The State and citizens at large went out of their way to glamorize enlisted service.

Deputy Mário Hermes (nephew of former President Hermes) buried his fellow congressmen with data on the French and German armies. Several volumes of Congress' 1915 annals are weighted down with evidence Hermes dredged up to convince Congress to adopt conscription.[105] While most politicians agreed that conscription had to be undertaken soon, disputes arose over how best to realize this goal. One of the most pressing issues was how to produce adequate draft rolls.

Since 1913, Young Turks heaped criticism on conscription's reliance on draft registration. Captain Francisco da Paula Cidade observed that there had been no progress in draft enrollment. Examining returns from Rio Grande do Sul, he found that enrollment totals dropped by more than 50 percent from 1900 to 1913. In 1912, Porto Alegre enrolled only 180 men out of 150,000 residents. The next year the total jumped to 1,070 only because draft boards used lists of graduates from secondary schools. Many states, and even the nation's capital, did not send any data on enrollment at all. This evidence was presented to convince Congress that draft enrollment could not be relied upon.[106] As the LAMB forecasted years earlier, the State eventually resorted to using civil records for conscription.

Propaganda and the betterment of conditions did not change public perceptions of enlisted service overnight. To ensure the necessity of undertaking a draft, the 1908 law allowed for voluntary enlistment in only one month per year. Volunteers had to be literate and single. They also had to meet more rigorous health standards, and to provide testaments of good conduct from local officials.

The Rio newspaper *A Razão* alleged that these restrictions were unconstitutional and that they acted only to open gaps in the ranks to force the draft's realization.[107] The Young Turks, who may have imagined draft opponents paying poor men to volunteer to foil the draft, had argued for the adoption of this strategy. One politician echoed this fear: "The army [is] composed of men that join the ranks for food and shelter, making it a nucleus of indolent and unemployed individuals. I cannot divine any other option than the full application of the draft lottery with dispositions that make praça reenlistment possible only under special circumstances. . . . It is necessary . . . to substitute volunteers with draftees. . . . The application of a draft law will bring a spirit of discipline, developing among inductees the faculty of judgement, stimulating patriotism and civic sentiment; and the man who entered the barracks an uncultivated individual will emerge transformed by dwelling with comrades of a higher social level than those presently in the army."[108] A 1915 editorial penned by a Young Turk concurred, "The national defense situation is in such a state that complete disarmament would be preferable to the maintenance of the sad caricatures of a navy and army that embarrass us."[109] In the past, the "soldiers of misfortune" had been treated with ambivalence by officers. To justify the draft, the Young Turks and their allies humiliated praças by disparaging them as pariahs that lent the barracks the "aspect of a penitentiary rather than a school to prepare men to defend their nation."[110] No wonder the sergeants who plotted to overthrow the government in 1915 planned first to execute the Young Turks who publicly impugned their military honor!

Officials knew from experience that the State could not depend on voluntary registration to obtain adequate draft rolls. One Young Turk advised "abandoning all other methods" and instead using the civil registry initiated in 1890.[111] By 1916, birth registries would include most men of military age, making the timing of the draft's execution propitious. Without this bureaucratic tool, it would have been very difficult to conduct a draft. Registration would continue, but boards made draft lists based mostly on civil birth and voter registries. Still, this method was inefficient and cumbersome. The names of those who had died as children (a sizeable number given infant mortality rates) appeared on draft lists, proving Leandro Gomes de Barros prophetic when in 1906 he joked that even the dead would be drafted![112] Young men who moved from their place of birth and enrolled for the draft or to vote elsewhere were unjustly liable to be called up in both places. Civil birth records were often poorly organized, especially in rural areas, making urban youths more susceptible to the draft. These factors partially explain the large numbers of men who failed to report, but despite many problems, the draft became an annual event that continues to this day in Brazil.

New taxes and systems of weights and measures had inspired public uprisings, but the draft threatened more than household purse strings. It threatened the home's inviolability and hallowed patriarchal privileges. The image of the enlisted career itself had to be overhauled to make it less threatening to the dignity of humble homes and families. Only in 1916 did Congress pass the enabling legislation and funding to carry out conscription. Amid the uncertainties of World War I, important factions of the political elite mobilized to lobby for military preparedness. The ideology of eugenics moved many to reject orthodox positivist and classic Liberal notions of the State's role in promoting public welfare. Army officers, medical officials, and intellectuals saw in the draft a means to attack a variety of social ills that dampened jingoistic hopes for Brazil's national destiny.

The draft would not only build the State's brute institutional power, but it also subverted institutions and conceptions of patriarchy, race, and states' rights that undergirded the Old Republic's oligarchic order. But more important was the negotiation of the draft with the broader public. Enlisted service had to be made an honorable masculine duty by at least paying lip service to praças' contributions to collective security. Authorities argued that a conscript's personal honor would be enhanced by a closer association with national honor. Military service played a critical role in an international restructuring of gender roles in which willingness to serve in peacetime became a badge of manhood for the citizenry. While these new models of manhood were gaining ground in 1916, it took time and effort before they gained broader acceptance.

pushed to equate
manhood = military service
+
national
honor

Chapter 10

Making the Barracks a "House"

and the Army a "Family"

Assessing the Conscription Lottery,

1916–1945

The national draft lottery placed the army's most basic labor relations on a track that shifted ties between the military and larger Brazilian society. Some of these changes began in the early 1900s, but the draft added new dimensions. The transition was gradual, but the 1916 draft provided a new foundation upon which reformers would remodel the barracks into a "house." It also extended the military's influence in society.[1] By consolidating the central State's power over the management of legitimate violence, conscription fortified the State's hand while weakening structures, beliefs, and practices that had underpinned coronelismo. This analysis confirms criticisms of traditional depictions of the Old Republic as a time of extreme federalism in which the central State was weak and largely noninterventionist.[2] Despite arguments that the draft would depoliticize the army, however, the institution's new strength would be turned against the Old Republic's political machine, and praças came to pose serious threats to political stability.

The transformation of army enlisted service from 1916 to 1945 is worthy of another book in its own right, but here a concise presentation to illustrate salient changes and continuities will bring together the themes of preceding chapters. To place these interpretations in context, it is vital first to briefly examine the army, conscription, and politics.

The ideal of military professionalism, espoused most fervently by the Young Turks, was predicated on the idea that officers should dedicate themselves to military matters and eschew politics.[3] Despite the hopes and claims of reformers, however, the push for modernization ultimately had a destabilizing affect on the army hierarchy. As Frank D. McCann argues, by the end of World War I many officers realized, "though vaguely at first, that the political system was set against army reform because such reform would endanger the system."[4]

While the draft slowly altered the character of enlisted service, the officer corps was being overhauled under a French military mission in 1919. Many Germanophile Young Turks, who were moving into the army's intermediate ranks, opposed contracting a French mission. But a new generation of junior officers, influenced by the platform of the 1915 Sergeants' Revolt, began to emerge.[5] The differences between these groups of officers became manifest during a series of Tenente (lieutenant) Revolts in the 1920s.

Many officers became disillusioned with President Epitácio Pessoa when he appointed the first civilian war minister in years. Controversy also beset former President Hermes da Fonseca when he returned from a five-year European hiatus to begin an inauspicious run for the presidency. In an attempt to bolster a lackluster campaign, a widely circulated newspaper published falsified letters attributed to the leading Republican Party candidate, Arthur Bernardes. The letters insulted Hermes by referring to him as a *"sargentão"* (big sergeant), and confirmed the continuing low status of praça rank despite the draft. These forged affronts to military honor provoked army protests, but the Republican political machines saw to it that Bernardes won the election handily. Still, acts of military dissension continued, and rumors of a coup plot spread. Elected president of the army's political lobby, the Military Club, Hermes overstepped when he urged an officer in Pernambuco by telegram to disobey presidential orders in 1922. For this act, Bernardes ordered Hermes's arrest and closed the Military Club.[6]

Junior officers expressed outrage at Bernardes's actions using the language of honor in rancorous debates with superior officers. The State justified the Military Club's closing based on laws designed to repress prostitution rings. Junior officers argued that Bernardes impugned military honor by treating officers like pimps.[7] Incensed junior officers, who had pinned their hopes for reform to Hermes's coat tails, led the first Tenente Revolt on July 5, 1922, in Rio and Mato Grosso. The mutiny was quickly subdued, but its dramatic flair captured the popular imagination. Twenty-eight officers and praças hemmed in Rio's Copacabana Fort refused to surrender. Instead, they sallied forth, each with a piece of the fort's Brazilian flag in their breast pocket. Eleven unflinchingly made a suicidal attack on loyalist forces. Most were killed or seriously injured.[8] This bravado won public respect for the resolute nationalists willing to die for their love of country.

Inspired by these martyrs, veterans of the first revolt and other officers continued to conspire. The second Tenente Revolt occurred on July 5, 1924, when 1,000 rebel army troops and state policemen took control of the city of São Paulo. The rebels held Brazil's second largest city for three weeks until the army's indiscriminate bombardment moved rebel forces to beat a retreat. Swollen to a force of some 6,000 men, the rebels headed southward by train and hoof. About one-sixth of these forces would eventually join another group of rebels in Rio Grande do Sul commanded by Captain Luís Carlos Prestes. These forces devised a bold plan to fight a guerilla war of movement against the State marching through Brazil's interior. For over two years, the "Prestes Column" marched to the interior of the Northeast. Their hopes of raising a popular army among the poor proved quixotic, but their pluck won the sympathy of a growing number of officers, troops, and reform-minded civilians. The tenentes became the heroes of reformers who longed to transform Brazil's corrupt political system and agro-export economy. Harried for months by the army and its allies, the Prestes Column retreated to Bolivia, where many continued to conspire. Though they represented only a small minority of the army's officers and praças, many rebels came to exert a powerful influence over Brazilian politics.[9]

In 1930, the break many tenentes had been waiting for appeared. A dispute between the Republican machines of São Paulo, Minas Gerais, and Rio Grande do Sul over the 1930 presidential election produced a rift within the political elite. The insider candidate of São Paulo's Republican Party, Júlio Prestes, won the election over an opposition candidate from Rio Grande do Sul, Getúlio Vargas. Vargas, however, did not accept defeat gracefully. He began to purchase arms and plot with tenente forces in exile as well as with army officers and opposition politicians across Brazil. As noted in chapter 7, Vargas had served briefly as a praça in Mato Grosso during the Acre crisis. He had a special respect and rapport with army officers and enlisted men, unlike most of his civilian counterparts. Most army officers still resented the hubris of civilian politicians.

Vargas won the support of a number of army officers, most importantly Colonel Góes Monteiro who led rebel troops. However, most army officers did not join the revolt. In Rio Grande do Sul, only one battalion offered sustained resistance, and some 300 officers there presented themselves as prisoners to rebel forces. While only a minority of officers joined the rebels, many army NCOs played a decisive role leading rebel units. Many privates also joined insurgent forces.[10]

Before Júlio Prestes could assume office, rebel forces won key victories in the South and Northeast. President Washington Luís maintained the loyalty of most officers, particularly the Young Turks, whose professional philosophy militated against political activism. However, loyalist forces were in retreat. To turn the tide, Washington Luís called up army reservists in Rio, but this move backfired and fomented public hostility toward the State.[11] When put to its first test, the reserve system did more to bring down the State than defend it. As rebel forces continued to advance, Washington Luís's own high command in Rio deposed him. Vargas and his forces were received with delirious cheers by the citizens of São Paulo and Rio. Whether they realized it or not, these soldiers were probably the first to receive such a triumphal and spontaneous welcome to the capital. The public image of soldiers was beginning to be more closely identified with reform and the disinterested protection of "national" interests.[12]

The so-called 1930 Revolution was as much of a defeat for the traditional army hierarchy as it was for Washington Luís's government. Many tenentes would go on to become powerful politicians in their own right over the next three decades. Tenentes and those army officers who championed Vargas's revolt were given promotions. The promotion of many rebel NCOs to the commissioned ranks angered loyalist officers who feared their careers were jeopardized.[13]

Vargas's victory also marked a stinging defeat for São Paulo's political elite, a dominant force during the Old Republic. Paulista leaders were used to managing their own affairs and resented Vargas's oversight. To increase the central State's power, Vargas imposed a military governor in São Paulo and most other states as a check on the power of coronéis. Still, rural oligarchs, especially in Minas Gerais, were some of Vargas's strongest allies. A consummate politician, Vargas adroitly played antagonistic interest groups against one another to achieve his goals.

In 1932, the Paulista oligarchy teamed up with one of the Young Turks' most distinguished representatives, Colonel Bertholdo Klinger. The Paulista rebels hoped to capitalize on resentment in the army officer corps and among coronéis to topple Vargas's regime. Klinger led the Paulista's Constitutionalist Revolt, but most soldiers and officers remained loyal to Vargas. Although quelling the revolt was difficult, the victory strengthened Vargas's hand. It also taught him to move more gingerly with São Paulo's wealthy elite. The revolt provided Vargas with a prospect to purge some 515 officers (about one in ten officers) through exile or forced retirement, easing some of the tensions in the ranks.[14]

In 1933, a constitutional assembly promulgated a new charter, and elected Vargas president, the first former army praça, who'd never held a commissioned rank, to hold the highest office in the land. Still, Brazil was rife with sedition. Vargas depended on the military's support, leaning heavily on General Góes Monteiro. In the 1930s, the army was highly politicized; coup plots and insubordinate acts abounded. Some officers and enlisted men joined in right-wing fascist organizations, while others joined leftist groups, including Brazil's Communist party (now headed by Luís Carlos Prestes, the hero of the Prestes Column).[15] In 1934, the leader of a seditious movement of army NCOs in São Paulo called himself the "Fulgencio Baptista of Brazil," referring to the mulatto sergeant that came to power in Cuba at the head of an army sergeants' strike.[16] Armed revolt by organizations on both the left and right provided Vargas with a pretext to expel or summarily imprison suspect officer and praça agitators. A coup attempt by Brazilian Communists in 1935 and a fascist putsch in 1938 helped to justify and to consolidate Vargas's assumption of dictatorial powers. In 1937, with army backing, he disbanded Congress, abolished all political parties, and promulgated his New State (*Estado Novo*).

Vargas's new charter further undercut the power of coronéis by instituting elements of a welfare state. He also extended the franchise to literate men and women and established a secret ballot which made it more difficult for politicians to manipulate elections. While State benefits and protections did not reach most workers, they did protect a portion of the urban middle and working classes. Perhaps more importantly, Vargas's propaganda showcased these programs. He skillfully publicized his image as a reformer and cultivated the epithet "father of the poor" to expand his popular appeal.[17] Beyond creating and distributing government jobs in an era of economic hardship, Vargas's reform and expansion of the civil service improved bureaucracy and enhanced the draft's efficiency.

Vargas pleased his military supporters with a number of measures. He subordinated state police forces to the War Ministry, ending the autonomy of militarized state police forces that had been used as a hedge against federal intervention in state politics during the Old Republic. The army also made efforts to depoliticize the ranks and innoculate praças against communist ideology.[18] Vargas also tightened the enforcement of the draft in his 1939 Military Service Law. Now all adult males were required to prove that they had a reservist card (issued only by draft authorities) before applying for the growing number of government jobs, registering to vote, or qualifying for State benefits. New penalties were imposed on those who dodged the draft and fees were exacted from those not required to serve.[19] Those young men who wanted to take advantage of the possibilities offered by the new federal patronage had to cooperate with draft authorities. Problems persisted, but the system's efficiency improved.

Vargas's military and foreign policy glamorized enlisted service. By 1936, army enlisted troop strength mushroomed to 74,284 men. The army's role in socializing young men had undergone a dramatic expansion. The growth of troop strength outpaced that of the population, but it represented only a small portion of the 3,467,354 men of military age (twenty to thirty) counted in the 1940 census.[20]

Vargas soon put his new draft laws to a severe test. By 1944, praça ranks numbered 153,158 men, led by more than 10,000 officers.[21] That year Brazil mobilized the Força Expedicionária Brasileira (FEB), the only Latin American expeditionary force to fight alongside the allies in Europe. Army health officials examined 107,609 men for the expedition, initially rejecting only 23,236. Political forces from the right to the left came together to urge public support of the draft and the FEB. Many draftees and reservists relied on family influence to secure exemptions, but some prominent citizens served as praças, such as millionaire João Lage who married into the wealthy São Paulo Matarazzo clan soon after returning from

Europe.[22] Vargas had proven that the draft could raise a large force in times of crisis. His innovations included paying benefits to FEB families to curb the financial onus of service. Meanwhile, the army established the Liga Brasileira de Assistência (LBA), headed by the FEB commander's wife, to facilitate correspondence and aid the families of soldiers on the home front.[23] Symbolically, the army "family" was taking care of its own.

In 1945, Brazil's expeditionary forces won a hard-fought victory over an Aryan foe in the battle of Monte Castelo in Italy. This triumph boosted national pride and eased the fears of many that Brazil's racial heterogeneity would prevent Brazil from becoming a major world power.[24] Reports from the front emphasized that the real heroes fighting in Italy had been the common soldiers. Journalists dubbed the campaign the war of the *pracinhas* (dear little praças).[25]

At war's end, Vargas found his legitimacy as a dictator crumbling after fighting in a "war to save democracy." Nervous about popular veterans, Vargas and some members of the officer corps saw to it that most FEB members (*febianos*) were quickly demobilized after an ebullient victory parade for the first contingent of returning soldiers in Rio even though most veteran praças were unabashed Vargas supporters. Crowds greeted the first group of returning veterans with "all the effusiveness usually reserved for immediate friends and relatives."[26] They swarmed the street so that soldiers had to march single file through a gauntlet of handshakes, kisses, and hugs. The populace now embraced soldiers as if they were family; the barracks had never seemed so close to the house. One columnist praised the mob's sense of Brasilidade and claimed that the FEB's reception had outstripped by far those for King Albert, Brazil's aviation hero Santos Dumont, the Prince of Wales, and Theodore Roosevelt. Some soldiers lost buttons, badges, and belt buckles to those in the crowds seeking souvenirs. This prompted another reporter to critique the parade's disorderliness in the language of house and street because the civic solemnity became an "extemporaneous Carnival." He added that "displays of affection should be reserved for the recesses of the home." Instead, the veterans "on the street [should be treated] with the respect due to heroes."[27] Like the critiques foreigners made of the Parguayan War victory parade in 1870, some felt the febiano parade lacked the decorum appropriate to patriotic celebrations.

Despite Vargas's efforts to discourage their organization, febianos formed Brazil's first vibrant veterans' association of praças and officers.

Members still march in annual parades across Brazil trying to recapture some of the nationalist euphoria that went unmatched until Brazil won World Cup soccer championships in 1958, 1962, 1970, and 1994. As if anticipating these triumphs, one journalist stated that Brazilians were familiar with celebrity restricted to victories in soccer or the success of a musical group, but not in battle in Europe. A national holiday honoring enlisted men, Soldiers' Day, was inaugurated in 1945, and Vargas's daughter and personal secretary, Alzira Vargas de Amaral Peixoto, organized an LBA fund to donate twenty homes to widows of febianos in Rio.[28] More than 500 pages of new legislation established a more comprehensive set of benefits for febianos and their families. Even so, many still failed to take advantage of these new government programs due to a lack of adequate information on aid (complicated by the geographic dispersion of veterans), bureaucratic red tape, and because the assistance went against the grain of traditional clientalistic politics.[29]

The very military that had kept Vargas in office forced him to step down. By 1945 the officer corps could dispense with Vargas because they had gained new status and respect in national politics. They restored democracy and would continue to portray themselves as guardians of national interests and freedoms. Hereafter, civilian politicians who did not treat officers with respect could pay a high political price. Civil-military relations were qualitatively different.[30]

After 1945 the draft system's efficiency improved, but it did not achieve the ideal of universal male conscription. To this day, middle- and upper-class youths can usually succeed in gaining exemption from the draft. In 1940, one suggestion for overcoming the aversion of the better educated to enlisted service was to create separate class-based units. This would keep the sons of the middle and upper classes from serving alongside their lower-class countrymen, undercutting the army's national integration ideology.[31] This idea shared a similar logic to the creation of Voluntário da Pátria units during the Paraguayan War, but the Vargas government rejected it. Unlike impressment, which attempted to separate the "unprotected" from the honorable poor, conscription came to mark the social distance between the working and the middle classes after 1916.

The distance between the rhetoric and practice of universal male conscription hindered efforts of less-privileged citizens to imagine themselves as equal members of a nation where all sacrificed for the common good.

Still, the new rhetoric, practices, and ideologies of universal conscription helped to mystify and partially camouflage the divisions of class, race, ethnicity, and gender. It also gave many common citizens new arguments to have their service recognized and to demand new protections and rights from the State. Vargas was able to enhance the conscription's efficiency in large part because of his broader reforms of State bureaucracy, but the pre–Estado Novo draft made Vargas's successes at draft reform possible.

Changing Patterns of Army Recruitment

One of the greatest frustrations in researching recruitment after the 1880s is a lack of data. It is obvious that the army kept track of recruitment statistics, but after years of searching, numerous visits to bureaus and archives, and conversations with army officers and researchers, it became clear to me that it would not be possible to find recruitment figures. The evidence available, however, does indicate that conscription had a significant impact on the regional distribution of recruitment and the composition of the lower ranks.

Law required newspapers to print the names of draftees. Unfortunately, no published source brought all of these names together. It is probable that national security concerns led the army and politicians to suppress the publication or distribution of aggregate data. The data in figure 10.1 is an exception, as these figures were published in a major regional newspaper. These numbers have to be interpreted with caution because the army was in the midst of a major transformation. It was not only overhauling recruitment, but also seeking to expand the size of its forces. Estimates of the number of men inducted in this and subsequent years is complicated by a number of factors. First, while infantry were only required to serve one year, those in the cavalry and artillery continued to serve a minimum two-year contract. Second, some men who qualified could choose to stay on, meaning that demand for new conscripts would be reduced. Even so, some major new recruitment trends are easily discerned, most notably an increasing tendency to recruit men from areas near local garrisons.

The most salient feature is the size of Rio Grande do Sul's troop contribution. Nearly one-third of all draftees hailed from this southernmost state, which garrisoned about one-third of the army's forces. In the 1800s, Rio Grande do Sul had depended on troops from the Northeast for about

Table 5. 1916 Draft Lottery Recruitment Quota, by State

	#	%		#	%
Rio Grando do Sol (S)	1,821	30.7	Pará (N)	154	2.6
Federal District (SE)	513	8.7	Maranhão (NE)	101	1.7
São Paulo (SE)	483	8.2	Alagoas (NE)	74	1.2
Bahia (NE)	449	7.6	Paraíba (NE)	39	0.6
Minas Gerais (SE)	432	7.3	Sergipe (NE)	35	0.6
Paraná (S)	356	6.0	Piauí (NE)	34	0.6
Santa Catarina (S)	300	5.1	Amazonas (N)	32	0.5
Pernambuco (NE)	295	5.1	Goiás (CW)	24	0.4
Rio de Janeiro (SE)	279	4.7	Espírito Santo (SE)	23	0.4
Mato Grosso (CW)	276	4.6	Rio Grando do Norte (NE)	23	0.4
Ceará (NE)	179	3.0	Total	5,922	100.0

Source: A Federação (Porto Alegre), 4 January 1917, 1; also, see O Correio da Manhã (Rio), 10 December 1916, 3.

one-third of its ranks; after 1916, it supplied all of the enlisted men who served there. When grouped with the other two states from its region, Santa Catarina and Paraná, one finds that two of five privates were now recruited from the South, an area characterized by a disproportionate number of European immigrants and their descendants. This was more than three times the region's share of national male population and twice the proportion of its 1870s contribution. This factor must have weighed into Vargas's calculations of his chances of militarily defeating Washington Luís in 1930. Although there was resistance to Vargas's 1930 coup by a battalion in Porto Alegre, it took him only three days to quell resistance to his movement in Rio Grande do Sul. The rebels' slogan "gaúchos don't fight gaúchos" was calculated to appeal to the regional identity of local troops. Many of the praças in these battalions, composed almost exclusively by Rio Grande do Sul natives, joined Vargas's cadres in 1930. In 1971, Alfred Stepan observed that the "recruitment policy of the Brazilian army has traditionally been that of drafting men from an area as close as possible to each garrison," but it is important to note that this tradition began only after 1916.[32]

Why was the South, particularly Rio Grande do Sul, required to pay such a large share of the tribute of blood? The congressional commission on land forces declared itself "frankly in favor" of the trend toward local service. They stressed that by "maintaining men in their states, it moderates the burden of service and facilitates mobilization considerably" of

Table 6. Regional Breakdown of the 1916 Draft Lottery Compared to 1920
Population Data and 1870–1882 Recruitment Data

	1916	%	% Male Population 1920 Census	% Recruits 1870–82
Northeast	1,229	20.8	35.0	52.5
Southeast	1,730	29.2	45.0	16.3
South	2,477	41.8	12.0	19.7
Cent. West	300	5.1	3.0	5.8
North	186	3.1	5.0	3.8
Foreign	0	–	–	1.9
Total	5,922	100.0	100.0	100.0

Sources: A Federação (Porto Alegre), 4 January 1917, 1; IBGE, Estatística Histórica do Brasil, 2nd ed. (Rio de Janeiro: IBGE, 1990), 34; appendix B.2, B.3, and B.6.

both recruits and reserves.[33] As Rio Grande do Sul would be the first line of defense against Brazil's most threatening rival, Argentina, this policy had obvious strategic advantages. Many leaders of Rio Grande do Sul, more keenly than their counterparts elsewhere, appreciated the need for a defense to deter invasion and police the borderlands.[34]

Another significant trend is the massive reduction in the Northeast's troop contribution. This region had supplied more than half of the nation's soldiery in the 1870s, but with the 1916 draft lottery, this proportion had dropped to one-fifth, well below the region's 35 percent share of male population in 1920. But even though the percentages of northeasterners recruited was reduced, more than half still served outside their home region mostly in garrisons in or around Rio.

The proportion of the Southeast's troop contribution nearly doubled that of the 1870s, but it was still well below the region's share of male population. The Capital District's large garrison continued to depend on troops from other states, and in this sense, Rio's battalions continued to "integrate" troops from across the country into a "national" military culture, conserving the army's self-proclaimed role as an "agent of national integration." Even though troops from across the nation served in Rio, three out of four recruits now remained in their home state.

The army's initial execution of conscription was far from a complete success. In 1918 the war minister who oversaw conscription's implementation observed that only 3,709 of 7,139 draftees called up had reported. But he felt that this was a good result considering Brazil's "extensive size, the difficulties of communication, and the Brazilian people's lack of faith in obligatory service, which has been attempted more than once since 1874."[35] Others concurred noting that even in Prussia, a nation with a dense population living in a relatively small area and with an "enviable unity of race," it had taken more than fifty years to make the draft run well.[36] By 1936, one officer noted that the number of those not reporting for the draft had fallen "appreciably." He ascribed this change to better conditions in the barracks, new attitudes, and more energetic draft enforcement.[37]

Conscription was intended to resolve problems that had burdened army discipline, but draft enforcement initially swamped it. In 1918, the STM heard 384 cases of draft dodging, 885 in 1919, and 814 in 1920. From 1921 to 1925, however, only 12 men accused of *insubmissão* (draft dodging) were convicted. As courts-martial became less zealous, officers complained that the draft was being "demoralized." In 1926, Major Pedro Cavalcanti warned that "progressively, the enforcement of the [draft] law has been loosened by increasing exemptions, and by [the impunity] of draft dodgers. He deplored the fact that the sons of privileged families, who should be setting an example, were using writs of habeas corpus to avoid military service.[38] Most Brazilians, however, could not afford or chose not to elude the draft through the civil courts.[39] In 1920, when a detachment marched in a parade given in honor of the visiting Belgian king, a Brazilian politician exclaimed to an officer in the grand stand, "Your battalions are so minuscule!" The officer lividly replied, "Yes they are, and they could be reduced to the complement of officers if one simple municipal judge decided to grant all soldiers a writ of habeas corpus." Bemoaning the "desertion of the flag" by Brazil's youth, Cavalcanti called for tougher laws to enforce the draft.[40]

Obviously, there were problems with the draft, but that it worked at all is perhaps the most telling sign of new attitudes toward enlisted service. Many units remained undermanned, but this was a period when army forces were in a phase of expansion from some 16,000 praças in 1915 to 43,812 by 1930.[41] The draft's ability to raise recruits was more efficient and less disruptive than impressment. While many still preached against the draft, the tumults that had occurred during the late empire were notably absent. New attitudes about a citizen's duty to perform military duty

Table 7. Numbers and Percentages of Recruits Required to Serve Outside Their Home State and Region

State	#	State	#	Region	#	%
Minas G.	342	Paraná	35	NE	649	39.6
São Paulo	252	Piauí	34	SE	809	49.4
Bahia	197	Amazonas	32	South	64	3.9
Rio de J.	187	Santa C.	29	CW	36	2.2
Pernambuco	123	E. Santo	28	North	81	4.9
Ceará	76	Goiás	24	Total	1,639	100.0
Alagoas	74	RGN	23			
Pará	49	Mato G.	12			
Maranhão	48	RGS	0			
Paraíba	39	Fed. Dist.	0			
Sergipe	35	Total	1,639			

Source: A Federação (Porto Alegre), 4 January 1917, 1.

emerged even among privileged sectors. Popular journalist João do Rio was impressed by the look and respectability of conscripts he visited after the first draft compared to those who served in previous years.[42]

How effective was conscription in recruiting a different class of soldier? Officers expressed a variety of opinions. In his 1929 address to Brazil's first eugenics conference, medical officer Colonel Dr. Arthur Lobo da Silva remarked, "It has already been a long time since army personnel [in Brazil and Argentina] have been constituted by the population's most infamous strata. . . . Some undesirables still appear, but most of our soldiers come from the laboring classes of society (small farmers, artisans, commercial employees, public employees, and so on) . . . Despite the [draft's] multiple defects, originating in the pitiful organization of the civil birth registry, which impedes a considerable number of boys from being called up, the new soldier finds in the barracks young men more or less well mannered, of good morals, and from different social classes."[43] Da Silva implies that the ideals of Olavo Bilac and the LDN had been realized.

Da Silva gathered data from his post in the Headquarters of Army Health. In 1928, he published "Anthropology in the Brazilian Army," a study of some 40,000 draftees between age twenty and twenty-two from across Brazil. Only two of five recruits were rural workers, but interestingly, they were not listed as sem ofício (without a skilled occupation), as almost 90 percent of troops were described in 1896 career records sur-

Table 8. Draftee Occupational Data, 1922–1923

Profession	Apt	Temporarily Exempt	Always Exempt	Total
Farmers/Rural Laborers	11,760	1,472	1,278	14,510
Urban Laborers	9,376	1,666	955	11,997
Artists	144	16	20	180
Commercial Emloyees	4,508	1,062	531	6,101
Public Employees	1,305	299	179	1,783
Liberal Professionals	222	54	23	299
Students	917	279	88	1,284
Sailors (reenlisting)	409	69	28	506
Army (reenlisting)	935	24	7	966
Without a Profession	817	129	67	1,013
Total	30,393	5,070	3,176	38,639*

Source: Derived from data in Colonel Dr. Arthur Lobo da Silva, "A Anthropologia no Exército Brasileiro," *Arquivos do Museu Nacional*, vol. 30, Rio (1928): quadro 7.
*This count is 36 less than the total presented in da Silva's graph, but his figures for draftees without a profession did not add up.

veyed in chapter 7. Thus, da Silva stresses that they were employed, "honorable" men. Since more than half of Brazil's populace lived in the countryside, rural men were underrepresented in the draft, reflecting the underdeveloped state of bureaucracy in rural areas where birth registration "appeared to be a myth." The reliance on civil birth registries to compose draft lists meant that the army tapped into a different sector of the population. Impressment drew heavily from those more likely to be undocumented: rural migrants, vagrants, and orphans. Now, these men were less likely to appear on draft rolls. Thus, the draft drew mostly from "state capitals and larger cities," and some urged that all troops be drawn from urban zones.[44]

Urban workers together with commercial and public employees constituted more than half of those inspected. The categories of commercial and public employee were rather vague, and could potentially range from a stock boy or a doorman to a bank manager or physician. For da Silva, most conscripts employed in commerce were "subaltern" employees from the "humble" classes, and those who volunteered tended to come from even more precarious backgrounds. For many recruits the barracks offered unknown luxuries. One recruit's 1924 memoir recorded that many conscripts had never worn boots, slept on a mattress, or used anything for covers other than a jute blanket. The draft also drew some students and professionals, but da Silva noted that those who were wealthier or well connected almost always found a way of exempting themselves.[45]

Da Silva's data shows that less than 5 percent of those who passed the physical examination were reenlisting soldiers or sailors. Now the armed forces were rotating many more younger men through the ranks for one or two years of training. In this manner, the army greatly extended its incorporation of a broader cross-section of the male population, drawing more heavily from the "honorable" urban poor. Less than 3 percent of those called up were listed as unemployed, and as da Silva suggested, most of the unemployed were volunteering. Enlisted service ceased to be a career that depended heavily on the "criminally idle."

In 1930, the governor of Paraíba renewed efforts to "moralize" the draft. He reported that "the abuse of arranged exclusions is what reduces to a ridiculous minimum the list of young men apt for the barracks—already . . . the draft lottery in this state is approaching reality. The result: Paraíba did not have one reported draft dodger [this year]."[46] The draft oscillated between crackdowns and lax enforcement, but one must take this official self-promotion with a grain of salt.

Most interpretations of the draft have emphasized its shortcomings. José Murilo de Carvalho found that in Brazil's first military enlistment zone in 1938, 28,753 of 40,074 men called up did not report for their required health inspection. Of the men who did report, only 6,398 were inducted.[47] Clearly, many who did not report were purposely dodging the draft, but the draft system had tremendous bureaucratic problems. New publicity strategies and bureaucratic development would slowly improve draft compliance, and the barracks appeared to be inching away from the street toward the house. Draft authorities learned that it was vital to call up many more men than they intended to conscript to achieve often less-than-satisfactory results. The fact that they only inducted 6,398 men (as Carvalho observed) may have been because that was all the men they required from the first enlistment zone. Even under much-improved conditions and stricter standards of enlistment in 1984, the army selected 727,345 of 1,407,211 enrolled. Of these only 358,548 were judged apt for service, and 138,543 were eventually incorporated. Medical exams excluded 70 percent of those drafted.[48] These figures demonstrate the draft lottery's continuing problems with gaining fuller public cooperation, but they do not appear to justify assertions that before 1945, "The only way to leave military service, not only for officers, but also for NCOs and for most enlisted men, was either by expulsion or by completing 25 to 30 years of service."[49] In the light of da Silva's evidence on the low reenlistment rates (5 percent of recruits in 1922–23), it seems difficult to hold that conscripts served for twenty-five years. An inspector for the rural sanitation service at Rio's Vila Militar surveyed 699 praças: 47 were aged seventeen to nineteen, 558, twenty to twenty-five; 64, twenty-six to thirty; and 30, thirty-one to forty.[50] By law, men over age thirty-five were not to serve as privates. Clearly NCOs served for many years, but most conscripts served brief terms.

Despite attempts to enforce standards, army officers continued to complain about their recruits' health and education. In 1918, an article "Obtuse Recruits" griped that some volunteers and draftees were "truly retarded." After more than four months of training they still did not know their left from their right.[51] As late as 1940, General Eurico Gaspar Dutra complained that Brazilians had demonstrated a "visceral rebellion" against enlisted army service. He went on to note that three of five draftees were illiterate and half, physically unfit.[52] But poor health should not obscure changes in the composition of the lower ranks in terms of recruits' social status.

In da Silva's 1922–23 survey, only one in five soldiers did not pass the physical examination; they were either temporarily exempted until they recovered from an illness or permanently excused from service. The leading cause of rejection was weakness of constitution followed by venereal disease; diseases or defects of the eyes, ears, nose and throat; respiratory problems; inadequate height (the minimum was 1.52 meters); and physical defects. Army health statistics raised the concerns of officers and health officials about consequences of venereal disease for national defense and the nation's "race." One 1936 article "Caring for the Race" explained, "On the day Brazilians are a sexually educated people, Brazil will no longer be an agglomeration of ethnicities without a characteristic profile and without the ability to take advantage of the possibilities that our future and our greatness demand."[53] Sexual diseases allegedly hindered the formation of a eugenic and homogenized "national race." According to the *Boletim de Educação Sexual* in 1935, "Brazil's greatest problem is combating venereal disease," and it called for a national Sex Day dedicated not to sex but to sex education.[54]

Recruits' physical inadequacies and diseases were fairly evenly spread through occupational and racial categories, but intriguingly, whites had the highest rejection rate. Perhaps this occurred because whites were better able to use influence to be excused from service. One officer recounted a story he heard being told by a railway worker who feared losing his job because he had been drafted. When he went for his health inspection, he found a doctor to whom he had "appealed" for assistance. The doctor falsely evaluated the railman as having tuberculosis, thereby exempting him.[55] It is difficult to know how common this practice was.[56]

Draft health inspections confirmed the findings of civilian public health experts in the 1910s. The draft made the medical community more conscious of the wretched health of Brazil's poor — protected and unprotected alike. Studies showed that more than 90 percent of recruits suffered from parasites.[57] The social knowledge provided by troops' health statistics fed criticism of the Old Republic's political order, which resisted the expansion of State intervention in public health. If Brazil hoped to field an army capable of fending off Argentines, much less Europeans, they had to develop their human resources.

As officials began to organize the first draft lottery, civilian physicians popularized the phrase that "Brazil is an immense hospital." Newspapers carried stories of their public lectures on the sorry state of public health among the poor. Many civilian physicians involved in the sanitation movement came to support conscription as a public health initiative. Like draft advocates, health reformers wanted more centralized federal regulation. Both groups faced largely the same opponents, since objections to both conscription and the creation of a national health ministry were rooted in the constitutional principle of states's rights. Soon after a draft was implemented, health reformers would win their battle to establish a centralized health ministry in 1919.[58] Civilian health officials treated soldiers, and many reservists found jobs in public health services. In these cases, promises that veterans would be given preference when competing for federal jobs were met, indicating an affinity between health and military reforms.[59]

Lobbyists had stressed the draft's utility for spreading the gospel of hygiene and promoting race "improvement." At least one officer would use data from health inspections to "prove" this assertion. His arguments provide insight into an era in which Brazilians were rethinking ideas of Brasilidade in terms of race and were using the armed forces as a microcosm of the nation. The army claimed it would "make Brazilians" out of recruits, meaning healthy and disciplined citizens. Officers used health statistics and other evidence to establish the army's role in developing a healthier, more homogeneous, and more cohesive populace.

army can "health" ify nation

The Army, the Draft, and Eugenics

In the 1920s, soldiers became the object of health and anthropological studies conducted by the army's medical corps and civil officials linked to the Rural Sanitation movement. In the post–World War I era, some officers seemed obsessed with Brazil's genetic and racial development, just as many in the post–World War II era became obsessed with economic development.[60] Officers made alliances with civilian eugenists, but eugenic thought was far from monolithic. In Brazilian prisons, anthropomorphic measures were used by criminologists to determine physical traits that would supposedly indicate a proclivity for antisocial behavior. Self-styled army "anthropologists" used similar measures to prove the draft was a eugenic engine for race "improvement."[61]

Army "scientists" discovered in recruit health inspections an exotic parade of common Brazilian culture that they studied with a distance akin to foreign anthropologists. Captain Dr. Alfredo Brandão examined three hundred tatoos on draftees in Maceió and Recife. Most tatoos were religious symbols (the most popular being of King Solomon). More "worldly" reenlisting soldiers had "more developed" tatoos, generally relating to the profession of arms (cannons, swords, rifles); one had the Brazilian flag tattooed on his forearm, difficult to interpret expressions of popular nationalism and identification with the army. For some, tatoos may have been a way of resisting the impersonal uniformity of army life, asserting an indelible mark of individuality. Tatoo culture was cultivated by military enlisted men around the globe during the era of major military mobilizations in the 1900s, but Dr. Brandão believed that tatoos revealed "either individual ignorance or backward social origins." He supported this hypothesis by arguing that most recruits with tatoos came from the countryside.[62] Reformers studied their subjects from a posture of assured superiority, but these sometimes-sneering nationalists aimed to socialize draftees into the "national life."

Unlike England and the United States, Brazil did not dismantle its conscription system after World War I. To the contrary, efforts were made to bolster it, and to expand the army's enlisted forces. Dr. Belisário Augusto de Oliveira Penna's *The Army and Sanitation* (1920) clearly linked the draft to sound eugenic practices. Penna linked the efforts of civilian public health experts to those of the army by actively supporting the LDN's efforts to implement and encourage public cooperation with the draft.[63] Penna, like many army officers, was a severe critic of the Old Republic's political and social order. "We extinguished black slavery and then proclaimed a regime governed by the people and for the people and the result is a generalized slavery to the regime of illness, ignorance, loans, taxes. . . . We have arrived at a point of putridness that urges an energetic reaction from the good elements remaining . . . to save our nationality, in imminent risk of disaggregation, first, and later by absorption by other peoples."[64]

Like the poet and draft advocate Olavo Bilac, Penna feared national dissolution. Public health would be a way to stir nationalist fervor, "The propaganda communicated intelligently in schools, high schools, factories, barracks, and farms in simple clear language . . . [will make public] health an object of a true and even religious cult."[65] Penna cited Herbert Spencer's maxim, "To be a good animal is the first condition for success in life; to be a nation of good animals is the first condition for national prosperity." Penna argued that many young men sought exemptions from the draft because of the poor health conditions in the barracks. The army had to provide more sanitary lodging, deliver better health care, combat alcoholism, and prevent the spread of syphilis by deterring contacts between soldiers and unregulated prostitutes. Presumably, this concern also extended to intercourse among troops, but eugenists were largely silent on this issue compared to their predecessors. Perhaps they sought to protect the public image of enlisted service by remaining quiet on the issue. For Penna, physicians would play a special role in the struggle to improve Brazil's "race" by treating praças ill with preventable diseases while teaching about hygiene.[66] As Nancy Ley Stepan stated, "Throughout the 1920s, eugenics was associated with patriotism and the call for a larger role for Latin America in world affairs. In Brazil, more specifically, the subjects of wartime readiness and discipline, of control and order, of Brazilian capacities and racial capabilities, were much on the minds of the elites."[67] While Stepan noted the link between military preparedness and racial concerns, little notice has been given to how officers used eugenics to prove the draft's vigor for race "improvement."

Draft records record a rare wealth of statistical data on young Brazilian males. Colonel Dr. Arthur Lobo da Silva demonstrated a keen interest in defining "Brazilian types," because as he believed, "even one hundred years into the future, there will not be a [single] Brazilian type."[68] He advocated that the army develop an "obligatory anthropometric service" to gather data on variations in draftee body types. Modeled after the service set up by the United States military during World War I, these methods originated in the studies of Cesare Lombroso and others.

Da Silva's enthusiasm for anthropometric measures stemmed from a desire to establish eugenic standards to gauge Brazil's racial "progress." He followed standards established by biological anthropologists like Roquette Pinto who worked at the prestigious Museu Nacional in Rio.[69] A draftee's height, weight, and chest would be measured when he had his health inspection, and once again upon his discharge. The data was used, according to a French eugenist formula, to calculate "robustness" and measure the efficiency of army training in race improvement. Like most French and Italian physicians, Brazilian eugenists accepted a neo-Lamarkian interpretation of genetic science or the belief that environment had an impact on genetic development. In 1929, da Silva gathered evidence from 7,820 inductees, and found that 90 percent of these soldiers had improved their robustness upon discharge. Although eugenists lavished much of their literature on women's hygiene, with conscription, the State touched in a more profound way the lives of much larger numbers of young men.[70]

In "Anthropology of the Army," da Silva indirectly suggests the draft's eugenic benefits for the "whitening" of Brazil's "race." He outlined five steps in Brazil's march toward whiteness: the decline of the "savage" (Indian) population, the gradual "extinction" of the African, increasing "white" immigration from Europe, and the amenable climate of southern Brazil (southerners would be less tan one would surmise). In his survey of draftees, da Silva found that nearly 59 percent were white; 29 percent, mestizo; 10 percent, black; and 1 percent, Indian.[71] Interestingly, da Silva noted that whites were initially the least "robust" group, but upon discharge, they had the highest rates of improved robustness. The data seems to contradict the idea that whites were genetically superior, but it could also be read as an indication that whites responded "better" to rigorous exercise, proper diet, hygiene, and basic medical treatment. If the draft improved the robustness of whites more than nonwhites, da Silva insinuates that robust white veterans would thus be more likely to pass on their eugenically improved genes to the next generation. Why else would da Silva preface his article with a discussion of whitening and racial homogenization before analyzing the draft's eugenic benefits? He concluded that the relative weakness of entering white recruits was due to the different jobs that blacks, mestizos, and caboclos generally practiced, suggesting that nonwhites tended to perform more strenuous physical labor.[72] Not all officers shared da Silva's views on the draft and race. Many civilian eugenists who supported the draft discarded race as a means of explaining the poor health of Brazilians. As Dr. Belisário Penna flatly put it when addressing the Military Club on public health, "Race has nothing to do with it."[73]

Some of the eugenic rhetoric later subsided among officers. In 1935, Góes Monteiro, Vargas's right-hand man who had led the rebel army during the 1930 Revolution, at the very least gave lip service to the dismissal of biological determinism, "Before suggesting education as the only advisable path for our real progress, we cite the judicious words of Alberto Torres as a rebuttal to the issue of race, 'It would simply be a vain pretension of ethnic nobility to affirm that the Brazilian black or Indian is inferior to the white.'"[74] Racist practices and beliefs, however, lingered in the army and larger civilian society: many became enshrined in national myth and popular culture.

In 1929, Colonel da Silva echoed Olavo Bilac's jingoism. He stressed the army's importance as a national school of "civics, physical [fitness], hygiene, moral improvement, and as a factor of eugenics or the betterment of individuals and the race." Army bases would develop draftees' brains by teaching illiterates how to read and write while instructing all about Brazil's laws and history.[75] After all, fears of ethnic and racial divisions within Brazil had been revived in the 1930s. Even after World War II, some still warned that further steps were needed to prevent the "disfigurement of our ancestral physiognomy" and "to accelerate the fusion of those heterogeneous elements [namely Italians, Germans, Japanese, and other groups] in the national organism."[76] Some officers made laudatory claims that the army had returned a large number of newly literate soldiers to the community, stating that the army had "made them Brazilians."[77] This rhetoric placed the army at the center of nationalist revivalism: a factory of "true" Brazilian citizens. Evidence indicates that regimental schools were not very effective in promoting primary instruction, even though some specialized primers were prepared.[78] Claims that Italo-, Nipon-, and Tueto-Brazilian recruits, who did not speak Portuguese, had quickly learned the language are more believable.[79]

While primary instruction may have been poor, most officers did insist that enlisted men be indoctrinated in the ritual and cultural forms of nationalism. Officers complained, for instance, that soldiers could not sing the national anthem. They produced military song books to instruct soldiers in the army's musical heritage, and placed a greater emphasis on reverence for the flag and national holidays. For many, this was their first exposure to patriotic culture.[80] Again, these practices would be found with greater regularity in urban centers, but General Rondon was praised for his maintenance of a flag pavilion even when stringing telegraph line through the Amazon.[81]

While da Silva's arguments for the draft lottery are tainted with the racist goal of whitening, others used eugenic arguments to reject aspects of biological determinism. Gilberto Freyre turned some racist fictions on their head by arguing that Africans were "eugenically" sound. Interestingly, Freyre's idea for his first book came when he spied a group of bedraggled Brazilian sailors in New York while he was studying at Columbia University with Franz Boas. He thought to himself that "it was not simply mulattos and cafuzos who I judge best represented Brazil, but *ill mulattos and cafuzos.*"[82] For Freyre, the illnesses that affected Brazilians did not have their origins in genetics, but in social conditions. Once again, military and public health concerns inspired a rethinking of race and nationality.

Freyre reasoned that race mixture in Brazil had created a people uniquely adapted to their tropical environment, establishing a "racial democracy." This analysis emphasized that racism was not a prominent feature in Brazilian culture. He contrasted race relations in Brazil favorably against those of the United States. Although Freyre trivialized the racism that minimized the opportunities of nonwhites, he created a more inclusive and positive national identity that celebrated Brazil's miscegenation, as did Latin American intellectuals in other nations in this era.[83] Freyre did not invent the concept of racial democracy, but he gave it greater coherence, intellectual legitimacy, and a nationalist impetus. Most Brazilians, including army officers, would embrace the ideology of racial democracy as a quality that proudly distinguished Brazil from other nations.[84] Like America's Horatio Alger myth, the myth of racial democracy has tenaciously withstood an onslaught of studies that demonstrate its fallacies. The tenacity of both myths likely lies in their ability to help their citizens to imagine themselves members of a distinct, leveled, and homogenized national community.

Still some officers espoused racist rhetoric that suggested the superiority of Caucasians, "In the miscegenation of races and peoples that constitute the substratum of Brazil's race we find that always the European element dominates in this melting pot which in the past brought us a European culture and carries us toward a North-American culture today."[85] In accordance with this school of thought, the 1942 instructions for entrance to the military academy and military preparatory schools established restrictions on the basis of race, religion, family background, and ideology. This meant that Jews, blacks, the sons of immigrants, and those whose parents had divorced or had suspect ideological views were barred from the main gateway to a commissioned officer's rank—a reversal of less-discriminatory entrance policies and a crass move to whiten the officer corps.[86] Even the mulatto author Lima Barretto (a novelist, conscription opponent, and civilian employee of Rio's army arsenal) believed the army was more color blind than other institutions at the turn of the century. He wrote, "I am beginning to believe the only moral thing in this land is still the army, which respects the merit of candidates." However, he also noted that, because he was "mulatto or black," he was offended when whites inquired whether he was really an employee of the arsenal clerical staff.[87]

In its propaganda, officers claimed that the army had been a bastion of racial tolerance, embracing Freyre's apology for Brazil's racially stratified patriarchal society.[88] To support this point, propagandists referred to the support of army officers like Colonel Sena Madureira for abolition in the 1880s and to the fact that the army had always incorporated all races.[89] President Vargas showcased Afro-Brazilian Carnival as a tourist attraction and symbol of Brazil's unique national heritage, but he also maintained a presidential honor guard drawn largely from blond, blue-eyed German immigrants from the state of Santa Catarina to impress upon foreign dignitaries that Brazil was a white nation. Ambivalence typified the way the army, the State, and the broader public embraced more inclusive ideals of national and racial identity.[90] The practice of racial inclusion did not live up to the rhetoric of racial democracy.

Praças also expressed awareness of racial and national identity. A black sergeant and febiano revealed to a reporter in 1945 that the Germans had nicknamed him the "black eagle" for his intrepid leadership of his platoon. He added, "There I was a Brazilian and a representative of the black race."[91] It is interesting to note that the sergeant emphasized that "there" (in Italy) he was both a Brazilian and a representative of the black race, possibly indicating that in Brazil these two identities were not as palpable or separable for him.

Even though the army's position on race was often hypocritical, the inclusion of a broader cross-section of the "respectable" poor in public service from all races meant that common citizens could make claims for services from the State. Petitions for government help or intercession had long been based on services rendered to the State.[92] Thus, enlisted service indirectly legitimated a more inclusive political system and the establishment of social welfare programs. This is similar to scholarly observations that conscription's dissemination in North Atlantic nations pushed the expansion of franchise and social welfare systems.[93] The growing reliance on the urban working classes to fill the army's lowest ranks complemented the emergence of urban populism in Brazil in the 1930s — even though active-duty praças to this day are prohibited from voting. Fears that praça ranks would be politicized by the vote undergirded this policy.

Civilian attitudes toward soldiers were also changing. One newspaper chain began to publish medical advice on how to gain weight to pass military health inspections because many frustrated young men were rejected by the army because of their slight physiques.[94] One officer reported that a large landholder he befriended believed men who had served in the army were better employees because they were "punctual and had a sense of duty." An editorial noted that the citizens of the small town of Pouso Alegre, Minas Gerais, feared the new barracks established there, but soon they found that the local soldiers were well behaved and respectful. They also spurred local commerce. The army did provide a new source of

13. Smartly uniformed army praças outside a newly inaugurated construction site for a barracks compound in 1922. The band photo illustrates the improving image and conditions of soldiering. Companhia Construtora de Santos. Quartel do Quitauna, Osasco, São Paulo Armario 12.2.9, 10 de Outubo de 1922, no. 4 *Courtesy of Biblioteca Nacional, Divisão de Inconografia. Photo developed from archival originals by Claudio de Carvalho Xavier.*

industrial-style training. It taught men to follow a schedule, to be more hygienic, and to take a new approach to performing tasks that may not have been common to many workers. It is difficult to say how generalized this feeling was, but even novelist Graciliano Ramos, a political prisoner during the Estado Novo and hardly a friend of the army, wrote that in his rural town in Alagoas, "the best workers, the most capable ones, had been soldiers."[95]

The Labor Ministry's bulletin reminded unions and industrialists that in the past the tradition of vagrants in the military was so common that veterans were considered indolent and unserviceable for civilian employment. But in 1944, all citizens could take pride in the soldier's uniform because it "denotes his physical robustness and his perfect mental equilibrium."[96] Members of the poor also voiced favorable attitudes toward the draft, which facilitated and motivated some sons of very poor families to get work papers allowing them to enter the documented working class.[97] Ex-praças probably did bring some of their education and habits home. Health care and hygienic education in the barracks probably did have a positive influence on public health while promoting the spread of patriotic culture. Even so, many ex-soldiers had a hard time readapting to civilian life; hygiene and patriotism were not the only things recruits learned in the barracks. As noted earlier, some recruits became adepts of leftist and right-wing groups, and some gave themselves over to debauchery. The control elites hoped to exert over the poor through the draft, penitentiaries, and other public institutions seemed illusory.

Remodeling the Barracks

The enlisted ranks' changing composition was accompanied by a linguistic repositioning that resonated with the ideology of the house. Army officers began to describe the relationships of obedience and hierarchy with praças in terms of the family and love.[98] In 1920, the war minister reasoned that if the State asked all families to present their sons for the draft, the army had to make the barracks an "extension of the home" where superiors exercised a fatherly authority.[99] The authority of officers was accorded the natural respectability and legitimacy of society's most fundamental institution.

Before conscription, it is difficult to imagine officers stating: "It is, thus, the obligation of every instructor to make himself loved by his soldiers."[100] When impressment filled the army's ranks with men from the dangerous classes, officers tended to espouse the draconian eighteenth-century philosophy of Frederick the Great, "Soldiers should fear their officers more than the enemy." Benedict Anderson and Doris Sommer stress the value of "love" in expressing nationalist sentiments as opposed to other identities.[101] Others have noted, however, that on the battlefield, it is the bonds of personal relationships that soldiers most often mention as their motivation to risk their lives, not abstract notions of patriotism.[102] While these two sentiments are in no way mutually exclusive, it is in the remembrance of fallen comrades that the love of country is most strongly expressed. War memorials to unknown soldiers are intended to represent the "ultimate sacrifice" as a selfless expression of love for one's fatherland and people.[103] Brazilian rhetoric reflected a transition in the development of more inclusive nationalist ideology that sought to control and develop honorable poor masculine youths for national defense.

The draft gave officers the freedom to rebuild the barracks in the form of a house that sheltered the "respectable" extended fraternal family of the nation. As Captain Gerardo Lemos do Amaral put it, "The army is a family that lives in the shadow of the flag. . . . Trusting each one of his comrades as if he were a brother, the military family will always be prepared . . . to emerge victorious."[104] In this manner, propagandists moved the barracks from the realm of the street into that of the house. They remodeled the barracks into a national house, an "honorable" vessel that protected and developed national masculine virtue.

Even the Catholic church, which had not supported conscription (as noted earlier, some priests had been implicated in efforts to undermine the draft in the 1870s), blessed new attitudes toward the draft and soldiers. One cleric published a book for soldiers that drew examples of valor and rectitude from sacred texts with incisive subtitles: "insidious deserters"; "an army defeated by the sin of one soldier"; "victorious over the enemy but defeated by women"; and "the height of devotion, immolating oneself for others." This familial and religious rhetoric was in no way unique to Brazil. The U.S. Navy waged a similar campaign to better sailoring's image. As the southern prohibitionist politician and Navy Secretary Josephus Daniels preached in 1914, "I am the father of more than 50,000 young men . . . and there is nothing more upon my heart than to see them of strong Christian character, living clean lives for home and kindred and country." In 1890, the army translated an Italian book on a soldier's moral education, and its language likely influenced that of Brazilian reformers: "The army should be considered a school where future *fathers of families* learn order and respect for the law" (emphasis added).[105]

The extent to which the public and soldiers embraced State propaganda is difficult to gauge. Private Oswaldo Barroso's 1924 memoir is a rare document of a draftee's experiences during the interwar period. Called up from rural São Paulo, Oswaldo maligned the lottery, arguing that coronéis manipulated draft boards. The recruit's memoir, however, revealed him to be well educated, indicating that even the more privileged poor and members of the lower middle class were often unable to escape the draft. Oswaldo suggests that "the biggest propagandists against the institution are those soldiers who spend a year in the barracks" because of the poor food, medical treatment, and conditions. But he was fascinated by the transformation that conscripts undergo. At first, they are skittish, awkward, and

14. Overview of newly constructed barracks in Osasco, São Paolo. Many new barracks were being built outside of major urban centers in the 1910s and 1920s, where soldiers were more isolated from the temptations of city life and the agitations of urban politics. Companhia Construtora de Santos. Quartel do Quitauna, Osasco, São Paulo, Armario 12.2.9, 10 de Outubro 1922, no. 97. *Courtesy of Biblioteca Nacional, Divisão de Inconografia. Photo developed from archival originals by Claudio de Carvalho Xavier.*

become emaciated because they are too disoriented to eat well. For Barroso, recruits from the countryside had always "feared and hated soldiers, and when they first don a uniform they seem scared of themselves." But after a few months, their faces become self-confident. Oswaldo noted that draftees received "a bath of civilization" and became "more aware, robust, and adroit with daily exercise. In short, they are already different men that obey officers out of a sense of discipline rather than terror." By wearing uniforms, marching in unison, and shaving their heads, draftees give themselves over to the regiment's "mass anonymity." Barroso felt that this socialization transformed not only rustics into "warriors," but even "the most timid bourgeois."[106]

Oswaldo expressed conflicted views on status in the barracks. On the one hand, "In the opinions of most officers, those who frequent the barracks are pariahs, people who do not have a place to fall down dead." On the other hand, "Conscripts come from everywhere and officers from many walks of life, here [in the barracks] they agglomerate in a paradoxical and unusual promiscuity . . . blacks and whites, mulattos and blonds, rich and poor elbow one another at every turn. They live the same existence. The representatives of all social classes are leveled. The black man dresses himself, feeds himself, and has the same treatment as white men. They eat at the same table together. On the base, social prejudice does not exist."[107] Like most recruits in any army, Oswaldo had mixed feelings about his experience. Many resented the lack of freedom, poor food, the arrogance of superiors, and the indignities thrust upon those of lowest rank. While Barroso was offended by his superiors's hubris (he believed most officers were less educated than himself), he also seemed struck by the paradoxical equalities that barracks life imposed — particularly in terms of race. His assertion that the army leveled classes and races while making men more robust seems lifted directly from Bilac and presaged views expressed by Freyre in the 1930s. While he does not speak of the army as a family, he was impressed by the comradeship that barracks life inspired. Like most Brazilians exposed to militarist propaganda, Oswaldo did not swallow these precepts whole. Rather he filtered them through his own experience and came to mixed conclusions.

As Oswaldo Barroso's remarks indicate, conscription had pushed the army over a threshold that transformed its relationship to civil society. Likewise, the image of soldiering in popular music took on a different caste from the days of Leandro Gomes de Barros and Domingos Caldas Barbosa. Most popular song lyrics in the 1940s portrayed enlisted life in a romantic or humorous way.[108]

Army crime rates confirm assertions that the composition, discipline, and conditions of service in the enlisted ranks had undergone a transformation after 1916. By the 1920s, rates of desertion, insubordination, assaults, and homicide dropped drastically as the enlisted ranks were in a phase of expansion and the army hierarchy was buffeted by the Tenente Revolts (appendix A.1).

As had President Marshal Floriano Peixoto, Vargas also employed summary punishments and the military court system to prosecute those who conspired or those suspected of conspiring against him. Enlisted men who were caught up in seditious plots could expect rough treatment, but insurgent officers and educated civilians were usually treated slightly better.[109] Even so Vargas's penal justice practices routinely violated the human rights not only of the poor, but also members of the middle and upper classes. The guarantees of the home even for the privileged were weakened as the State challenged the fortress of patriarchal authority. Vargas relied heavily on military stockades to hold and interrogate suspected criminals and political enemies when consolidating his power under the Estado Novo. But he did not systematically send criminals to settle frontiers even though some continued to support a policy of penal colonization of the Amazon.[110]

The roots of military law's periodic insertion into the civil justice system in Brazil and many other nations are poorly illuminated, and they deserve greater attention from researchers who hope to understand State building and the military's expanding role in the 1900s. This study illustrates but a small piece of dramatic institutional changes linked to enlisted service in Brazil. These transitions had ramifications that went far beyond the army. Not only were other institutions burdened by the army's changing roles, but these changes were linked to broader social issues. New ideas about defense stimulated reconceptualizations of "race," proper manhood, public hygiene, and citizenship. The draft replaced impressment, breaking down traditional practices that had given coronéis a virtual monopoly in the patriarchal "protection" market. These profound but largely unnoticed changes challenged many patriarchal precepts and practices that undergirded the Old Republic's institutional and ideological order. Without them, it is much more difficult to imagine urban populism's rise in the 1930s and coronelismo's decline.

Conclusions

Army, Masculine Honor,
Race, and Nation

The complaints, civil disobedience, rhetoric, and humor generated by army recruitment in Brazil from 1864 to 1945 illuminate conflictual transitions in notions of honor, masculinity, penology, citizenship, national identity, sexuality, and the limits of public power. This process sped up in the 1910s when an influential group of educated Brazilians formed a consensus that a draft would help resolve a variety of threats to national strength and unity, ranging from regionalism to public hygiene, racial "degeneration," and national defense. Meanwhile, the State and pro-conscription civil organizations worked to convince the "respectable" poor that enlisted service was honorable. To execute a draft and other "progressive" reforms it was essential to alter common perceptions of "honorable" manhood.[1]

The spread of modern military practices to Brazil and other nations in the 1900s challenged patriarchal privileges, political practices, institutions, and conceptions of status. But, even if the distance between the ideal and the practice of universal male conscription was often great, the leveling and homogenizing rhetoric that accompanied it popularized a more inclusive conception of national identity. The following sections ponder themes analyzed in preceding chapters: the army, masculine honor, race, and nation.

Army

The transition from impressment to conscription distanced enlisted service from some of the most commonly used tropes employed to describe praça status: slavery, criminality, marginality, and depravity. Improving conditions and terms of service reinforced by vigorous rhetoric and propaganda slowly began to change public attitudes toward the enlisted ranks. If the army had not made efforts in the 1890s to restrict its role in Brazil's penal justice system, the draft's success would have been much more difficult, if not impossible, to imagine.

In 1916, the draft consolidated a number of alterations in the enlisted man's contract and the army's role in penal justice. Through the draft, officials opted to discipline what they regarded as a more salvageable portion of the population, the "honorable" urban poor. Thereby, the State abdicated much of its role in disciplining the unprotected poor and non-homicidal criminals. The draft made the army responsible for educating and disciplining a much larger cross-section of Brazilian young men from modest families. The weight of these institutional changes differed not only in terms of strata of the poor, but also by region. These points illustrate that caution needs to be used when generalizing about the State's expanding role in disciplining the lower classes as slavery declined in Brazil.

The Brazilian case seems similar to the observation Edward L. Ayers made of the American South: "When the Civil War destroyed slavery, it destroyed the basic structure that gave shape to the South. Slavery had sealed off vast numbers of people from the state and market economy, and when the walls of slavery fell nothing stood ready to replace them. Neither slavery nor true free labor could prevail, neither master nor the state exercised the control they wished."[2] In Brazil, the decline of bondage was more gradual than in the United States, but the Brazilian State did not develop institutions similar to the Freedmen's Bureau in order to smooth the transition of slave to citizen. Impressment filled an important niche in the twilight world between slavery and the emergence of free labor and a more inclusive ideal of citizenship. It shaped in significant ways, the arduous negotiations between former slaveowners, ex-slaves, the State, and the free poor in Brazil.

Conscription challenged traditional Brazilian conceptions of honor, much as the penitentiary system threatened the honor of poor white convicts in the postbellum American South. The states of the South abandoned their antebellum penitentiary system because it would punish whites alongside blacks. Instead, racially segregated convict lease programs were instituted to provide cheap labor to incipient industries. These programs were soon replaced by segregated chain gangs employed directly by state officials.[3] The Brazilian army continued to be a destination for "criminals" and vagrants of all races after slavery's abolition in 1888. For most of Brazil's poor whites, racial integration in the army or in prison did not in itself challenge their sense of honor, but vulnerability to impressment and conscription did. These institutional differences deepen our understanding of the extent to which American and Brazilian governments policed racial and class boundaries, which influenced the evolution of race relations and racial identification.

Army impressment fed a coercive federal labor and protopenal system after slavery's abolition in 1888, but in the 1890s, the army began shortening minimum enlisted-service contracts. As a result, it slowly came to depend less heavily on impressment, and voluntarism increased. The army also freed praças from routine police work, closed down its apprentice schools, and withdrew from its role as a permanent warden of large numbers of civilian convicts.

Eric J. Hobsbawm argued that the progress of nationalism in Europe advanced in step with the growth of schools and universities.[4] In Brazil and many other nations, militaries were modernized before compulsory primary schooling could be effectively implemented.[5] Because States cannot modernize all institutions concurrently, the sequence of institutional modernization indicates much about how a political elite views its populace. In Brazil, elite fears of the populace's racial inferiority seems to have made military modernization a higher priority than education in the 1910s. The preference for military modernization also helps to explain the military's influence in Brazil and many other developing nations.

Basic bureaucratic State building proved an invaluable and largely unrecognized ally of conscription. The State ultimately relied on the civil birth registry (established in the early 1890s) to compile draft lists in 1916. Without this tool, it would have been difficult to implement conscription before the 1910s. The reliance on the civil registry also shifted more and more of the onus of military service to the poor born and raised in urban centers. This differed substantially from recruitment in Russia, where the Red Army, like its imperial predecessor, continued to rely heavily on peasant conscripts.[6] By the 1930s, when the exodus of rural migrants began to inundate city slums, Brazilian army officers questioned the wisdom of recruiting rural men at all. By recruiting more men from urban areas, officers hoped to stem some rural-urban migration to ease the pressure it placed on urban infrastructure.[7] Besides, poor urban youths had greater access to the few educational opportunities available (which expanded more rapidly under Vargas's rule), making them easier to train in modern warfare.

The efforts to focus conscription on urban populations were paralleled by significant regional redistributions of recruitment. The troubled Northeast had provided the bulk of the army's manpower before 1916, but the draft decidedly shifted the weight of recruitment southward. Because of the larger proportions of Europeans and their descendants in Brazil's south, conscription "whitened" the enlisted ranks. Henceforth, most men served in their home states, remaining closer to their homes and families. Local recruitment saved transportation costs and facilitated the mobilization of reserves. This trend would continue to the point that by the 1960s, army bases drew most draftees directly from the localities where they served. If Alfred Stepan's hypothesis—that localized recruitment made the "loyalty of local units" more "open to question in times of great national political conflict"—is correct, this new recruitment pattern belied some of the army's claims to be an agent of national integration.[8] Even so, the army clings to the slogan "the army—agent of national integration" because it portrays the army as the linchpin of national unity and racial cooperation.

Conscription also began to change the composition of praça ranks. Draftees were now drawn from families of the "honorable" urban poor, and fewer and fewer vagrants and "criminals" were inducted. This transition occurred slowly, but the draft was becoming a fact of life that the honorable urban poor of Brazil came to accept, even if many resented that members of the middle and upper classes continued to use influence to exempt themselves. More and more poor Brazilians became keen to pass their health inspections as enlisted service became a desirable status that could offer opportunities. As a poor octogenarian interviewed in rural Maranhão stated in the 1980s, "These days everyone wants to go to war, but back then nobody wanted to."[9] The draft did not level all classes, as Olavo Bilac had prophesied, but it did more to level the working classes. Vulnerability to the draft came to mark the lower limits of middle-class status, but some sons of the middle-class did not manage to secure exemptions, and others served because they desired to do so.

Unlike the United States, where Civil War veteran benefits expanded to become a vehicle of Republican party patronage, most Paraguayan War veterans never saw promised benefits. Theda Skocpol argues that wartime mobilization and conscription, not the pressure of trade union movements, formed the basis of America's first experiments with social welfare programs. Even in Europe, wartime service and concern about the health of future citizen soldiers became powerful justifications for the welfare State's creation and expansion. The great global military mobilizations of the first half of the 1900s pushed the wealthy and political leaders in North Atlantic nations and Japan to make concessions to less prosperous citizens who made the personal and familial sacrifices to defend national honor.[10] The privileged of these nations faced the real prospect of losing their wealth or property to foreign incursions or disruptions of trade. The great mobilizations and sacrifices of war pressured States to provide new protections and rights to citizens who served as soldiers. These pressures on Latin American elites increased, but they were never as extensive as those experienced in the North Atlantic and Japan. The Brazilian state failed to develop an alternative system of adequate protections and benefits for praças that might have competed with the coronel system until after 1945. The febianos organized the first vital veteran organization for praças and officers that could apply political pressure to protect their interests. Up until then, the low regard for praças, the small percentage of citizens who actively voted, and the relatively meager scale of military mobilizations made the organization of an institution similar to the Veterans of the Grand Army of the Republic difficult to conceive. Future research on the comparative development of welfare systems should give this factor greater consideration.[11]

Impressment had reinforced the power of coronéis over their clients by forcing poor families and individuals to seek local patrons for protection from dragooning. By drafting an increasing proportion of the honorable poor, the army began to erode the virtual monopoly held by coronéis (local political bosses) on the protection market. In 1918, two years after the first draft, the central State abrogated the National Guard and under the Estado Novo both state and municipal police forces were subordinated to the War Ministry.[12] Thus the draft undermined important foundations of regional political organization and labor relations of both the empire and the Old Republic.

All of these changes were facilitated by the abolition of slavery, urbanization, and the incipient industrialization that slowly altered the character and structure of Brazil's labor market and political relationships. Personalist relationships began to give way to more bureaucratic forms in the anonymity of burgeoning cities. The jobs, reforms, and State patronage promulgated by Vargas's Estado Novo affirmed the federal government's new role as an important patron of the honorable poor. These changes mellowed negative attitudes toward enlisted service. Even though Vargas's reforms were largely palliative and his social safety net rescued few, his propaganda celebrated the newly won rights and respectability of workers.[13] This helped secure Vargas a populist urban political base that re-elected him president in 1950 after he was thrown from power in 1945. The inclusion of a greater percentage of honorable poor Brazilians in State service lent legitimacy to the social programs and more inclusive electoral politics of urban populism, just as it made authoritarian military rule in Brazil from 1964 to 1985 plausible.

Conscription, perhaps more than any other reform, pushed the State to construct new institutions of penal justice, although they would be slow in developing. The army's changing roles in larger society altered important institutional strategies of disciplining and cultivating model citizens. This transformation also influenced important conceptions of appropriate manhood in relation to personal, family, and national honor.

Masculine Honor

National honor, often symbolized as a virtuous female, had to be defended from foreign interlopers and traitors.[14] Nationalists tapped the loyalty and pride that men of honor should "naturally" feel for their family. As one Brazilian army song of the 1860s warned, "A bad people armed for war comes to conquer us and rape our wives . . . to deflower our daughters." Conversely, this "wife stealing" logic could serve as a stimulus, "All brave soldiers returning from the cursed [Paraguayan] war brought home in his backpack a beautiful mestizo backland woman (cabocla)."[15] These metaphors implied that men of defeated nations were cuckolds unable to defend their collective honor and that the victors affirmed their virility with the spoils of sexual conquests. With the rise of nationalism, this rhetoric became more pronounced because it fetishistically promoted the heterosexual nuclear family as the primary building block of social order and metaphor for the nation. National honor is thus linked to—and charged with—deep-seated preoccupations with sexual dominance symbolized by women and the family. Since ancient times, leaders of patriarchal societies often utilized the sexualized imagery of honor to justify and to promote war mobilizations.[16] These metaphors could come to fuller closure in Brazil only with conscription's implementation, because impressment filled the ranks with men associated with "dishonorable" conduct.

Authorities used impressment to define traits and behaviors associated with honorable manhood for poor freemen. Not every man identified with these ideals and some defiantly thumbed their noses at these values. Nonconformists could see their rejection of these stereotyped performances as acts of rugged individuality, and in turn, question the manhood of conformists. Competing ideas of appropriate manhood were at work among groups and within individuals.

For most poor freemen in the late 1800s, honorable manhood was most consistently defined against stereotypes of women, children, convicts, and most of all, slaves. "Men" would not behave like or let themselves be denied rights withheld from these subordinated groups. For example, the rights to wear shoes and bear arms were markers of freedom forbidden to slaves. The freedom to come and go, assured to citizens in the Constitution, was also a marker of manly competence proscribed, not only to slaves and convicts, but also to many women and children. Responsible poor freemen were expected to marry, to exhibit their virility by fathering children, and then to protect and provide for their dependents. This was crucial in part because it was widely believed that men were "natural" sexual aggressors whose organisms required sexual release, without which, a "mummification" of passion occurred, imperiling their health and psyches. By contrast, women and children were "naturally" sexually passive and required "protection." This was an ideal most explicitly espoused by more privileged men, but most poor freemen and women also viewed marriage as a touchstone of honorable status and shared a language of gender stereotypes. Again the vast majority of male slaves were denied the sanction of marriage and life as a head of household.

Poor freemen generally associated floggings and servile duties with the dishonorable status of slavery. "Men" were expected to resist physical or

15. "The Fantasms of the Present" depicted "national honor" as a beautiful woman on her knees besieged by specters labeled "war," "hunger," "Urquiza" (a powerful Argentine caudillo many feared would ally himself with Paraguay), and "cholera." The figure of a male Indian Tupi warrior interposed himself to defend Brazil's feminized honor. In this way, family and national honor are associated with the protection of honest women. From *O Arlequim*, July 14, 1867, 8. *Courtesy of the Biblioteca Nacional, Rare Works Division. Photo by Gilson Ribeiro.*

sexual aggression against themselves and their dependents by peers. If they submitted to beatings by a social superior, men could still demonstrate their manhood by being defiant and not demonstrating fear.[17] The right to vote required an adult male to head an independent household (unless a man held a medical or law degree or bore a military officer's rank). This independence was considered an essential requirement for the freedom of conscience required of a citizen to vote. The law assumed that a household dependent lacked this manly liberty. Thus, the rule was basically one male household head, one vote, rather than one man, one vote. This brief and far-from-complete list of attributes associated with "honorable" manhood reveals why impressment and conscription threatened the status of respectable poor freemen.[18] In the age of slavery and impressment, praças lost the ability to exercise most of these prerogatives prized by honorable free poor men.

The manumission of slaves and impressment sweeps for the Paraguayan War exacerbated disdain for enlisted army service. As slavery slowly and steadily declined in Brazil, vulnerability to impressment became an even more important distinction for the status-conscious free poor.[19] Being a free person, in and of itself, had less meaning without the existence of the dishonorable touchstone of slavery. Thus, work or conditions that smacked of servility became tainted. Enlisted army service held such a taint, and this study, as anthropologist Peter Fry perceptively characterized it, is essentially a story of the "purification" of praça status from an untouchable to an "embraceable" one. More than any other issue, except for the abolition of slavery, conscription touched upon the mutually constitutive conceptions of manhood, race, class, and nation in a profound way.

The decline of slavery, urbanization, and State building destabilized many of the ideas of manhood that held sway during the age of impressment. In his classic history of childhood, Phillippe Aries noted the importance of conscription for defining new ideas of a cohort of youthful manhood in Europe, "It was manly strength which, in boys, would express the idea of adolescence, and adolescence was foreshadowed in the eighteenth century by the conscript." Brazilian Reformers began to address the honorable poor's concerns by depicting enlisted service as a manly duty performed by responsible citizens. They rhetorically rebuilt the barracks into a "home" that housed the nation's fraternal "family" ready to defend national honor.

Army reformers finally grasped the importance of dominating the high ground of the symbolic geography and rhetoric of honor and masculinity. A telling indicator of this self-conscious effort began to appear in the early 1900s: the replacement of the Portuguese feminine definite article *a* by the masculine definite article *o* before the term praça when referring to soldiers.[20] Thus, *a praça* continued to refer to a public square and *o praça*, an enlisted man. Grammatically, reformers affirmed the masculinity of praças while attenuating enlisted service's direct association with the world of the street. One reporter took this obsession with the masculinity of soldiering one step further when he expressed chagrin that Brazil's World War II heroes were referred to in the diminutive as *pracinhas*: "Diminutives do not go well with heroism; one does not understand the tenderness of domestic epithets in the tumult of the street. So let us leave for other places and the other sex the softness of this more or less effeminate tenderness."[21]

Reformers' concern with securing the "manliness" of enlisted service did not stop with grammar, they sought to distance the barracks from its association with "perversion." As the military's political profile became more prominent in the unstable international environment of the 1930s, the conscripted military became more sensitive about protecting the image of enlisted service from associations with immorality. One telling incident in the 1930s that reveals this sentiment involved attempts to ban the distribution of a second edition of Adolfo Caminha's *Bom Crioulo,* the 1895 novel that depicted a romantic affair between a black sailor and a white cabin boy. When attempts to ban the novel's distribution failed, a navy historian discredited the historical accuracy of Caminha's plot.[22] If the army and navy wanted to draft the "sons of families," they had to assure the public that the barracks were moral "homes" and that officers acted like surrogate parents.

Efforts to suppress homosexuality in the ranks may be linked to conscription and the great mobilizations of the late 1800s and 1900s. In 1872, a Brazilian medical thesis linked the fate of "nations" throughout history to their management of prostitution and "unnatural" copulations. Conscripted militaries wanted to assure families that their sons would not be exposed to perversion or worse, sexual violation, in the ranks. When impressment filled the ranks, officials had no compunction about pressing suspected practitioners of sodomy. Despite the efforts of officers, propagandists, and even clergy to portray the barracks as a place of moral rectitude, the common suspicion that sexually segregated spaces encouraged homosexuality proved difficult to change, as did attempts to make same-sex intercourse equally shameful for both active and passive partners. As late as 1930, Nelson Werneck Sodré reported that among students of the military preparatory school: "Homosexuality, habitual in boarding schools, as in penitentiaries—this is one of the reasons these cloistered regimes should be condemned because they mutilate people—was only shameful when one was the passive partner, the active partner was seen almost as a demonstration of virility. The number of passive partners were few, but couplings were common, almost always inconsequential—most of the time for reasons of ostentation—among cadets. In two or three cases, these couplings were the object of rumors, provoking fights and jealousies; in one case, the passive partner was one of these exceptional cases of an indecisive nature between [a preference] for one sex or another."[23]

It seems possible that conscription and the great mobilizations of the 1900s became an important conduit in an international restructuring of sexual identity. More and more couples (be they hetero- or homosexual) were seen as equally active sexual partners; the old dichotomies of passive versus active, masculine versus feminine, and man versus boy were challenged.[24] Still, barracks culture moved some to prove periodically their sexual dominance. Documenting virility at times came at the expense of a comrade's honor. The "fights and jealousies" that same-sex couplings and disputes over women could cause undermined the discipline officers attempted to instill in their men. It seems probable that the desire to curb these disputes and maintain discipline is why courts-martial did not acquit praças who excused the murder of unfaithful wives as a defense of honor (unlike most civilian juries). Reformers linked homoerotic desire to psychological instability and violence. It is no coincidence that the black protagonist of *Bom Crioulo* killed his lover in a jealous rage. Reformers, like Caminha, tried to discourage the disruptive behavior associated with "sodomy" by stigmatizing both participants as "homosexuals," emasculating both the active and passive partners. These challenges to predominant conceptions of gender and sexuality paralleled significant political and economic transformations.

More than anyone, Getúlio Vargas undermined the power of the state-based political machines that dominated the Old Republic (1889–1930). An integral part of this transition involved a protracted attack on certain conceptions of manhood without dismantling patriarchy. Reform programs had to develop, disseminate, and popularize alternative visions of appropriate gender roles and new yardsticks to measure status and honor. Soldiering's new respectability was central to redefining gender roles in relation to honor.[25] More research is needed to determine the extent to which officers instructed their troops about homosexuality as an "illness" linked to racial degeneration and sexually transmitted diseases. Remapping manhood within the geography of honor in relation to enlisted service was thus bound up in the nationalist project of race improvement. For many reformers, as Olavo Bilac urged, a soldier's personal honor had to be sublimated by and subordinated to his proud association with national honor as an agent of the State.

In multiracial societies, ideas of nation, citizenship, and military service took different trajectories. The American South limited enlisted service to white men during the Civil War (1860–65), although plans to mobilize bondsmen were debated. The Union army reluctantly bestowed this privilege on blacks, and even then, it was careful to segregate them from white troops. There was no equivalent to the racial violence unleashed during the New York draft riots of 1863, either during Brazil's mobilization for the Paraguayan War or thereafter.[26] The integration of basic State institutions like the army meant that the juncture of race, manhood, and nation would be mobilized differently in Brazil. In the United States, army service continued to be seen as an honorable duty associated with racial privilege and republican manhood, especially in the South. Racist southerners often targeted black soldiers in uniform for racial violence. Thus, it is not startling that draft propaganda in the United States during World War I relied heavily on gender ridicule to shame "slackers": men who dodged the draft or who did not buy war bonds.[27] Because of soldiering's low status in Brazil, racial segregation was impracticable; therefore, conscription's propagandists took a different tact.

From 1868 to 1878 in Cuba, an ultimately unsuccessful insurgent army fighting for national independence from Spain made slavery's abolition one of its goals. Thus, the movement attracted volunteers from many slaves and free men of color into its ranks, some of whom became high-ranking officers. This strategy pushed Spanish loyalists to legislate the gradual abolition of slavery with the Moret Law (1870) — similar to Brazil's 1871 Free Womb Law implemented soon after the Paraguayan War. In both cases, war destabilized the underpinnings of the slave regime. Still most Cuban cane planters continued to support Spain out of fear of slave rebellion and to protect their investments in slave property. Some rebel officers tried to create a national identity that cut across the racial hierarchies that divided the Cuban-born and left them subject to Spanish imperialism. As the mulatto officer Antonio Maceo declared, *"Aquí no hay negritos ni blanquitos sino cubanos"* (here there are no little blacks or little whites, only Cubans). A group of rebel black and mulatto soldiers and officers repudiated the 1878 peace treaty that neither abolished slavery nor established Cuban independence.[28]

Only in the 1890s, after the 1886 abolition of Cuban slavery, would inspirational ideologues like José Marti organize a more explicitly multiracial struggle for independence. Cuban insurgents were ultimately defeated by U.S. military intervention in the so-called Spanish-American War 1899, and they remained subject to "legal" U.S. government intervention under the Platt Amendment until 1933. As in Brazil, racial prejudice and strife continued in Cuba after 1900, but the incorporation of black men as independence fighters and even high-ranking officers must have had an impact on how they viewed the nation-state and Cuban identity. Still, many high-ranking black officers were subordinated to eleventh-hour white converts to the Independence struggle. Brazil's history of war (even the Paraguayan War) never required the extensive mobilizations of men and resources that arose in the United States in the 1860s or Cuba in the 1890s. The experience of nonwhite soldiers in Brazil, Cuba, and the United States shaped their respective ideas of citizenship and exclusion and influenced the negotiation of racial and national identities.[29]

While abolition in Cuba made a more nationalistic war for Independence possible, in Brazil, it facilitated the bloodless republican army coup of 1889. In Brazil, Cuba, and the United States, military mobilizations weakened both slavery and the surrounding political and social order constructed to accommodate the slave regime. In these three countries, the relationship between warfare, enlisted service, abolition, and citizenship had different formulations, but in all cases, belief in racial hierarchies hampered efforts to imagine a leveled and homogenized "race" as the basis of an organic nation-state. Conscription pushed authorities, soldiers, intellectuals, and citizens to grapple with and to adjust the meaning of these ideas.

During World War I, the rhetoric of hygiene, eugenics, nationalism, and militarism began to fuse in support of conscription. European and North American imperialism, partially unmasked by the barbarity of World War I and the violation of the territory of neutral nations, convinced many influential Brazilians that they could not hesitate to establish a modern system of military training and mobilization. Far from corrupting young men, the army would help train a more effective labor force and turn conscripts away from a life of vice, indolence, and crime. It would also supposedly alleviate ethnic, regional, and class tensions that threatened to divide Brazil by bringing men of different backgrounds together. Conscription would advance efforts to develop a stronger sense of national identity. Advocates argued that the draft would improve public health by promoting recruits' physical and intellectual well-being through rigorous exercise, training, and primary instruction. After all, if the State hoped to preserve Brazil's national integrity, it had to take stock of and develop its human resources.

The rhetoric surrounding the draft helped to alleviate the fears expressed by many that Brazil's diverse racial composition and climate would prevent it from becoming a truly modern, united, and "civilized" nation-state. The military, rather than public schools, orphanages, or reformatories, would be the State's point institution to spread the gospel of hygiene, nationalism, physical fitness, and morality to the lower classes during the Old Republic. Eugenics justified the draft's adoption in Brazil, whereas Chile and Argentina began peacetime conscription in 1901 before eugenic thought began to supplant positivism.

Eugenists supported the draft based on its hygienic and potential genetic benefits for the "race." For some, this implied an acceleration of the whitening process, but for others, the racist assumptions that undergirded eugenics were turned on their head. Influential nationalist intellectuals rejected strict biological racism and argued that the mixture of Indians, Africans, and Europeans had produced a "eugenically" sound race ideally adapted to Brazil's tropical environment. The poor hygiene and lack of education among Brazil's lower classes had their origins in social and economic conditions, not in genetics or climate.[30] This ideology helped to undermine the Spencerian ideas that buttressed the domination of politics by "white" oligarchical elites (the coronéis) with little regard for popular consent.

Conscription also produced data on the poor public health of Brazil's young men. This social knowledge gave new scientific authority to officers and health officials, which some used to criticize the oligarchic regime of Brazil's Old Republic and the tenets of classical liberalism. Eugenic "science" undermined the authority of positivist thinkers who had criticized obligatory military, public health, and education laws. Eugenists generally supported a more activist State that would act on a variety of societal problems related to health, education, and economic development. They questioned the validity of positivism and the legitimacy of oligarchic rule in Brazil with arguments based on "modern" social, military, and health sciences. Most coronéis had defended the federalist principle of states' rights, as enshrined in the 1891 Constitution, to frustrate recruitment reform and the establishment of a federal health ministry. The establishment of a national health ministry in 1918 and conscription in 1916 indicates how officers and medical professionals' interests sometimes converged to subvert the authority of coronéis. Reformers organized new types of grassroots organizations — such as the National Defense League (LDN) — that lobbied Congress for legislation. These World War I-era defeats reveal the weakening grip of coronéis. They paved the way for Getúlio Vargas's later efforts to concentrate more political power in the federal government and to expand the prerogatives of State action in society and the economy far beyond those prescribed by classical liberal philosophy.

The World War II victories won by Brazilian troops over Aryan foes in 1945 were taken by some as evidence that Brazil's racial diversity would not deter it from rising as a major world power. Many nationalists voiced new confidence in the populace's "hidden energies."[31] They described Brazil's diverse racial heritage as an advantage rather than an impediment to national destiny. The ideology of racial democracy denied the racial prejudice that continued to exclude many nonwhites from desirable jobs and political leadership. Instead, racial democracy promoted a unifying sense of national solidarity and race harmony that has proven difficult to dislodge. By the 1910s, comparisons with the tense race relations that typified the United States became a key part of a Brazilian sense of superiority and distinctiveness — the essence of nationalist sentiment.[32]

Nation

Militaries in nations across the world strive to place themselves at the center of ongoing struggles to shape national memories and imaginations. Most solemn national holidays are marked by the participation of the military as symbolic participants, if not central actors. Militaries supply nations with the majority of their martyrs whose deaths are attributed to their love of country. The Brazilian army's self-portrayal as the linchpin of "national integration" began to gain greater acceptance among influential sectors of the civilian population in the 1900s. Their number included the folklorist and literary critic Sílvio Romero, who in 1912 praised the army and President Marshal Hermes da Fonseca's drive to undermine the power of the oligarchic coronéis. This nationalist mystique helped to justify the draft's execution, and it would also vindicate the army's periodic intervention in civilian politics as an entity above the fray of myopic partisan politics.[33]

16. Monument to the pracinhas (veterans of World War II), Rio de Janeiro. This modernist statue features the common soldier, using racially neutral features. *Photo by author, developed by Gilson Ribeiro.*

The changing status of enlisted service is perhaps best captured by the giant modernistic monument in Rio that celebrates the febiano triumph in Italy. Unlike most previous war memorials, it does not glorify individual officers, but instead privileges the ill-defined, nearly homogeneous, and racially neutral physiognomies of unknown praças. In stone, at least, "Brazilians" are symbolically homogenized into a single, if poorly delineated, "race." Never before was the anonymous praça so publicly glorified, so respected, or so closely associated with national honor.

Conscription slowly did away with the more picaresque "soldiers of misfortune" who had been the mainstays of Brazil's traditional army. With the draft, soldiering and the army came to be more closely identified with a moralizing sense of national identity and unity. More respectable young men of all races and ethnic groups served together in praça ranks.

The nationalist fervor that championed the draft stimulated reconsideration of national identity and culture. In the 1910s, 1920s, and 1930s, many of Brazil's intellectuals—influenced by modernism and regional-ism—revisited some of the romantic ideals forwarded by the folklorist Sílvio Romero to define Brasilidade. They embraced folk culture, which mixed European, African, and Indian traditions as "authentic" artifacts of a unique national culture. But most rejected the biological and climatic determinism that had haunted Romero's visions of Brazil's national des-tiny and those of most of his contemporaries.[34]

This point brings us back to the colonial bard, praça, and priest, Do-mingos Caldas Barbosa, whose biography and songs introduced this book. Nationalist intellectuals apotheosized Domingos as a pioneer of a truly Brazilian national consciousness and music. His was a story that celebrated the triumph of talent over mixed-racial heritage and birth outside wedlock. His mixed race, military service, and Catholicism were ripe for intellectuals recasting nationalist ideals and icons. Not surprisingly, a new collection of Domingos's works appeared in 1944.[35] To the delight of this new genera-tion of folklorists, he embodied the nationalist ideal of "racial democracy," which held that racial tolerance had been rooted in Brazil's unique colonial experience. But, no one paused to ponder how enlisted service's shifting status had altered the significance of Domingos's martial metaphors in his song "Soldier of Love." As the days of the "soldier of misfortune" drew to a close, the meanings of these martial metaphors were lost on more and more listeners, just as cordel literature, the phonograph, and the radio would begin to squeeze out the influence of Brazil's rich oral traditions.

I hope this study suggests the importance of analyzing impressment, conscription, and the cultural nexus of house and street as innovative com-parative approaches to issues of citizenship, family, honor, gender, and na-tion. As one of the last widely accepted forms of corvée labor, conscription links the history of coercive and free labor systems as well as open and auto-cratic political systems. Studies of its adoption by different cultures should offer rich new insights into the development of political and social rights, identities, and attitudes. As new studies of masculinity and whiteness dem-onstrate, new questions and hypotheses emerge when scholars examine categories that are relegated to the realm of "traditional" history. New in-terpretative doors can be unlocked when the methods of cultural and social history, buttressed by other approaches, are applied to the study of military mobilizations and the societies that employ these tribute labor systems.

Appendix A

Military Crime Data

Table A.1 Most Numerous Types of Army Praça Crime

Year	Desertion	Insubordination	Physical Wound	Homicide	Abandon Post	Allow Prison Escape	Petty Theft	Total # of Praças
1869	115	26	19	23	0	15	10	—
1870	126	20	30	10	0	11	4	10,383
1871	391	34	72	22	0	17	22	14,726
1872	593	27	43	24	6	19	8	—
1873[a]	555	58	65	25	7	66	16	14,918
1875	320	105	78	10	10	24	13	14,581
1877	288	113	81	9	23	24	13	—
1878	238	85	66	5	8	17	3	15,043
1879[a]	303	127	59	18	17	35	5	14,912
1880[a]	424	222	132	32	41	79	17	—
1881[a]	96	54	32	8	10	13	9	13,516
1882	142	71	67	14	13	15	4	11,369
1883	224	63	46	12	21	32	16	—
1884	247	79	53	13	14	30	4	—
1885	274	94	66	5	8	30	5	—
1886	293	45	58	13	10	37	12	—
1887	228	53	58	20	16	26	6	—
1888	258	58	58	41	19	17	19	—
1891[b]	527	61	54	25	1	33	18	18,826
1892[b]	367	49	62	10	7	45	24	18,052
1893[b]	354	60	54	18	4	11	10	24,887
1894[b]	309	24	10	9	7	17	5	28,120
1895[b]	381	24	21	22	0	20	13	19,698
1896[b]	1,024	68	49	32	7	27	14	17,699
1897[b]	568	59	50	25	10	34	11	20,035
1898[b]	798	121	33	16	2	18	10	14,901
1899	893	31	33	16	4	16	8	14,983
1900	823	32	33	13	3	18	15	14,989
1901	825	73	47	9	11	22	12	14,705

Table A.1 *continued*

Year	Desertion	Insubor-dination	Physical Wound	Homicide	Abandon Post	Allow Prison Escape	Petty Theft	Total # of Praças
1902	495	63	47	16	0	3	10	15,184
1903	468	38	36	14	5	7	10	15,884
1904	518	53	17	16	10	5	2	18,446
1905	474	33	36	21	8	11	7	15,900
1906	416	31	18	9	2	10	1	15,907
1907	417	37	30	23	4	14	3	18,297
1908	382	31	33	16	5	24	2	—
1909	321	18	26	24	3	14	9	16,339
1910	297	14	37	28	10	7	3	—
1911	349	18	21	12	1	6	8	—
1912	363	27	51	24	1	2	12	—
1913	303	29	41	23	5	3	2	—
1914	371	17	34	13	1	7	1	—
1915	341	16	46	23	1	11	7	—
1916	224	47	69	38	3	26	6	—
1917	180	17	18	22	1	9	21	—
1918	377	9	10	10	1	0	10	—
1919	333	19	25	22	1	18	7	—
1920	334	26	0	9	2	3	9	—
1921	73	18	11	1	1	4	7	—
1922	59	4	3	2	0	0	5	—
1923	57	29	6	8	1	8	15	—
1924	44	20	3	6	2	3	9	—
1925	72	9	6	8	1	6	4	—
Total	19,252	2,559	2,153	887	348	969	496	—

Sources: RRMGu, (1870–1926), annexos.

[a]Figures reflect more than one year of data.

[b]Years in which no distinction was made between army and navy crimes; figures include numbers from both branches.

Table A.2 Distribution of STM Crime by Armed Force and Rank

	Army Officer	Army Praça	Navy Officer	Navy Praça	Police Officer[b]	Police Praça[b]	Civilian	Total
1869	55	230	2	60	1	10	20	378
1870	29	242	6	63	1	29	6	376
1871	44	659	4	65	0	29	0	801
1872	21	757	1	36	1	35	0	851
1873[a]	23	880	8	39	0	25	0	975
1875	24	757	1	36	1	35	0	854
1877	4	657	5	44	0	22	0	732
1878	13	490	7	44	3	23	0	580
1879[a]	21	664	10	58	1	34	0	788
1880[a]	28	1,143	5	93	1	60	0	1,330
1881[a]	7	268	2	20	0	8	0	305
1883	8	373	1	43	0	20	0	445
1884	7	471	0	52	0	22	0	552
1885	19	525	2	65	0	24	0	635
1886	8	539	4	93	0	17	0	661
1887	17	528	1	53	0	16	0	615
1888	20	496	4	77	0	52	0	649
1889[a]	32	540	3	77	0	23	0	675
1891	16	619	2	38	2	115	0	792
1892	5	537	2	63	0	76	0	683
1893	8	409	2	43	3	96	0	561
1894	32	330	15	40	0	24	15	456
1895	60	423	53	13	9	46	0	604
1896	58	990	12	40	7	203	11	1,321
1897	36	650	9	54	10	78	5	842
1898	91	820	8	65	1	78	0	1,063
1899	70	1,026	8	118	1	53	0	1,276
1900	38	997	2	80	2	66	0	1,185
1901	44	1,046	5	64	8	59	0	1,226
1902	38	698	5	101	1	47	0	890
1903	26	610	9	106	1	78	0	830
1904	24	672	7	161	1	72	0	937
1905	55	641	24	143	0	72	0	935
1906	24	522	5	119	0	77	0	747
1907	24	637	3	111	2	81	0	858
1908	17	520	4	121	1	61	0	724
1909	7	443	2	106	2	56	0	616
1910	15	410	12	103	2	45	0	587
1911	16	457	13	53	0	38	0	577
1912	12	538	12	85	0	84	0	731

Table A.2 *continued*

	Army Officer	Army Praça	Navy Officer	Navy Praça	Police Officer[b]	Police Praça[b]	Civilian	Total
1913	15	489	3	149	0	128	0	784
1914	17	498	9	129	0	140	0	793
1915	8	548	6	131	3	64	0	760
1916	19	437	7	99	1	13	0	576
1917	14	305	14	54	0	6	0	393
1918	14	819	1	57	3	22	0	916
1919	8	1,357	4	118	0	14	0	1,501
1920	11	1,231	3	119	0	121	0	1,485
1921	11	248	5	71	0	26	0	361
1922	2	85	17	43	0	23	0	170
1923	25	152	17	65	1	48	4	312
1924	14	101	0	43	0	36	0	194
1925	27	120	0	42	1	52	1	243
Total	1,281	30,604	366	3,965	71	2,782	62	39,131
%	3.3	79.8	1.0	10.3	0.1	7.2	0.1	100.0

Sources: RRMGu, (1870–1926), annexos.

[a]Figures reflect more than one year of data.

[b]Also includes some cases of National Guard praças. Police praças and officers tried by courts-martial were those who served in the Corte, later renamed the Federal District under the Republic.

Table A.3 Military Police Inquiries for 1896 Crimes in the National Archive

	# of cases	Percentage
Crimes Against Military Honor and Duty		
Desertion	6	2.0
Simple Desertion	2	.66
Aggravated Desertion	3	1.0
Desertion in War Time	28	8.9
First Simple Desertion	152	48.3
Second Simple Desertion	22	7.0
Third Simple Desertion	8	2.5
First Aggravated Desertion	17	5.4
Second Aggravated Desertion	4	1.3
Third Aggravated Desertion	1	.33
Insubmission	2	.66
Abandonment of Duty	2	.66
Drunkenness	1	.33
Indiscipline	9	2.9
Total	257	81.28

Table A.3 *continued*

	# of cases	Percentage
Crimes Against Personal Security and Life		
Aggression	1	.33
Physical Offenses	1	.33
Mutual Injuries	2	.66
Light Injuries	1	.33
Injuries	5	1.66
Grave Injuries	1	.33
Attempted Homicide	2	.66
Attemped Suicide	2	.66
Involuntary Homicide	1	.33
Homicide	8	2.50
Total	24	7.79
Crimes Against Property		
Theft	1	.33
Damaging Property	1	.33
Total	2	.66
Crimes Against the Military's Administrative and Economic Order		
Administrative Falsification	2	.65
Crimes Against the Republic's Internal Security		
Insubordination	20	6.3
Allowing a Prisoner to Escape	5	1.66
Flight	2	.66
Total	27	8.62
Abuse of Military Authority		
Abuse of Authority	3	1.0
Overall Total	315	100.0

Source: RRMGu, (1896), annexos.

Appendix B

Army Recruitment Data

Table B.1 Army Enlisted Recruitment by Region

Region	Recruits 1850–61	%	Recruits 1865–70	%	Recruits 1870–82	%
Northeast	13,832	52.7	43,997	48.2	9,713	52.4
Southeast	5,834	22.2	30,868	33.8	3,021	16.3
South	3,587	13.7	8,042	8.8	3,641	19.7
Central West	1,546	5.9	3,840	4.2	1,079	5.8
North	1,456	5.5	4,551	5.0	712	3.9
Paraguay	0	0.0	0	0.0	342	1.9
Total	26,255	100	91,298	100	18,508	100

Source: Data derived from RRMGu (1851, 1852, 1853, 1854, 1856, 1857, 1858, 1859, 1860, 1861, 1862, 1871, 1872, 1875, 1877, 1878, 1880, and 1883) in statistical appendices ("annexos").

Table B.2 1871 and 1873 Recruitment Quota by Region Compared to Percentage Slave and Free Population in 1872

Region	Recruit Quota	% National Recruits	% National Free Pop.	% National Slave Pop.
Northeast	2,215	48	49.3	31.2
Southeast	1,645	37	37.1	59.5
South	310	7	7.5	6.3
Central West	110	2	2.5	1.1
North	190	4	3.6	1.9
Total	4,500	100	100.0	100.0

Source: RRMGu (Rio: Typ. Universal de Laemmert, 1872 and 1874), annexos. Nineteenth-century Brazilians did not distinguish between the North, Northeast, South and Southeast as they did in the 1920s. Even so, provinces are divided into regions according to twentieth-century conventions for the sake of analysis: the North comprises Pará and Amazonas; the Northeast, Maranhão, Ceará, Piauí, Rio Grande do Norte, Paraíba, Pernambuco, Sergipe, Alagoas, and Bahia; the Southeast, Espírito Santo, Rio de Janeiro, São Paulo, Minas Gerais, and the Côrte; the Central West, Mato Grosso and Goiás; and the South, Paraná, Santa Catarina, and Rio Grande do Sul. See Figure 1.

Table B.3 Regional Distribution of Brazil's Male Population (Figures in Thousands)

Region	1854[a]	%	1872	%	1890	%	1900	%	1920
Northeast	3,732.8	48.6	2,363	46	2,957	41	3,364	38	5,508
Southeast	3,051.3	39.7	2,101	41	3,145	43	4,000	45	6,988
South	378.7	4.9	373	7	729	10	915	11	1,798
Central West	265	3.5	112	2	160	2	188	2	393
North	250	3.3	174	4	247	4	365	4	757
Total	7,677.8	100.0	5,123	100	7,238	100	8,832	100	15,444

Source: Derived from IBGE, *Estatística Histórica do Brasil,* 2nd ed. (Rio: IBGE, 1990), 31, 34.
[a]Population in this column includes men and women.

Table B.4 Regional Distribution of Army Officers and Troops

Region	1871	%	1880	%	1891	%	1900	%
Northeast	2,269	13	4,055	27	5,099	25	3,426	19
Southeast	3,867	22	3,228	21	5,279	26	5,717	32
South	4,265	24	4,882	32	7,248	35	7,035	39
Central West	2,650	15	2,105	14	2,079	10	1,188	7
North	970	5	1,004	6	683	3	499	3
Other	3,723	21	30	0	0	0	0	0
Total	17,744	100	15,304	100	20,388	99	17,865	100

Source: Data derived from RRMGu, (Rio: Typ. Univ. de Laemmert, 1871 and 1872; Type. Carioca, 1875; Typ. Nacional 1875, 1877, 1878, 1880, and 1883), annexos. Officers account for approximately 10 percent of these figures.

ble B.5 Provincial Distribution of Recruitment 1850–61

vince (Region)	# Men	% Men	% 1854 Pop.	Province (Region)	# Men	% Men	% 1854 Pop.
) Grande do Sul (S)	3,133	11.9	2.7	Rio de Janeiro (SE)	951	3.6	15.6
nambuco (NE)	3,019	11.5	12.3	Paraíba (NE)	938	3.6	2.7
ìia (NE)	2,808	10.7	14.3	São Paulo (SE)	826	3.2	6.5
rte (SE)	2,650	10.0	*	Alagoas (NE)	711	2.7	2.6
ranhão (NE)	1,975	7.5	4.7	Goiás (CW)	567	2.2	2.4
ará (NE)	1,683	6.4	5.0	Rio Grande do Norte (NE)	566	2.1	2.5
á (N)	1,160	4.4	2.7	Amazonas (N)	298	1.1	0.6
uí (NE)	1,150	4.4	2.0	Espírito Santo (SE)	265	1.0	0.7
nas Gerais (SE)	1,142	4.3	16.9	Santa Catarina (S)	249	1.0	1.4
gipe (NE)	980	3.8	2.4	Paraná (S)	204	0.8	0.9
to Grosso (CW)	980	3.8	3.8	Paraguay (foreign)	0	0.0	0.0
				Total	26,255	100	100

rce: IBGE. *Estatística Histórica do Brasil,* 2d ed. (Rio: IBGE, 1990), 31.
gures for the province and capital district of Rio de Janeiro combined.

ble B.6 Provincial Distribution of Recruitment for the Paraguayan War (1872)
ercentages rounded)

vince (Region)	# Men	% Men	Pop.	Province (Region)	# Men	% Men	Pop.
ìia (NE)	15,297	16.8	13.6	Mato Grosso (CW)	3,298	3.6	.6
rte (SE)	11,467	12.5	2.7	Piauí (NE)	2,705	3.0	2.0
) prov. (SE)	7,861	8.6	8.1	Alagoas (NE)	2,656	2.9	3.5
rnambuco (NE)	7,136	7.8	8.4	Paraíba (NE)	2,454	2.7	3.7
) Paulo (SE)	6,504	7.1	8.3	Sergipe (NE)	2,254	2.4	2.4
ará (NE)	5,648	6.2	7.1	Paraná (S)	2,022	2.2	.9
aranhão (NE)	4,536	5.0	3.6	Santa Catarina (S)	1,537	1.7	1.6
) Grande do Sul (S)	4,483	4.9	4.4	Rio Grande do Norte (NE)	1,311	1.4	2.4
nas Gerais (SE)	4,070	4.5	20.8	Espírito Santo (SE)	966	1.1	.9
á (N)	3,827	4.2	2.7	Amazonas (N)	724	0.8	.6
iás (CW)	542	0.6	1.7	Total	91,298	100	100

rce: Recruitment figures derived from RRMGUP (1872), annexos; population data drawn from IBGE, *Estatística Histórica do sil,* 2nd ed. (Rio: IBGE, 1990), 34.

Table B.7 Provincial Distribution of Recruitment 1870–82

Province (Region)	# Men	% Men	% 1874 Pop.	Province (Region)	# Men	% Men	18 Po
Rio Grande do Sul (S)	3,232	11.9	4.4	Sergipe (NE)	547	3.0	
Ceará (NE)	2,106	11.4	7.1	Maranhão (NE)	524	2.8	
Corte (SE)	2,014	10.9	3.2	Goiás (CW)	391	2.1	
Bahia (NE)	1,714	9.3	14.0	Rio de Janeiro (SE)	364	2.0	8
Pernambuco (NE)	1,648	8.9	8.4	Minas Gerais (SE)	308	1.7	2
Paraíba (NE)	1,427	7.7	3.7	Santa Catarina (S)	244	1.3	
Mato Grosso (CW)	668	3.6	0.6	São Paulo (SE)	229	1.2	4
Piauí (NE)	606	3.3	2.0	Paraná (S)	165	0.9	
Rio Grande do Norte (NE)	578	3.1	2.3	Amazonas (N)	140	0.8	
Pará (N)	572	3.1	2.8	Espírito Santo (SE)	106	0.6	
Alagoas (NE)	563	3.0	3.4	Paraguay (foreign)	342	1.8	
				Total	18,508	100.0	10

Sources: See sources for table B.4.

Table B.8 Percentages of Pressed Troops (P), Volunteers (V), Reenlistments (R), and Others (O) by Region 1850–61 and 1870–82.

Region	1850–61					1870–82				
	P	V	R	O	Total	P	V	R	O	Total
Northeast	64	16	13	7	100	34	59	7	—	100
Southeast	62	20	8	10	100	45	45	10	—	100
South	35	33	16	16	100	21	73	6	—	100
C. West	23	31	26	20	100	14	58	28	0	100
North	60	30	5	5	100	58	40	2	0	100
Other	0	0	0	0	100	—	37	63	0	100
Overall Average	57	21	13	9	100	33	58	9	—	100

Sources: See sources for table B.4. "Others" incorporates two substitutes and six National Guardsmen designated for army service for 1870–82. For 1850–62, it includes the category of *contratados* or recruits contracted by recruitment agents paid a salary and/or a commission.
(—) Less than 1 percent.

Appendix C

Populations of Public Disciplining Institutions

Table C.1 Population of Major Civil Prisons[1]

	1871	1876	1881	1886	1891	1895	1900	1905	1910	1915	1919	1923
Alagoas	—	—	—	—	—	—	—	—	85	150	143	180*
Amazonas	—	—	—	—	—	—	—	—	—	—	—	51
Bahia	402	410	571	544	548	—	—	—	—	—	—	351
Rio Capital	225	259	479	638	884	468	171	177	172	878	—	—
Ceará	225	408	259	235	—	—	—	—	—	67	131	106
Espírito Santo	—	—	—	—	—	—	—	—	—	—	—	52
Minas Gerais	316	—	423	—	302	—	—	1,617*	2,180*	—	—	111
Mato Grosso	25	384	72	—	—	—	—	—	—	—	—	—
Maranhão	—	—	—	—	—	—	—	—	—	67	131	146
Pará	—	—	—	216	—	—	—	—	—	—	—	74
Paraíba	127	—	350	214	—	—	160	85	95	175	98	175
Pernambuco	351	c.400	c.400	371	—	—	735	—	—	—	—	382
Piauí	—	—	—	—	—	—	—	—	—	87	83	81
Rio Province	—	189	311	157	—	—	—	—	—	—	—	—
Rio Grande do Norte	—	—	—	—	—	—	—	—	—	27	37	54
Rio Grande do Sul	594	—	—	330	—	—	—	—	294	602	—	—
São Paulo	381	—	252	977*	—	—	—	—	—	—	—	—

Source: Data for 1915, 1919, and 1923 derived from José Gabriel de Lemos Brito, Os sistemas penitenciárias do Brasil, 3 vols., (Rio: Imp. Nacional, 1924–27); for specific cites on data culled from governors' reports see endnote listed above.

*Data for these years, includes population of all or nearly all of a state or province's prison population combined.

Table C.2 Fernando de Noronha's Convict Population, Selected Years
1865–1920

	Military	Civilian		Total
		Men	Women	
1865	278	1,400	ni	1,678
1869	248	988	21	1,257
1873	231	1,154	29	1,414
1879	278	1,364	36	1,678
1881	257	1,375	36	1,688
1886	251	1,216	ni	1,436
1896	112	260	ni	372
1899	0	232	ni	232
1920	0	447	ni	447

Sources: RRMGuP, (1870, 1874, and 1880), annexos; on simplification of notes for governors' reports, see note 1 for Appendix C. Pernambuco: (March 1, 1881), 26; (February 19, 1900: police chief's annexo), 13; (March 6, 1921), 19; for 1865 see Morais, *Prisões,* 35.
ni — no information.

Table C.3 Population of Army Apprentice Schools

	1871–72	1875	1880	1885	1890	1895	1899
Bahia	146	152	50	50	62	80	0
Goiás	0	0	40	34	35	0	0
Mato Grosso	ni	82	11	50	50	ni	79
Minas Gerais	0	0	25	40	43	80	0
Pará	50	96	18	49	50	50	0
Pernambuco	128	120	50	50	50	80	0
Rio (Artisans)	203	232	100	104	265	250	250
(Artillery)	504	430	319	280	198	0	0
Rio Grande do Sul	58	50	50	49	50	77	79
Total	1,089	1,162	663	706	753	617	408

Sources: On simplification of notes for governor's reports, see note 1 for Appendix C. Pernambuco: (March 1, 1871), 13; (March 1, 1876), 31; (March 1, 1881), 112; (March 6, 1886), 10. Rio Grande do Sul: (March 14, 1871), 36; (May 8, 1886), 15. Minas Gerais: (1881), 28; (June 15, 1891), 32. Mato Grosso: (May 3, 1881: police chief's annexo), 19. Pará: (February 18, 1876), 27–28; (February 15, 1881), 90; (March 25, 1881), 20. RRMGuP (1877) 28–29, 30–31; RRMGuP (1880), 15–18; RRMGuP (1885), 15–18; RRMGuP (1886), 20, 22; RRMGuC, (1891), 20; RRMGuC (1896), 42–48; and RRMGuC (1899), 62, 64.
ni — no information.

Notes

Unless otherwise cited, English translations of original Portuguese works are my own.

Introduction

1 Morais Filho, *Serenatas e seraus* 1: introduction; Barbosa, "A Ternura Brasileira," "Zabumba," and "A Portugueza Abrazileirada," in *A Viola de Loreno,* 14–16, 225–30, 257, 298–99.
2 Dauril Alden, *Royal Government in Colonial Brazil,* 70 n.32; "Representação dos presos que haviam vindo de Lisboa e Porto como degredados para Moçambique, Angola, e outras partes, pedindo a s.a.r. lhes concedesse a graça de mandar sentar praça nos regimentos da linha onde muitas deles já haviam servido," Rio, 1821, bnr-smor, Exército, pa. II-34, 25, 16; Varnhagen, "Biografia de Domingos Caldas Barbosa," 49.
3 Morais Filho, *Serenatas e seraus,* 1:xii–xiv.
4 Matos, *A poesia popular na república das letras,* 50–3; Anderson, *Imagined Communities;* Sommer, *Foundational Fictions.*
5 Romero, *Cantos populares do Brasil,* introduction.
6 Lima Barreto's tragic nationalist, Policarpo, stated, "It is prejudiced to suppose that every man who plays the guitar is a social outcast. . . . We are the ones who abandoned this genre, but it was honored in Lisbon in the previous century with Father [Domingos] Caldas who had an audience of nobility." Policarpo and his neighbor, a general, consult a Brazilian folklore scholar to "develop the cult of traditions, [and] maintain them always alive in memory and custom." Lima Barreto, *Triste fim do Policarpo Quaresma,* 12, 22. As Hermano Vianna demonstrates, however, even though many members of the elite developed a taste for erudite European music, they continued to be exposed to popular Brazilian musical forms at social gatherings (*The Mystery of Samba,* chapter 3).
7 Belmondy, "O nosso soldado," *O Alvorada,* March 1878, 3, in bnr-smor.
8 Hebe Maria Mattos de Castro *Das cores do silêncio,* 31–40; Fraga Filho, *Mendigos, moleques, e vadios,* 165–67; Gilmore, *Manhood in the Making.*
9 Chiavenato, *Genocídio Americano;* Menezes, *Guerra do Paraguai.*
10 Kraay, "Shelter of the Uniform," 637–57.
11 Prado Junior, *Colonial Background of Modern Brazil,* 361–85.

12 Cope, *The Limits of Racial Domination;* Martinez-Alier, *Marriage, Class and Colour;* Eduardo Silva, *Prince of the People,* chap. 7.

13 Mattoso et al., "Trends and Patterns."

14 President Nilo Peçanha's African heritage was often parodied in political cartoons. Lustosa, *Histórias de presidentes,* 56. "Whiteness" in Brazil deserves closer scrutiny; see for example Roediger, *The Wages of Whiteness.* A new study moving in this direction is Barickman's "Citizenship, Kinship, Slavery, and Household in the 1835 Parish Censuses from Bahia."

15 Schwartz, *Sugar Plantations in the Formation of Brazilian Society;* Kuznesof, "Ethnic and Gender Influences on "Spanish" Creole Society," 153–201.

16 da Matta, *A casa e a rua,* 31–69; idem, *Carnavais, malandros, e heróis,* 35–66; Gilberto Freyre presaged some of da Matta's insights in *Sobrados e macumbos,* 1:215–6.

17 On the importance of family, see Kuznesof and Oppenheimer, "The Family and Society in Latin America," 215–34. Donna J. Guy emphasized the need for more studies of masculinity in "Future Directions in Latin American Gender History."

18 *Collecção das leis do Império do Brasil* (Rio: Typ. Nacional, 1831), III:215–6.

19 Graham, *House and Street,* 3–27; Carvalho, *Os bestializados,* 126–39; Holloway, "A Healthy Terror," 640; Scheper-Hughes, *Death Without Weeping,* 76–92; Chalhoub, *Trabalho, lar, e botequim;* idem, *Visões da liberdade;* Abreu Esteves, *Meninas perdidas;* Caulfield, *In Defense of Honor.* On Iberian society see, for example, Julian Pitt-Rivers, "Honor and Social Status."

20 Timothy Coates, "Exiles and Orphans," 113–15; Pearson, "The Crowd in Portuguese India," 42. The Iberian words *praça* and *plaza* to designate an enlisted man differs from the Germanic term for a private. As Habermas noted, privates were "without rank and without the particularity of a special power to command interpreted as 'public.'" This reveals distinct linguistic and conceptual approaches to private and public power within Europe. Habermas, *The Structural Transformation of the Public Sphere,* 5.

21 On bordellos and their relationship to nation building, see Margaret Rago, *Do cabaré ao lar;* Guy, *Sex and Danger.*

22 Macedo, "Da prostituição em Geral," 115–21, 167; also, Almeida, *Homosexualismo,* 76–85.

23 *Relatório do Presidente da Província Henrique Pereira da Lucena* (Recife: M. Figeroa de F. e Filhos, 1875), 35.

24 McCann, "The Nation in Arms," 211–43. On veterans, see Eduardo Silva, *Prince,* 38–40; Soares, *A negregada instituição,* 185–96.

25 Stern, *The Secret History of Gender;* Guttman, *The Meanings of Macho.*

26 Von der Goltz, *The Nation in Arms,* 7–8.

27 Lovemen, *For la Patria,* 78, 86.

28 See, for example, essays in Joseph and Nugent, eds., *Everyday Forms of State Formation.*

29 An important exception to this generalization in the case of impressment is Lemisch, *Jack Tar Versus John Bull;* other important studies emphasize the significance of military mobilization for state building (Moore, *Conscription and Conflict in the Confederacy*). Tilly, "War Making and State Making as Organized Crime," 169–86. Tilly built on Frederic C. Lane's "Force and Enterprise in the Creation of Oceanic Commerce," in *The Tasks of Economic History* 10 (1950): 190–231; and "The Economic Meaning of War and Protection," in *Venice and History: The Collected Papers of Frederic C. Lane* (Baltimore: Johns Hopkins Press, 1966 [1942]).

Chapter 1 "Nabbing Time"

1 The U.S. Navy also pressed men. Lemisch, *Jack Tar Versus John Bull.*

2 See, for example, Aluísio Azevedo's depiction of urban slum residents fighting off policemen in *O Cortiço,* 88–89.

3 Impressment, while not as gruesome as the Atlantic passage, exhibits certain parallels to the slave trade. See, for example, testimony collected in Conrad, *Children of God's Fire,* chap. 1. On Indian slaving, see Monteiro, *Os Negros da terra.*

4 Nilo Val, "Notas sobre a história militar do Brasil," in *A Defeza Nacional* 83 (June 1920): 370. The navies and armies of Europe depended on impressment of vagabonds and subjected peoples. Napoleon occupied some regions for the sole purpose of dragooning. Forrest, *Conscripts and Deserters,* 19; on Portugal, Selvagem, *Portugal militar,* 202.

5 Cipolla, *Guns, Sails, and Empires.*

6 Boxer, *The Portuguese Seaborne Empire,* chap. 8; on Spain, Perry, *Crime and Society in Early Modern Seville,* chap. 5.

7 McNeill, "The Age of Gunpowder Empires"; Boxer, *The Portuguese Seaborne Empire,* 301–2.

8 Boxer, *The Portuguese Seaborne Empire,* 312.

9 Boxer, *Golden Age of Colonial Brazil,* 85–86; Ribeiro, *O Capitão de Infantaria Portuguez,* 2:157–84.

10 Coates, "Exiles and Orphans," 60–1.

11 See Boxer, *Golden Age of Colonial Brazil,* 54.

12 Bender, *Angola Under the Portuguese,* 73.

13 Coates, "Exiles and Orphans," 70.

14 Coates, "Exiles and Orphans," 64; Boxer, *Portuguese Seaborne Empire,* 314.

15 Coates, "Exiles and Orphans," 113–18; Bender, *Angola Under the Portuguese,* 60–61.

16 Duffy, *The Army of Frederick the Great,* 62; Russian public parks prohibited both dogs and army privates. Bushnell, *Mutiny Amid Repression,* 6.

17 Coates, "Exiles and Orphans," chap. 1; Bender, *Angola Under the Portuguese,*

73, 48; Robert Hughes, *The Fatal Shore,* 19–42; Pike, "Penal Servitude in the Spanish Empire, 21–40; Perry, *Crime and Society,* chap. 5.

18 On dangerous "soldier-exile" revolts, see Bender, *Angola Under the Portuguese,* 62–63; Coates, "Exiles and Orphans," 35–36.

19 McBeth translates the code in "The Politicians Versus the Generals," 256–60.

20 Cerqueira, *Reminiscencias da Guerra do Paraguay,* 5.

21 Alcântara, ed., *Legislação militar,* 203–4.

22 Boxer suggests that the need for *soldier exiles* increased in the 1700s and 1800s in *The Portuguese Seaborne Empire,* 313.

23 Boxer, *The Portuguese Seaborne Empire,* 311–12.

24 The Portuguese abrogated penal transportation in 1954. Bender, *Angola Under the Portuguese,* 93.

25 Alden, *Royal Government in Colonial Brazil,* 70 n. 32.

26 Robert Hughes, *The Fatal Shore,* 67.

27 Morton, "The Military and Society in Bahia," 249–69; Kraay, "Soldiers, Officers, and Society"; Kraay, "As Terrifying as Unexpected," 501–27.

28 Boxer, *Golden Age of Colonial Brazil,* 141.

29 Morton, "The Military and Society in Bahia," 263–64.

30 Kraay notes that in Bahia, African-born slaves were not freed to fight as soldiers in "Slavery, Citizenship, and Military Service," 228–56; Jorge Prata de Souza found that African-born slaves were recruited in Rio in *Escravidão ou morte,* 96–97. See also A. J. R. Russell-Wood, *The Black Man in Slavery and Freedom in Colonial Brazil* (New York: St. Martin's Press, 1982).

31 Sodré, *A história militar do Brasil,* 55.

32 Ferreira Lins, "A legião de São Paulo no Rio Grande do Sul," 168–69; Peregalli, *Recrutamento Militar no Brasil Colonial,* 99–101.

33 Peregalli, *Recrutamento Militar no Brasil Colonial,* 68, 118–37, 162.

34 Ibid., 138–47.

35 Barman, *Brazil,* chap. 4; Lynch, *The Spanish American Revolutions;* Lasso, "Haiti as an Image of Popular Republicanism; Ferrer, *Insurgent Cuba.*

36 Pang, *In Pursuit of Honor and Power.*

37 McBeth, "Brazilian Generals, 1822–1865," 125–41.

38 Schulz, *O Exército na política,* 28; José Murilo de Carvalho, "As Forças armadas na primeira república," 117–23.

39 *ASB,* vol. 2–3, *sessão* 30 July 1874, 237.

40 McBeth, "The Politicians Versus the Generals," 60–61.

41 Ibid., 155–65.

42 Ibid., 92–95.

43 *Collecção das decisões do império do Brazil de 1822,* 128–49.

44 Karasch lists sources on slaves who served in campaigns in the early 1800s in *Slave Life in Rio de Janeiro,* 79–80 n. 56.

45 Kuznesof, "Clans, the Militia, and Territorial Government," 189–93.

46 Flory, *Judge and Jury in Imperial Brazil,* 50–2; Marcus Joaquim Maciel de Carvalho, "Hegemony and Rebellion in Pernambuco," 75–78; Marson, *O Império de Progresso,* 207–8.

47 Letter from Delegate Manoel Antonio da [illegible] Reis to the governor, Barra Mansa, Feb. 6, 1847, APERJ, fu. PP, col. 103, pa. 18, ma. 30, doc. 8.

48 Marson, *O Império de Progresso,* 108–19; Marcus Joaquim Maciel de Carvalho, "Hegemony and Rebellion in Pernambuco," 78; Kraay cautions that most rebels pressed after the 1837 Sabinada Revolt were discharged soon after their induction, in Kraay, "Soldiers, Officers, and Society," 231–32.

49 For one Brazilian observer, this system was modeled after the equally unsavory British ship hulk prisons. IHGB, attributed to Cypriano José Barata de Almeida, "Dissertação abreviada sobre o horrível masmona — presiganga — existente no Rio de Janeiro," la. 48, doc. 12, May 26, 1829; on British hulks, Robert Hughes, *Fatal Shore,* 41–2; Bandeira Filho, *Informações sobre o Presídio de Fernando de Noronha,* annexos.

50 McBeth, "The Politicians Versus the Generals," 161.

51 Cited in Marcus Joaquim Maciel de Carvalho, "Hegemony and Rebellion in Pernambuco," 78.

52 Barman, *Brazil;* David Bushnell and Neill Macauley, *Latin America in the Nineteenth Century* 2nd ed. (New York: Oxford Univ. Press, 1994), 163–69.

53 Barman, *Brazil,* 150–88; Kraay, "The Politics of Race in Independence-Era Bahia," 30–56.

54 Barão de Itapicuru-Mirim, *Informações sobre a fixação das forças de terra para o anno de 1836 a 1837 apresentadas a Assemblea Legislativa de 1835* (Rio: Typ. Nacional, 1835), 4–6; McBeth, "The Politicians Versus the Generals," 182; Berrance de Castro, *A milícia cidadã,* 183–84.

55 Rodrigues et al., *A guarda nacional no Rio de Janeiro;* Uricoechea, *O minatauro imperial;* and Berrance de Castro, *A milícia cidadã.*

56 Rodrigues et al., *A guarda nacional no Rio de Janeiro,* 14–15; Meznar, "The Ranks of the Poor," 336–40.

57 Leal, *Coronelismo;* Raimundo Faoro, *Os Donos do Poder,* 5th ed. (Porto Alegre: Globo, 1979), I:378–79; Richard Graham, *Patronage and Politics in Nineteenth Century Brazil,* 89–97; Rodrigues et al., *A guarda nacional no Rio de Janeiro;* Berrance de Castro, *A milícia cidadã;* Carvalho, *A construção da ordem,* 165–178, 359–79.

58 Kraay, "As Terrifying as Unexpected," 502–3.

59 General V. Benício da Silva, ed., *A evolução militar do Brasil,* 289–91.

60 Flory, *Judge and Jury in Imperial Brazil,* 159–60.

61 For example, Kraay, "As Terrifying as Unexpected," 502, 508–15.

62 Marson noted that during the Praieira Revolt, Liberals and Conservatives competed for recruits through wage offers. Marson, *O Império de Progresso,* 63.

63 Assunção, *A Guerra de bem-te-vis,* 18; Maria de Lourdes Monaco Janotti, *A Balaiada* (Saõ Paulo: Ed. Brasiliense, 1987), 43–62.

64 Assunção, "Histórias do Balaio: Historiografia, memória oral, e as origens da Balaiada," *História Oral* 1:1 (June 1998):67–89.

65 Assunção, *A Guerra de bem-te-vis,* 171.

66 Ibid., 166, 174.

67 Berrance de Castro, *A milícia cidadã,* 233–42.

68 Letter from Police Chief Januário Francisco Coelho to the Governor of Rio de Janeiro, Mar. 22, 1844, APERJ, fu. PP, col. 8, pa. 2, ma. 2.

69 Letter from Commandante Superior da Guard Nacional Fabiano Pereira Barros to Governor Silveira Motta, Feb. 8, 1860, Rio, APERJ, fu. PP, col. 8, ma. 7.

70 For a guardsman's discharge see, for example, Letter from João Pedro Carvalho Moniz to the War Minister, Mar. 6, 1874, Porto Alegre, ANR, ma. IG¹ 200, fo. 1129.

71 Taunay, *Memórias,* 94–95. In 1859, a senator expressed concern that an officer's son was subject to "humiliating" corporal punishments before being recognized as a cadet. *ACB,* 1859, 3:74–76.

72 Joaquim and Juarez Távora chaffed under the thumb of NCOs who abused their authority over them. Juarez Távora, *Uma vida e muitas lutas,* 80–87; also, Lins de Barros, *Memórias de um revolucionário,* 12–13.

73 John Schultz, "The Brazilian Army and Politics," 50–64.

74 Engajamentos, Marinheiros Irlandeses para o Brasil, October 2, 1851, Liverpool, ANR, ma. IM 550, fo. 367, 385–86.

75 Barman, *Brazil,* 234.

76 "Recrutamento e engajamento," *O Militar,* July 11, 1854, 3.

Chapter 2   Raising the "Pagan Rabble"

1 For a list of the war's plentiful historiography, see Reber, "The Demographics of Paraguay," 289–90, n. 1; for a more recent assessment of the war's impact on Brazil, Costa Perez, *A espada de Dâmocles.*

2 Even some black freemen volunteered. Eduardo Silva, "O Príncipe Obá, um voluntário da pátria," 67–75; Schwarcz, *As barbas do Imperador,* chap. 11.

3 Abente, "The War of Triple Alliance," 47–69.

4 The decree is reproduced in Duarte, *Os Voluntários da Pátria,* 200–3.

5 5,000 Voluntários were provincial policemen. Ibid., 225.

6 Ibid., 217.

7 Wartime mobilization is beset by the numbers game. Reber figures that Paraguay mobilized 70,000 to 80,000 troops. Reber, "The Demographics of Paraguay," 308–10; for Brazil's official numbers, see *RRMGUP* (1872), annexos. Júlio José Chiavenato makes widely cited unsubstantiated claims that mobilization led to a "40 percent decline in Brazil's black population — in

only six years a million blacks vanished." He makes estimates without citing sources. Chiavenato: *O negro no Brasil*, 11, 199; id., *Genocídio Americano* and id., *Os Voluntários*. Kraay critiques these numbers and argues that official army and navy statistics were accurate in "Slavery." A forthcoming dissertation by Vitor Izecksohn at the University of New Hampshire argues that official army numbers were low, and based on data from provincial officials, he feels the actual number of slaves freed for army service may have reached 7,000. Jorge Prata de Souza also feels that official numbers were low for Rio de Janeiro, *Escravidão ou morte*. General Tasso Fragoso added official wartime mobilization figures to army troop strength before the war to assay 111,651 troops, Fragoso, *História da Guerra*, 5:260–64; General Paulo de Queiroz Duarte counted 135,580 deployed, but he cites no sources in *Os Voluntários da Pátria*, 210–18.

8   Police correspondence, April 13, 1867, Rio, ANR, SPCOA, ma. IJ⁶517, no fo. nos.; on slave prices, see Graden, "From Slavery"; Souza, *Escravidão ou morte*, chap. 4; Salles, *Guerra do Paraguai*, 68; Kraay, "Slavery, Citizenship, and Military Service," 239–46.

9   *O Arlequim* no. 5, May 1865, 5.

10 *RRMGuP* (1872), annexos. Cartoons hint that wealthy men presented unhealthy slaves as recruits: *O Arlequim*, October 13, 1867, 4; id., May 1867, 5.

11 In Rio Grande do Sul, an 1867 list by a commission enlisting volunteers for the army recorded a number of slaves who were presented as substitutes for sons or valued employees. Others presented themselves as substitutes for nephews or younger brothers. *AHRGS*, la. 204, ma. 3, AMD, 1863–88, no fo. nos.

12 Comparatively little attention has been paid to the mobilization of Brazilian women. On Paraguayan women, see Ganson, "Following Their Children into Battle," 335–71.

13 "Liberty and Oppression," *A Semana Illustrada*, September 3, 1865, 1972. One officer observed that women stripped the bodies of fallen enemies, and one heroic black woman distinguished herself by administering first aid to the wounded during a battle. Taunay, *A retirada da Laguna*, 97, 99.

14 Taunay, *A retirada da Laguna*, 135–36, 203; also, "Catalina, the Indian. This woman died dressed as a man at the battle of Paysandu," *A Semana Illustrada*, March 12, 1865, 1775. In peacetime, the War Ministry paid only for the transportation of the women and children of troops. See Correspondence from the War Minister to the President of Maranhão, January 26, 1881, São Luis, ANR, ma. IG¹26, no. fo. nos.

15 One officer's wife accompanied him. Correspondence of the War Ministry with the President of Ceará, April 12, 1865, Fortaleza, ANR, ma. IG¹40, no fo. nos.

16 Letter from the President of Ceará to the War Ministry, September 30, 1865, Fortaleza, ANR, ma. IG¹40, no fo. nos.; and ibid., October 12, 1865, no fo.

nos. Brazilian women had a battle hymn, "Canção da Mulher Brasileira." Peixoto, *Cancioneiro militar.*

17 Letter from Rio's Police Chief to the War Ministry, April 13, 1867, Rio, ANR, SPCOA, ma. IJ⁶517, no fo. nos. On Mato Grosso, see Volpato, *Cativos do sertão,* 64–5; Lucena Filho found evidence of a similar ratio of guardsmen "captured" by third parties for wartime duty in the *Journal do Recife,* November 4, 1865; see Lucena Filho, "Pernambuco," 93–94.

18 ASB, vol. April–June, *sessão* June 5, 1870, 86–87.

19 Graden, "From Slavery," 179–81; Lucena Filho, "Pernambuco," 89–91.

20 *O Cabrião,* São Paulo, September 15, 1867, 392 in BNR-SMOR.

21 Cited in Graden, "From Slavery," 182; Lucena Filho, "Pernambuco," chap. 4.

22 Editorial, *O Voluntário,* July 29, 1865, 2.

23 This remark is based on periodicals consulted in the BNR-SMOR: *O Cabrião, Mosquito, A Semana Illustrada, A Vida Fluminense, Mephistopheles,* and *O Arlequim.* For a different view of Brazilian wartime press coverage, see Silveira, *A batalha de papel.*

24 Volpato, *Cativos do sertão,* 64–65; Lucena Filho, "Pernambuco," 111–14; on substitute auctions, see, for example, satire in *O Cabrião,* December 2, 1866, 76; Letter from Francisco Fragoso to the Police Chief, October 18, 1866, Rio, ANR, ma. IJ⁶517, no fo. nos.

25 Rio de Janeiro's police chief complained about the 7th National Guard Battalion in Guaratyba: Letter from the Police Chief of Rio de Janeiro Province to the Justice Ministry, Rio de Janeiro, October 23, 1867, ANR, SPCOA, ma. IJ⁶517, no fo. nos.; also, Letter from Recruitment Agent Lieutenant Colonel José Lucas Raposo da Camara to the Governor of Pernambuco, December 20, 1865, Ingaseira, APEP, li. OE-20, fo. 73–74. On the trials of hunting down designated guardsmen, see Letter from Police Lieutenant Joaquim Herculano Caldos to Governor Francisco de Paula Silveira Lobo, October 22, 1866, Gamelina, APEP, li. PM-79, no fo. nos.

26 Marson, *Revolução Praieira,* 110–12; Circular Letter from War Minister João Lustoso da Costa Paranagua to the Province of Rio de Janeiro, October 2, 1867, Rio, APERJ, fu. PP, col. 8, pa. 11, ma. 13. On voluntary associations organized to "protect" the families of men at the front, ibid. January 13, 1868.

27 Cerqueira, *Reminiscencias,* 2–5.

28 ASB, vol. April–June, *sessão* June 5, 1870, 86–87.

29 "Minas," *O Diário do Povo,* January 6, 1869, 2.

30 *O Mosquito,* October 24, 1869, 5; also in BNR-SMOR, see: *O Cabrião,* November 18, 1866, 64; ibid., December 2, 1866, 76; ibid., May 26, 1867, 268; and ibid., September 15, 1867, 392; *A Semana Illustrada,* August 6, 1865, 1939.

31 Letter from Lieutenant Frederico Augusto Vellozo da Silveira to Governor Barão de Villa Bella, January 8, 1868, Granito, APEP, li. OE-20, fo. 130;

Letter from Major Antonio Dornellas Camara to Vice Governor Abilio José Tavares da Silva, ibid., April 26, 1867, fo. 108–10.

32 Letter from the War Minister Barão de Muritiba to the Governor of Rio de Janeiro, December 18, 1869, Rio, APERJ, fu. PP, col. 9, pa. 11, ma. 13.

33 Officers made lists of "recruitable" convicts in Brazil's largest penal colony. Letter from Tenente Coronel José Soares to Governor Francisco Paula de Silveira Martins, Fernando de Noronha, December 18, 1866, APEP, li. FN-12, no fo. nos.; for petitions of convicts Manoel Pereira de Alencar, Joaquim Gonçalves da Silva, and José Joaquim d'Almeida, see ibid., December 10, 1866; December 4, 1866; and December 3, 1866.

34 Correspondence from the President of Ceará to the War Ministry, September 11, 1867, Fortaleza, ANR, ma. IG¹40, no fo. nos.

35 ASB, vol. April–June, sessão June 5, 1870, 85–86.

36 Izechzohn, "O cerne da discórdia," 121–24; on Pedro II's image and declining popularity during the war, see Schwarcz, As barbas, 306–17.

37 Souza, Escravidão ou morte; Salles estimated that libertos never exceeded ten percent of the front line forces in Salles, Guerra do Paraguai, 66; Conrad cited the often quoted number of 20,000 slaves manumitted to fight in The Destruction of Brazilian Slavery, 76; for a fuller review see, Kraay, "Slavery, Citizenship, and Military Service"; on Afro-Argentine soldiers, see Andrews, The Afro-Argentines of Buenos Aires, 113–37. Also see chapter 2, note 7 on higher estimates.

38 O Diário do Povo, October 18, 1867, 1–2.

39 Letter from War Minister Baron de Muritiba to the Governor of Rio de Janeiro, Rio, June 10, 1870, APERJ, fu. PP, col. 8, pa. 12, ma. 15, no doc. nos.

40 My thinking here is influenced by Greenberg's Honor and Slavery and more generally in the United States, Roediger's The Wages of Whiteness.

41 Dionysio Cerqueira lamented that an all-black unit of volunteers commanded by black officers was dissolved at the front. Most were sent to serve as hospital orderlies, reproducing Brazil's racial hierarchy by delegating servile and less heroic duties of lesser prestige to blacks. Cerqueira, Reminiscências, 71–72.

42 Reports of Brazilian troops active in Paraguay in 1867 show that one-fourth to one-third of the deployed troops were consistently listed as "ill." On November 30, 1967, for example, 10,881 were listed as "ill," 25,883 as "ready," and 3,239 as "employed." RRMGUP (1968), 80; Eduardo Silva, "O Príncipe Obá," 74.

43 Taunay, A retirada da Laguna, 144–45.

44 Ibid., 152.

45 Peñalba, "Draft Dodgers, War Resisters, and Turbulent Gauchos," 476.

46 Ibid., 470–78.

47 Foucault, Discipline and Punish, chap. 1.

48 Younger cadets were shocked by this castigation and questioned its legality

among themselves. Cerqueira reflected, "We were young and did not understand the responsibility that weighed on the chief commander of a greenhorn army." Cerqueira, *Reminiscencias,* 57–61.

49   Taunay, *A retirada da Laguna,* 176.

50   Silva, ed., *Consultas do Conselho do Estado,* 119–21.

51   Cited in Izecksohn, "O cerne da discórdia," 185.

52   Ibid., 101–2, 109–11, 131–35.

53   V. de Barros, "Queixa," Ilha do Governador, Rio de Janeiro, July 19, 1868, ANR, SPCOA, ma. IJ⁶517, no fo. nos.; a Conservative police chief of Pará requested imperial police to aid him in maintaining the peace in Barcarena, Pará, where Liberals were "well armed" and the local police delegate was not "trust worthy." Rio's police chief obliged the request, informing his men to obey the orders of Pará's police. Letter from the Police Chief of Pará to the Police Chief of the Côrte, September 9, 1868, Belém, ANR, SPCOA, ma. IJ⁶517, no fo. nos.

54   On Liberals, see Peter M. Beattie, "Transforming Enlisted Army Service in Brazil," chap. 2.

55   ASB, vols. I–II, *sessão* June 28, 1869, 334.

56   Ibid., 329.

57   Pessoa, *A idéia repúblicana no Brasil,* 37–62. Passage translated by and cited in Emilia Viotti da Costa, *The Brazilian Empire,* 73.

58   "The Official Rejoicing," *The Anglo-Brazilian Times,* July 23, 1870, 2; "La Fête du 10 Juillet," *Ba-Ta-Clan,* July 16, 1870, 1–2.

59   On the fragility of the grandstands, see auto de exame por Miguel José Távares, Rio, July 5, 1870, ANR, SPCOA, ma. IJ⁶518, no fo. nos.

60   Lima, *O movimento da Independência,* 420–25.

61   "A Country Worth Fighting For," *The Anglo-Brazilian Times,* August 22, 1870, 3; Silva, "O Príncipe Obá," 69–70.

62   "O Symbolo do Brazil," *Brazil-Americano,* July 7, 1875, 2; see also the popular song by Francisco Ponzio Sobrinho, "O sertanejo patriotico," 1870, n.p., in BNMR. The cartoons found in the Paraguayan newspapers *El Centinela* and *Cabichui* are replete with these images; Peter M. Beattie, "National Identity and the Brazilian Folk," 7–43.

63   Taunay stated that he often argued for the French army and political system over the Prussian with Military Academy comrades in the 1860s. Taunay, *Memórias,* 98; Doria noted that Prussia's victory over France proved the importance of well-prepared troops in *Estudos sobre a promoção nos exércitos;* Nunn, *Yesterday's Soldiers,* 131–36.

64   *Revista do Exército Brasileiro,* Rio de Janeiro, 1882, 1, in AHE.

65   "O recrutamento e Sr. Deputado Buarque de Macedo," *Imprensa Academica,* São Paulo, July 28, 1868, 1, in BNR-SMOR. A senator echoed this idea, "The military spirit is a condition for the life of nations; without it, China was defeated by a handful of Tartars; India allowed its two hundred million

inhabitants be dominated by the English; Mexico by three hundred Spaniards, and Peru by Pizarro." *O Globo*, August 21, 1874, 2.

66 Peter M. Beattie, "National Identity and the Brazilian Folk," 7–45. For an in-depth analysis of ideas of the frontier and nation among intellectuals, see Lima, *Um sertão chamado Brasil*. Rio:

Chapter 3   The "Law of the Minotaur"?

1 Stepan, *The Hour of Eugenics*, 3.
2 Taunay, *Extracto do discurso*; Skidmore, *Black into White*.
3 Costa, *The Brazilian Empire*, 75; Richard Graham, *Patronage and Politics*, chap. 7.
4 See, for example, Barcellos, "Dos systemas penitenciarios"; in unpublished Bib.; Salvatore and Aguirre, "Penitentiaries, Visions of Class, and Export Economies," 194–223.
5 Costa, *The Brazilian Empire*, 74, chap. 8.
6 RRMGUP (1870), 25; ibid. (1872), 2–3; *Relatório do Presidente de Província Dr. José Evaristo da Cruz Gouvêa à assemblea da Paraíba*, Paraíba: n.p., September 16, 1871, 6.
7 Cited in Eduardo Silva, *Prince of the People*, 124.
8 Naval Minister correspondence, letter 86, "Inspecção do Arsenal de Marinha de Matto Grosso," May 7, 1883, Corumbá, ANR, ma. XM-842, no fo. nos. Examples of illegal flogging in the army are found in chap. 8.
9 *O Globo*, August 14, 1874, 2.
10 On initiation rites, see Celso Castro, *O espírito militar*.
11 RRMGUP (1872), 6.
12 RRMGUP (1874), 4.
13 Liberals accused Conservatives of exploiting Parliamentary rules to limit debate on recruitment and electoral reform in the *Câmara*. *O Globo*, August 19, 1874, 3; *O Diário do Rio de Janeiro*, September 1, 1874, 4. Conservatives claimed that the methods were vital for the bill's timely passage because the *Câmara* had already debated it for three years. *O Diário do Rio de Janeiro*, June 1, 1874, 1. See figure 8.
14 *O Diário do Rio de Janeiro*, February 28, 1874, 1; *Jornal do Commércio*, February 25, 1874, 2.
15 *A República* contradicted itself on this point, "Do not think that he [the common Russian citizen] only lives for war; on the contrary, he cuts off his fingers and blinds himself to avoid becoming a soldier." *A República*, February 24, 1874, 2.
16 *O Globo*, August 14, 1874, 2.
17 *O Diário do Rio de Janeiro*, June 8, 1874, 2.
18 See, for example, Costa, *The Brazilian Empire*; Graham, *Patronage and Politics*; Silva, *Prince of the People*.

19 Eugen Weber noted that the French who had invented conscription began to adopt Prussian models by 1868 in *Peasants into Frenchmen*, 292.

20 *ASB*, vol. April–June, *sessão* June 5, 1870, 90.

21 *Diário do Rio de Janeiro*, September 20, 1874, 1–2.

22 *ASB*, vol. April–June, *sessão* June 1, 1870, 7; ibid., *sessão* June 2, 1870, 77–78.

23 *ASB*, vol. July, *sessão* July 1, 1870, 7.

24 *ASB*, vol. April–June, *sessão* June 5, 1870, 85–86.

25 *ASB*, vol. July, *sessão* July 1, 1870, 7.

26 *O Diário do Rio de Janeiro*, June 8, 1874, 2; *ASB*, vol. July, *sessão* July 1, 1870, 7.

27 Nabuco echoed this idea, *O Diário do Rio de Janeiro*, September 1, 1874, 2.

28 *O Globo*, August 13, 1874, 2.

29 *O Globo*, August 19, 1874, 3.

30 *O Globo*, August 14, 1874, 2.

31 *ASB*, *sessão* May 29, 1874, 1:131.

32 *O Diário do Rio de Janeiro*, June 8, 1874, 2.

33 *O Globo*, August 18, 1874, 2.

34 *A Sintinela do Sul*, July 7, 1867. Reproduced in Izecksohn, "O Cerne da discórdia," 211.

> Junqueira—one of [conscription's] advantages is that it is equal for all provinces. . . . There are . . . provinces that do not present troops in proportion to their population.
> Saraiva—For example, Minas Gerais . . .
> Silveira Lobo—That is not so, [Minas] has given much.
> Junqueira—. . . the noble senator . . . represents one of the most important southeastern provinces, where armed service is not among the most sought after [careers], seeks to impede this project's passage which is eminently leveling, and thus, it should be even more appealing to the senator's liberal ideals."[35]

35 *O Globo*, August 14, 1874, 2.

36 Junqueira reasoned, "The free native population cannot be the basis of the [recruitment] distribution because the current statistics [1872 census] are far from accurate. Therefore, it is established that the draft boards will make the count; and it is without foundation to combat this system by saying that in many provinces it will be a sophism." "Assemblea de 13 de Agosto," *O Globo*, August 14, 1874, 2.

37 *ASB*, vol. 3–5 (1873), 202–6; *O Globo*, August 14, 1874, 2.

38 See law 2556 of September 26, 1874, *Collecção das leis do Império do Brazil* (Rio: Imprensa Nacional, 1874), 64–74.

39 See law 5881, Article 115, ibid., 1876, 1:168–69, 189; *Collecção das leis do Império do Brasil* (Rio: Typ. Nacional, 1876), 236.

40 *O Globo*, August 14, 1874, 2.

41 *O Globo,* August 19, 1874, 2.

42 See law 2556 of September 26, 1874, *Collecção das leis do Império do Brazil* (Rio: Imprensa Nacional, 1874), 64–66.

43 Junqueira felt that exempting students would upset the balance between urban and rural recruitment. *O Diário do Rio de Janeiro,* June 7, 1874, 1; *O Globo,* August 14, 1874, 2.

44 *O Globo,* August 14, 1874, 2.

45 *O Diário do Rio de Janeiro,* July 15, 1874, 2.

46 *O Globo,* August 14, 1874, 2; E. P. Thompson, "Time, Work-Discipline, and Industrial Capitalism," 59–97. In 1882, the war minister called for the creation of regimental schools to teach soldiers Portuguese grammar, French, geography, history, and math. He claimed that some were already operating in Rio and the provinces, and he asked that the officers who taught these courses be compensated. RRMGUP (1882), 9.

47 One senator linked police and army recruitment reform. Army and police praças involved in crime became an increasing embarrassment. *O Diário do Rio de Janeiro,* June 8, 1874, 1; Holloway, "A Healthy Terror," 664–69.

48 "Assemblea de 13 de Agosto," *O Globo,* August 14, 1874, 2.

49 Ibid.

50 *O Diário do Rio de Janeiro,* September 20, 1874, 1–2.

51 Ibid., September 2, 1874, 1–2.

52 Ibid.

53 Ibid., June 8, 1874, 2.

54 Malerba, *Os brancos da lei.* On fears of militarism's influence on exports, see Rebouças, *Agricultura nacional,* 96–99.

55 ASB, *sessão* May 30, 1874, 1:133; *O Globo,* August 19, 1874, 2.

56 *O Diário do Rio de Janeiro,* September 2, 1874, 1–2.

57 *O Diário do Rio de Janeiro,* June 8, 1874, 2; *O Globo,* August 18, 1874, 2.

58 *O Globo,* August 19, 1874, 2.

59 *O Globo,* August 13, 1874, 2.

60 *O Diário do Rio de Janeiro,* June 9, 1874, 2.

61 Schowalter, *Railroads and Rifles;* Brazil, Argentina, and Chile began to acquire large stocks of breech-loading rifles in the mid-1890s when Brazil began to lower minimum service contracts. See, for example, the nervous letter from Argentina's war minister to his president reporting Brazil's order of 120,000 mausers, Carta de Pablo Riccheri a Uriburu, December 24, 1894, Berlin, AGN, Fundo Uriburu, *legajo* 8, 2532.

62 *O Globo,* August 13, 1874, 2; ibid., August 14, 1874, 2; *Mephistopheles,* September 6, 1874, 2.

63 Salvatore and Aguirre, "The Birth of the Penitentiary in Latin America." On the "progressive march toward civilization" and the Recruitment Law, see *Diário do Rio de Janeiro,* February 28, 1874, 1.

Chapter 4 Whipping a Dead Letter

1 *A Reforma,* August 1, 1875, 2. The information came from *A Folha Official de Alagoas* which transcribed the justice of the peace's official report. In a Pernambucan parish a protestor ripped up recruitment notices and replaced them with a call to protest on the day the draft board sat. Letter from the Delegate of São Bento to the Police Chief, July 5, 1875, APEP, li. PC-144, fo. 77.

2 There are important exceptions, such as Frank D. McCann's "The Nation in Arms," 211–43; Richard Graham, *Patronage,* 27–9.

3 Nelson Werneck Sodré provided the classic analysis of a professionalizing army officer corps allied with an emerging bourgeoisie in conflict with the landed elites. He states that the attempts to implement conscription in 1875 were "foiled in the face of political resistance" without more specifics. Sodré, *A história militar,* 142; John Henry Schulz, "The Brazilian Army," 120–25; William S. Dudley concurred, "The landed elite would presumably not undertake to strengthen the army through an equitable recruitment law, if there were any chance it would weaken their position." Dudley, "Reform," 170.

4 Meznar, "The Ranks of the Poor," 335–51.

5 Teresa A. Meade provides a thoughtful analysis of the structures and traditions of urban protest in Rio in *"Civilizing" Rio: Reform and Resistance in a Brazilian City, 1889–1930* (University Park: Pennsylvania State University Press, 1997). Meade, like most social and labor historians — with the exception of Edgar Carone, have paid scant attention to the protests against conscription. Resistance to conscription and impressment provides a means of linking analysis of rural and urban traditions of popular protest over a broad sweep of time.

6 *RRMGuP* (1875), 8.

7 *O Globo,* September 5, 1874, 4.

8 On republicans and the army, see Magalhães Junior, *Deodoro a espada contra o império,* 1:136–37.

9 "Assemblea geral do Senado sessão 65," *O Globo,* August 18, 1874, 2.

10 Harrod, *Manning,* 34–38.

11 Assunção, *A Guerra de bem-te-vis,* 18, 165–76.

12 See Junqueira's blast at Liberals from Minas in *O Globo,* August 14, 1874, 2.

13 *Relatório do Presidente Henrique Pereira de Lucena* (Recife: M. Figueiroa de F. e Filhos, 1875), 7; Barman, "The Brazilian Peasantry Reexamined," 401–22; Meznar, "Deference and Dependence," 191–247.

14 *O Alvorada,* Ano I, no. 4, April 1878, 2. See accusations leveled against Liberal leaders in *Diário de Pernambuco,* December 4, 1874, 2. The governor paid for steamship passages for six Jesuits to Lisbon, Letter from Police Chief Democrito Calvalcante d'Albuquerque to Governor Lucena, Janu-

ary 21, 1875, Recife, APEP, li. PC-142, fo. 119. On impressment of rioters, see Letter from Antonio Raymundo Lins Caldas to Governor Henrique, January 4, 1875, Limoeiro, APEP, li. OE-20, fo. 369.

15 Correspondence from the President of Paraíba to the War Minister, April 13, 1875, Paraíba ANR, ma. IG¹57, no fo. nos.; also see men remitted for army service from Pernambuco in Letter from the Police Chief Antonio Francisco Correia d'Araujo to Governor Henrique Pereira de Lucena, December 18, 1874, Recife, APEP, li. PC-140, fo. 371; ibid., December 9, 1874, fo. 379; ibid., December 21, 1874, fo. 414.

16 Correspondence from the President of Paraíba to the War Ministry, May 17, 1875, Paraíba, ANR, ma. IG¹57, no fo. nos.; "O recrutamento na Paraíba," *O Globo*, February 12, 1875, 2; *Diário de Pernambuco*, December 2, 1874, 2; Meznar, "The Ranks of the Poor," 350 n. 50.

17 *O Globo*, February 12, 1875, 2; Meznar, "The Ranks of the Poor, 350; Letter from Police Chief Democrito to Governor Lucena, January 29, 1875, Recife, APEP, li. PC-142, fo. 156.

18 These phrases are cited in Meznar, "The Ranks of the Poor," 347–51. Fears of re-enslavement were not unfounded; see, for example, Freitas, "Slavery and Social Life."

19 *RRMGUP* (1877), 13.

20 Correspondence from the President of Mato Grosso to the War Ministry, December 31, 1884, ANR, ma. IG¹246, fo. 973; for another example, see *Constituição*, September 13, 1872, 1; also see Flory, *Judge*, 188–89 and Graham, *Patronage*, 89–93.

21 *A Reforma*, July 20, 1875, 2.

22 Ibid.

23 *A Reforma*, August 1, 1875, 2. The location of the place names twice re- moved by newspapers rereporting the same story leads to confusion. Bert Barickman recognized Igreja Nova as a rural district north of Salvador near another district known as Palomé, not Salomé. I am not certain of the location or accuracy of the place name Porto Real do Colegio parish. I thank the sharp eyes of Dain Borges for catching this mix-up.

24 "Ofício do Vice-Presidente," in *Relatório apresentado à Assemblea legislativa da Bahia* (Salvador: Jornal da Bahia, 1876), 1–3; Correspondence from the President of Bahia to the War Ministry, December 1, 1875, Salvador, ANR, ma. IG¹128, fo. 1129–30; Ibid., April 3, 1876, fo. 27–9.

25 *Relatório do Presidente da Província Francisco da Faria Lemos à assemblea cearense* (Fortaleza: Typ. Cearense, 1876), 5.

26 In 1912, Governor Nogueira Acioli fell from power when his military police forces fired on a protest march of women, producing a violent popular reaction that ousted the oligarch in three days. Carone, *A República Velha*, 2:291–92.

27 On the etiquette of female protest in another setting see Stern, *The Secret*

History of Gender; on the importance of honor for reciprocity networks in contemporary Brazil see Scheper-Hughes, *Death Without Weeping,* 102–5; on military salaries see McCann, "The Nation in Arms," 219–21.

28 Correspondence from the War Ministry to the President of Bahia, December 21, 1875; ANR, ma. IG^{1}128, fo. 1109, 1112; "Ofício do Vice-Presidente Dr. José Eduardo Freire de Carvalho," in *Relatório apresentado à assemblea legislativa da Bahia* (Salvador: Typ. Jornal da Bahia, 1876), 1–3.

29 *Relatório do Presidente da Província João Paulo Carvalho de Moraes* (Recife: March 1, 1876), 27–8.

30 Ibid. Conflicts over registration are noted in Paraíba, *Relatório do Presidente da Província Dr. Silvino Elvidio Carneiro de Cunha* (Paraíba, 1875).

31 *Relatório do Presidente da Província Dr. Sebastião José Pereira à assemblea legislativa de São Paulo* (São Paulo, 1876), 47; Moura, *Saindo das sombras,* 99.

32 Minas Gerais, *Relatório do Presidente da Província Barão da Villa da Barra apresentado à assemblea legislativa* (Ouro Preto, 1876), 6, 36.

33 *Relatório do Presidente da província José Antônio de Azevedo Castro* (Porto Alegre, 1876), 13.

34 *Jornal de Aracaju,* October 16, 1875, 2.

35 Ibid.; Weber, *Peasants into Frenchmen.*

36 *Jornal de Aracaju,* October 16, 1875, 1–2.

37 "Sorteio militar [ad]," *Jornal de Aracaju,* December 25, 1875, 4.

38 Letter to War Minister Duque de Caxias from the Juiz de Direito of the first civil district, vara civil, November 10, 1875, Rio, AHE, ca. 116 R-7. I thank my friend Mara Loveman for generously sharing this source with me.

39 *Relatório que ao S. Senador João Florentino Meira de Vasconcellos apresentou ao Dr. José Francisco Netto no acto de passar-lhe a administração da província de Minas Gerais* (Ouro Preto, 1881), 6.

40 Correspondence from the President of Minas Gerais to the War Ministry, October 15, 1884, Ouro Preto, ANR, ma. IG^{1}216, fo. 654. Similarly, a "large number of women" attack the draft board in Vargem Alegre parish. Interestingly, this report states that "these women were accompanied by a large number of men." This was a gender role reversal as women are normally described as accompanying men. Correspondence from the President of Minas Gerais to the War Ministry, October 1, 1884, ANR, ma. IG^{1}216, fo. 655. In 1896, the governor of Minas Gerais reflected: "*Mineiros* hate the uniform. Conscription will not work, and was evaded while our women tore up enlistment records. Sending recruiting agents does not work well either." ASB (July 15, 1892), 369. Cited in Wirth, *Minas Gerais in the Brazilian Federation,* 189.

41 Correspondence from the President of Minas Gerais to the War Ministry, March 9, 1877, Ouro Preto, ANR, ma. IG^{1}215, fo. 331; Correspondence from the President of Bahia to the War Ministry, August 24, 1875, Salvador, ANR, ma. IG^{1}128, fo. 1083; Correspondence from the President of Minas

Gerais to the War Ministry, April 28, 1875, Ouro Preto, ANR, ma. IG¹214, fo. 195; Correspondence from the President of Bahia to the War Ministry, December 1, 1875, Salvador, ANR, ma. IG¹128, fo. 1129–30; ibid., April 3, 1876, fo. 27–29; Correspondence from the President of Mato Grosso to the War Ministry, June 2, 1875, Cuiabá, ANR, ma. IG¹245, fo. 388.

42 When they were fined, parish authorities claimed that the laws regulating enrollment were unclear. Their fines were eventually suspended. Correspondence from the President of Mato Grosso to the War Ministry, May 3, 1878, Cuiabá ANR, ma. IG¹245, fo. 531; and June 7, 1880, fo. 564; see a similar case in Nossa Senhora das Neves in Mauhá Rio de Janeiro in 1880. Letter from the President of Rio de Janeiro to the War Ministry, October 5, 1880, Niteroi, ANR, ma. IG¹148, no fo. nos.

43 *RRMGuP* (1877), 13–14.

44 Correspondence from the President of Bahia to the War Ministry, April 3, 1876, Salvador, ANR, ma. IG¹128, fo. 27.

45 In 1890, Apiai had 279 registered voters; most were *lavradores* (farmers who owned or rented plots of land). AESP, Registro da Câmara de Apiai, 1875–1895; see similar lists in AMD 1863–1888, AHRGS, la. 204, ma. 3, no fo. nos.

46 Letter from Espírito Santo's governor, Candido Luiz Maria da Oliveira, reprinted in *RRMGuP* (1885), Annexo T.

47 *Relatório do Presidente da Província Francisco de Farias Lemos à assemblea legislativa* (Ouro Preto: April 13, 1886), 54–56.

48 *Relatório do Presidente da Província André Augusto de Padua Fleury apresentado à assemblea legislative cearense* (Fortaleza: April 1, 1881), 28.

49 *Relatório do Presidente da Província Joaquim da Costa Barradas à assemblea legislativa cearense* (Fortaleza: n.p., 1886), 36; see also Correspondence from the President of Maranhão to the War Ministry, São Luíz, January 26, 1887, ANR, ma. IG¹27, no fo. nos.

50 Correspondence from the President of Rio Grande do Sul to the War Ministry, March 3, 1881, Porto Alegre, ANR, ma. IG¹201, fo. 284–88.

51 Pompéia, *Crônicas do Rio,* 65–67.

52 See the assertions on the army's right to take part in State administration in *O soldado,* March 22, 1881 in AHE.

53 Alfred Stepan, *The Military in Politics,* 12; Hayes, *The Nation in Arms,* 46–70; McCann, "The Nation in Arms," 504–7.

54 Cited in Hahner, *Civilian-Military Relations in Brazil,* 75.

55 The army's advanced educational institutions endured numerous reforms in the late 1800s, making it difficult to speak of "a" military academy. I use the term to describe the nucleus of higher army education in Rio.

56 Barreto, *Triste fim de Policarpo Quaresma,* 42; Celso Castro, *Os militares e a República.*

57 Taunay, *Memórias,* 94.

58 Magalhães Junior, *Deodoro a espada contra o império,* 1:180–81.

59 Hahner, *Civilian-Military Relations in Brazil*, 12–19; Magalhães Junior, *Deodoro a espada contra o império*, 1:206–46.

60 Magalhães Junior, *Deodoro a espada contra o império*, 1:316. For a typical request for army soldiers to repress rebellious slaves see, for example, Correspondence between the War Ministry and the President of Rio de Janeiro Province, March 28, 1885, ANR, Nictheroy, ma. IG¹147, fo. 555. For a critique of the army's claims to be a bastion of abolitionism, see Kraay, "Recruitment."

61 I borrow this phrase from Barreto, *Triste fim de Policarpo Quaresma*, 95.

62 See the call for a draft lottery in the most widely circulated republican newspaper of Rio Grande do Sul. "Recrutamento," *A Federação*, February 21, 1889, 1. I thank my friend Roger Kittleson for sharing this citation.

Chapter 5

"And One Calls This Misery a Republic?"

1 Dain Edward Borges, *The Family in Bahia Brazil*

2 Daniel J. Hughes, *The King's Finest*, 11–23.

3 Letter from Rui Barbosa to the editor, December 20, 1890, ACRB, pa. *La Prensa*. Cited in de Carvalho, *Os bestializados*, 169 n. 11.

4 Da Cunha, *Rebellion in the Backlands*, 207, 249–51.

5 Ibid., 223; Peter M. Beattie, "National Identity and the Brazilian Folk."

6 Pang and Seckinger, "The Mandarins of Imperial Brazil"; José Murilo de Carvalho, *A construção da ordem* and *Teatro de sombras*.

7 Rodrigues, *A guarda nacional*, 301–12.

8 ASB, *sessão* August 11, 1896, 3:423.

9 On Brazil's early labor movement, Maram, *Anarquistas, immigrantes;* Carvalho, *Os bestializados*, 52–64; Carone, *A República Velha*, 153–54.

10 *O Operário*, January 20, 1889, 1–2. I thank Roger Kittleson for this citation.

11 *Echo Popular,* March 11, 1890, 2.

12 Lauro Sodré, *Crenças e opiniões* (Belém: Typographia do Diário Oficial, 1896), 241. Cited in Carvalho, *Os bestializados*, 50.

13 Rodrigues, *A guarda nacional*, 313–26.

14 *O Echo Popular,* May 31, 1890, 1.

15 *A Voz do Povo*, Rio de Janeiro, August 28, 1892, 1 in AEL; Letter from [illegible] to Dr. Gregorio Enriques Lopes, October 20, 1893, Rio, AGCRJ, AM, codice (197) 39-4-10.

16 *O Echo Popular,* May 29, 1890, 1.

17 Ibid., May 29, 1890, 2.

18 Ibid., May 31, 1890, 1.

19 RRMGUC (1891), 9.

20 Mello, *O Governo provisório*, 1:202–4; Carone, *A República Velha*, 2:85–87; Carneiro, *História das revoluções brasileiras*, 62–73. Floriano's supporters

in Alagoas and Bahia were skittish because the revolt coincided with the exile of students who opposed Floriano's regime, Telegram from Governor Bezouro to Floriano Peixoto, August 7, 1892, Macieó, ANR, Arquivo Floriano Peixoto, ca. 8L-1; Telegram from General Lima e Silva to Floriano Peixoto, September 13, 1892, ibid.; Telegram from Benjamin Barroso to Senator Bezerra, January 1, 1892, Fortaleza, ibid.

21 Law #39 of January 30, 1892 is reproduced in Lobo Viana, ed., *Guia Militar,* 1:109.

22 "Relatório do General Luis Henrique Ewbank," March 28, 1892, AHE, se. 4 ca. 1-C, pa. 2. See also the rebel manifesto, *O Lidador,* March 26, 1892, 1.

23 Love, *Rio Grande do Sul,* 36–75.

24 Steven Topik, *Trade and Gunboats: The United States and Brazil in the Age of Empire.*

25 Hahner, *Civilian-Military Relations in Brazil,* 125–48; Topik, *Trade and Gunboats.*

26 Barreto, *Triste fim de Policarpo Quaresma,* 85, 103.

27 *A Revista Illustrada,* March 1893, 4–5.

28 *ASB, sessão* August 12, 1896, 3:434–38; ibid., *sessão* August 13, 1896, 3:458–59.

29 *ASB, sessão* August 12, 1896, 3:438.

30 *ASB, sessão* August 13, 1896, 3:453.

31 Da Cunha, *Rebellion in the Backlands,* 180.

32 See, for example, Levine, *Vale of Tears;* on Padre Cícero, see della Cava, *Miracle at Joaseiro.*

33 Da Cunha, *Rebellion in the Backlands,* 283.

34 Carvalho, *Os bestializados,* 66–74.

35 Da Cunha, *Rebellion in the Backlands;* Peter M. Beattie, "National Identity and the Brazilian Folk."

36 Leal, *Coronelismo.*

37 *ASB, sessão* July 10, 1899, 2:87.

38 Ibid., 85. Senator Pires Ferreira noted that the 1892 penalties had not been applied. *ASB, sessão* August 12, 1896, 3:2.

39 *A Nação,* December 31, 1903, 1.

40 Ibid., 29 December 1903, 1; ibid., December 30, 1903, 1; ibid., January 1, 1904, 1; ibid., January 4, 1904, 1.

41 The naval minister cited law #478 of December 9, 1897, article one, paragraph six, letters a, b, and c. *A Voz do Trabalhador,* January 4, 1903, 1.

42 *A Larva,* January 8, 1904, 8.

43 *ASB*, appendix, *sessão extraordinária* January 7, 1904, 21.

44 Ibid., 30, 32.

45 Foucault's idea of multivocal "discourses" overemphasizes the convergence of these dialogues, implying an unrelenting sense of domination. His work, however, does illuminate the give and take between the dominant and sub-

ordinate groups, particularly in terms of the debate on family honor in this study. Foucault, *The History of Sexuality*, 25–35.

46 Carone, *A República Velha*, 2:211–29; Carvalho, *Os bestializados*, 126–39.

47 Abreu Esteves, *Meninas perdidas*, 25–32, 83–114; Caufield and Abreu Esteves, "Fifty Years of Virginity in Rio de Janeiro, 47–74; Caulfield, *In Defense of Honor;* Carvalho, *Os bestializados*, 52–53, 98.

48 Mendes, *Actual agitação militarista*, 3; Mendes, *O ensino público e o despotismo sanitário;* Mendes, *A Liberdade espiritual e a vacinação obligatória;* Mendes, *Mais um attentado de depotismo sanitário*.

49 *O Echo Popular*, May 31, 1890, 2.

50 *Correio da Manhã*, November 6, 1904, 1. Cited in Carvalho, *Os bestializados*, 100–101; Mendes cited in Cruz Costa, *O positivismo na República*, 38; *Correio da Manhã*, November 10, 1904.

51 An ensign in Salvador led a revolt on November 17, 1904 in sympathy with Rio's revolt. Relatório do Quartel General do Commandante do Terceiro Districto Militar General de Brigada Antonio Vicente Ribeiro Guimarães, November 22, 1907, Salvador, AHE, se. 4, ca. 1A, H-11, pa. 4.

52 For a cadet's account of the Vaccine Revolt, see Klinger *Narrativas Autobiográficas*.

53 Chalhoub, *Cidade febril*. "Serviço de Prophylaxia da Febre Amarela, Secção da Polícia dos Focos Terceira Zona," December 31, 1905, Rio, ACOC-FOC, BP/SR/1905.20.40, doc. (3+0+0) Relatório sobre a campanha contra a febre amarela 1905–1911, *pa*. 02, no *fo*. nos.

54 *RRMGUC* (1904), 3–5.

55 Osorio Filho, *O espírito das armas brasileiras*, XXXII.

56 Viveiros, *Rondon conta sua vida*, 376–425; Bederman, *Manliness and Civilization*.

57 See, for example, Osorio Filho's association of Scouting, *tiros*, and the LDN in *O espírito das armas brasileiras*, 222–26, XXVI–XXXII. McCann, "Nation in Arms," 226–29; on gun clubs and nationalism in Germany, see Mosse, *The Nationalization*, 148–60.

58 Nancy Leys Stepan, *The Hour of Eugenics*, 16, 36; Borges, *The Family in Bahia Brazil*.

Chapter 6 The Troop Trade and the Army as a Protopenal Institution in the Age of Impressment

1 Scott, *Hidden Transcripts*. Interestingly, the one article Scott cites on the topic addresses Latin America: Fick's "Black Peasants and Soldiers in the St. Domingue Revolution."

2 Richard Graham, *Patronage and Politics*, 27–33; Kraay, "Soldiers, Officers, and Society," chap. 6; Holloway, *Policing Rio de Janeiro;* Soares, *A negregada instituição*, 225–30; Fraga Filho, *Mendigos moleques, e vadios*, 119–25;

Molas, *Historia social del gaucho;* Slatta, *Gauchos and the Vanishing Frontier;*
Wells, "Yucatán: Violence and Social Control on Henequen Plantations";
Guy P. C. Thomson, "Los Indios y el servicio militar en el México decimonónico," 207–51; Salvatorre, "Reclutamiento militar, disciplinamento y
proletización," 25–47.

3   This section summarizes arguments made in greater detail in Peter M. Beattie, "Transforming Enlisted Army Service in Brazil," chap. 6.

4   Correspondence from the Governor of Minas Gerais to the War Minister,
April 8, 1873, Ouro Preto, ANR, ma. IG¹214, fo. 94.

5   In 1885, all northeastern provinces except Maranhão had more troops than
their budgeted levels. War Ministry Correspondence with the President of
Maranhão, July 15, 1885, Rio, ANR, ma. IG¹27, no fo. nos.

6   Peixoto, *Memórias de um velho soldado,* 72–73.

7   On the transfer of incorrigible troops, see Correspondence from the Governor of São Paulo to the War Ministry, August 28, 1873, Santos, ANR, ma.
IG¹160, fo. 173–74; War Ministry Correspondence, September 9, 1873, Rio
de Janeiro, ANR, ma. IG¹160, fo. 172.

8   Kraay finds that in Bahia most recruits appeared to be taken in the coastal
areas near urban centers in "Soldiers, Officers, and Society," 225; Rio
Grande do Sul with scattered regiments seems to have drawn more evenly
from urban centers and rural municipalities. "Relações nominal dos actuaes
encarregados de recrutamento no exercício de 1863–64," May 1863, Porto
Alegre, AHRGS, AMD, la. 204, ma. 3.

9   *O Globo,* August 14, 1874, 2; Mappa dos individuos voluntários e recrutados na Província do Rio de Janeiro que assentaram praça no exército do 1
de Junho de 1859 a 29 de Fevereiro de 1860, Niteroi, APERJ, fu. PP, col. 8,
pa. 7, ma. 7, no fo. nos.; Mappa do Tenente Francisco Manoel Villas rela-
tando os presos existentes nas prisões do quartel do corpo da polícia da
província, Niteroi, APERJ, fu. PP, col. 168, pa. 12, ma. 30, no fo. nos. For
similar examples from Pernambuco, see Letter from Corporal Antonio
Schalopprink to the Chief of Police, October 1, 1874, Recife, APEP, li.
PC-140, fo. 67; on police officers assigned as recruitment agents from Ca-
ruaru to Nazereth, see Mappa dos 16 oficiaes do Corpo de Polícia que se
achão addidos, Recife, November 26, 1866, Recife, APEP, li. PM-79, no
fo. nos.

10 Rebouças, *Agricultura Nacional,* 95–99.

11 Barickman, *A Bahian Counterpoint,* 134–35. On regional politics under the
Old Republic, scholars contrast the relative cohesion of political elites in
Minas Gerais and São Paulo to Pernambuco, Bahia, and Rio Grande do Sul.
More work on the late empire may reveal if these traits pre-dated the Republic, and recruitment patterns may offer evidence to support this hypothesis. Levine, *Pernambuco in the Brazilian Federation;* Eul-Soo Pang, *Bahia in
the First Republic;* Love, *São Paulo in the Brazilian Federation;* idem., *Rio*

Grande do Sul; Wirth, *Minas Gerais in the Brazilian Federation;* Flory, *Judge and Jury in Imperial Brazil,* 94, 104–5, 180, 188–89.

12 Rebouças, *Agricultura Nacional,* 98–99.

13 Rio Branco, *Informações sobre o estado de lavoura.*

14 Moura notes that army recruitment and the designation of rural workers to perform temporary National Guard duty was often used for political revenge in São Paulo in *Saindo das sombras,* 94–99.

15 ASB, *sessão* August 11, 1896, 2:421. Peter M. Beattie, "Transforming Enlisted Army Service in Brazil," chap. 6 and 7.

16 Assunção, *A guerra de bem-te-vis,* 18, 165–76; Villela, *Canudos,* 45–46.

17 Albuquerque Jr., *A invenção do nordeste e outras artes,* 69–93; Greenfield, "The Great Drought and Elite Discourse," 375–400. Also see Lima, *Um Sertão chamado Brasil.* In the 1800s, Brazilians tended to divide their nation in two: whether between south and north, coast and *sertão* (hinterland), or "civilization" and "barbarism." In the 1900s, however, Brazilians began to discern five regions: North, South, Northeast, Southeast, and Central West. Recruitment patterns generally confirm the usefulness of this latter grouping.

18 Rebouças, *Agricultura nacional,* 98–99. Rebouças outlines the same region as Dermeval Peixoto did at the turn of the century.

19 Correspondence from the Governor of Ceará with the War Ministry, December 24, 1877, Fortaleza, Ceará, ANR, ma. IG¹42, no fo. nos.

20 Gerald Michael Greenfield, "O comportamento dos migrantes," 219–43; idem., "The Great Drought and Elite Discourse."

21 Correspondence from the Governor of Ceará to the War Ministry, December 24, 1877, Fortaleza, Ceará, ANR, ma. IG¹42, no fo. nos.

22 *O Alvorada,* April 1878, 2, in BNR-SMOR; *O Militar,* July 11, 1854, 3 in AHE.

23 An example of a slave who "passed" as a volunteer on the advice of members of a press gang, Letter from War Minister Baron de Muritiba to the Governor of Rio de Janeiro, June 10, 1870, Rio, APERJ, fu. PP, col. 8, pa. 12, ma. 15, no doc. nos.

24 Editorial, *Pedro II,* April 15, 1883, 1, in a newspaper clipping found in Naval Ministry Correspondence, ANR, ma. XM-842, no fo. nos.

25 The survey of 315 court martial cases from 1896 analyzed in the following chapter confirms the continued predominance of Northeasterners in the ranks during the republic. The location of courts-martial show that more than two-thirds of all Northeasterners were tried outside of their home region. This confirms that the army continued to facilitate the strategic diaspora of Northeasterners through its troop trade in the 1890s. Peter M. Beattie, "Transforming Enlisted Army Service in Brazil," chap. 6.

26 *RRMGUC* (1914), 3–4.

27 *Relatório do Presidente do Pernambuco João Pedro Carvalho de Moraes* (Recife: Typ. Figueroa de Faria e Filhos, 1876), 27; Kraay, "Recruitment," 22–23.

28 Forrest demonstrates the importance of local economy, political influence, geography, and culture in shaping recruitment in France in *Conscripts and Deserters;* on impressment and social control see, for example, Richard Graham, *Patronage and Politics.*

29 Nelson Werneck Sodré provided the classic analysis of a professionalizing army officer corps allied with an emerging bourgeoisie in conflict with the interests of the land-based regional oligarchies who dominated the political process. Sodré simply states that the attempts to implement conscription in 1875 were "foiled in the face of political resistance" without specifying the nature of this struggle in *A história militar,* 142; John Henry Schulz, "The Brazilian Army and Politics," 120–25. William S. Dudely largely concurred with Sodré, stating, "The landed elite would presumably not undertake to strengthen the army through an equitable recruitment law, if there were any chance it would weaken their position." Dudely, "Reform," 170; Meznar, "The Ranks of the Poor," 335–51; Kraay, "Soldiers, Officers, and Society," 243–54.

30 Alfred Stepan, *The Military in Politics,* 20.

31 On the Rurales, see Vanderwood, *Disorder and Progress.*

32 The arguments presented here summarize more extensive explorations of evidence in Beattie, "Conscription Versus Penal Servitude," 847–78.

33 Letter from Emilio de Cerqueira Lima to the Police Chief, January 18, 1874, Porto Feliz, Secretária da Polícia, AESP, *ordem* 2560, ma. 1; Letter from Delegate Antonio Eugenio do Amaral, January 24, 1874, Botucatá, ibid.; for a similar case from Minas, see Correspondence from the Governor of Minas Gerais to the War Ministry, July 28, 1874, Juiz de Fora, ANR, ma. 1G¹214, fo. 151.

34 Petition from Francisco de Souza de Barros to the Governor of Rio de Janeiro, December 29, 1959, Valença, APERJ, fu. PP., col. 8, ma. 7. One officer recalled that many soldiers were "disorderly drunken criminals" sent to serve from a prison cell. Nélson de Melo, depoimento, CPDOC/FGV, História Oral, Rio (1983), 4–5.

35 *Relatório do Presidente Henrique Pereira de Lucena* (Recife: M. Figeroa de F. e Filhos, 1875), 35–36.

36 Prado Junior, *The Colonial Background of Modern Brazil,* 361–85.

37 Evaristo de Morais, *Prisões,* 49.

38 Ibid., 12–13; Wines, *The State of Prisons and Child-Saving Institutions,* 552–54; Moreira, "Entre o deboche e a rapina," 121–58.

39 Evaristo de Morais, *Prisões,* 15.

40 In 1876, Pernambuco had 42 jails; 22 were private properties; 13, provincial; 5, municipal; 1, national (Fernando de Noronha); and 1, clerical. The gov-

ernor noted that "except for the Casa de Detenção, these jails do not conform to constitutional precepts." *Relatório do Presidente João Pedro Carvalho de Moraes,* 20. On Rio Grande do Sul in 1866, see Letter from the Police Secretary of Rio Grande do Sul to the Police Chief of the Corte, December 29, 1866, Porto Alegre, ANR, SPCOA, ma. 1J⁶517, no fo. nos. A description of a small municipal jail in the interior of Bahia can be found in Raulino, *O sentenciado 304,* 8–9; "Police Chief's annexo" in *Relatório do Presidente Francisco de Faria Lemos* (Fortaleza: Typ. Cearense, 1876), 7; on poor security, see Letter to Pernambuco's Governor from the Police Chief, January 29, 1875, Villa de Gamelleira, APEP, li. PC-140, fo. 101; and ibid., fo. 165–71.

41 Brito, *Os sistemas penitenciárias,* 1:309–17; Wines, *The State of Prisons and Child-Saving Institutions,* 554.

42 Lemos Brito, *Os sistemas penitenciárias,* 2:70–85; Robert Hughes, *The Fatal Shore,* chap. 6.

43 Huggins, *From Slavery to Vagrancy,* 105–8; Gerald M. Greenfield, "O comportamento dos migantes," 219–33; Joan E. Meznar, "Orphans and the Transition from Slave to Free Labor," 499–503.

44 Letter from Police Delegate Manoel Honrato de Barros to Police Chief Antonio Francisco Correia d'Araujo, Termo de Barreiros, December 19, 1874, APEP, li. PC-140, fo. 438.

45 See, for example, Letter from the Police Chief Antonio Francisco Correia d'Araujo to Governor Henrique Pereira de Lucena, December 16, 1874, Recife, APEP, li. PC-140, fo. 363; ibid., December 17, 1874, fo. 368; ibid., October 17, 1874, fo. 197.

46 See Kraay's discussion of this negotiation in "Soldiers, Officers, and Society," chap. 8; on fear of troops, see Villela, *Canudos,* 31.

47 *RRMGuC* (1913), 6.

48 On impressment levels see Peter M. Beattie, "Transforming Enlisted Army Service in Brazil," chap. 6.

49 *RRMGuC* (1914), 3–4.

50 *RRMGuP* (1871), 3.

51 Rodrigues et al., *A guarda nacional,* 301–12.

52 Letter from Police Delegate Francisco Joaquim Cavalcante to Galvão to Police Chief Antonio Francisco Correia d'Araujo, December 9, 1874, Igaurassu, APEP, li. PC-140, fo. 336; Letter from Police Delegate José Alves Marinho Falcão to Police Chief, December 14, 1874, Brejo, ibid., fo. 382; Letter from the District Attorney Graciliano Auguost Cesár Mandelo to the Police Chief, October 28, 1874, Villa Bella, ibid., fo. 216.

53 Governor of Maranhão's Correspondence with the War Ministry, January 22, 1875, São Luis, ANR, ma. IG¹26, no fo. nos.; for an example from Ceara, see "Relatório do Chefe da Polícia," in *Relatório do Presidente da Província apresentado à assemblea cearense* (Fortaleza: Typ. Cearense, 1876), 6.

54 The Prussophile junior officers, known as the Young Turks, also insisted that the "action of the army should not have the character of police operations." *A Defeza Nacional,* October 10, 1914, 2; Capella, "As malhas de aço no tecido social."

55 RRMGC (1913), 9–11.

56 Carone, *A República Velha,* 2:242; Diacon, "Searching for a Lost Army," 409–36.

57 Augusto Fausto de Souza, "Fortificações no Brasil," 5–140; Morais, *Prisões,* 6, 10; Holloway, *Policing Rio de Janeiro,* 74; also see, for example, Cadeias e Prisões Civis e Militares, Rio de Janeiro, AGCRJ, codice (363) 40-2-60.

58 On the British transportation system, see Robert Hughes, *The Fatal Shore;* on the French, see Gordon Wright, *Between the Guillotine and Liberty,* 82–152; on the Portuguese, see Coates, "Exiles and Orphans"; Bender, *Angola,* chap. 3.

59 See, for example, Letter from Tenente Coronel José Soares [illegible] to Governor Francisco Paula da Silveira Martins, Fernando de Nornoha, December 18, 1874, APEP, li. FN-12, no fo. nos.; ASB, *sessão* May 29, 1874, 1:131.

60 Fluery, "Parecer," 5.

61 *Relatório do Presidente João Pedro Carvalho de Moraes* (Recife: M. Figeroa de F. e Filhos, 1876), 29.

62 Evaristo de Morais, *Prisões,* 35.

63 As late as 1923, the naval prison on the Ilha das Cobras held "fifteen [civilian] convicts from Rio's Casa de Corecção." Brito, *Os sistemas,* 1:306.

64 Evaristo de Morais, *Prisões,* 76.

65 War ministers harped on the problem of troop shortfalls, RRMGUP (1870), 25; ibid. (1872), 2–4; ibid (1874), 3–5.

66 Evaristo de Morais, *Prisões,* 76; RRMGUP (1882), 23–24.

67 During the same period, 52 minors were remitted to the naval apprentice school. *Relatório do Presidente Dr. Luiz Hollanda Cavalcanti de Albuquerque,* (Niteroi: n.p., 1876), chart #7.

68 Evaristo de Morais, *Prisões,* 77; *Relatório da Repartição dos Negócios do Ministério Marinha ao Parlamento,* 17.

69 Holloway, "A Healthy Terror," 648, 668; Soares, *A negregada instituição;* on capoeiras in the early republic, see Carvalho, *Os bestializados,* 87–90; *O Diário do Rio de Janeiro,* September 2, 1874, 1–2.

70 Naval Ministry Correspondence on Enlistment and Reenlistment, March 6, 1872, Rio ANR, ma. XM 268, no fo. nos. *Relatório do Senador João Florentino Meira de Vasconcellos Netto* (Ouro Preto: n.p., May 4, 1881), 28; on police repression and capoeiras, see Holloway, *Police;* idem., "A Healthy Terror"; Soares, *A negregada instituição.*

71 Naval Ministry Correspondence on Recruitment, September 21, 1876, Rio ANR, ma. XM 874, no fo. nos.

72 See copies of police report in Naval Ministry Correspondence on Recruitment, June 13, 1876, Rio ANR, ma. XM 874, no fo. nos.

73 Navy Ministry Correspondence on Recruitment, June 9, 1876, Rio ANR, ma. XM 874, no fo. nos.

74 Navy Ministry Correspondence on Recruitment, June 9, 1876, Rio ANR, ma. XM 874, no fo. nos. Army correspondence from the Côrte does not mention this initiative.

75 Holloway, "'A Healthy Terror,'" 668; Kraay, "The Protection of the Uniform," 637–57; also Kraay, "Slavery," 228–56.

76 RRMGUC (1892), 15–17; *Relatório apresentado ao Presidente da República dos Estados Unidos do Brasil pelo Ministro de Estado dos Negócios da Marinha Vice Almirante Antônio Coutinho Gomes Pereira* (Rio: Imp. Nacional, 1919).

77 Miguel Calmon, *Discursos pronunciados nas sessões do Senado Federal de 29 a 30 de Dezembro, 1927* (Rio: Imprensa Nacional, 1928), 13.

78 José Murilo de Carvalho observed that the police used the Vaccine Revolt as an excuse to clean up the streets, deporting "criminals" with little regard for their involvement in the revolt, see Carvalho, *Os bestializados,* 113–26; on the Chibata Revolt, see Morel, *A Revolta da Chibata,* 161–77; on the Canudos Rebellion, see Calmon, *Discursos,* 19; for a damning report on political prisons during the Tenente Revolts, see Everardo Dias, *Bastilhas Modernas 1924–26.*

79 Isaac Noberto de Carmo, ANR, STM, ca. 13.342, (1904), 20.

80 Foucault, *Discipline and Punish;* Max Weber, *Economy and Society;* Max Weber, *The Theory of Social and Economic Organization;* Anderson, *Imagined Communities;* E. P. Thompson, "Time, Work-Discipline," 58–97; Howard, *The Causes of War,* 182; Weber, *Peasants into Frenchmen,* chap. 17; Charles Tilly, "The Emergence of Citizenship," 223–36; Hagen, *Soldiers in the Proletarian Dictatorship;* Harrod, *Manning the New Navy;* Frevert, "Das jakobinische modell."

81 See the comparison of army and police forces in José Murilho de Carvalho, "As forças armadas na primeira república," 181–83; Hahner, *Civilian-Military Relations,* chap. 7.

82 Lieutenant Castro Ayres, "O Orçamento da Guerra," *A Defeza Nacional,* n. 5, ano I, February 10, 1914, 138.

83 Edward L. Ayers, *Vengeance and Justice.*

Chapter 7 Brazilian Soldiers and Enlisted Service in the Age of Impressment

1 The 315 records surveyed came from across Brazil in ANR, STM, 1896. On where these trials originated, see Peter M. Beattie, "Transforming Enlisted Army Service in Brazil." Regulations required a copy of a defendant's career

record, and in two of three cases, they appear in court-martial transcripts. These copies came from regimental logs which neither I nor Hendrik Kraay have found. Kraay's survey of soldiers in Bahia yields similar results. Kraay, "Soldiers, Officers, and Society," chap. 7; idem., "Recruitment."

2 Fortunato, pro. 243, ANR, STM, cx. 13205, (1896); also, Manoel Francisco, pro. 507, ANR, STM, cx. 13210, (1896); Prisco Manoel dos Santos ("son of Jacino"), pro. 351, ANR, STM, cx. 13208, (1896); José Maria da Silva ("son of João José"), pro. 61, ANR, STM cx. 13201, (1896); on slave surnames, Schwartz, *Sugar Plantations*, 401–2.

3 WMC, September 1, 1877, Rio, ANR, SPCOA, ma. 1J⁶519, no fo. nos.

4 Fernando Vieira Ferreira, pro. 329, ANR, STM, cx. 13208, (1896).

5 Antônio Ferreira da Silva, pro. 456, ANR, STM, cx. 13264, (1900).

6 José Peixoto, pro. 328, ANR, STM, cx. 13207, (1896).

7 Leonel Cardoso de Menezes e Souza was expelled for admitting to participating in sedicious movements—pro. 1139, ANR, STM, cx. 13269, (1900), 4.

8 See, for example, Harris, *Patterns of Race in the Americas;* see also Harris, "Racial Identity in Brazil," 21–28; Skidmore, "Bi-Racial U.S."

9 Instituto Brasileiro de Geografia e Estatística [IBGE], Conselho Nacional de Estatístico, *O Brasil em números*, (Rio: IBGE, 1966), 25.

10 David Bushnell also found the literacy rates among Russian soldiers to be "remarkably" high compared to the general population, and suggests that there were low standards for determining literacy. Bushnell, *Mutiny*, 4–5.

11 Peixoto, *Memórias*, 123.

12 Childs, "A Case of 'Great Unstableness,'" 717–40; Stein, *Vassouras*, 161–69.

13 See Peixoto's description of Rio's São Christóvão borough in *Memórias*, p. 19; on Urca in Rio, see Peregrino, *História e projeção*.

14 Complaint of Manuel Cavalcante d'Albuquerque contra Eduardo José Teixeira, November 10, 1865, Fortaleza Tamandaré, APEP, li. OE-20.

15 Peixoto, *Memórias*, 59. This practice seems similar to the privilege given to trusted slaves who were allowed to farm their own provision grounds, allowing some to establish a private residence and marry. Barickman, "A Little Piece of Ground," 649–88; Jacintho Franco de Godoy, pro. 219, ANR, STM, cx. 13205, (1896), 7. On guidelines for off-base living, see Lobo Viana, *Guia Militar*, 2:133–34; Meznar gives examples from Paraíba in "The Ranks of the Poor," 342–44. Sandra Lauderdale Graham shows that employers often barred live-in domestics from having private residences in *House and Street*, 61.

16 Sandra Lauderdale Graham, *House and Street*, 73. On the history of the marriage promise in Brazil, see for example, Faria, *A colônia em movimento*.

17 Alfredo Baptista Jardineiro, pro. 385, ANR, STM, cx. 13390, (1908), 43.

18 Letter from Octavio Augusto Borges to Rui Barbosa, January 30, 1910, Santa Rita de Cassia, Minas Gerais, ACRB, CR216/5.

19 Hildebrando Bayard de Melo, *No Exército do meu tempo,* 5–6; for another example, see Paula da Cidade, *Síntese de tres séculos de literatura militar brasileira,* 474.

20 José Maria da Silva, pro. 61, ANR, STM, CX. 13201 (1896); James Scott, *Domination.*

21 Peixoto, *Memórias,* 44–45; on uniforms, see *O Alvorado,* March 1878, 1–2; Karasch, *Slave Life,* 130; Brandão, "A Tatuagem na cirurgia militar," 266–71.

22 On the pride of backlander's from the Northeast see, for example, Villela, *Canudos,* 49; on pride in black and African heritage see, for example, Eduardo Silva, *Prince of the People,* 26–31.

23 Ignacio Fabber, pro. 690, ANR, STM, CX. 13346, (1904), 25. The government forced Paraguayan prisoners of war to work on the telegraph and rail lines of Rio de Janeiro. A large group of POWs fled this onerous service in 1870. Letter From Guilherme Capanema to the Police Chief Antonio Carneiro de Campos, June 9, 1870, APERJ, fu. PP., col. 183, pa. 31, ma. 66, no fo. nos. Letter from Juiz de Paz Joaquim José de Sousa Barreto to Governor of Rio de Janeiro José Tavares Bastos, September 7, 1866, Passo Freis, APERJ, fu. PP., col. 8, pa. 10, ma. 12, no fo. nos.

24 Bandeira Filho, *Informações,* 23–24, 28; Fleury, "Parecer."

25 Ministério de Guerra, Correspondence with the Ministry of Agriculture, 1880–1886, ANR, ma. IG^{1}604; Correspondence with the Ministério de Justiça, 1872–1886, ibid.

26 Sergeant Ernesto Carlos Schmidt, pro. 412, ANR, STM, CX. 13262, (1900), 91–2; Vicente Antônio da Silva, pro. 124, ANR, STM, CX. 13338, (1904), 24–25.

27 Nélson de Melo, (depoimento), CPDOC/FGV, História Oral, Rio, (1983), 6; Eduardo Silva, *Prince of the People,* 121.

28 *Relatório do Presidente André Augusto de Padua Fleury,* (Fortaleza: n.p., April 1, 1881), 26. In 1862 the war minister admitted that there were not enough first-line troops to conduct regular garrison duties. They had to be aided by National Guard troops on Sundays. Letter from War Minister Marques de Caxias to the Governor of Rio de Janeiro, May 20, 1862, APERJ, fu. PP., col. 8, pa. 8, ma. 8.

29 Carvalho, *Dever militar e política partidiária,* 30–31.

30 Sodré, *História Militar,* 198–200; Paula da Cidade, "Verbetes," 25–35; *O Alvorada,* November 15, 1878, 6–7.

31 Paula da Cidade, "Verbetes," 35.

32 Leal, "Depoimento," 8.

33 *O Alvorada,* April 1878, 2–3.

34 Joaquim Tomaz Alves, pro. 384, ANR, STM, ca. 13389, (1908), 64; see a nearly identical complaint in *O Alvorada,* March 15, 1879, 1.

35 Domician Ernesto Dias Cardoso, pro. 707, ANR, STM, CX. 13216, (1896), 6.

36 Villela, *Canudos,* 71–72.

37 "Um desertor," *O Estado de São Paulo*, December 9, 1915, 2; "Vencimentos do exército," *O Nihilista*, April 6. 1883, 2.

38 *O Alvorado*, March 1878, 1–2.

39 Barickman, *A Bahian Counterpoint*, 46; see also his discussion of diet.

40 Morley, *The Diary of Helena Morley*, 214. I thank Katherine McCann for sharing this citation with me.

41 Lobo Viana, *Guia militar*, 2:14.

42 Ataliba Telles de Menzes Rodrigues and Roque Fagundes, pro. 368, ANR, STM, cx. 13389, (1908).

43 *O Alvorada*, no. 7, n.d., 7–8 in BNR-SMOR. One officer was tried for not paying his troops and withholding their Sunday wine ration, Clementino Velasco Molina, São Borja, Rio Grande do Sul, pro. 155, ANR, STM, cx. 13238, (1898).

44 Battlefield promotions were often temporary, RRMGuP (1870), 23–24.

45 RRMGuP (1882), 23–24.

46 One sergeant missed taking his entrance exam before reaching the age limit because of the Canudos War; he had to appeal his case directly to the war minister Villela Junior, *Canudos*, 91–4.

47 Scott Mainwaring, *The Catholic Church and Politics;* Serbin, "Priests, Celibacy, and Social Conflict."

48 McCann, "The Nation in Arms."

49 On Vargas's brief service as a praça, see Levine, *Father,* 14–15.

50 Letter from Almeida Novaes, March 3, 1908, Rio, ANR, SPCOA, ma. IJ⁶385, no fo. nos. Letter from Alfredo Pinto Vieira de Melo, April 4, 1908, ibid. On conflicts with Italian immigrants, see ibid., April 17, 1877, ma. IJ⁶519. On Lusophobia, see Report from the President of Maranhão to the War ministry, August 9, 1875, São Luís, ANR, ma. IG¹26, no fo. nos. Also, Telegram from General Leite Castro to War Minister Marechal Eneas, October 19, 1893, Recife, AHE, 4th section, cx. H-11; Letter from the Police to the War Ministry, December 12, 1877, Uruguaiana, ANR, cx. 201, fo. 669; Cabo Joaquim Victoriano Fortaleza, pro. 54, ANR, cx. 13809, (1915).

51 Sebastião Francelino, pro. 22, ANR, STM, cx. 13200, (1896).

52 The examples above are taken from: Alexandre Farias, pro. 117, ANR, STM, cx. 13257, (1896), 5; Mario Alves de Souza e outros, pro. 249, ibid., cx. 13259, (1896), 74; Luiz da Silva Guedes, pro. 424, ibid., cx. 132563, (1896), 7; Canuto Antônio de Oliveira, pro. 249, ibid., cx. 13259, (1896), 4.

53 Francisco dos Santos III, pro. 688A, ANR, STM, cx. 13346, (1904).

54 Sodré, *Narrativas militares*, 255–70.

55 Eduardo Silva, *Prince of the People*. See John Chasteen's analysis of regional and national identity in the borderlands of Brazil's south in *Heroes*. I had hoped to find more evidence of popular nationalism among soldiers similar to that Florencia Mallon found among peasant National Guardsmen in Mexico and Peru; Mallon, *Peasant and Nation*.

56 Taunay, *A retirada;* Peter M. Beattie, "National Identity and the Brazilian Folk," 25–27.

57 Cunha, *Rebellion in the Backlands,* 249–51, 282; Sodré, *O naturalismo.*

58 See, for example, Volpato, *Cativos do Sertão,* 205–19.

59 Almeida, *Homosexualismo,* 75–86; Macedo, "Da prostituição," 115.

60 Sandra Lauderdale Graham, *House and Street,* 55–9.

61 *A Defesa Nacional,* January 10, 1916, 113.

62 Captain Francisco César da Costa Mendez, Manaus, pro. 223, ANR, STM, cx. 13784, (1912), 50.

63 Lott cited in Sodré, *A história militar,* 376–77; Kraay, "Soldiers, Officers, and Society," 372–83. Even leftist leaders complained about this, Lacerda, *História de uma covardia,* 35. See da Matta's analysis of the phrase "Do you know who you are talking to?" to assert authority in *Carnavais.*

64 *Relatório do Presidente Barão de Taquary,* (Fortaleza: n.p., 1871), 10.

65 On Cuiabá, see Volpato, *Cativos do sertão,* 189; Letter from Delegate Beleano de Araujo Ferrasto to Police Chief Joaquim José d'Amaral, January 7, 1874, AESP, Secretária da Polícia, *ordem* 2560, ma. 1. One police delegate asked that the nomination of active duty army officers to police commands be halted unless they retired from the army. Letter from Minister of War Carlos de Araujo Buarque to the Governor of Rio de Janeiro, June 23, 1864, fu. PP., APERJ col. 8, pa. 9, ma. 10, no fo. nos.

66 Correspondence from the Governor of Bahia to the War Ministry, September 25, 1876 and September 29, 1876, Salvador and Rio, ANR, ma. IG[1]128, fo. 80–88; Eduardo Silva, *Prince of the People;* see also the report on gangs of criminals in Rio made up of veterans. Police correspondence, February 26, 1868, ANR, SPCOA, ma. IJ[6]517, no fo. nos.

67 "Desertor," *O Diário do Rio de Janeiro,* February 2, 1874, 2.

68 Holloway, "A Healthy Terror," 671.

69 "Vagabundo," *O Diário do Rio de Janeiro,* February 2, 1874, 2.

70 "Norte do Império," *O Diário do Rio de Janeiro,* February 3, 1874, 2.

71 Fraga Filho, *Mendigos, moleques, e vadios.*

72 Similarly in Cuiabá during the Paraguayan War, civic leaders, who feared soldiers and the spread of cholera, forced praças to live on the opposite side of the river from the city in an encampment. Many stayed on after the war to form a new city borough there. Volpato, *Cativos do sertão,* 104.

73 Schulz, "The Brazilian Army," 137.

74 Eduardo Silva, *Prince of the People,* 39–40. See Barreto's story of veterans and petitions, "A matemática não falha," in *Bagatelas,* 177–84.

75 Letter from the Finance Minister of Rio de Janeiro to War Minister Barão de Muritiba, August 12, 1870, Niteroi, APERJ fu. PP., col. 8, pa. 12, ma. 15, no fo. nos. For a similar plea for a land title from a veteran impoverished by drought in Ceará, see Requerimento de José Caetano de Oliveira, April 1877, Fortaleza, ANR, IG[1]585, doc. 28. For biting Liberal criticisms of the

handling of veteran benefits, see *ASB*, vol. April–June, *sessão* June 2, 1870, 78; ibid., *sessão* July 15, 1871, 108–10.

76 *ASB*, vol. 2, *sessão* June 28, 1907, 2:286–87.

77 *A Razão*, March 2, 1920, 1; Dias, *Bastilhas modernas*.

78 Letter from the Governor of Minas Gerais to the War Minister, March 13, 1872, Ouro Preto, ANR, ma. IG¹214, no fo. nos.; Letter from the Governor of Bahia to the War Ministry, January 28, 1875, Salvador, ANR, ma. IG¹128, no fo. nos.

79 Scheper-Hughes, *Death Without Weeping*; Reis, *A morte é uma festa*.

80 The navy minister noted, "Recruitment is almost unnecessary because the Navy Apprentice Schools supply sufficient personnel each year." Letter from the Barão de Angra Chefe do Quartel Geral da Marinha to the Navy Ministry, June 19, 1871, Rio ANR, XM 268, no fo. nos.

81 João da Cruz Rangel, 12.1 *Repartiçao do Ajudante General, Mappa estatístico do Corpo de Imperiaes Marinheiros do anno de 1836 a Dezembro 1884*, ANR, GIFI, cx. 5C-486, fo. 488; *RRMGUP* (1871–1885), annexos.

82 Nélson de Melo, (depoimento), CPDOC/FGV, História Oral, Rio, (1983), 6; Zachory Morgan's forthcoming dissertation from Brown University on the navy promises to reveal much about race and enlisted service. Also Nascimento, *A ressaca da marujada*.

83 *RRMGUP* (1872), annexo B; similar incomplete reports for 1879, 1880, and 1881 registered 398, 254, and 290 deaths respectively. Correspondence with the Corpo de Saude, March 24, 1875, Rio, ANR, ma. IG⁶15, fo. 13; ibid., March 22, 1880, Rio, fo. 2; ibid., March 15, 1881, Rio, fo. 2; and ibid., March 20, 1882, Rio, fo. 9.

Chapter 8 Days of *Cachaça*, Sodomy, and the Lash

1 I make this argument in greater detail in Peter M. Beattie, "Conflicting Penal Codes."

2 Carvalho, *Dever militar*, 31.

3 *O Alvorada*, May 1, 1879, 7; ibid., April 15, 1879, 1.

4 Carone, *A República Velha*, 1:162.

5 McAlister, *The Fuero Militar in New Spain*; Archer, *The Army in Bourbon Mexico*.

6 See, for example, *ASB*, vol. July *sessão* July 15, 1871, 108–9.

7 *Relatório do Presidente da Província João Pedro Carvalho de Moraes*, (Recife: M. Figueroa de F. e Filhos, 1876), 26.

8 *O Alvorada*, March 1878, 5.

9 *Collecção das leis da República do Brasil*, 1:19.

10 *Código penal e disciplinar da armada*, 79–101.

11 Flory, *Judge and Jury*.

12 *Código penal e disciplinar da armada*, 23.

13 Peixoto, *Memórias*, 107–12; *Código penal e disciplinar da armada*, 9–15.

14 João Correa de Araujo, pro. 392, ANR, STM, cx. 13390, (1908), 64.

15 José Francisco Cardoso, pro. 42, ANR, STM, cx. 13200, (1896), 6–7.

16 See, for example, Fausto, *Crime e cotidiano*, 233–35, 246, 256–69.

17 João Claudio de Santa Anna, pro. 176, ANR, STM, cx. 13203 (1896).

18 Sandra Lauderdale Graham, *House and Street*, 15–20, 74–77.

19 Hahner, *Poverty and Politics*, 56; Holloway, *Policing*; Bretas, *A guerra nas ruas*.

20 José Maria da Silva, pro. 61, ANR, STM, cx. 13201 (1896); For a nearly identical case, see Antônio Gonçalves de Oliveira, pro. 114, ibid., (1896).

21 Peixoto, *Memórias*, 49.

22 Narcizo Coelho Vianna, pro. 427, ANR, STM, cx. 13263, (1900), 4.

23 *Código penal e disciplinar da armada*, 13–15.

24 Tenente Alfredo Baptista Jardineiro, pro. 385, ANR, STM, cx. 13390, (1908), 7.

25 Brigido Justiniano d'Oliveira, pro. 69, ibid., cx. 13338, (1904), 9.

26 *O Alvorada*, March 15, 1879, 6–7; see also the response, ibid., April 1, 1879, 6–7.

27 "As mulheres dos soldados," *O Indicador Militar*, May 1, 1862, 144–46.

28 Frederick S. Harrod shows how the U.S. Navy regularized the captain's mast where commanders distributed punishment for petty offenses to reduce the burdensome increase in courts-martial in the 1920s. Harrod, *Manning the New Navy*, 115–28.

29 See complaints that many officers, the "sons of patronage," never served in frontier regiments, but remained in Rio, hampering the ability of frontier regiments to conduct necessary duties. *O Alvorada*, January 15, 1879, 2; ibid., February 1, 1879, 5.

30 Peixoto, *Memórias*, 108.

31 Carvalho, *Os bestializados*, 101–3, 106.

32 José dos Santos, pro. 529, ANR, STM, cx. 13342, (1896).

33 Frederick S. Harrod uses crime data to measure the U.S. Navy's success in modernizing its recruitment, training, and efficiency. Harrod, *Manning the New Navy*, 112–28.

34 Sebastião Gregorio da Silva, pro. 681, ANR, STM, cx. 13345, (1904), 20–21.

35 Manoel Pereira Nunes, pro. 66, ANR, STM, cx. 13338, (1904), 17; José Thimoteo dos Santos, Pro. 417, ibid., cx. 13263, (1900), 30–31; Austerlino Elias de Aguiar, pro. 735, ibid., cx. 13349, (1904), 16; João Antônio de Oliveira, pro. 301, ibid., cx. 13260, (1904), 18; Eduardo José Ramos, pro. 125, ibid., cx. 13257, (1900), 19; Severino Izidoro de Paixão, pro. 477, ibid., cx. 13265, (1900), 22; Manoel Basílio da Silva, pro. 1098, ibid., cx. 13269, (1900), 17.

36 Francisco da Silva Segundo, pro. 413, ANR, STM, cx. 13391, (1908), 67.

37 Francisco Mendes, Lupercio Manoel Thomaz de Camargo, Severo Goulart, and Sérgio Lourenço, pro. 19, ANR, STM, CX. 13393, (1909), 8, 90.

38 Villela Junior, *Canudos,* 71–73, 97–98.

39 José Bernardo de Salles, pro. 143, ANR, STM, CX. 13258, (1900), 56.

40 Naderio de Roza, pro. 357, ANR, STM, CX. 13261, (1900), 20; similarly João Baptista dos Santos claimed that he was persecuted by his company sergeant after refusing to wash his NCO's tunic. Pro. 685, ibid., CX. 13345, (1904), 4.

41 *O Alvorada,* June 1, 1879, 2–3; Carta Anonima ao Ministério da Guerra, n.d. Cuiabá, ANR, ma. IG²44, no fo. nos.

42 João Martins da Costa, pro. 8, ANR, STM, CX. 13335, (1904), 18.

43 João da Silva Porto, pro. 488, ANR, STM, CX. 13265, (1900), 22; João Martins da Costa, pro. 8, ibid., CX. 13335, (1904), 18; João Barbosa da Fonseca, pro. 1095, ibid., CX. 13269, (1900), 22–23.

44 Antônio de Mello Albuquerque, pro. 1025, ANR, STM, CX. 13268, (1900), 5, 26.

45 Jorge dos Santos, pro. 9, ANR, STM, CX. 13335, (1904), 21.

46 Adelino Cesár do Amaral, pro. 408, ANR, STM, CX. 13209, (1896), 24; Marcelino José dos Santos, pro. 489, ibid., CX. 13266, (1900), 21–22; Manoel de Souza Mendez, pro. 356, ibid., CX. 13261, (1900), 17; João Alfredo da Costa, pro. 679, ibid., CX. 13345, (1904), 23.

47 *O Alvorada,* April 1878, 2.

48 RRMGuP (1872), 2–3.

49 José Noqueira da Silva, pro. 387, ANR, STM, CX. 13262, (1900), 22.

50 Narcizo Coelho Viana, pro. 427, ANR, STM, CX. 13263, (1900), 14–15.

51 José Aggripino de Oliveira, pro. 605, ANR, STM, CX. 13267, (1900), 5–6.

52 José Zeferino da Hora, pro. 653, ANR, STM, CX. 13342, (1904).

53 Manoel Bezzerras, pro. 180, ANR, STM, CX. 13340, (1904), 13; Vicente Alves, pro. 50, ibid., CX. 13337, (1904), 20–21; Glycero Pedro da Costa, pro. 700, ibid., CX. 13347, (1904), 26.

54 Antônio Pereira de Oliveira, pro. 211, ANR, STM, CX. 13204 (1896); see also, Paulino Martins de Freitas, pro. 49, ibid., CX. 13200 (1896); João Baptista dos Santos, pro. 491, ibid., CX. 13209 (1896).

55 Correspondence from the Governor of Mato Grosso to the War Ministry, June 10, 1874, Cuiabá, ANR, ma. IG¹244, fo. 320.

56 The navy's data for deserters who were captured or who returned of their own free will from 1870 to 1884 totaled 1,311. STM data for the same years only reviewed 377 cases of navy desertion. This suggests that three out of four sailors were punished with sword blows rather than jail terms. Navy Secretary João da Cruz Rangel, 12.1 *Repartiçao do Ajudante General, Mappa estatístico do Corpo de Imperiaes Marinheiros do anno de 1836 a Dezembro 1884,* ANR, GIFI, CX. 5C-486, fo. 488 (fo. not in order); RRMGuP (1871–85), annexos.

57 Manoel da Costa Ribeiro, pro. 478, ANR, STM, CX. 13265, (1900), 20.

58 Martinho Elenterio dos Santos, pro. 474, ANR, STM, CX. 13264, (1900), 11.

59 *Jornal do Brasil,* December 8, 1988; see also José Murilho de Carvalho's biting commentary on this interview, "A Cidadania a porrete," in ibid., *Cuaderno B, 6.*

60 Caminha, *Bom Crioulo.*

61 Antônio Borges Enrique, pro. 68, ANR, STM, CX. 13340, (1904), 11.

62 See Hendrick Kraay's discussion of desertion amnesty in "Reconsidering Recruitment."

63 *RRMGuP* (1880), 5–6.

64 *RRMGuP* (1872), 3–4; Greenfield, "The Great Drought and Elite Discourse," 375–400.

65 Annual provincial crime statistics can be found in governor's reports to provincial and state legislatures.

66 Manoel João da Silva, pro. 695, ANR, STM, CX. 13216, (1896).

67 Pedro Antônio de Barros, pro. 582, ANR, STM, CX. 13213, (1896).

68 Antônio Francisco Maciel, pro. 731, ANR, STM, CX. 13216 (1896).

69 *Collecção da decisões do império do Brazil,* 59, 90.

70 Antônio Pereira, pro. 67, ANR, STM, CX. 13338, (1904), 48–51.

71 Sodré, *Memórias,* 41.

72 Ibid., 50.

73 Besse, "Crimes of Passion," 653–66; Chalhoub, *Trabalho,* 142–64.

74 Joaquim Ferreira, pro. 463, ANR, CX. 13824, (1916), 35.

75 For similar clashes in the U.S. Navy, see Chauncey, "Christian Brotherhood."

76 Letter from Police Chief Antonio Francisco Correia d'Araujo to Governor Henrique Pereira de Lucena, November 10, 1874, Recife, APEP, li. PC-140, fo. 237; see also ibid., December 29, 1874, fo. 441; Magalhães, *Diário íntimo,* 198–99, 202–3.

77 Almeida, *Homosexualismo,* 75–76, 85.

78 Caminha likely read Herman Melville's novels, which also hinted at homosexuality among sailors: *Billy Budd; Sailor: An Inside Story; Moby Dick: or, the White Whale; White Jacket or the World in a Man of War.*

79 Peter M. Beattie, "Conflicting Penal Codes," 65–85; Joan Scott, "Gender," 1067–70.

80 Almeida, *Homosexualismo,* 76–85. One should not assume that no shame tainted the active partner. Although he studies sodomy in a distant time and place, Geoffrey Spurling emphasizes this point in "Honor, Sexuality, and the Catholic Church," 45–67.

81 João Estacio, Sao Gabriel, pro. 236, ANR, STM, CX. 13224, (1897), 47.

82 See, for example, Green, *Beyond Carnival;* Parker, *Beneath the Equator.*

83 David M. Halperin, "Sex Before Sexuality"; Chauncey, "Christian Brotherhood or Sexual Perversion?" 189–211; Peter Fry notes that homosexual

identities emerged in the cities of southern Brazil in the late 1960s in *Para inglês ver,* 93–94.

84 Manoel Cardoso de Nascimento, pro. 396, ANR, STM, CS. 13390, (1908), 59.

85 Antônio Moreira Ignacio, pro. 750, ANR, STM, CX. 13349, (1904), 10. In 1894, Aggripino Antônio da Costa was imprisoned for eight days, performing guard duties at midday while at march, for allowing a corporal to enter a barrack under his watch to attempt to intoxicate one of his comrades for libidinous ends. Aggripino Antônio da Costa, pro. 434, ANR, STM, CX. 13309, (1896), 6–7.

86 *Código penal e disciplinar da Armada,* 58.

87 João Francisco d'Almeida, pro. 294, ANR, STM, CX. 13812, (1916), 66–67.

88 Manoel Martins dos Santos, Rio, pro. 113, ANR, STM, CX. 13818, (1916); for similar cases, see ibid. José Dominguez dos Santos, CX. 13203, (1896); Antônio Manoel Rodriguez, CX. 13214, (1896); Manuel Epaminondas Lessa, Itaguai, Rio Grande do Sul, pro. 218, CX. 13822, (1916).

89 Parker, *Beneath the Equator,* 27–51. Talisman Ford argues that Brazilian sexologists's conceptions of "deviant" sexuality was far from unified from 1900 to 1940. She notes that Brazilian medical treatises on homosexuality tended to maintain a passive/active dichotomy (Ford, "Passion is in the Eye of the Beholder"). Professional military attitudes about homosexuality may have provided another conduit of international influence that condemned both active and passive partners in same sex intercourse as Adolfo Caminha's *Bom crioulo* suggests.

Chapter 9 "Tightening Screw" or "Admirable Filter"?

1 Carone, *A República Velha,* 1:158–85, 2:242–43; Carone echoes some of Gilberto Freyre's analysis of urban sectors and the military in *Casa Grande;* McCann, "The Nation in Arms," 211–20.

2 Carone, *A República Velha,* 2:242.

3 Ramsaur, *The Young Turks;* Capella, "As malhas de aço no tecido social"; Pedro Tórtima, "Polícia e justiça de mãos dados," chap. 2.

4 *ACB, sessão* November 14, 1907, 7:678.

5 "Nono Batalhão," *Jornal do Ceará,* May 22, 1907, 2.

6 McCann, "The Nation in Arms," 226–29.

7 *ACB, sessão* November 11, 1907, 7:465.

8 *O Estado de São Paulo,* January 9, 1908, 1.

9 *ACB, sessão* November 11, 1907, 7:465.

10 *ACB, sessão* November 14, 1907, 7:671–72; Peter M. Beattie, "Transforming Enlisted Army Service in Brazil."

11 *RRMGUC* (1903), 3–4.

12 *ACB, sessão* November 12, 1907, 7:521.

13 Ibid.

14 Carone, *A República Velha,* 1:163.

15 *ACB, sessão* November 14, 1907, 7:692; *ACB, sessão* October 21, 1907, 7:716–17.

16 Love, "Political Participation in Brazil," 9.

17 *ACB, sessão* 14 November 1907, 7:690.

18 *Collecção da leis da República dos Estados Unidos do Brazil de 1908,* 1:11.

19 *ACB, sessão* December 6, 1907, 7:223–27, 229.

20 *Collecção das leis da República dos Estados Unidos do Brazil de 1908,* 1:11–33.

21 *ACB, sessão* October 21, 1907, 6:716–17.

22 *ACB, sessão* November 14, 1907, 7:692.

23 Letter from Police Chief Alfredo Pinto Vieira de Melo to the War Ministry in Rio, December 29, 1908, Rio, ANR, SPCOA, ma. IJ⁶519, no fo. nos.

24 *ACB, sessão* October 21, 1907, 6:720–21, 774.

25 Carone, *A República Velha,* 2:242–43.

26 *ASB, sessão* December 10, 1915, 9:142.

27 *Jornal do Commércio,* November 13, 1908. Cited in Carone, *A República Velha,* 1:163. The privileged Recife law student Assis Chateaubriand volunteered to serve in 1909 to improve his stamina. Fernando Morais, *Chatô, 59.*

28 McCann, "The Nation in Arms."

29 McCann describes the ceremony in "The Nation in Arms," 228.

30 *RRMGUC* (1913), 8.

31 *RRMGUC* (1915), 9.

32 *ACB, sessão* November 14, 1907, 7:692.

33 *A Defeza Nacional* 63 (December 1918), 106–7; ibid. 17 (November 1914), 148.

34 Rodrigues et al., *A guarda nacional,* 418–21, 443–47.

35 Benedict Anderson singles out the import of "print capitalism" in *Imagined Communities,* 37–65.

36 Lêmos Terra, *Memórias de lutas,* 40–42, 166.

37 Barreto, *Triste fim de Policarpo Quaresma,* 62.

38 See, Cunha, *Rebellion in the Backlands,* 102–4. Lêmos Terra, *Memórias de lutas,* 41–42, 144.

39 Leandro Gomes de Barros, "O tempo de hoje. O sorteio militar," pamphlet (Guariba, Paraíba: P. Baptista, 1916 [1906]), 12–15, in BNMR.

40 Ibid., 15.

41 Matta, *Carnavais,* 35–118.

42 Leandro Gomes de Barros, "O sorteio militar," pamphlet, in BNMR.

43 "Olho na rua," *Jornal do Ceará,* December 30, 1907, 1.

44 Ibid., 1–2.

45 Olavo Bilac, "Chronica," *Kosmos,* November 1907, 1–3.

46 Associação de Empregados no Commercio do Rio de Janeiro, *Sorteio mili-*

tar; *A Luz Social,* February 3, 1907, 1 in AEL; Gomes, *A invenção do trabalhismo,* 85–95.

47 I thank Celso Castro for generously sharing the following citations: *Jornal do Brasil,* June 1, 1908; *Correio da Manhã,* June 6, 1908, 1.

48 This comment is interesting because Olavo Bilac, who would later become a key draft supporter, had authored several patriotic public school texts. Bilac and Netto, *Contos Pátrios.* This patriotic primer went through fifty editions by 1968. Bilac also penned *Altravez do Brazil (narrativas) Livros de leitura para o curso médio das escolas primárias.* In a speech to educators, Bilac revealed his animus toward labor, "I elevate you to this divine charter, in order that you be . . . a generator of patriots and not anarchists." Bilac, *Últimas conferencias e discursos,* 62; anarcho-syndicalists harped on public and private education's patriotic content and military training classes. See, "Bellicosidades," *A Plebe,* September 22, 1917, 2, in AEL. A *febiano* credited his public education as the font of his patriotic sentiments strengthened by his army service, Altino Bondesan, *Um pracinha paulista,* 29–30.

49 Again I thank Celso Castro for sharing these citations. The Federação Operária's meetings are reported in *Jornal do Brazil,* 13, 20, and January 27, 1908.

50 One tract lambasted antimilitarists who: "appeal to the weak spirit of women to better persuade" their husbands and sons to resist conscription. Assumpção, *Serviço militar obrigatório,* 8; for the Anti-Militarist League's manifesto, see *Não Matarás,* March 1908 in AEL.

51 *Não Matarás,* March 1908, 1, in AEL.

52 RRMGUC (1914), 3–4; McCann, "The Nation in Arms," 229; Peter M. Beattie, "Transforming Enlisted Army Service in Brazil," 288–92; Edgar Carone, *Movimento operário,* 122–23.

53 Jagunço, "Alistamento e sorteio," *A Voz do Trabalhador,* January 13, 1909, 2. The same edition cited *La Voz de España,* which denounced registration figures in São Paulo as fraudulent. An Italian language periodical explained how to avoid conscription. "Soldati per Forza," *Avanti!* February 7, 1908, 1, in AEL; "Desertore," ibid.; "L'Antimilitarismmo nelle canzoni militari," ibid., February 20, 1908, 1.

54 "A lei do sorteio: um habeau corpus," *Correio da Manhã,* January 16, 1908, 1.

55 Rui Barbosa, "Plataforma," in *Obras Completas* (Bahia: n.p., 1910), 75, 77. Cited in Morel, *A Revolta da Chibata,* 16–17.

56 Love, "Political Participation," 9.

57 Morel, *A Revolta da Chibata,* 63–145.

58 Quote reproduced in Morel, *A Revolt da Chibata,* 63.

59 More, *A Revolta da chibata,* 158–60. Nascimento, *A ressaca da marujada.*

60 Confidential letter from Belfort de Oliveira to Rui Barbosa confessing the former's regret at not denouncing the drama of 400 sailors, August 8, 1910, Amazonas CR 1071/2, ACRB; ibid. May 30, 1911.

61 Morel, *A Revolta da Chibata,* 161–77.

62 See the court-martial of the officer who led the attack on Manaus. Capitão de Corveta Francisco Cesar da Costa Mendez, pro. 223, ANR, STM, CX. 13262, (1912).

63 Carone, *A República Velha*, 2:291–92; Morel, *A Revolta da Chibata*, 271–77.

64 Álvaro Otávio de Alencastre, *O problema nacional* (Rio: 1917), 25. Cited in Skidmore, *White into Black,* chap. 3.

65 Todd A. Diacon, *Millenarian Vision;* idem., "Bring the Countryside Back In." 560–92.

66 Peter M. Beattie, "National Identity and the Brazilian Folk," 12–31; Skidmore, *Black into White,* chap. 4. On Immigration, see Jeffrey Lesser, *Negotiating National Identity.*

67 Luebke, *Germans in Brazil,* 219–23.

68 *O Estado de São Paulo,* December 19, 1920, 2; ibid., December 20, 1915, 2; ibid., December 21, 1915, 1; ibid., December 22, 1915, 2; ibid., December 23, 1915, 1; *Correio da Manhã,* December 19, 1915, 1; ibid., December 20, 1915, 1; ibid., December 21, 1915, 1; ibid., December 22, 1915, 1. See also the investigating officer's memoirs, Naronha, *Narrando a verdade.* One demand made by the sergeants was the right to the family benefits enjoyed by officers. The war minister insisted that the State could not afford to "assume the responsibility of protecting the families of battalion sergeants because from then on there would not be a sergeant who would not marry." Carone, *A República Velha,* 2:316–19.

69 *Correio da Manhã,* April 7, 1919, 3–4; ibid., April 8, 1916, 3; ibid., April 12, 1916, 3.

70 Carone, *A República Velha,* 2:318–21.

71 *O Estado de São Paulo,* December 23, 1915, 3. Reprinted from *O Paiz.*

72 Nancy Leys Stepan, *The Hour of Eugenics;* Gilberto Hochman, *A era do saneamento.*

73 Gentil Falcão, *A Defesa Nacional.* Labor newspapers harped on floggings in the military. *Não Matarás,* March 1908, 1, in AEL.

74 Bilac's enemies on the left criticized his change of position of this issue. See, for example, "Está salva a honra da Pátria," *O Cosmopolita,* October 28, 1916, 2, in AEL; "O militarismo," ibid., May 1, 1917, 3. On the reaction of Brazilian intellectuals and leaders to World War I, see Skidmore, *Black into White,* chap. 3.

75 Bilac, *A Defesa Nacional,* 41.

76 Ibid., 133.

77 Ibid., 133–34.

78 Ibid.

79 Ubaldo, *A greve militar,* 3.

80 On the fetishes of novelists, politicians, and physicians for the heterosexual nuclear family as the normative foundation of nation-states, see: Sommer, *Foundational Fictions,* 33–51; Jurandir Freire Costa, *Ordem médica,* 35–77;

Chauncey, "Christian Brotherhood"; Magalhães Junior, *Olavo Bilac e sua época;* Green, *Beyond Carnival,* 56–57.

81 The journalist João do Rio was impressed by the new aspect of soldiers he observed. Rio, *No tempo de Wencesláo,* 217–35; Peter M. Beattie, "Transforming Enlisted Army Service in Brazil," 168–69. British counselor in Brazil Authur Peel reported the "frenzied enthusiasm" for and "popular attraction" to Bilac's ideas, which were spread "far and wide." November 21, 1915, Petrópolis, PRO, FO317/2294/104910. On the United States, see Shenk, "Work or Fight."

82 "A trinidade maléfica: pátria, guerra, e cazerna," *A Tribuna do Povo,* December 7, 1916, 1, in AEL.

83 Bilac, *A Defesa Nacional,* 24.

84 Excerpt from Olavo Bilac's October 9, 1915 address to students of the Faculdade de Direito de São Paulo, reproduced in Bilac, *A Defesa Nacional,* 23–28.

85 Anderson, *Imagined Communities.*

86 Bilac, *A Defesa Nacional,* 38.

87 *Boletim do Diretório da Liga de Defesa Nacional,* Nov 1917, 2.

88 Bilac, *A Defesa Nacional,* 38.

89 Nancy Leys Stepan, *The Hour of Eugenics,* 17, 35–39, 63–101.

90 A 1916 editorial praised Brazil's youth for its vigor, playing soccer instead of crowding cafés and flop houses. *Correio da Manhã,* October 25, 1916, 1.

91 Bilac, *A Defeza Nacional,* 27. See also, Belsário Penna, *O exército e sanidade;* Nancy Leys Stepan, *The Hour of Eugenics,* 46–54; McCann, *A nação armada,* 15–48; Carone, *A República Velha,* 1:162–70.

92 Leitão de Carvalho, *A Defeza Nacional,* February 10, 1914, 140.

93 Bilac, *A Defeza Nacional,* 75, 80; Osorio Filho, *O espírito das armas,* 26–32.

94 "O problema militar," *Correio da Manhã,* October 5, 1916, 1.

95 Hayes, *The Nation in Arms.* On the importance of military "lore," see Nunn, *The Time of the Generals.*

96 *O Estado de São Paulo,* November 29, 1915, 1; *Não Matarás,* March 1908, 2, in AEL referred to an editorial by the war minister in *Jornal do Commércio* that made this accusation. It did not cite the date of publication.

97 Deputy Mario Hermes praised the support of carioca newspapers, "*O Paiz, A Rua, o Imparcial,* and *Correio de Manhã* [which] have dedicated columns of . . . support [for conscription]." ACB, *sessão* June 30, 1916, 3:415.

98 Labor bashed Rui Barbosa and Olavo Bilac for changing their positions on conscription. *Tribuna do Povo,* October 28, 1916, 2; "Sobre o sorteio," ibid., October 19, 1916, 2; "Serviço Militar Obrigatório," ibid., 2.

99 ACB, *sessão* July 26, 1915, 7:338. On the PRC: ACB, *sessão* July 19, 1915, 7:781–805; ACB, *sessão* August 19, 1915, 9:1018. A labor newspaper claimed that more than thirty "libertarian" workers' organizations had formed an anarchist alliance against the war and the draft. *A Plebe,* June 2, 1917, 4, in AEL.

100 *O Estado de São Paulo,* December 22, 1915, 3–4.

101 On labor militancy from a gender perspective, see Wolfe, *Working Men, Working Women,* chap. 1; Maram, "The Immigrant," 178–210; French, *The Brazilian Workers' ABC,* chap. 1.

102 Leandro Gomes de Barros, "Echos da Pátria," "A Guerra," and "Canto de Guerra," Recife: n.p., 1917, 10, in BNMR.

103 Ibid., 6, 10.

104 See the numerous editorials and speeches delivered by Osorio Filho in support of scouting, tiros, and the draft reprinted in *O espírito das armas.*

105 ACB, *sessão* June 30, 1916, 3:409–578.

106 ACB, *sessão* July 26, 1915, 7:321–22.

107 "O sorteio militar em cheque," *A Razão,* December 28, 1916, 1.

108 ACB, *sessão* July 26, 1915, 8:340–41.

109 "Limpa tudo," "Radium," *O Estado de São Paulo,* November 28, 1916, 1.

110 Estevão Leitão de Carvalho, "Outro aspecto do nosso voluntariado," *A Defeza Nacional,* February 1914, 142.

111 Da Cidade, *A Defeza Nacional* 7, April 1914, 218–19.

112 Oswaldo Barroso observed that the dead, officers, and women were called up. Barroso, *Memórias de um recruta,* 40.

Chapter 10 Making the Barracks a "House" and the Army a "Family"

1 McCann, "The Nation in Arms," 240; José Murilho de Carvalho, "As forças armadas," 141.

2 See, for example, Topik, *The Political Economy of the Brazilian State;* Font, *Coffee, Contention, and Change;* Diacon, "Searching for a Lost Army"; Nísia Trindade Lima and Gilberto Hochman, "Condenado pela raça."

3 On the "professional" perspective, see Leitão de Carvalho, *Dever Militar.*

4 McCann, "The Formative Period," 737–65, 753.

5 Carone, *A República Velha,* 2:352–53; McCann, "The Nation in Arms," 233.

6 Carone, *A República Velha,* 2:339–68.

7 Sodré, *A história militar,* 202–8.

8 Carneiro, *História das Revoluções Brasileiras;* Drummond, *O Movimento tenentista,* 77–88.

9 Prestes, *A Columna Prestes,* 111–55; Corrêa, *A Rebelião de 1924 em São Paulo;* Carone, *O Tenentismo;* Diacon, "Searching for a Lost Army."

10 Leitão de Carvalho, *Dever Militar,* 133–34; Coutinho, *General Góes Depõe;* Young, "Military Aspects of the 1930 Revolution," 180–96; Murilho de Carvalho, "Armed Forces and Politics," 192–223.

11 Carone, *A República Velha,* 2:435.

12 See the comments of a poor black woman on Vargas and her praise of volunteer soldiers as "men." Jesus, *Bitita's Diary.*

13 Rachum, "The 1930 Revolution."

14 Carvalho, "Armed Forces and Politics," 208.

15 See, for example, Paulo Sérgio Pinheiro, *Estratégias da ilusão*, 308–26.

16 Pérez, "Army Politics and the Collapse," 59–76; Carvalho, "Armed Forces and Politics," 197.

17 See, for example, Levine, *The Vargas Regime;* Id., *Father of the Poor?*

18 "Voto do General Góes Monteiro," December 3, 1935, Rio, CPDOC/FGV, GV-35.12.03/3, 0645/1–0647/2.

19 Carvalho, "Armed Forces and Politics," 202.

20 War Minister Góes Monteiro suggested that the State should extend the draft to women, but this innovative idea was not pursued. Carvalho, "Armed Forces and Politics," 202, 211; Id., "As forças armadas," 113–88.

21 See the table on army forces in Carvalho, "Armed Forces and Politics," 211.

22 Altino Bondesan, *Um pracinha paulista*, 9–19; Morais, *Chatô*, 448. The Brazilian Communist Party praised the *febianos* in *Tribuna Popular*, May 27, 1945; ibid., June 13, 1945; ibid., July 18, 1945. Others called on praças to turn their arms against Vargas and capitalism; "Basta de carne brasileira para as canhões imperialistas," *Luta Proletária*, January 1945, 1; ibid., June 1945, 1, in AEL.

23 On FEB recruitment, see Osvaldo Cordeiro de Farias, CPDOC/FGV, CFa 43.9.20, pa. III–1, 5–6. See the many letters to the LBA asking for aid and expressing pride in sons who were soldiers fighting for Brazil's "national honor." Ibid. pa. 1.

24 On new confidence in the "hidden energies" of Brazil's people, see *Jornal do Brasil* 22 (July 1945), 5; Silveira and Mitke, *A luta dos pracinhas*.

25 On the historiography of the FEB, see Neves, "A Força Expedicionária Brasileira."

26 Ferraz, "A história dos veteranos"; letter paraphrased and cited in McCann, *Brazilian-American Alliance*, 441.

27 McCann, "*Força Expedicionária Brasileira,*" 1–11. On the crowd's affection, *Jornal do Brasil*, July 18, 1945, 5–6; "A festa de emoção," ibid., July 20, 1945, 5; "O Dia do soldado, o dia do Brasil," ibid., July 22, 1945, 5. Nilson Costa, *Vida e luta*, 125.

28 *Jornal do Brasil*, July 22, 1945, 5; ibid., August 25, 1945, 6; ibid., August 26, 1945, 6; ibid., July 1, 1945, 8.

29 Ferraz, "A história dos veteranos."

30 Carvalho, "Armed Forces and Politics," 202–3: Alfred Stepan, *The Military in Politics;* Skidmore, *Politics in Brazil.*

31 Carvalho, "Armed Forces," 202.

32 Alfred Stepan, *The Military in Politics*, 17–20.

33 This report was reprinted in *A Federação*, January 4, 1917, 1.

34 *A Federação*, January 4, 1917, 1.

35 RRMGuC (1918), 12.

36 *A Defeza Nacional*, February 10, 1917, 149.

37 *RRMGUC* (1936), 22.

38 "O sorteio militar em cheque," *A Razão,* December 28, 1916, 1–2.

39 See a rail worker's brief recollection of his military service. Levine and Crocitti, eds., *The Brazil Reader,* 217.

40 *Jornal do Commercio,* September 12, 1926, 3; *A Defeza Nacional,* October 10, 1920, 65. Also see Sueann Caulfield's analysis of this parade and ideas of modernity in *In Defense of Honor.*

41 Carvalho, "Armed Forces and Politics," 211.

42 During the 1932 Constitutionalist Revolt, men who did not sign on for the rebel army were held in disdain by friends and relatives, and young women refused to talk to them. Interview of Isreal Días Novaes, MISSP, oral history section, Revolução Constitutionalista 1932, *fita* 20.18; Rio, *No tempo de Wenceslâo,* 217–35.

43 Coronel Dr. Arthur Lobo da Silva, "Acção eugenica dos exercitos," 3–4.

44 Peter M. Beattie, "Transforming Enlisted Army Service in Brazil," chap. 7. On contemporary recruitment, see Alfred Stepan, *The Military in Politics,* chap. 1; Colonel Dr. Arthur Lobo da Silva, "A Anthropologia," 23, 37–38. On recruiting only from cities, see *A Defeza Nacional,* January 10, 1917, 113–14.

45 Barroso, *Memórias,* 124–25; Colonel Dr. Arthur Lobo da Silva, "A Anthropologia," 36; Henrique B. Duffles Teixeira Lott noted that some medical students served as conscripts in his company in 1917 in *Depoimento* (Rio: CPDOC / FGV-História Oral, 1982), 45.

46 *Relatório do Governador Dr. Alvaro Pereira de Carvalho ao congresso do estado da Paraíba* (Paraíba: n.p., 1930), 115.

47 Carvalho cites AHE, cx. 66, *Relatório da Directoria de Recrutamento referente ao ano de 1939,* Gabinete do Ministério, *armário* 20; Carvalho, "Armed Forces and Politics," 202. I was unable to consult this source because it was in a basement archive that was closed due to flooding and has only recently been reopened in the AHE. Mara Loveman has recently completed research for her dissertation in this archive.

48 "Alistados denunciam maus-tratos," *Folha de São Paulo,* September 29, 1985, 24.

49 Carvalho, "Armed Forces and Politics," 202; Barroso's memoir also indicates that conscripts were regularly mustered out of service in 1924. Barroso, *Memórias.*

50 Penna, *O exército e sanidade,* 58–59.

51 *A Defeza Nacional* 58 (July 10, 1918), 306–7; "O sorteio militar em perigo . . . ," ibid., July 1919, 343–49 and August 1919, 387–91.

52 *RRMGUC* (1940), 36, 132; cited in McCann, "The Nation in Arms," 234, 7.

53 Sex Day also had a hymn. *Boletim de Educação Sexual,* March 1935, in AEL.

54 Ibid. The *Boletim* declared November 20, 1936, Brazil's first national Sex Day. Similar fears of venereal disease and military service gripped many

nations, including the United States, in the 1900s. See Brandt, *No Magic Bullet.*

55 *A Defeza Nacional* 41 (February 10, 1917), 149.

56 Colonel Dr. Arthur Lobo da Silva, "A Anthropologia," *quadro* 7 in index.

57 Penna uses several surveys but does not cite them in *O exército e sanidade*, 53–58.

58 "O Brasil é um imenso hospital," *Correio da Manhã*, November 1, 1916, 1; Lima and Hochman, "Condenado pela raça," 23–40.

59 Penna groused when reservists working for him were called up to march in the parade marking Brazil's centennial in 1922. Letter from Penna to Carlos Chagas, 22 September 1921, Rio, ACOC-FOC, BP/SPRE/1921.09.22, pa. 01.

60 Alfred Stepan, *The Military in Politics;* McCann, *A Nação armada*, 74–109; Hilton, "The Armed Forces and Industrialists," 629–71.

61 *A Defeza Nacional* 208 (April 1931): 251–55. On the use of anthropometric measures, see Schwarcz, *O espectáculo das raças.*

62 *Medicina Militar* 7 (May 1917): 266–71.

63 Letter from the President of the LDN [illegible] Barros to Belisário Penna, October 29, 1929, Rio, ACOC-FOC, BP/CO/1918.20.40, pa. 01; Letter from the LDN to Belisário Penna, n.d., Rio, ACOC-FOC, BP/CO/1921.11.23, pa. 3; Brazilian observers puzzled over Winston Churchill's failed efforts to preserve peacetime conscription in Britain. *Correio da Manhã*, March 8, 1919, 1.

64 Letter from Belisário Penna to the Governor of Pernambuco Dr. Sergio Loreto, July 24, 1923, n.p., ACOC-FOC, BP/CO/1921.11.23, pa. 3.

65 Penna, "Propaganda Sanitária," Rio, n.d., ACOC-FOC, BP/PI/900.20.40.

66 Penna, *Exército*, 6, 48, 63–65. See Penna's address to Brazil's Young Men's Christian Association, August 31, 1918, Rio, ACOC-FOC, BP/PI/1896.04.20.

67 Nancy Leys Stepan, *The Hour of Eugenics*, 36, 50. Similar fears gripped U.S. authorities. Brandt, *No Magic Bullet*, chapters 1 and 2.

68 Colonel Dr. Arthur Lobo da Silva, "A Anthropologia," 3–43.

69 See Pinto's collection of anthropomorphic data, manuscripts, and photography on recruits from the late 1910s and early 1920s in MN/UFRJ/SAB, col. Roquette Pinto, fichas antropométricas; ibid., fotografia antropométrica, file 596.

70 Colonel Dr. Arthur Lobo da Silva, "Acção eugenica," 2–14; Penna, *O exército e sanidade*, 57–62. This diverges from Nancy Leys Stepan's view in *The Hour of Eugenics* that Latin American eugenists focused on the health, hygiene, and child-rearing abilities of women. On men, eugenists, and alcoholism, see Matos, "O bar é o meu lar."

71 Colonel Dr. Arthur Lobo da Silva, "A Anthropologia," 3–19.

72 Colonel Dr. Arthur Lobo da Silva, "Acção eugênica," 9.

73 Penna, *O exército e sanidade,* 17.

74 *RRMGUC* (1935), 31.

75 Colonel Dr. Arthur Lobo da Silva, "Acção eugênica," 2–14.

76 *Jornal do Brasil,* July 2, 1945, 1. On these fears and nonblack minorities, see Lesser, *Negotiating National Identity.*

77 *RRMGUC* (1926), 11.

78 Barroso noted that literate recruits were matched with illiterate ones to teach literacy, but the army supplied no materials or classrooms, and officers often suspended classes. Barroso, *Memórias,* 172; José Ribas Cadaval, *Notícia explicativa sobre o método intuitivo Cadaval para ensinar crianças, e com mais vantagens, adultos a ler, escrever, e contar em sessenta lições; . . . (especialmente para o soldado brasileiro . . .)* (Rio: Imp. Nacional, 1908); H. O. G. e J. A. C., *A educação do soldado* (Belem: Liv. Florente, 1919).

79 *A Defeza Nacional* (August 10, 1918), 354; Penna, "[unpublished] Diary of a visit to Rio Grande do Sul," ACOC-FOC, BP/Produção Intelectual, 5–7.

80 Diacon, "Bringing the Countryside Back In"; *Hynos patrioticos e canções militares* (n.p.: Typ. Bruquense, 1917).

81 Sodré, *Narrativas Militares,* 57.

82 Freyre, *Casa Grande e Senzala,* 23.

83 Nancy Leys Stepan, *The Hour of Eugenics,* 166–70; Viotti da Costa, *The Brazilian Empire,* chap. 9; Jeffery Needell, "Identity, Race, Gender." On the overt nature of racism from a poor black woman's perspective in the 1920s and 1930s in Brazil, see Jesus, *Bitita's Diary.*

84 Mara Loveman, "Race and Nationality in Brazilian Army Thought."

85 Speech text in Farias, CPDOC/FGV, CFa 44.09.20tv, pa. I–22.

86 Carvalho, "Armed Forces and Politics," 205. In the 1920s, Sodré studied at the army preparatory school with a Black and a Bororó Indian student, *Memórias,* 46–48.

87 Barreto placed second on an exam for a scrivener's post in the army arsenal. When soon thereafter an arsenal employee died, he was awarded a post. Barreto, *Diário íntimo,* 25, 30.

88 Freyre later wrote an apology for the army's role in Brazilian society and supported the military dictatorship from 1964 to 1985. Freyre, *Ordem e progresso;* Guimarães da Costa, *Formação democrática.*

89 For a critique of army abolitionism, see Kraay, "The Shelter," 228–50.

90 On the paradoxical ways that the poor black woman Carolina Maria de Jesus wrote about race and national identity, see Levine, *The Life and Death of Carolina Maria de Jesus.*

91 "O regresso da FEB," *Jornal do Brasil,* July 26, 1945, 6.

92 Richard Graham, *Patronage and Politics,* 79–85; Kraay, "Officers, Soldiers, and Society," 179–93.

93 Conscription's critics and proponents often noted that it was the "man

on foot that made democracies." Some argued that democracies arise when the value of infantryman for warfare increased. Nickerson, *The Armed Horde.*

94 Morais, *Chatô,* 281.

95 *A Defeza Nacional,* November 10, 1920, 135; "A conscripção em Minas," *Correio da Manhã,* February 16, 1919, 3; E. P. Thompson, "Time," 59–97; Needell, "Identity, Race, Gender"; Ramos, *Memórias do Cárcere,* 1:64.

96 *Boletim do Ministério do Trabalho, Indústria e Comércio* (July 1944): 275–83. I thank my friend Tom Jordan for sharing this citation.

97 Levine, *The Life and Death,* 133, 139.

98 Vanda Maria Ribeiro Costa, "Com rancor," 174–200.

99 McCann, "The Nation in Arms," 234–35.

100 "Objeto de educação moral do soldado," *A Defeza Nacional* (September 1938), 295. Cited in Costa, "Com rancor," 175–76.

101 Anderson, *Imagined Communities;* Sommer, *Foundational Fictions.*

102 Kellet, *Motivação para o combate.*

103 See, for example, Winter, *Sites of Memory.*

104 *A Defeza Nacional* (September 1938), 291; cited in Costa, "Com rancor," 176.

105 Harrod, *Manning,* 26–31, 34–48; Even the private sector was slow to invest in advertising. Morais, *Chatô,* 142; Corsi, *Educação moral,* 30; Bitten-court, *Guia prático do reservista;* Bocaiuva Cunha, *O que os brasileiros devem saber;* Juracy de Assis Machado, *Tu e o serviço militar;* Tavares, *Como ficar quite;* Sousa, *Lança de David;* Igreja Católica no Brasil, Bispos, *Circular Coletiva.*

106 Barroso, *Memórias,* 92–93, 123–27, 190–91.

107 Ibid., 124, 150.

108 This assertion is based on songs that deal with praças from 1918 to 1950 in the BNMR. Francisco Telles, "O voluntário especial (recruta do setimo ao amigo João da Costa Filho)" (Rio: Oficinas da casa viuva guerreiro, n.d.); Claudinor Cruz and Pedro Caetano, "Um praçinha na Itália (para car-naval)" (Rio, n.p., 1946); Zé Trinidade and Aloysio Silva Araujo, "Recruta 23" (Rio, Ed. Irmãos Vitale, 1952).

109 Carvalho, "Armed Forces and Politics," 198.

110 Western colonization was a goal that the military government of the 1960s supported with land grants to individuals without criminal records. José Carlos Ataliba Nogueira argued that convicts could settle the Amazon in "Pena sem prisão," *Revista dos Tribunais* (1938). For a political prisoner's memoir, see Ramos, *Memórias do cárcere;* Colonel Octávio Costa, *Exército como fator.*

111 More attention has been given to this issue in Spanish America. See Brian Loveman, *The Constitution of Tyranny.*

Conclusions

1 Joan Scott, "Gender," 1067–70; Duetsch, "Gender and Sociopolitical Change," 259–306.
2 Ayers, *Vengeance*, 183; Rebecca J. Scott, "Defining," 70–102.
3 Ayers, *Vengeance*; Lichtenstein, "Good Roads and Chain Gangs," 85–110. Mary Ellen Curtin, *Black Prisoners and Their World.*
4 Hobsbawm, *The Age of Revolution*, 166.
5 Dávila, " 'Perfecting the Race,'" 179–92.
6 In Soviet Russia, peasants and workers began to see military service as an avenue of social mobility, whereas under the Russian monarchy, peasants and workers loathed military service. Hagen, *Soldiers,* 327–37.
7 Xavier de Oliveira, *O Exército e o sertão;* Barros, *O exército e o êxodo rural;* Levine and Sebe, *The Life and Death,* 139; Eugen Weber notes a similar effect on rural to urban migration in France in *Peasants into Frenchmen,* chap. 17.
8 Alfred Stepan, *The Military in Politics,* 12–29; Colonel Octávio Costa, *Exército como fator.*
9 Assunção, *A Guerra de Bem-te-vis,* 166, 174.
10 Tilly, "The Emergence of Citizenship," 223–36.
11 Skocpol, *Protecting Soldiers and Mothers,* 39. Also see essays in Skocpol and Rueschemeyer, eds., *States, Social Knowledge;* and Titmuss, *Essays on the Welfare State,* chap. 4. Jaime A. de Araújo Oliveira and Sonia M. Fleury Teixeira note that the first Brazilian government worker pension plans in the 1920s were inspired by pensions for military officers in *(Im)previdência social,* 19–22. Barbara Weinstein notes that the impetus for worker benefits in São Paulo began with programs designed to help rebel soldiers and to win industrial laborers' support for the Constitutionalist Rebellion of 1932 in *For Social Peace in Brazil.* Molloy, *Politics of Social Security.*
12 Carvalho, "Armed Forces and Politics," 193–223.
13 Levine, *Father of the Poor.*
14 José Murilo de Carvalho, *A Formação das Almas,* chap. 4; Peter M. Beattie, "Conflicting Penile Codes," 65–70.
15 Peixoto, *Cancioneiro militar,* 38, 74–75.
16 Some of these same sentiments could inform racial or class solidarities instead of leveling national ones, such as the exaggerated fears of black men raping white women in the American South after abolition. Hodes, *White Women, Black Men,* 198–208; see also, for example, Trexler, *Sex and Conquest.*
17 Steve J. Stern observes this kind of manly resistance among plebeian men in colonial Mexico, *The Secret History,* chap. 7.
18 Barickman, "Citizenship, Kinship, Slavery"; Graham, *Patronage and Politics,* chap. 1.
19 Greenberg, *Honor and Slavery.*
20 Peter Fry's comments on Peter M. Beattie, "Masculinidade, raça, e nação: a

questão do sorteio militar 1870–1930," presentation to the Núcleo da Cor, Instituto de Filosofia e Ciências Sociais, Universidade Federal do Rio de Janeiro, June 20, 1999.

21 *Journal do Brasil,* July 22, 1945, 5.

22 Beattie, "Conflicting Penile Codes," 78.

23 Sodré, *Do Tenentismo,* 40. Sodré echoed vintage concerns: Herculano Augusto Lassance Cunha, *Dissertação sobre a prostituição*; Macedo, "Da prostituição," 115–21, 167; Almeida, *Homosexualismo,* 75–76, 85. On changing ideas of sexuality in the 1920s and 1930, see Green, *Beyond Carnival,* chap. 2.

24 On changing conceptions of heterosexual partnership see, for example, Besse, *Restructuring Patriarchy,* chap. 3; Peter M. Beattie, "Conflicting Penile Codes," 65–85. On the Argentine army, see Guy, *Sex and Danger,* chap. 6.

25 Other historians have noted that conceptions of female honor also slowly changed as more prosperous women took on new roles outside the home. Caulfield, "In Defense of Honor," chap. 3; Caulfield and Esteves, "Fifty Years of Virginity," 63–65; Borges, *The Family in Bahia.*

26 Bernstein, *New York City Draft Riots.*

27 Shenk, "Work or Flight"; Ira Berlin et al., *Slaves No More;* Ayer, *Vengeance.* Conscription was incompatible with serfdom, Wirtschafter, *From Serf to Russian Soldier,* xiv–xix.

28 Martinez-Alier, *Marriage, Class, and Colour.*

29 Rebecca J. Scott, *Slave Emancipation in Cuba;* Robert, "Slavery and Freedom, 181–92; Helg, *Our Rightful Share;* Andrews, *Blacks and Whites in São Paulo;* Kelley, *Race Rebels;* Ferrer, *Insurgent Cuba;* Kraay, "The Shelter," 249–50.

30 Dain Borges, "Puffy, Ugly, Slothful," 235–56; Skidmore, *Black into White.*

31 *Jornal do Brasil,* February 22, 1945, 5.

32 Skidmore, *White into Black;* Needell, "Identity, Race, Gender."

33 Winter, *Sites of Memory;* Freyre, *Ordem e progresso,* 2:740–41; Romero, *A bancarrota;* Hayes, *The Nation in Arms;* Alfred Stepan, *The Military in Politics;* Loveman, *For la Patria.*

34 Skidmore, *White into Black.*

35 Barbosa, *A Viola de Loreno.*

Appendix C

1 To simplify lengthy citations of governors' reports to provincial (after 1889 "state") governments, I have listed sources found on microfilm in the periodical section of the Biblioteca Nacional by locale, date, prisons listed, and page number. Often data is found in appendixes to reports written by police chiefs as noted below. Ceará: Casa de Detenção (July 4, 1871), 6–7; (May 31, 1876: police chief's annexo), 6; (April 1, 1881: police chief's annexo), 62–3; (September 9, 1886: police chief's annexo), 7. Pernambuco

includes Casa de Detenção and after 1900 the state Penal Colony of Fernando de Noronha: (March 1, 1871), 9; (March 1, 1876: police chief's annexo), 4; (March 1, 1881), 25; Reported 32 deaths in 1885; (July 3, 1886), 15; (March 6, 1900: police chief's annexo), 6. Bahia includes the Cadeia de Prisão com Trabalho, the Casa de Correçao, and the Prisão de Galês in the Navy Arsenal up to 1881: (March 1, 1871: police chief's annexo), 17–8; (March 1, 1876); (April 3, 1886), 43; (April 7, 1892), 8–12. Rio Grande do Sul: Casa de Correcção (March 14, 1871), 81; Cadeia Civil da Capital (March 7, 1886), 123; (September 22, 1926), 8. São Paulo: Casa de Correcção and Cadeia da Capital: (February 5, 1871), 11, 14; (February 2, 1876); (January 13, 1881), 156; in 1886 São Paulo includes Cadeia de Capital (171 prisoners), Limoeira (112), Pindamonhangaba (117), Mogymirim (131), Queluz (134), Campinas (312), (February 15, 1886: annexo 8), 12, 22–30. Minas Gerais: Cadeia da Capital (March 2, 1871: police chief's annexo); (May 4, 1881), 29. Minas: (1891) 29; includes Minas's 110 jails in 1906 and 1911 (1906: police chief's annexo), 47; (1911: police chief's annexo), 8. Mato Grosso includes Cadeia da Capital and in 1876 Presos Correcionais: (August 20, 1871), 12; (May 3, 1876), 11, 17; (May 3, 1881: police chief's annexo), mapa #1; (September 7, 1921), 56. Pará (March 25, 1886), 78. Rio (Capital District): Casa de Detenção, in 1886 includes Casa de Correcção and Prisão Civil, in 1896 Casa de Detençao and Casa Correcção, in 1901, 1906, and 1910 only the Casa de Correcção, in 1916 Casa de Correcção and Casa de Detenção: (1871), 29; (1877), 267; (1881), 155; (1886), 117–18, 126; (1891) 96, 100; (1896), 84, 87; (1901), 151–54; (March, 1906), 68; (April 1911), 70; (April, 1916), 81–82, 88. Paraíba: Cadeia da Capital (October 16, 1871), 8; Cadeia da Capital and de Pombal for 1881 only (September 21, 1881), 11; Cadeia da Capital only (August 1, 1886: police chief's annexo), 20–21; (October 1, 1901), 15; (September 1, 1906), 6; (September 1, 1911), 6. Rio de Janeiro (province/state): (October 22, 1876), mapa 2; (June 3, 1881: police chief's annexo), 24; Casa de Detenção only (August 6, 1886), 52.

Glossary of Portuguese Terms

Afilhadagem. Protection granted a godson, broadly used to describe clientelism.

Alferes. Ensign.

Anspeçada. A praça rank between private and corporal.

Assentamento. A praça's career record.

Assentar praça. To become an active-duty army praça.

Aquilombado. Resident of a runaway-slave community (*quilombo*).

Blanco(a). White.

Caboclo(a). The color and appearance of person with a mixture of Indian and white blood. It can also imply hinterland origins.

Caçada humana. Literally, "manhunts." Frequently used to describe army impressment practices.

Cachaça. Brandy made from sugarcane.

Cafuzo/a. An individual of mixed Indian and African heritage.

Camarada. Soldier assigned to perform personal services for an officer, akin to a domestic servant.

Capitão(aes) do Mato. Bounty hunter who tracked down runaway slaves for a living.

Capoeira. A uniquely Afro-Brazilian martial art, dance, and musical form developed by slaves and maroons. By the nineteenth century, capoeira had developed into distinct countercultural organizations formed by slaves and freemen in urban centers for mutual protection and support. Also a practicioner of capoeira.

Carioca. Native of Rio de Janeiro.

Casaca. (frock coat) A denigrating term used by the army to describe the civilian political elite.

Casado(a). A married person.

Chibata. Brutal corporal punishment applied to navy praças.

Conciliação. A period of cooperation, literally "conciliation," between Liberal and Conservative party politicians in the mid-nineteenth century.

Conselho de Guerra. Court-martial.

Conselho Supremo Militar de Justiça. Supreme Military Council of Justice. The high court of military justice from 1808 to 1893.

Coronel/coronéis. Rural political boss. The term derived from the fact that many held the rank of colonel in the National Guard.

Coronelismo. Exercise of power by local magnates.

Degredo. A sentence of temporary or permanent exile commonly awarded by Portuguese courts.

Degredado(a). An individual sentenced to temporary or permanent exile.

Desprotegido. Unprotected ones. Individuals who lacked a patron who could protect them from impersonal authority.

Desarranchar. To be given permission to live off base.

Desterro. Punishment of exile within Brazil.

Deus é grande mas o mato é maior. God is great, but the wilderness is greater. Expression commonly used by those who escaped authorities by fleeing to Brazil's vast wilderness.

Doutor. A title of great respect usually reserved for those who graduated from one of Brazil's highly exclusive law or medical faculties, but it was also used to venerate powerful or respected men without a degree. In army usage, doutores referred to officers who were educated at the military academy.

Florianistas. Supporters of President Marshal Floriano Peixoto.

Furriel. A rank between corporal and sergeant.

Foro Militar. Military court jurisdiction.

Fula. Dark black color and appearance of people originating from Guinea.

Galés. Literally, "galleys." Sentence commonly applied to slaves convicted of felonies in the nineteenth century that required them to work and wear irons while jailed.

Gaúcho(a). Native of Rio Grande do Sul.

Indiática. Indian in color and appearance.

Insubmissão. The crime of draft dodging.

Insubmisso. Draft dodger.

Jacobino. Jacobin. Radical Republican wing.

Jovem turcos. Young Turks. Term for progressive junior officers, many of whom studied in Germany, who pushed for the national draft lottery and military modernization in general.

Juiz de Órfão. Municipal judge whose jurisdiction included orphaned minors.

Juiz de Paz. Justice of the peace.

Jurar Bandeira. An oath of allegiance sworn to the flag by all who served in the armed forces.

Leva. A convict laborer; also refers to groups of men dragooned and transferred to army compounds to serve as soldiers.

Liberto(a). A manumitted slave; the army used the term to designate bondsmen who were freed on the condition that they fight on the front during the Paraguayan War (1864–70).

Linhas de tiro. Swiss-style sharp-shooting clubs formed by members of the elite and middle-class after 1900.

Malta. Slang used to describe capoeira gangs and their members.

Mestiço. Mestizo.

Mil-réis. Currency of Brazilian empire and Old Republic.

Modinha. Popular song form, a favorite of Domingos Caldas Barbosa.

Moreno(a). Light brown.

Operário militar. Artisan employed by an army arsenal.

Ordenança. Third-line security force composed of free males between the ages of eighteen and forty-five who did not serve in the army or militia.

Palmatório. Perforated wooden paddle commonly used to strike the palms and soles for corporal punishment.

Pardo(a). Dark brown.

Pataqueiro. Literally, "cheap actor." Men hired to perform the National Guard duty of wealthier men.

Pistolão. Big shot, a patron, literally, "big pistol."

Povo. The common folk.

Povo fardado. Literally, "the people in uniform." This phrase is a popular Brazilian rendition of the concept of the citizen-soldier.

Praça. Noncommissioned soldiers (from privates to sergeants) in the army, police, and navy.

Pranchada. Blow delivered with the broad side of a sword or a *prancha*, designed for corporal punishment in the army.

Preto(a). Black.

Quilombo. Maroon or runaway-slave community.

Recrutas à pau e corda. "Club and rope recruits," a phrase commonly used to denigrate pressed recruits during the Paraguayan War.

Reinol(óis). Native to Portugal.

Recrutado. Recruited. In nineteenth-century Brazil, it referred to a soldier that had been pressed into military service.

Recrutamento. Recruitment. In the 1800s it carried a strong connotation of impressment.

Salvações. The "salvations" or toppling of state governments that opposed the government of President Marshal Hermes.

Sem Ofício. A person without a skilled trade.

Sertão. Sparsely populated hinterlands.

Sertanejo. Native of the *Sertão.*

Soldado. The rank of private.

Subdelegado. Subdeligate a parish-based police authority.

Tarimbeiro. Literally, "barracks bunk." Army slang for a group of old-school officers who had no specialized higher military education but learned their profession in regiments.

Tempo de Pegação or *Tempo de Pega.* "Nabbing time." Popular phrase describing recruitment sweeps that characterized mobilizations for major regional conflicts or international campaigns.

Tenente. Lieutenant.

Tributa de sangue. The tribute of blood or military service.

Voluntários da Pátria, also *Voluntário.* Volunteers of the fatherland. A special army corps with special privileges promulgated in 1865 to attract men to volunteer to fight during the Paraguayan War (1864–70).

Voluntários agenciados. "Volunteers" recruited by agents paid on commission.

Bibliography

Archives

ACOC-FOC — Arquivo da Casa de Oswaldo Cruz, Fundação Oswaldo Cruz. Rio.
ACRB — Arquivo da Casa de Rui Barbosa. Rio.
AGCR — Arquivo Geral da Cidade do Rio de Janeiro.
AGN — Archivo General de la Nación. Buenos Aires, Argentina.
AEL — Arquivo Edgar Leuenroth. Campinas, São Paulo.
AESP — Arquivo do Estado de São Paulo. São Paulo.
AHE — Arquivo Histórico do Exército. Rio.
AHRSG — Arquivo Histórico do Rio Grande do Sul. Porto Alegre.
ANR — Arquivo Nacional. Rio.
APEP — Arquivo Público do Estado de Pernambuco. Recife.
APERJ — Arquivo Público do Estado do Rio de Janeiro. Rio.
BNMR — Biblioteca Nacional de Música. Rio.
BNR-SMOR — Biblioteca Nacional Seção de Manuscritos e Obras Raras. Rio.
CPDOC — Centro de Pesquisa e Documentação, Fundação Getúlio Vargas. Rio.
IBGE — Instituto Brasileiro de Geografia e Estatística. Rio.
IHGB — Instituto Histórico e Geográfico Brasileiro. Rio.
MN/UFRJ/SAB — Museu Nacional. Universidade Federal do Rio de Janeiro. Setor de Antropologia Biológica.
MISSP — Museu de Imagen e Som. São Paulo.
PRO — Public Records Office. London, England.

Dissertations and Unpublished Papers

Almeida, Cypriano José Barata de [attributed]. "Dissertação abreviada sobre o horrível masmona — presiganga — existente no Rio de Janeiro," in IHGB, lata 48, doc. 12, 26 May 1829.
Aufderheide, Patricia Ann. "Order and Violence: Social Deviance and Social Control in Brazil, 1780–1840," Ph.D. diss., University of Minnesota, 1975.
Barcellos, Alfredo A. Vieira. "Dos systemas penitenciarios e da sua influencia sobre o homem." Rio: Tese de Medicina, 1875.
Barickman, B. J. "Citizenship, Kinship, Slavery, and Household in the 1835 Parish Censuses from Bahia: Santiago do Iguape." Paper presented to the Social Science History Conference, New Orleans, November 1997.

Capella, Leila Maria Corrêa. "As malhas de aço no tecido social: A revista *A Defesa Nacional* e o serviço militar obrigatório." Dissertação de Mestrado, Universidado Federal Fluminense 1985.

Carvalho, Marcus Joaquim Maciel de. "Hegemony and Rebellion in Pernambuco, Brazil 1821–1835." Ph.D. diss., University of Illinois, 1989.

Caulfield, Sueann. "In Defense of Honor: The Contested Meaning of Sexual Morality in Law and Courtship, Rio de Janeiro, 1920–1940." Ph.D. diss., New York University, 1994.

Coates, Timothy J. "Exiles and Orphans: Forced and State-Sponsored Colonizers in the Portuguese Empire, 1550–1720." Ph.D. diss., University of Minnesota, 1993.

Dávila, Walter Jerome José. "'Perfecting the Race': Education and Social Discipline in Brazil's Vargas Era, 1930–1945." Ph.D. diss., Brown University, 1998.

Dudley, William S. "Reform and Radicalism in the Brazilian Army, 1870–1889." Ph.D. diss., Columbia University, 1972.

Ferraz, Francisco César Alves. "A história dos veteranos da FEB pós-guerra." Paper presented to the Brazilian Studies Association, Recife, 21 June 2000.

Ferreira Lins, Maria de Lourdes. "A legião de São Paulo no Rio Grande do Sul, 1775–1822." Dissertação de Mestrado, Universidade de São Paulo, 1977.

Ford, Talisman. "Passion is in the Eye of the Beholder: Sexuality as Seen by Brazilian Sexologists, 1900–1940," Ph.D. diss. Vanderbilt University, 1995.

Graden, Dale T. "From Slavery to Freedom in Bahia, Brazil 1791–1900. Ph.D. diss., University of Connecticut, 1991.

Izecksohn, Vitor. "O cerne da discórdia: A guerra do Paraguai e o núcleo profissional de exército." Dissertação de Mestrado, Instituto Universitario de Pesquisas do Rio de Janeiro, 1992.

Kraay, Hendrik. "Soldiers, Officers, and Society: The Army in Bahia, Brazil, 1808–1889," Ph.D. diss., University of Texas, Austin, 1995.

Loveman, Mara. "Questions on the Vargas Era from the Old Republic: Race and Nationality in Brazilian Army Thought." Paper presented at the Brazilian Studies Association, Recife, Brazil, 20 June 2000.

Lucena Filho, Márcio. "Pernambuco e a Guerra do Paraguai: O recrutamento e os limites da ordem." Dissertação de Mestrado, Universidade Federal de Pernambuco, 2000.

Matos, Izilda Santos de. "O bar é o meu lar." Paper presented to the XX Encontro de ANPOCS (n.p., n.d., photocopy).

McBeth, Michael C. "The Politicians Versus the Generals: The Decline of the Brazilian Army During the First Empire." Ph.D. diss., University of Washington, 1972.

Meznar, Joan E. "Deference and Dependence: The World of Small Farmers in a Northeastern Community, 1850–1900." Ph.D. diss., University of Texas at Austin, 1986.

Moreira, Paulo Roberto Staudt. "Entre o Deboche e a Rapina: Os cenários sociais da criminalidade popular em Porto Alegre, 1868–1888." Dissertação de Mestrado, Universidade Federal do Rio Grande do Sul, 1993.

Neves, Luis Felipe da Silva. "A Força Expeditionária Brasileira: Uma perspectiva histórica." Dissertação de Mestrado, Universidade Federal do Rio de Janeiro, 1992.

Schulz, John Henry. "The Brazilian Army and Politics, 1850–1894," Ph.D. diss., Princeton University, 1973.

Serbin, Kenneth P. "Priests, Celibacy, and Social Conflict: A History of Brazil's Clergy and Seminaries," Ph.D. diss., University of California, San Diego, 1993.

Shenk, Gerald Edwin. " 'Work or Fight': Selective Service and Manhood in the Progressive Era," Ph.D. diss., University of California, San Diego, 1992.

Tórtima, Pedro. "Polícia e justiça de mãos dados: a conferência judiciaria policial de 1917." Dissertação de Mestrado, Universidade Federal Fluminense, 1988.

Warren, Michael A. "Ordem e Civilização: The Modernization of Brazilian Naval Yards in the Nineteenth Century," Ph.D. diss., Tulane University, 1997.

Periodicals

O Alvorada. Jaguarão and Rio Grande, Rio Grande do Sul.
The Anglo-Brazilian Times. Rio de Janeiro.
O Arlequim. Rio de Janeiro.
Aurora. Rio de Janeiro.
Avanti! São Paulo.
Ba-Ta-Clan. Rio de Janeiro.
Boletim do Diretório Central da Liga de Defesa Nacional. Rio de Janeiro.
Boletim de Educação Sexual. Rio de Janeiro.
Brazil-Americano. Rio de Janeiro.
A Bruxa. Rio de Janeiro.
Cabichui. Asunción, Paraguay.
O Cabrião. São Paulo.
Constituição. Fortaleza, Ceará.
Correio da Manhã. Rio de Janeiro.
Cosompolita. Rio de Janeiro.
A Defeza Nacional. Rio de Janeiro.
Diário de Notícias. Rio de Janeiro.
Diário de Pernambuco. Recife.
O Diário do Povo. Rio de Janeiro.
O Diário do Rio de Janeiro. Rio de Janeiro.
O Echo Popular. Rio de Janeiro.
El Centinela. Asunción, Paraguay.
O Estado de São Paulo. São Paulo.

A Federação. Porto Alegre, Rio Grande do Sul.
O Globo. Rio de Janeiro.
O Indicador Militar. Rio de Janeiro.
Jornal de Aracaju. Aracaju, Sergipe.
Jornal do Brazil. Rio de Janeiro.
Jornal do Ceará. Fortaleza, Ceará.
Jornal do Commércio. Rio de Janeiro.
Kosmos. Rio de Janeiro.
A Larva. Rio de Janeiro.
O Lidador. Corumbá, Mato Grosso.
Luta Proletária. N.p.
A Luz Marítima. Rio de Janeiro.
A Luz Social. São Paulo.
O Malho. Rio de Janeiro.
Medicina Militar. Rio de Janeiro.
Mephistopheles. Rio de Janeiro.
O Militar. Rio de Janeiro.
Mosquito. Rio de Janeiro.
A Nação. Rio de Janeiro.
Não Matarás. Rio de Janeiro.
O Nihilista. Rio de Janeiro.
O Operário. Porto Alegre, Rio Grande do Sul.
Pedro II. Fortaleza, Ceará.
A Razão. Rio de Janeiro.
A Reforma. Porto Alegre, Rio Grande do Sul.
A República. Rio de Janeiro.
Revista do Exército Brasileiro. Rio de Janeiro.
A Revista Ilustrada. Rio de Janeiro.
Revista Militar. Rio de Janeiro.
Revista dos Tribunaes. São Paulo.
A Semana Illustrada. Rio de Janeiro.
O Soldado. Rio de Janeiro.
O Telegrapho. São Luis, Maranhão.
Tribuna Popular. Rio de Janeiro.
A Tribuna do Povo. Viçosa, Alagoas.
A Vida Fluminense. Rio de Janeiro.
O Voluntário. Diamantina, Minas Gerais.
A Voz do Trabalhador. Rio de Janeiro.

Published Documents and Collections

Alcântara, José de., ed. *Legislação militar.* Lisboa: Imprensa Nacional, 1861.

Bandeira Filho, Dr. Antônio Herculano de Souza. "Informações sobre presídio de Fernando de Noronha: relatório apresentado ao governo." Rio: n.p., 1880.

Código penal e disciplinar da Armada: Regulamento processual e formulário do processo criminal militar. Rio: Imprensa Nacional, 1914.

Collecção das decisões do império do Brazil de 1822. Rio: Imprensa Nacional, 1887.

Collecção das leis da República dos Estados Unidos do Brasil. Rio: Imprensa Nacional, 1890–1930.

Collecção das leis do Império do Brazil. Rio: Imprensa Nacional, 1830–1874.

Instituto Brasileiro de Geografia e Estatística [IBGE], Conselho Nacional de Estatístico. *O Brasil em números.* Rio: IBGE, 1966.

———. *Estatística Histórica do Brasil.* 2nd ed. Rio: IBGE, 1990.

Nascimento e Silva, M. J. do, ed. *Consultas do Conselho do Estado sobre os negócios relativos ao Ministério da Guerra 1867–1872.* Rio: Imprensa Nacional, 1885.

Recenseamento do Brazil: Realizado em primeiro de setembro de 1920. 2 vols. Rio: Typ. de Estatística, 1922.

Relatório[s] da Repartição dos Negócios do Ministério da Guerra apresentado ao Congresso [RRMGuC]. Rio: Imprensa Nacional, 1891–1940.

Relatório[s] da Repartição dos Negócios do Ministério da Guerra apresentado ao Parlamento [RRMGuP]. Rio: Imprensa Nacional, 1850–1889

Secondary Sources

Abente, Diego. "The War of Triple Alliance: Three Explanatory Models." LARR 22, no. 2 (1987): 47–69.

Abreu Esteves, Martha de. *Meninas perdidas: os populares e o cotidiano do amor no Rio de Janeiro da Belle Époque.* Rio: Paz e Terra, 1989.

Albuquerque, Durval Muniz de, Jr. *A invenção do nordeste e outras artes.* Recife: Ed. Massangana, 1999.

Alcinio, Padre Rogério. *Clevelândia do norte.* Rio: Biblioteca Nacional, 1971.

Alden, Dauril. *Royal Government in Colonial Brazil: With Special Reference to the Administration of the Marquis of Lavradio, Viceroy, 1769–1779.* Berkeley: University of California Press, 1968.

Almeida, José Ricardo Pires de. *Homosexualismo (a libertinagem no Rio de Janeiro).* Rio: Laemmert, 1906.

Almeida, Manuel Antônio de. *Memoirs of a Militia Sergeant.* Translated by Ronald W. Sousa. New York: Oxford University Press, 1999 [1854–55].

Anderson, Benedict. *Imagined Communities: Reflections on the Origin and Spread of Nationalism.* Rev. ed. New York: Verso, 1991.

Andrews, George Reid. *The Afro-Argentines of Buenos Aires, 1800–1900.* Madison: University of Wisconsin Press, 1991.

———. *Blacks and Whites in São Paulo Brazil 1888–1988.* Madison: University of Wisconsin Press, 1991.

Archer, Christon I. *The Army in Bourbon Mexico, 1760–1810*. Albuquerque: University of New Mexico Press, 1977.

Ariés, Phillippe. *Centuries of Childhood: A Social History of Family Life*. Translated by Robert Baldick. New York: Vantage Books, 1962.

Associação de Empregados no Commercio do Rio de Janeiro. *Sorteio militar: representação dirigida ao congresso nacional*. Rio: Typ. do Jornal do Commercio, 1907.

Assumpção. *Serviço militar obrigatório*. Belo Horizonte: Imp. do Estado de Minas Gerais, 1912.

Assunção, Matthias Röhrig. *A guerra de bem-te-vis: a Balaiada na memória oral*. São Luís: Serviço de Imprensa e Obras Gráficas do Estado, 1988.

———. "Histórias do Balaio: Historiografia, memória oral, e as origens da Balaiada," *História Oral* 1, no. 1 (June 1998): 67–89.

Ayers, Edward L. *Vengeance and Justice: Crime and Punishment in the Nineteenth Century South*. New York: Oxford University Press, 1984.

Azevedo, Aluísio. *O Cortiço*. 19th ed. São Paulo: Editora Ática, 1988 [1890].

Bandeira Filho, Dr. Antonio Herculano de Souza. *Informações sobre o presidio de Fernando de Noronha*. Rio: n.p., 1880.

Barbosa, Domingos Caldas. *A viola de Loreno*. Edited by Francisco de Assis Barbosa. Rio: Civilização Brasileira, 1980.

Barickman, B. J. *A Bahian Counterpoint: Sugar, Tobacco, Cassava, and Slavery in the Reconcôncavo, 1780–1860*. Stanford, Calif.: Stanford University Press, 1998.

———. "A Little Piece of Ground They Call *Roça:* Slave Provision Grounds in Nineteenth Century Bahia," *HAHR* 74, no. 4 (1993): 649–88.

Barman, Roderick J. *Brazil: The Forging of a Nation 1798–1852*. Stanford, Calif.: Stanford University Press, 1988.

———. "The Brazilian Peasantry Reexamined: The Implications of the Quebra-Quilos Revolt, 1874–75," *HAHR* 57, no. 3 (August 1977): 401–24.

Barreto, [Alfonso Henrique de] Lima. *Bagatelas*. Sao Paulo: Brasiliense, 1956.

———. *Diário íntimo*. Rio: Ed. Mérito, 1953.

———. *Triste fim de Policarpo Quaresma*. Rio: Edioro, Coleção Prestígio, n.d. [1980s, originally published in 1915].

Barros, Colonel Hygino de. *O exército e o êxodo rural*. Rio: Biblioteca do Exército, 1959.

Barroso, Oswaldo. *Memórias de um recruta*. São Paulo: Monteiro Labato, 1924.

Beattie, J. M. "The Pattern of Crime in England 1660–1820." *Past and Present* 62 (February 1974): 47–95.

Beattie, Peter M. "Conflicting Penile Codes: Modern Masculinity and Sodomy in the Brazilian Military, 1860–1916." In *Sex and Sexuality in Latin America*, edited by Dan Balderston and Donna J. Guy, 65–85. New York: New York University Press, 1997.

———. "Conscription Versus Penal Servitude: Army Reform's Influence on the

Brazilian State's Management of Social Control, 1870–1930." *Journal of Social History* (Summer 1999): 847–78.

——. "The House, the Street, and the Barracks: Reform and Honorable Masculine Social Space in Brazil." HAHR 76, no. 3 (August 1996): 439–73.

——. "National Identity and the Brazilian Folk: The Image of the *Sertanejo* in Taunay's *A retirada da Laguna.*" *Review of Latin American Studies* 4, nos. 1–2 (1991): 7–43.

Bederman, Gail. *Manliness and Civilization: A Cultural History of Gender and Race in the United States, 1880–1917.* Chicago: University of Chicago Press, 1995.

Bender, Gerald J. *Angola Under the Portuguese: The Myth and the Reality.* Berkeley and Los Angeles: University of California Press, 1978.

Bernstein, Iver. *The New York City Draft Riots: Their Significance for American Society and Politics in the Age of the Civil War.* New York: Oxford University Press, 1990.

Berlin, Ira, et al. *Slaves No More: Three Essays on Emancipation and the Civil War.* New York: Cambridge University Press, 1992.

Berrance de Castro, Jeanne. *A milícia cidadã: a guarda nacional de 1831 a 1850.* São Paulo: Cia. Ed. Nacional, 1977.

Besse, Susan K. "Crimes of Passion: The Campaign Against Wife Killing in Brazil, 1910–1940" *Journal of Social History* 22, no. 4 (Summer 1989): 653–66.

——. *Restructuring Patriarchy: The Modernization of Gender Inequality in Brazil 1914–40.* Chapel Hill: University of North Carolina Press, 1996.

Bilac, Olavo. *Atravéz do Brazil (narrativas) livros de leitura para o curso médio das escolas primárias.* Rio: Francisco Alves, 1910.

——. *A defeza nacional.* Rio: Ed. Biblioteca do Exército, 1965.

Bilac, Olavo, and Coelho Netto. *Contos pátrios para alumnos das escolas primárias.* Rio: Francisco Alves, 1904.

——. *Últimas conferencias e discursos.* São Paulo: Livraria Francisco Alves, 1924.

Bittencourt, Alvaro. *Guia prático do reservista ou o manual do recruta de mar e terra.* Rio: J. Cardoso e Mello, 1928.

Bondesan, Altino. *Um pracinha paulista no inferno de Hitler.* São Paulo: Ed. Guaíra, n.d.

Borges, Dain Edward. *The Family in Bahia Brazil, 1870–1945.* Stanford: Stanford University Press, 1992.

——. "Puffy, Ugly, Slothful, and Inert: Degeneration and Brazilian Social Thought, 1880–1940." JLAS 25 (1993): 235–56.

Boxer, C. R. *The Golden Age of Colonial Brazil 1695–1750: Growing Pains of a Colonial Society.* Berkeley and Los Angeles: University of California Press, 1962.

——. *The Portuguese Seaborne Empire 1415–1825.* 2d ed. Exeter, Mass.: Carcanet, 1991.

Brandão, Captain Dr. Alfredo. "A tatuagem na cirurgia militar." *Medicina Militar* (May 1917): 266–71.

Brandt, Allan M. *No Magic Bullet: A Social History of Venereal Disease in the United States since 1880.* New York: Oxford University Press, 1985.

Bretas, Marcos Luiz. *A guerra nas ruas: povo e polícia na cidade do Rio de Janeiro.* Rio: ANR, 1997.

Brito, José Gabriel Lemos de. *Os sistemas penitenciárias do Brasil.* 3 vols. Rio: Impresa Nacional, 1924–27.

Burns, Bradford E. "The Destruction of a Folk Past: Euclydes da Cunha and Cataclysmic Culture Clash." *Review of Latin American Studies* 3, no. 1 (1990): 17–36.

Bushnell, John. *Mutiny Amid Repression: Russian Soldiers in the Revolution of 1905–1906.* Bloomington: Indiana University Press, 1985.

Calmon, Miguel. *Discursos pronunciados nas sessões do Senado Federal de 29 a 30 de Dezembro, 1927.* Rio: Imprensa Nacional, 1928.

Caminha, Adolfo. *Bom Crioulo: The Black Man and the Cabin Boy.* Translated by E. A. Lacey. San Francisco: The Gay Sunshine Press, 1982 [1895].

Carneiro, Glauco. *História das revoluções brasileiras.* 2d ed. Rio: Record, 1989.

Carone, Edgar. *Movimento operário no Brasil (1877–1944).* 2d ed. São Paulo: Difusão Editorial, 1984.

———. *A República Velha.* Vol. 1. *Instituições e classes sociais 1889–1930.* 5th ed. São Paulo: Editora Bertrand, 1988.

———. *A República Velha.* Vol. 2. *Evolução política (1889–1930).* 4th ed. Rio: Difusão Editorial, 1983.

———. *O tenentismo: Acontecimentos, personagens, e programas.* São Paulo: Difusão Editorial, 1975.

Carvalho, General Estevão. *Dever militar e política partidária.* São Paulo: Companhia Editôra Nacional, 1959.

Carvalho, José Murilo de. "Armed Forces and Politics in Brazil, 1930–45." HAHR 62 (May 1982): 193–223.

———. *Os bestializados: O Rio de Janeiro e a República que não foi.* São Paulo: Companhia das Letras, 1991.

———. *A construção da ordem e Teatro de sombras.* Rio: Ed. Universidade Federal do Rio de Janeiro, 1996.

———. "As forças armadas na primeira república: o poder desestabilizador." *Cadernos do Departamento de Ciencia Politica* 1 (1973): 113–88.

———. *A formação das almas: o imaginário da república no Brasil.* São Paulo: Companhia das Letras, 1990.

Carvalho, Marcus Joaquim Maciel de. "Os índios de Pernambuco no ciclo da insurreições liberais, 1817/1848: ideologias e resistência." *Revista da Sociedade Brasileira de Pesquisa Histórica,* no. 11 (1996): 51–69.

Castro, Celso. *O espírito militar: um estudo de antropologia social no Academia Militar das Agulhas Negras.* Rio: Jorge Zahar Ed., 1990.

———. *Os militares e a República: um estudo sobre cultura política e ação política.* Rio: Jorge Zahar Ed., 1995.

Castro, Hebe Maria Mattos de. *Das cores do silêncio: os significados da liberdade no sudeste escravista, Brasil século XIX.* ANR, Rio: 1995.

Caulfield, Sueann. *In Defense of Honor: Sexual Morality, Modernity, and Nation in Early Twentieth Century Brazil.* Durham, N.C.: Duke University Press, 2000.

Caulfield, Sueann, and Martha de Abreu Esteves. "Fifty Years of Virginity in Rio de Janeiro: Sexual Politics and Gender Roles in Juridical and Popular Discourse, 1890–1940." LBR 30 (fall 1993): 47–74.

Cava, Ralph della. *Miracle at Joaseiro.* New York: Columbia University Press, 1970.

Cavalcante Brandão, Bernice, et al. *A polícia e a força policial no Rio de Janeiro.* Rio de Janeiro: Série Estudos–Pontífica Universidade Católical/Rio de Janeiro, 1981.

Cerqueira, Dionysio. *Reminiscências da Guerra do Paraguay.* Rio: Livraria F. Briguet and Cia., n.d.

Chalhoub, Sidney. *Cidade febril: cortiços e epidemias na Corte imperial.* São Paulo: Cia. das Letras, 1996.

———. *Trabalho, lar, e botequim: o cotidiano dos trabalhadores no Rio de Janeiro da belle epoque.* São Paulo: Ed. Brasilense, 1986.

———. *Visões da liberdade: uma história das últimas décadas da escravidão na Corte.* São Paulo: Companhia das Letras, 1990.

Chasteen, John Charles. *Heroes on Horseback: A Life and Times of the Last Gaucho Caudillos.* Albuquerque: University of New Mexico Press, 1995.

Chauncey, George, Jr. "Christian Brotherhood or Sexual Perversion? Homosexual Identities and the Construction of Sexual Boundaries in the World War One Era." *Journal of Social History* 18 (winter 1985): 189–211.

———. *Gay New York: Gender, Urban Culture, and the Making of the Gay Male World 1890–1940.* New York: Basic Books, 1994.

Chiavenato, Júlio José. *Genocídio Americano: a Guerra do Paraguai.* 2d ed. Rio: Ed. Brasiliense, 1978.

———. *O negro no Brasil: da senzala à Guerra Paraguai.* 14th ed. São Paulo: Brasiliense, 1982.

———. *Os voluntários da pátria e outros mitos.* São Paulo: Global Editora, 1983.

Childs, Matt D. "A Case of 'Great Unstableness': A British Slaveholder and Brazilian Abolition." *The Historian* 60, no. 4 (summer 1998): 717–740.

Cidade, Francisco de Paula da. "Verbetes para um diccionário bio-bibliográfico militar brasileiro." *Revista Militar Brasileira* 24, no. 1 (June): 25–35.

Cipolla, Carlo M. *Guns, Sails, and Empires: Technological Innovations and the Early Phases of European Expansion, 1400–1700.* New York: Pantheon Books, 1965.

Clausewitz, Karl Von. *On War.* Translated by Colonel Joseph I. Green. New York: Random House, 1943.

Conrad, Robert E. *Children of God's Fire: A Documentary History of Black Slavery in Brazil.* University Park: Pennsylvania State University Press, 1984.

———. *The Destruction of Brazilian Slavery, 1850–1888.* Berkeley: University of California Press, 1972.

Cope, Douglas. *The Limits of Racial Domination: Plebeian Society in Colonial Mexico City, 1660–1720.* Madison: University of Wisconsin Press, 1994.

Corrêa, Anna Maria Martinez. *A rebelião de 1924 em São Paulo.* São Paulo: Hucitec, 1976.

Corsi, Carlo. *Educação moral do soldado (obra traduzida e adaptada às condições actuaes do exército brasileiro . . .)* Rio: Imprensa Nacional, 1890.

Costa, Cruz. *O positivismo na república, notas sobre a história do positivismo no Brasil.* São Paulo: Ed. Nacional, 1956.

Costa, Emilia Viotti da. *The Brazilian Empire: Myths and Histories.* Chicago and London: University of Chicago Press, 1985.

Costa, Jurandir Freire. *Ordem médica e norma familiar.* 3d ed. Rio: Graal, 1989.

Costa, Nilson. *Vida e luta de um pracinha.* Campina Grande: n.p., 1950.

Costa, Colonel Octávio. *Exército como fator de integração nacional.* Rio: Imprensa do Exército, 1967.

Costa, Samuel Guimarães da. *Formação democrática do exército brasileiro.* Rio de Janeiro: Biblioteca do Exército, 1957.

Costa, Vanda Maria Ribeiro. "Com rancor e efeito: Rebeliões militares na década de 30," 174–200. Rio: FGV-CPDOC, 1984.

Costa, Wilma Perez. *A espada de Dâmocles: o exército e a crise do império.* São Paulo: Hucitec-Unicamp, 1996.

Coutinho, André Ribeiro. *O capitão de infantaria portuguez.* 2 vols. Lisbon: Régia Oficina Sylviana e a Academia Real, 1751.

Coutinho, Lourival. *General Góes depõe.* Rio: Livraria Ed. Coelho Branco, 1956.

Cruz Rangel, João da. *12.1 Repartiçao do Ajudante General, Mappa estatístico do Corpo de Imperiaes Marinheiros do anno de 1836 a Dezembro 1884,* ANR, GIFI, CX. 5C–486, fo. 488.

Cunha, Lassance, *Dissertação sobre prostituição em particular na cidade do Rio de Janeiro.* Rio: Typ. Imparcial do F. Paula Brito, 1845.

Cunha, Ranulfo Bocaiuva. *O que os brasileiros devem saber sobre o serviço militar.* Rio: Calvino Filho, 1933.

Curtain, Mary. *Black Prisoners and Their World, Alabama, 1865–1900.* Charlottesville: University of Virginia Press, 2000.

da Cunha, Euclydes. *Rebellion in the Backlands.* Translated by Samuel Putnam. Chicago: University of Chicago Press, 1944.

da Matta, Roberto. *A casa e a rua: espaço, cidadania, mulher e morte no Brasil.* Rio: Ed. Guanabara, 1987.

———. *Carnavais, malandros, e heróis: para uma sociologia do dilema brasileira.* Rio: Jorge Zahar Ed., 1979.

Diacon, Todd A. "Bringing the Countryside Back In: Recovering the History of Federal Army's Pursuit of the Prestes Column in Brazil 1924–27." JLAS 27 (1995): 560–92.

——. *Millenarian Vision, Capitalist Reality: Brazil's Contestado Rebellion, 1912–1916*. Durham, N.C.: Duke University Press, 1991.

——. "Searching for a Lost Army: Recovering the History of the Federal Army's Pursuit of the Prestes Column in Brazil, 1924–27." *The Americas* 54, no. 3 (January 1998): 409–36.

Dias, Everardo. *Bastilhas modernas 1924–26*. São Paulo: Empresa Ed. de Obras Sociais Literárias, n.d.

Donzelot, Jacques. *The Policing of Families*. London: Hutchinson, 1979.

Doria, Antônio de Sousa. *Estudos sobre a promoção nos exércitos*. Rio: Typ. Popular, 1871.

Downing, Brian M. *The Military Revolution and Political Change: Origins of Democracy and Autocracy in Early Modern Europe*. Princeton, N.J.: Princeton University Press, 1992.

Drummond, José Augusto. *O movimento tenentista: a intervenção dos oficiais jovens (1922–1935)*. Rio de Janeiro: Graal, 1986.

Duarte, Paulo de Queiroz. *Os voluntários da pátria na Guerra do Paraguai*. Rio: Biblioteca do Exército, 1981.

Dudley, William S. "Institutional Sources of Officer Discontent in the Brazilian Army, 1870–1889." HAHR 55 (February 1975): 44–65.

——. "Professionalization and Politicization as Motivational Factors in the Brazilian Army Coup of 15 November 1889." JLAS 8 (February 1976): 101–25.

Duetsch, Sandra McGee. "Gender and Sociopolitical Change in Twentieth Century Latin America." HAHR, 71, no. 2 (1991): 259–306.

Duffy, Charles. *The Army of Frederick the Great*. Vancouver: David and Charles, 1974.

Engel, Magali. *Meretrizes e doutores: saber médico e prostituição no Rio de Janeiro 1840–1890*. São Paulo: Ed. Brasiliense, 1988.

Falcão, Gentil. *A defesa nacional ou o regulamento do sorteio em linguagem popular*. Rio: Tip. do Jornal do Commercio, 1923.

Faria, Sheila de Castro. *A colônia em movimento: fortuna e família no cotidiano colonial*. Rio: Nova Fronteira, 1988.

Fausto, Boris. *Crime e cotidiano: a criminalidade em São Paulo*. São Paulo: Ed. Brasiliense, 1984.

——. *A revoluçao de 1930: historiografia e história*. São Paulo: Editora Brasiliense, 1972.

Faoro, Raimundo. *Os donos do poder*. 5th ed. Porto Alegre: Globo, 1979.

Ferrer, Ada. *Insurgent Cuba: Race, Nation, and Revolution, 1868–1898*. Chapel Hill: University of North Carolina Press, 1999.

Fick, Carolyn. "Black Peasants and Soldiers in the St. Domingue Revolution: Initial Reactions to Freedom in the South Province." In *History from Below: Studies in Popular Protest and Popular Ideology in Honour of George Rudé*, edited by Frederick Krantz. Montreal: Concordia University Press, 1985.

Flory, Thomas. *Judge and Jury in Imperial Brazil, 1808–1871*. Austin: University of Texas Press, 1981.

Fluery, Conselheiro Padua. *Parecer sobre o presídio de Fernando de Noronha*. Rio: Imprensa Nacional, 1880.

Font, Maurício. *Coffee, Contention, and Change in the Making of Modern Brazil*. Cambridge: Basil Blackwell, 1990.

Forjaz, Maria Cecília Spina. *Tenentismo e política: tenetismo e camadas médias urbanas na crise da Primeira República*. Rio: Paz e Terra, 1977.

Forrest, Alan. *Conscripts and Deserters: The Army and French Society During the Revolution and Empire*. New York: Oxford University Press, 1989.

Foucault, Michel. *Discipline and Punish: The Birth of the Prison*. Trans. Alan Sheridan. New York: Pantheon Books, 1977.

———. *The History of Sexuality: An Introduction*. Translated by Robert Hurley. New York: Penguin, 1978.

———. *The History of Sexuality. Vol. 1*. New York: Vintage Press, 1990 [1976].

Fraga Filho, Walter. *Mendigos, moleques, e vadios na Bahia do século XIX*. São Paulo: Ed. Hucitec, 1996.

Fragoso, Augusto Tasso. *História da guerra entre a Tríplice Aliança e o Paraguai*. 5 vols. Rio: Imprensa do Estado Maior do Exército, 1924.

Freitas, Judy Bieber. "Slavery and Social Life: Attempts to Reduce Free People to Slavery in the Sertão Mineiro, Brazil 1850–1871," JLAS 26, no. 3 (Oct. 1994): 597–619.

French, John D. *The Brazilian Workers' ABC: Class Conflict and Alliances in Modern São Paulo*. Chapel Hill: University of North Carolina Press, 1992.

Frevert, Ute. "Das jakobinische modell: Allgemeine Wehrphlict und Nationsbildung in Preaßen-Deutschland." In *Militär und Gesellschaft im 19. und 20. Jahrhundert*, edited by Ute Frevert. Kletta Cott, 1997.

Freyre, Gilberto. *Casa grande e senzala: formação da família brasileira sob o regime patriarcal*. Rio: José Olympio, 1978 [1933].

———. *Ordem e progresso*. 3d. ed. 2 vols. Rio: José Olympio Ed., 1974.

———. *Sobrados e macumbos: decadência do patriarcado rural e desenvolvimento do urbano*. 7th ed. Rio: José Olympio, 1985 [1936].

Fry, Peter. *Para inglês ver: identidade e política na cultura brasileira*. Rio: Jorge Zahar Ed., 1982.

Fundação, Getúlio Vargas. *A Revolução de 1930 e seus antecendentes: coletânea de fotografias organizada pelo Centro de Pesquisa e Documentação de História Comtemporânea do Brasil*. Rio: Ed. Nova Frontiera, 1980.

Ganson, Barbara J. "Following Their Children into Battle: Women at War in Paraguay, 1864–1870." *Americas* 66, no. 3 (1990): 335–71.

Gilmore, David D. *Manhood in the Making: Cultural Concepts of Masculinity*. New Haven, CT: Yale University Press, 1990.

Gomes, Angela de Castro. *A invenção do trabalhismo*. 2d ed. Rio: Relume-Dumará, 1994.

Graham, Douglas H., and Sérgio Buarque de Hollanda Filho. *Migrações internas no Brasil 1872–1970*. São Paulo: Inst. de Pesquisas Econômicas, 1984.

Graham, Richard. *Patronage and Politics in Nineteenth Century Brazil*. Stanford, Calif.: Stanford University Press, 1990.

Graham, Sandra Lauderdale. *House and Street: The Domestic World of Servants and Masters in Nineteenth-Century Rio de Janeiro*. New York: Cambridge University Press, 1988.

Green, James N. *Beyond Carnival: Male Homosexuality in Twentieth Century Brazil*. Chicago: University of Chicago Press, 1999.

Greenberg, Kenneth S. *Honor and Slavery*. Princeton, N.J.: Princeton University Press, 1996.

Greenfield, Gerald Michael. "O comportamento dos migantes e as atitudes das elites durante a Grande Seca do nordeste, 1877–79." *Cadernos de Estudos Sociais* 5, no. 2 (1989): 219–43.

——. "The Great Drought and Elite Discourse in Imperial Brazil." HAHR 72, no. 3 (1992): 375–400.

Guttman, Matthew C. *The Meanings of Macho: Being a Man in Mexico City*. Berkeley: University of California Press, 1996.

Guy, Donna J. "Future Directions in Latin American Gender History." *Americas* 51, no. 1 (July 1994): 1–9.

——. *Sex and Danger: Prostitution, Family, and Nation in Argentina in Buenos Aires*. Lincoln: University of Nebraska Press, 1991.

Habermas, Jürgen. *The Structural Transformation of the Public Sphere: An Inquiry into a Category of Bourgeois Society*. Translated by Thomas Berger. Cambridge: MIT Press, 1996.

Hagen, Mark Von. *Soldiers in the Proletarian Dictatorship: The Red Army and the Soviet Socialist State, 1917–1930*. Ithaca, N.Y.: Cornell University Press, 1990.

Halperin, David M. "Sex Before Sexuality: Pederasty, Politics, and Power in Classical Athens." In *Hidden from History: Reclaiming the Gay and Lesbian Past*, edited by Martin Duberman, et al. New York: Meridian Press, 1989.

Hahner, June E. *Civilian-Military Relations in Brazil 1889–1898*. Columbia: University of South Carolina Press, 1969.

——. *Poverty and Politics: The Urban Poor in Brazil, 1870–1920*. Albuquerque: University of New Mexico Press, 1986.

Harris, Marvin. *Patterns of Race in the Americas*. New York: Walker, 1964.

——. "Racial Identity in Brazil." LBR 1, no. 2 (1964), 21–28.

Harrod, Frederick S. *Manning the New Navy: The Development of a Modern Naval Enlisted Force, 1889–1940*. Westport, CT: Greenwood Press, 1978.

Hayes, Robert Ames. *The Nation in Arms: The Brazilian Corporate Mystique*. Tempe: Arizona State University Press, 1989.

Helg, Aline. *Our Rightful Share: The Afro-Cuban Struggle for Equality, 1886–1912*. Chapel Hill: University of North Carolina Press, 1995.

Hilton, Stanley E. "The Armed Forces and Industrialists in Modern Brazil: The Drive for Military Autonomy, 1889–1954." HAHR 62, no. 4 (1982): 629–71.

Hobsbawm, Eric. "Introduction: Inventing Tradition." In *The Invention of Tradition*, edited by E. Hobsbawm and T. Ranger. New York: Cambridge University Press, 1992.

———. *The Age of Revolution in Europe, 1789–1848*. London: Cardinal, 1973.

Hochman, Gilberto. *A era do saneamento: as bases do política de saúde pública no Brasil*. São Paulo: Hucitec, 1998.

Hodes, Martha. *White Women, Black Men: Illicit Sex in the Nineteenth Century South*. New Haven, Conn.: Yale University Press, 1991.

Holloway, Thomas H. "The Brazilian Judicial Police in Florianópolis, Santa Catarina, 1841–1871." *Journal of Social History* 20, no. 4 (1987): 733–56.

———. "A Healthy Terror: Police repression of *Capoeiras* in Nineteenth-Century Rio de Janeiro." *HAHR* 69, no. 4 (1989): 637–676.

———. *Policing Rio de Janeiro: Repression and Resistance in a Nineteenth-Century City*. Stanford, Calif.: Stanford University Press, 1993.

Howard, Michael. *The Causes of War*. London: Unwin, 1983.

Hsi-Huey, Liang. *The Rise of Modern Police and the European State System from Metternich to the Second World War*. New York: Cambridge University Press, 1992.

Huggins, Martha. *From Slavery to Vagrancy*. New Brunswick, N.J.: Rutgers University Press, 1985.

Hughes, Daniel J. *The King's Finest: A Social and Bureaucratic Profile of Prussia's General Officers, 1871–1914*. New York: Preager Press, 1987.

Hughes, Robert. *The Fatal Shore*. New York: Random House, 1987.

Igreja Católica no Brasil. Bispos. *Circular Coletiva do Exms. e Revms. arcebispos das provincias ecclessiasticas no Brasil*. Rio: Typ. Leuzinger, 1917.

Janotti, Maria de Lourdes Monaco. *A Balaiada*. São Paulo: Ed. Brasiliense, 1987.

Jesus, Carolina Maria de. *Bitita's Diary: The Childhood Memories of Carolina Maria de Jesus*. Ed. Robert M. Levine and trans. Emanuelle Oliveira and Beth Joan Vinkler. Armonk, N.Y.: M. E. Sharp, 1998.

Joffily, Geraldo Ireneo. *O Quebra Quilo: a revolta dos matutos contra os doutores*. Brasília: Thesaurus, 1977.

Johnson, John J. *The Military and Society in Latin America*. Stanford, Calif.: Stanford University Press, 1964.

Joseph, Gilbert, and Daniel Nugent, eds. *Everyday Forms of State Formation*. Durham, N.C.: Duke University Press, 1994.

Karasch, Mary C. *Slave Life in Rio de Janeiro, 1808–1850*. Princeton, N.J.: Princeton University Press, 1987.

Keegan, John. *The Illustrated Face of Battle: A Study of Agincourt, Waterloo, and the Somme*. London: Jonathan Cape, 1976.

Kelley, Robin. *Race Rebels: Culture, Politics, and the Black Working Class*. New York: Free Press, 1994.

Kellet, Anthony. *Motivação para combate*. Trans. Delcy G. Dourawa. Rio: Biblioteca do Exército, 1987.

Klinger, Bertholdo. *Narrativas autobiográficas*. 6 vols. Rio: Edições O Cruzeiro, 1951.

Knight, Alan. "Popular Culture and the Revolutionary State in Mexico, 1910–1940." HAHR 74, no. 3 (1994): 393–444.

Kraay, Hendrik. "The Politics of Race in Independence Era Bahia: The Black Militia Officers of Salvador, 1790–1840. In *Afro-Brazilian Culture and Politics, Bahia 1790s to 1990s*, ed. Hendrik Kraay. Armonk, N.J.: M. E. Sharp, 1998.

——. "Reconsidering Recruitment in Imperial Brazil" *Americas* 55, no. 1 (July 1988): 1–33.

——. "The Shelter of the Uniform: The Brazilian Army and Runaway Slaves, 1800–1888" *Journal of Social History* 29, no. 3 (March 1996): 637–57.

——. "Slavery, Citizenship, and Military Service in Brazil's Mobilization for the Paraguayan War." *Abolition and Slavery* 18, no. 3 (December 1997): 228–56.

——. "As Terrifying as Unexpected: The Bahian *Sabinada* 1837–38." HAHR 72, no. 4 (1992): 501–27.

Kuethe, Allan J. *Military Reform and Society in New Granada, 1773–1808*. Gainesville: University Presses of Florida, 1978.

Kuznesof, Elizabeth Ann. "Clans, the Militias, and Territorial Government: The Articulation of Kinship with Polity in Eighteenth Century São Paulo." In *Social Fabric and Spatial Structures in Colonial Latin America*, edited by David Robinson. Ann Arbor, Mich.: Published by University Microfilms International for the Department of Geography, Syracuse University, 1979.

——. "Ethnic and Gender Influences on "Spanish" Creole Society in Colonial Spanish America." *Colonial Latin American Review* 4, no. 1 (1995): 153–201.

——. *Household Economy and Urban Development: São Paulo, 1765 to 1836*. Dellplain Latin American Studies, no. 18. Boulder: Westview Press, 1986.

Kuznesof, Elizabeth Ann, and Robert Oppenheimer. "The Family and Society in Latin America: An Historiographical Introduction," *The Journal of Family History* 10, no. 3 (fall 1985): 215–34.

Lacerda, Maurício de. *História de uma covardia*. Rio: Nova Fronteira, 1980.

Leal, Aristedes. "Depoimento." Seção de História Oral. Rio: CPDOC, 1977.

Leal, Victor Nunes. *Coronelismo: The Municipality and Representative Government in Brazil*. Translated by June Henfrey. New York: Cambridge University Press, 1977.

Lasso, Marixa. "Haiti as an Image of Popular Republicanism in Caribbean Colombia. Cartagena Province (1811–1828)." In *The International Impact of the Haitian Revolution*, ed. David Geggus. Columbia: University of South Carolina Press, forthcoming.

Lemisch, Jesse. *Jack Tar Versus John Bull: The Role of New York's Seamen in Precipitating the Revolution*. New York: Garland Publishing, Inc., 1997.

Lêmos Terra, Ruth Brito. *Memórias de lutas: literatura de folhetos do nordeste 1893–1930.* São Paulo: Global Ed., 1983.

Lesser, Jeff. *Negotiating National Identity: Immigrants, Minorities, and the Struggles for Ethnicity in Brazil.* Durham, N.C.: Duke University Press, 1999.

Levine, Robert M. *Father of the Poor? Vargas and His Era.* New York: Cambridge University Press, 1998.

———. *Pernambuco in the Brazilian Federation, 1889–1937.* Stanford, Calif.: Stanford University Press, 1978.

———. *Vale of Tears: Revisiting the Canudos Massacre in Northeastern Brazil, 1893–97.* Berkeley: University of California Press, 1992.

———. *The Vargas Regime: The Critical Years 1934–1938.* New York: Columbia University Press, 1970.

Levine, Robert M., and John Crocitti, eds. *The Brazil Reader.* Durham, N.C.: Duke University Press, 1999.

Levine, Robert M., José Carlos, and Sebe Bom Meihy. *The Life and Death of Carolina Maria de Jesus.* Albuquerque: University of New Mexico Press, 1995.

Lewin, Linda. *Politics and Parentela in Paraíba: A Case Study of Family-Based Oligarchy in Brazil.* Princeton, N.J.: Princeton University Press, 1987.

Lichtenstein, Alex. "Good Roads and Chain Gangs in the Progressive South. The Negro Convict Is a Slave." *The Journal of Southern History* 59, no. 1 (February 1993): 85–110.

Lima, Nísia Trindade. *Um sertão chamado Brasil: intelectuais e representação geográfica de identidade nacional.* Rio: Ed. Revan, 1999.

Lima, Nísia Trindade, and Gilberto Hochman. "Condenado pela raça, absolvida pela medicina: o Brasil descoberto pelo movimento sanitarista da primeira república." In *Raça, Ciência e Sociedade,* edited by Marcos Chor Maio and Ricardo Ventura Santos. Rio: Fundação Oswaldo Cruz/Centro Cultural Banco do Brasil, 1996.

Lima, Oliveira. *O movimento da Independência: o império brasileiro 1821–1889.* 2d ed. São Paulo: Melhoramentos, n.d.

Lins de Barros, João Alberto. *Memórias de um revolucionário.* 2d ed. Rio: Ed. Civilização Brasileira, 1954.

Lobo Viana, José Feliciano, ed. *Guia Militar.* 2 vols. Rio: Imprensa Nacional, 1897.

Love, Joseph. *Rio Grande do Sul and Brazilian Regionalism, 1882–1930.* Stanford, Calif.: Stanford University Press, 1971.

———. *São Paulo in the Brazilian Federation, 1889–1937.* Stanford, Calif.: Stanford University Press, 1980.

———. "Political Participation in Brazil, 1881–1969." LBR 7 (winter 1970): 3–24.

Loveman, Brian. *The Constitution of Tyranny: Regimes of Exception in Spanish America.* Pittsburgh, Pa.: University of Pittsburgh Press, 1993.

———. *For la Patria: Politics and the Armed Forces in Latin America*. Wilmington, Del.: Scholarly Resources, 1999.

Luebke, Frederick C. *Germans in Brazil: A Comparative History of Cultural Conflict during World War I*. Baton Rouge: Louisiana State University Press, 1987.

Lustosa, Isabel. *Histórias de presidentes: a república no Catete*. Petropolis: Vozes, 1989.

Lynch, John. *The Spanish American Revolutions, 1808–1826*. London: Weidenfeld and Nicholson, 1973.

Macedo, Francisco Ferraz de. "Da prostituição em geral." Rio: Academica, 1872.

Machado, Juracy de Assis. *Tu e o serviço militar; alistamento, convocação, insubmissão, e desersão de praças*. Porto Alegre: Editora da Livraria do Globo, 1941.

Machado, Maria Helena P. T. *Crime e escravidão: trabalho, luta, e resistência nas lavouras paulistas 1830–1888*. São Paulo: Brasilense, 1987.

Magalhães, José Vieira Couto de. *Diário íntimo*. Edited by Maria Helena P. T. Machado. São Paulo: Cia. Das Letras, 1998.

Magalhães, Raimundo, Jr. *Deodoro a espada contra o império*. 2 vols. São Paulo: Cia. Ed. Nacional, 1957.

———. *Olavo Bilac e sua época*. Rio: Cia. Ed. Americana, 1974.

Mahan, Alfred Thayer. *The Influence of Seapower Upon History, 1660–1883*. New York: Harper and Brothers, 1907 [1890].

Mainwaring, Scott. *The Catholic Church and Politics in Brazil, 1916–1985*. Stanford, Calif.: Stanford University Press, 1986.

Malerba, Jurandir. *Os brancos da lei: liberalismo, escravidão, e mentalidade patriarcal no Império do Brasil*. Maringá: Ed. da University Estadual de Maringá, 1994.

Mallon, Florencia E. *Peasant and Nation: The Making of Post Colonial Mexico and Peru*. Berkeley: University of California Press, 1995.

Malloy, James M. *The Politics of Social Security in Brazil*. Pittsburgh, Penn.: University of Pittsburgh Press, 1979.

Maram, Sheldon C. *Anarquistas, immigrantes, e o movimento operário no Brazil*. Rio: Paz e Terra, 1979.

———. "The Immigrant and the Brazilian Labor Movement, 1890–1920." In *Essays Concerning the Socioeconomic History of Brazil and Portuguese India*, edited by Dauril Alden and Warren Dean, 178–210. Gainesville: University Presses of Florida, 1977.

Markoff, John, and Silvio Barreto. "Professional Ideology and Military Activism in Brazil: A Critique of a Thesis of Alfred Stepan," *Comparative Politics* 17, no. 1 (1985): 175–91.

Marson, Izabel Andrade. *O Império de progresso: Revolução Praieira (1842–1855)*. 3d ed. São Paulo: Ed. Brasiliense, 1987.

Martínez-Alier, Verena. *Marriage, Class, and Colour in Nineteenth-Century Cuba*. Ann Arbor: University of Michigan Press, 1974.

Matos, Cláudia Neiva de. *A poesia popular na república das letras*. Rio: Ed. Universidade Federal do Rio de Janeiro, 1994.

Mattoso, Katia, Herbert S. Klein, and Stanley Engerman. "Trends and Patterns in the Prices of Manumitted Slaves: Bahia, 1819–1888." *Slavery and Abolition* (May 1986).

McAlister, Lyle N. *The Fuero Militar in New Spain, 1764–1800*. Gainesville: University Presses of Florida, 1957.

McBeth, Michael C. "Brazilian Generals, 1822–1865: A Statistical Study of Their Careers." *Americas* 44, no. 2 (1987): 125–41.

McCann, Frank D. *The Brazilian-American Alliance, 1937–1945*. Princeton, N.J.: Princeton University Press, 1973.

———. "The *Força Expedicionária Brasileira* in the Italian Campaign 1944–45." *Army History* 26 (spring 1993): 1–11.

———. "The Formative Period of Twentieth-Century Brazilian Army Thought, 1900–1922." HAHR 64, no. 4 (1984): 737–65.

———. "The Military." In *Elites and Masses in Modern Brazil*, edited by Michael L. Conniff and Frank D. McCann, 47–80. Lincoln: University of Nebraska Press, 1989.

———. "The Nation in Arms: Obligatory Military Service during the Old Republic." In *Essays Concerning the Socioeconomic History of Brazil and Portuguese India*, edited by Dauril Alden and Warren Dean. Gainesville: University Presses of Florida, 1977.

———. *A Nação armada: ensaios sobre a história do exército brasileiro*. Recife: Ed. Guararapes, 1982.

———. "Origins of the 'New Professionalism' of the Brazilian Army." *Journal of Inter-American Studies and World Affairs* 21, no. 4 (1979): 505–22.

McKinley, Silas Bent. *Democracy and Military Power*. New York: Vanguard Press, 1941.

McNeill, William H. "The Age of Gunpowder Empires, 1450–1800." In *Essays on Global and Comparative History*. Washington, D.C.: American Historical Association, 1989.

Meade, Teresa A. *"Civilizing" Rio: Reform and Resistance in a Brazilian City 1889–1930*. University Park: Pennsylvania State University Press, 1997.

Mello, Almirante Custódio José de. *O governo provisório e a revolução de 1893*. 2 vols. São Paulo: Nacional Editora, 1938.

Melo, Hildebrando Bayard de. *No exército do meu tempo*. Rio: Biblioteca do Exército, 1987.

Melo, Plácido de. "A cruz e a espada: criação do serviço religioso para os quartéis." Speech of 26 July 1916 for the Clube Militar, published in *Pelo altar e pela pátria*.

Mendes, Raimundo Teixeira. *Actual agitação militarista pelo serviço militar obrigatório e a regeneração humana*. Rio: Typ. Jornal do Commercio, 1915.

———. *O ensino público e o despotismo sanitário.* Rio: Igreja Positivista do Brazil, 1910.

———. *A liberdade espiritual e a vacinação obrigatória.* Rio: Igreja Positivista do Brazil, 1902.

———. *Mais um attentado de despotismo sanitário: transporte violento ao hospital, sujeição à inaculações tirânicas, morte da víctima, profanação do cadaver.* Rio: Igreja Positivista do Brazil, 1909.

Menenez, Alfredo da Mota, *Guerra do Paraguai: como construímos o conflicto.* São Paulo: Ed. Contexto, 1998.

Meznar, Joan E. "Orphans and the Transition from Slave to Free Labor in Northeast Brazil: The Case of Campina Grande, 1850–1888." *Journal of Social History* (spring 1994): 499–515.

———. "The Ranks of the Poor: Military Service and Social Differentiation in Northeast Brazil, 1835–1875." HAHR 72, no. 3 (1992): 335–51.

Miller, Wilbur R. *Cops and Bobbies: Police Authority in New York and London 1830–1870.* Chicago: University of Chicago Press, 1977.

Molas, Ricardo Rodriguez. *Historia social del gaucho.* Buenos Aires: Ediciones Moue, 1968.

Monteiro, John Manuel. *Negros da terra: índios e bandeirantes nas origens de São Paulo.* São Paulo: Cia. das Letras, 1994.

Moore, Albert Burton. *Conscription and Conflict in the Confederacy.* Columbia: University of South Carolina Press, 1996 [1924].

Morais, Evaristo de. *Prisões e instituições penitenciárias no Brasil.* Rio: Liv. Ed. Conselheiro C. de Oliveira, 1923.

Morais, Fernando. *Chatô: O rei do Brazil.* São Paulo: Cia. das Letras, 1994.

Morais Filho, Alexândre José de Mello. *Serenatas e seraus.* 3 vols. Rio: Typ. H. Garnier, 1901–2.

Morel, Edmar. *A Revolta da Chibata.* 4th ed. Rio: Ed. Graal, 1986.

Morley, Helena. *The Diary of Helena Morley.* Translated by Elizabeth Bishop. New York: The Ecco Press, 1977 [1957].

Morton, F. W. O. "The Military and Society in Bahia, 1800–1821." JLAS 7, no. 2 (1975): 249–69.

Mosse, George L. *The Nationalization of the Masses: Political Symbolism and Mass Movements in Germany from the Napoleonic Wars through the Third Reich.* New York: H. Fertig, 1975.

Mott, Luiz. *Escravidão, homosexualidade, e demonologia.* São Paulo: Icone, 1988.

Moura, Denise Aparecida Soares. *Saindo das sombras: homens livres e pobres vivendo a crise do trabalho escravo 1850–1888.* Campinas: Unicamp, 1998.

Nascimento, Álavaro Pereira do. *A ressaca da marujada: recrutamento e disciplina na marinha de guerra, 1880–1910.* Rio: Arquivo Nacional, Rio de Janeiro, 2001.

Needell, Jeffery. "Identity, Race, Gender, and Modernity in the Origins of Gilberto Freyre's *Oeuvre.*" *American Historical Review* 100, no. 1 (February 1995).

Nickerson, Hoffman, *The Armed Horde 1793–1939: A Study of the Rise, Survival and Decline of the Mass Army.* New York: G. P. Putnam's Sons, 1942.

Nogueira, Cornélia. *Movimentos migratórios no Brasil e seu condicionantes económicos (1872–1980).* São Paulo: Financiadora de Estudos e Projetos, 1987.

Nogueira, José Carlos Ataliba. "Pena sem prisão." *Revista dos Tribunaes* (1938).

Noronha, General Abilio de. *Narrando a verdade: Contribuição para a história da revolta em São Paulo.* São Paulo: Monteiro Labato, 1924.

Nunn, Frederick M. *The Time of the Generals: Latin American Professional Militarism in World Perspective.* Lincoln: University of Nebraska Press, 1992.

——. *Yesterday's Soldiers: European Military Professionalism in South America, 1890–1940.* Lincoln: University of Nebraska Press, 1983.

Oliveira, Jaime A. de Araújo, and Sonia M. Fleury Teixeira. *(Im)previdência social: 60 anos de história da Previdência no Brasil.* Petrópolis: Vozes, 1985.

Oliviera, Xavier de. *O exército e o sertão.* Rio: A. Coelho Branco, 1932.

Osorio Filho, Fernando Luis. *O espírito das armas brasileiras: nossas guerras, factos e depoimentos (livro da mocidade).* Pelotas: Olavo Alves e Filho, 1918.

Pang, Eul-Soo. *Bahia in the First Republic: Coronelismo and Politics.* Gainesville: University Presses of Florida, 1979.

——. *In Pursuit of Honor and Power: Brazil's Noblemen of the Southern Cross.* Tuscaloosa: University of Alabama Press, 1988.

Pang, Eul-Soo, and Seckinger, Ronald. "The Mandrins of Imperial Brazil." *Comparative Studies in Society and History* 14 (March 1972): 215–44.

Parker, Richard G. *Beneath the Equator: Cultures of Desire, Male Homosexuality, and Emerging Gay Communities in Brazil.* New York: Routledge, 1999.

——. *Corpos, prazeres, e paixões: a cultura sexual no Brasil contemporâneo.* Trans. Maria Therezina M. Cavallari. 2d ed. São Paulo: Ed. Best Seller, 1991.

Paula da Cidade, General Francisco de. *Síntese de tres séculos de literatura militar brasileira.* Rio: n.p., 1959.

Pearson, M. N. "The Crowd in Portuguese India." In *Coastal Western India,* edited by M. N. Pearson. New Delhi: Concept Publishing Company, 1981.

Peixoto, Dermeval. *Cancioneiro Militar.* São Paulo: Escola do Lyceu Coração de Jesus, 1923.

——. *Memórias de um velho soldado: nomes, coisas e fatos de meio século atrás.* Rio: Biblioteca do Exército, 1960.

Penna, Belsário, and Augusto de Oliveira. *O exército e sanidade.* Rio: n.p., 1920.

Peñalba, José Alfredo Fornos. "Draft Dodgers, War Resisters, and Turbulent Gauchos: The War of the Triple Alliance Against Paraguay." *Americas* 38, no. 4 (1982): 463–79.

Peregalli, Enrique. *Recrutamento Militar no Brasil Colonial.* Campinas: Ed. da Universidade de Campinas, 1986.

Peregrino, Umberto. *História e Projeção des instituições culturais do* exército. Rio: Livraria José Olympio, 1967.

Pérez, Louis, Jr., "Army Politics and the Collapse of the Cuban Officer Corps: The Sergeants' Revolt of 1933," JLAS 6 (May 1974): 59–76.

Perry, Mary Elizabeth. *Crime and Society in Early Modern Seville*. Hanover, N.H.: University Press of New England, 1980.

Pessoa, Reynaldo Carneiro. *A idéia repúblicana no Brasil através dos documentos*. São Paulo: n.p., 1873.

Pike, Ruth. "Penal Servitude in the Spanish Empire: Presidio Labor in the Eighteenth Century." HAHR 58, no. 1 (February 1978): 21–40.

Pinheiro, Paulo Sérgio. *Estratégias de ilusão: a revolução mundial e o Brasil, 1922–35*. São Paulo: Companhia das Letras, 1991, 308–26.

Pitt-Rivers, Julian. "Honour and Social Status." In *Honour and Shame: The Values of Mediterranean Society*, ed. J. G. Peristiany. London: Weidenfeld and Nicolson, 1965.

Pompeia, Raul. *Crônicas do Rio*. Edited by Virgílio Moretzsohn Moreira. Rio: Biblioteca Carioca, 1996.

Prado Junior, Caio. *The Colonial Background of Modern Brazil*. Translated by Suzette Macedo. Berkeley: University of California Press, 1967.

Prestes, Anita L. *A columna prestes*. São Paulo: Ed. Brasiliense, 1991.

Rachum, Ilan. "The Brazilian Revolution of 1930: A Revision." *InterAmerican Economic Affairs* 29 (winter 1975): 59–84.

Rago, Magaret. *Do cabaré ao lar: a utopia da cidade disciplinar, Brasil, 1890–1930*. Rio: Paz e Terra, 1985.

Ramos, Graciliano. *Memórias do cárcere*. 2 vols. 27th ed. São Paulo: Ed. Record, 1994.

Ramsaur, E. E. *The Young Turks*. Princeton, N.J.: Princeton University Press, 1957.

Raulino, E. *O sentenciado 304 (leitura para as prisões)*. Bahia: Escola Typ. Salesiana, 1902.

Reber, Vera Blinn. "The Demographics of Paraguay: A Reinterpretation of the Great War, 1864–70." HAHR 68, no. 2 (1988): 289–319.

Rebouças, André. *Agricultura nacional*. Rio: Lamoureux, 1883 [1875].

Reis, João José. *A morte é uma festa: ritos fúnebres e revolta popular no Brasil do século XIX*. São Paulo: Cia. das Letras, 1991.

Ribeiro, Carlos Antonio Costa. *Cor e criminalidade: estudo e análise da justiça no Rio de Janeiro (1900–1930)*. Rio: Ed. Universidade Federal do Rio de Janeiro, 1995.

Rio Branco, Visconde de [José Maria da Silva Paranhos]. *Informações sobre o estado da lavoura*. Rio: Typ. Nacional, 1874.

Rio, João do. *No tempo de Wenceslão*. Rio: Villas-Boas, 1917.

Robert, Karen. "Slavery and Freedom in the Ten Years' War, 1868–1878." *Slavery and Abolition* 13 (December 1992): 181–92.

Rodrigués, Antônio Edmilson, et al. *A guarda nacional no Rio de Janeiro, 1831–1918*. Rio: Pontífica Universidade Católica do Rio de Janeiro, 1981.

Roediger, David R. *The Wages of Whiteness: Race and the Making of the American Working Class.* New York: Verso, 1991.

Romano, Roberto. *Brasil: igreja contra o estado.* São Paulo: Kairós, 1979.

Romero, Sílvio. *A bancarrota do regimen federativo, acção dissolvente das oligarquias, acção indespensável do exército.* Porto: Typ. A. J. Souza e Irmão, 1912.

———. *Cantos populares do Brasil.* 3 vols. 2d ed. Rio: Livraria Classica de Alves & Cia., 1897.

Russell-Wood, A. J. R. *The Black Man in Slavery and Freedom in Colonial Brazil.* New York: St. Martin's Press, 1982.

Salles, Ricardo. *Guerra do Paraguai: escravidão e cidadania na formação do exército.* Rio: Paz e Terra, 1991.

Salvatore, Ricardo D. "The Birth of the Penitentiary in Latin America." In *The Birth of the Penitentiary in Latin America,* edited by Ricardo D. Salvatore and Carlos Aguirre. Austin: University of Texas Press, 1996.

———. "Reclutamiento militar, disciplinamento y proletarización en la era de Rosas." *Boletín del Instituto de História Argentina y Americana* 3, no. 5: 25–47.

Salvatore, Ricardo D., and Carlos Aguirre. "Penitentiaries, Visions of Class, and Export Economies: Brazil and Argentina Compared." In *The Birth of the Penitentiary in Latin America,* edited by Salvatore and Carlos Aguirre, 194–22. Austin: University of Texas Press, 1996.

Scheper-Hughes, Nancy. *Death Without Weeping: The Violence of Everyday Life in Brazil.* Berkeley: University of California Press, 1992.

Schowalter, Dennis. *Railroads and Rifles: Soldiers, Technology, and the Unification of Germany.* Hamden, Conn.: Archon Books, 1975.

Schultz, John H. *O exército na política.* São Paulo: Edusp, 1994.

Schwarcz, Lilia Moritz. *As barbas do Imperador: Pedro II, um monarca dos trópicos.* São Paulo: Cia. das Letras, 1998.

———. *O espectáculo das raças: cientistas, instituições e questão racial no Brasil, 1870–1930.* São Paulo: Cia. das Letras, 1993.

Schwartz, Stuart B. *Sugar Plantations in the Formation of Brazilian Society: Bahia, 1550–1835.* Vol. 52 of *Cambridge Latin American Studies.* New York: Cambridge University Press, 1985.

Scott, James. *Domination and the Arts of Resistance: Hidden Transcripts.* New Haven, Conn.: Yale University Press, 1990.

Scott, Joan. "Gender: A Useful Category of Analysis." *American Historical Review* 95, vol. 1 (December 1986): 259–306.

Scott, Rebecca J. "Defining the Boundaries of Freedom in the World of Cane: Cuba, Brazil, and Louisiana after Emancipation." *American Historical Review* (February 1994): 70–102.

———. *Slave Emancipation in Cuba: The Transition to Free Labor, 1860–1899.* Princeton, N.J.: Princeton University Press, 1985.

Selvagem, Carlos. *Portugal militar: Compêndio de história militar e naval de Portugal.* Lisbon: Imprensa Nacional, 1931.

Sena Madureira, Antônio de. *Estudo da organisação militar dos principais estados da europa*. 2 vols. London: Officina Typ. de Guilherme Clowes e filhos, 1874 and 1876.

Silva, Coronel Dr. Arthur Lobo da. "Acção eugenica dos exercitos." Memória Apresentado ao Primeiro Congresso Brasileiro de Eugenia. Reprinted from *A Folha Médica*, 25 August 1929.

———. "A Anthropologia no Exército Brasileiro." *Archivos do Museu Nacional* 30 (1928): 3–43.

Silva, Eduardo. *Prince of the People: The Life and Times of a Brazilian Free Man of Colour*. Translated by Moyra Ashford. London and New York: Verso, 1993.

———. "O Príncipe Obá, um voluntário da pátria." In *Guerra do Paraguai 130 anos depois*, ed. Maria Eduarda Castro Magalhães Marques. Rio: Relume Dumará, 1995.

Silva, General V. Benício da., ed. *A evolução militar do Brasil: anotações para a história*. Rio: Biblioteca do Exército, 1958.

Silva, Joel, and Thassilo Mitke. *A luta dos pracinhas: a força expedicionária-FEB na II Guerra Mundial*, 3d ed. Rio: Ed. Record, 1993.

Silveira, Mauro César. *A batalha de papel: a guerra através da caricatura*. Porto Alegre: L and PM, 1996.

Skelley, Alan R. *The Victorian Army at Home: The Recruitment and Terms of the British Regular, 1859–1899*. Montreal: McGill-Queens University Press, 1977.

Skidmore, Thomas E. "Bi-Racial U.S. Versus Multi-Racial Brazil: Is the Contrast Still Valid?" JLAS 25 (1993): 573–86.

———. *Politics in Brazil, 1930–1964: An Experiment in Democracy*. New York: Oxford University Press, 1967.

———. *Black into White: Race and Nationality in Brazilian Thought*. 2d ed. Durham, N.C.: Duke University Press, 1992.

Skocpol, Theda. *Protecting Soldiers and Mothers: The Political Origins of Social Policy in the United States*. Cambridge, Mass.: Belknap Press, 1992.

Skocpol, Theda, and Dietrich Rueschemeyer, eds. *States, Social Knowledge, and the Origins of Modern Social Policies*. Princeton, N.J.: Princeton University Press, 1996.

Slatta, Richard. *Gauchos and the Vanishing Frontier*. Lincoln: University of Nebraska Press, 1983.

Soares, Carlos Eugênio Líbano. *A negregada instituição: os capoeiras no Rio de Janeiro*. Rio: Biblioteca Carioca, 1994.

Sodré, Nelson Werneck. *Do Tenentismo ao Estado Novo: memórias de um Soldado*. 2d ed. Petrópolis: Vozes, 1986.

———. *A história militar do Brasil*. 3d ed. Rio: Civilização Brasileira, 1979 [1964].

———. *Narrativas Militares*. Rio: Biblioteca do Exército, 1959.

———. *O naturalismo no Brasil*. Rio: Civilização Brasileira, 1965.

Sommer, Doris. *Foundational Fictions: The National Romances of Latin America*. Berkeley: University of California Press, 1991.

Sousa, Sacerdote Geraldo Antenor Pires de. *Lança de David, páginas para nossos soldados*. Petropolis: Vozes, 1937.

Souza, Augusto Fausto de. "Fortificações no Brasil: época da respectiva fundação, motivo determinado dela, sua importância defensiva, e valor actual." *Revista do Instituto Histórico Geográphico e Ethnográphico do Brasil* 48, no. 2 (1885): 5–140.

Souza, Jorge Prata de. *Escravidão ou morte: os escravos brasileiros na Guerra do Paraguai*. Rio: Associação Docentes da Universidade Éstácio de Sá, 1996.

Spurling, Geoffrey. "Honor, Sexuality, and the Catholic Church." In *The Faces of Honor: Sex, Shame, and Violence in Colonial Latin America*, edited by Lyman L. Johnson and Sonya Lipsett-Rivera. Albuquerque: University of New Mexico Press, 1998.

Stein, Stanley. *Vassouras: A Brazilian Coffee County*. Princeton, N.J.: Princeton University Press, 1985 [1958].

Stepan, Alfred. *The Military in Politics: Changing Patterns in Brazil*. Princeton, N.J.: Princeton University Press, 1971.

Stepan, Nancy Leys. *The Hour of Eugenics: Race, Gender, and Nation in Latin America*. Ithaca: Cornell University Press, 1991.

Stern, Steve J. *The Secret History of Gender: Women, Men, and Power in Late Colonial Mexico*. Chapel Hill: University of North Carolina Press, 1995.

Strachan, Hew. *Wellington's Legacy: The Reform of the British Army*. London: University of Manchester Press, 1984.

Straubhaar, Joseph Dean. "Mass Communications and the Elites." In *Modern Brazil: Elites and Masses in Comparative Perspective*, edited by Michael Conniff and Frank D. McCann. Lincoln: University of Nebraska Press, 1989.

Taine, Hippolyte. *Les Origenes de la France Contemporaire*. Paris: Hachette, 1891.

Taunay, Alfredo d'Escragnolle. *Memórias*. São Paulo: Instituto Progresso Ed., 1948.

———. *A retirada da Laguna*. Trans. Ramiz Galvão from the 3rd French ed., 5th Portuguese ed. São Paulo: Typ. Ideal, 1919 [1871].

———. *Extracto do discurso do Vice-Presidente da Sociedade Central de Immigração no senado na sessão de 10 de Setembro de 1886*. Rio: Typ. G. Leuzinger, 1886.

Távora, Juarez. *Uma vida e muitas lutas*. 3d ed. Rio: Coleção Documentos Brasileiros, 1973.

Tavares, Raul. *Como ficar quite com o serviço militar*. 5th ed. Rio: Graphica Guarany Ltd., 1943.

Thompson, E. P. "Time, Work-Discipline, and Industrial Capitalism." *Past and Present* 38 (December 1967): 59–97.

Thomson, Guy P. C. "Los Indios y el servicio militar en el México decimonónico. Leva o ciudadanía?" In *Indio, nación y comunidad en el México del siglo XIX*, edited by Antonio Escobar Ohmstede. Mexico City: Centro de Estudios Mexicanos y Centroamericanos, 1993.

Tilly, Charles. "The Emergency of Citizenship in France and Elsewhere." In *Citizenship, Identity, and Social History*, edited by Charles Tilly, 223–36. Cambridge, U.K., Cambridge University Press, 1996.

———. "War Making and State Making as Organized Crime." In *Bringing the State Back In*, edited by Peter Evans, Dietrich Rueschemeyer, and Theda Skocpol. Cambridge, U.K., Cambridge University Press, 1985.

Titmuss, Richard M. *Essays on the Welfare State*. London: George Allen and Unwin Ltd., 1958.

Topik, Steven. "Middle-Class Brazilian Nationalism, 1889–1930: From Radicalism to Reaction." *Social Science Quarterly* (June 1978): 93–104.

———. *The Political Economy of the Brazilian State 1889–1930*. Austin: University of Texas Press, 1987.

———. *Trade and Gunboats: The United States and Brazil in the Age of Empire*. Stanford, Calif.: Stanford University Press, 1996.

Torres, Moysés Augusto. *Memórias de um sargento do exército*. Rio: Livraria Editora Cátedra, 1974.

Torres, Rosa Maria Gusmao de Sampaio. "Aspects of Daily Military Life in the 1920s." *South Eastern Latin Americanist* 28, no. 2 (1984): 17–22.

Trexler, Richard. *Sex and Conquest: Gendered Violence, Political Order, and the European Conquest of the Americas*. Ithaca, N.Y.: Cornell University Press, 1995.

Trochim, Michael R. "The Brazilian Black Guard: Racial Conflict in Post-Abolition Brazil." *Americas* 44 (January 1988): 285–300.

Ubaldo, Domingos. *A greve militar*. N.p., 1916.

Uricoechea, Fernando. *O minatauro imperial*. Rio de Janeiro: Difusão Editorial, 1978.

Vanderwood, Paul J. *Disorder and Progress: Bandits, Police, and Mexican Development*. 2d ed. Wilmington, DE: Scholarly Resources Inc., 1992.

Varnhagen, F. A. de. "Biografia de Domingos Caldas Barbosa." In *Revista do Instituto Histórico e Geográfico*. Vol. 14. 2d ed. (1879): 47–60.

Vianna, Hermano. *The Mystery of Samba: Popular Music and National Identity in Brazil*. Edited and translated by John Charles Chasteen. Chapel Hill: University of North Carolina Press, 1999.

Villela Junior, Marcos Evangelista da Costa. *Canudos: memórias de um combatente*. São Paulo: Ed. Marco Zero, 1988.

Viveiros, Esther de. *Rondon conta sua vida*. Rio: Livraria Sao José, 1958.

Volpato, Luiza Rios Ricci. *Cativos do sertão: vida cotidiana e escravidão em Cuiabá em 1850–1888*. São Paulo: Ed. Marco Zero, 1993.

Von der Goltz, General Baron Colmar. *The Nation in Arms: A Treatise on Modern Military Systems and the Conduct of War*. Translated by Philip A. Ashworth. London: Hodder and Stoughton, 1914 [1883].

Weber, Eugen. *Peasants into Frenchmen: The Modernization of Rural France 1870–1914*. Stanford, Calif.: Stanford University Press, 1976.

Weber, Max. *The Theory of Social and Economic Organization*. Translated by A. M. Henderson and Talcott Parsons. New York: Oxford University Press, 1947.

———. *Economy and Society: An Outline of Interpretive Sociology*. Translated by Ephriam Fischoff, et al. 2 vols. Berkeley: University of California Press, 1978.

Weinstein, Barbara. *The Amazon Rubber Boom, 1850–1920*. Stanford: Stanford University Press, 1983.

———. *For Social Peace in Brazil: Industrialists and the Remaking of the Working Class in São Paulo, 1920–1964*. Chapel Hill: University of North Carolina Press, 1996.

Wells, Allan. "Yucatán: Violence and Social Control on Henequen Plantations." In *Other Mexicos: Essays on Mexican Regional History*, edited by Thomas Benjamin and William McNellie. Albuquerque: University of New Mexico Press, 1984.

Wines, Enoch Cobb. *The State of Prisons and Child-Saving Institutions in the Civilized World*. Cambridge, U.K.: John Wilson and Son, 1880.

Winter, Jay. *Sites of Memory, Sites of Mourning: The Great War in European Cultural History*. New York: Cambridge University Press, 1995.

Wirth, John D. *Minas Gerais in the Brazilian Federation, 1889–1937*. Stanford, Calif.: Stanford University Press, 1978.

Wirtschafter, Elise Kimerling. *From Serf to Russian Soldier*. Princeton, N.J.: Princeton University Press, 1990.

Wolfe, Joel. *Working Women, Working Men: São Paulo and the Rise of Brazil's Working Class*. Durham, N.C.: Duke University Press, 1993.

Wright, Gordon. *Between the Guillotine and Liberty: Two Centuries of the Crime Problem in France*. New York: Oxford University Press, 1983.

Young, Jordan. "Military Aspects of the 1930 Revolution." HAHR 44 (May 1964): 180–96.

Index

Cavalry, 54, 162, 246
Calmon, Miguel, 147
Camarada duty, 67, 79, 158, 160, 187, 188, 189
Caminha, Adolfo, 192, 199, 200, 202, 277, 278
Candido, João, 223
Canudos War of 1896–1897, 35, 112, 113, 115, 168, 225, 226, 228; conditions, 163, 188, 189; veterans, 173
Capoeira(s), 145, 146, 147, 171, 195
Carnival: 59, 60, 161; and the confusion of status, 218; and tourism, 260; as a trope, 244
Carone, Edgar, 207
Carvalho, Estevão Leitão de (general), 161
Carvalho, José Murilho de, 117, 252
Catholic Church: army chaplains, 168, 264; and elections, 86; Jesuits, 1, 177; missions, 19; priests, 3, 58, 61, 70, 71, 74, 83, 84, 92, 98, 229, 230, 277, 284; seminarians, 74; and slaves for the Paraguayan War, 41; and social mobility, 165; and State relations, 64, 69, 71, 83, 264; and ultramontanism, 83
Caxias, Marshal Duke de (Luis Alves de Lima e Silva), 34, 53, 54, 57, 70, 78, 86, 93, 133, 142, 181
Ceará, 44, 51, 58, 86, 88, 94, 115, 116, 135, 161, 169, 196, 209, 218, 224; and the Great Drought of 1877–79, 131, 132
Censorship, 97, 108
Census, 72, 73, 86, 93, 139, 155, 221, 243
Cerqueira, Dionísio, 47
Chagas, Carlos (doctor), 227
Chibata Revolt of 1910. See Anti-Flogging (Chibata) Revolt of 1910
Chile, 281
Citizenship (civic duty), 74, 84, 85,

92, 100, 104, 167–69, 191, 209, 210, 229, 237; and discipline, 150; and flogging, 192; and the household head, 275; and military service, 230, 232, 249, 258, 259, 267, 272, 280, 284
Civil registry, 92, 235, 236, 251, 270. See also Institutional capacity
Civilian Party (Civilista Party), 222. See also Antimilitarists
Civilization: as a trope, 80, 82, 211, 281. See also Barbarism
Class, 63, 229, 235; bourgeoisie, 207, 265; and conscription, 230, 231, 271; and marriage, 182; middle, 121, 207, 227, 242, 245, 264, 266, 271; and nationalism, 209, 246; and political persecution under Vargas, 266; segregation, 245; tensions, 121, 227, 280; upper, 31, 245, 266, 271; working, 99, 104, 119, 220, 232, 235, 242, 245, 251, 261, 266, 271. See also Free poor; Honor
Coates, Timothy Joel, 23
Colonization, 20, 21; and enlisted military service, 22
Congress, 102, 104, 107, 114, 120, 134, 174, 208, 210, 215, 220, 222, 224, 228, 235, 236, 242, 282
Conscription. See Military recruitment
Conselheiro, Antônio (Antonio Vicente Merdes Maciel), 112, 255
Conselho Suprema Militar de Justiça (CSMJ), 179, 180. See also Suprema Tribunal Militar (STM)
Conservative Party: representatives, 31, 33, 34, 45, 52, 57–59, 64, 69, 70, 72, 74, 75, 77, 78, 83, 86, 87, 91, 92, 98, 114, 132, 145
Constant Botelho de Magalhães, Benjamin (colonel), 95

Constitution: of 1824, 28, 33, 102, 138; of 1891, 102, 106, 115, 142, 211, 212, 281
Constitutionalist Revolt of 1932, 242
Contestado Revolt of 1912–1916, 163, 186, 225, 226, 228, 231
Cordel literature, 217–19, 284. *See also* Music lyrics
Coronéis (political bosses), 31, 32, 73, 113, 114, 168, 207, 210, 222, 224, 225, 237, 238, 242, 254, 267, 272, 281, 282; attitudes toward conscription, 81, 82, 104, 130; and manipulation of conscription, 264; and opposition to conscription, 234
Corruption, 36, 52
Council of State (Council of Ministers), 31, 34, 56, 57
Crime: 2, 17, 80; and anthropomorphic measures, 255; and the army, 136, 140, 141, 199, 203; capoeira, 145; convicts, 136, 141; decline in the army after 1916, 266; of deflowering, 119, 158; and enlisted military service, 13, 18, 19, 22, 23, 80, 175, 176, 195–203, 252, 271, 280; spousal abandonment, 158; as a trope, 268
Crown, 18, 19, 22, 23, 26
Cuba, 242, 279, 280

da Cunha, Euclydes, 99–101, 113, 114, 168, 197, 198, 226
da Matta, Roberto, 8, 14
Debatable lands, 24, 28, 29
Debt peonage, xx, 126
Desertion and deserters, 1, 4–5, 25, 26, 46, 54–56, 67, 129, 140, 153, 159, 172, 175, 186, 191–93, 196, 266; and court-martial, 185; and navy data, 192; root causes, 186, 187, 189, 191–94; in wartime, 188
Dictatorship, 61, 273
Discharge(s), 47, 53, 65, 67, 78, 79,

83, 161, 170, 171, 175, 190, 191; in the navy 174
Draft. *See* Military recruitment
Dragoon. *See* Military recruitment
Dutra, Eurico Gaspar (general), 253

Election(s): 32, 86; fraud, 65, 69, 70, 71, 86; law, 64, 65, 76; and limited suffrage, 213, 275; and military recruitment, 57, 58, 70, 71, 73, 212, 213, 273; and populism, 281; presidential election of 1910, 222; secret ballot, 227; and universal male suffrage, 65
England (English), 22, 23, 24, 59, 139, 143, 211, 233. *See also* Britain
Enlistment bounties, 19
Espírito Santo, 78, 86, 94
Estado Novo (new state), 242, 246, 262, 267, 272, 273
Eugenics: 13, 14, 199, 221, 227, 231, 232, 250, 278, 280: and conscription, 121, 232, 237, 253–63, 281; and gender, 257; neo-Lamarckian genetic theory, 121, 257
Europe: conscription, 211; defensive needs and expenditure, 141, 151; myth of military invincibility, 120

Falcão, Gentil (lieutenant), 220, 228, 229
Family, 8, 9, 13, 14, 22, 50, 69, 72, 74, 84, 88, 89, 98, 104; companionate relationships, 202; and conscription, 221, 229; and febiano benefits, 243; honor, 37, 42–44, 73, 74, 76, 88, 99, 105, 119, 122, 137, 169, 176, 229, 277; and national identity, 273, 274; and praça benefits, 174, 175; and praças, 157, 158; and public order, 169, 273; and security, 146; and the State, 47, 72, 76; as a trope, 120, 228, 229, 231, 244, 263
Fatherhood, 48, 84, 105, 162, 169, 264
Favela(s), 173

Gun clubs (*cont.*)
tics, 216; and lobbying for conscription, 228

Habeas corpus, 59, 114, 133, 222, 249
Habermas, Jürgen, 298 n.20
Hervé, Gustave, 230
Hobsbawm, Eric J., 270
Holidays: religious, 166; patriotic, 166
Holland (Dutch), 94, 211
Holloway, Thomas, 172
Homicide, 139, 140, 195, 196; and dishonorable discharges, 196; and prison populations, 143
Honor, 7, 8, 13, 14, 37, 53, 63, 74, 76, 96; and class, 182, 208; and conscription, 218, 252; contested ideas of, 178; and family, 8, 14, 119, 197; and family security, 89, 137, 197, 219; and the free poor, 75, 197; and law enforcement, 141; and marital status, 182, 201; and masculinity, 178, 197, 200, 237, 268, 275, 284; and military discipline, 198; and nations, 8, 14, 40, 43, 44, 63, 284; and race, 8, 14, 63; and sexual roles, 201, 277; and social geography, 82, 117, 278; and violent crime, 196–98
House and street, the (metaphor), 8, 10, 38, 51, 73, 84, 88, 98, 152, 170, 228, 229, 233, 244, 252, 264, 284; inviolability of the home, 8–9, 22, 58, 84, 104, 117, 119, 120, 122, 170, 196, 197, 220, 229, 236, 266; and scholarly literature, 9, 298 n.19
Household economy, 74, 89
Humor, 2, 4, 59, 60, 96, 108, 109, 218, 219, 266, 268

Identification, career record descriptions, 154; and desertion, 155; photographs, 154; and race, 154, 155
Immigration (immigrants), 20, 21, 62–64, 65, 76, 94, 149, 221, 232, 260; and military recruitment, 130; and national unity, 226, 258
Impressment. *See* Military enlisted service; Military recruitment
Indentured servitude, xx, 126, 159
Indian (Asian), 19, 22–24
Indian(s) (indigenous population), 7, 19–21, 26, 32, 44, 55, 61, 101, 121, 159; and Brasilidade, 284; Indian-descent and army racial categories, 155; Indian Protection Society, 211; as a national symbol, 275; and racial democracy, 259; and sexuality, 199; and whitening, 257
Infantry: 145, 246; fixed units, 194
Institutional capacity, 125, 136–38, 142, 236, 237; and conscription, 243, 246
Institutional fit, 148, 150, 237, 243
Institutional reform, 148, 150, 151; and the military as a priority, 149, 243
Insubordination, 172
Insurgency, 147, 223
International military organizational race, 210–12
Invalids of the Fatherland, 172, 174
Italy (Italian), 20, 21, 121, 226, 232, 258, 261

Jacobino(s), 103, 104, 106, 108, 113, 115, 117, 120, 173, 212
Japan (Japanese), 20, 101, 120, 151, 210, 226, 232, 258, 272; percentage of population in the armed forces, 141
Jews, 260
João VI (King Dom), 27, 28, 144, 179
Judicial system: 138; criminal sentences, 138, 139; district attorney, 140; Juiz de Orphãos, 145
Junqueira, José de Oliveira (war minister), 66–68, 71, 73–79, 82, 90, 91

Justice(s) of the Peace, 28–29, 33, 70, 71, 81, 86, 92, 93
Juveniles, 144. *See also* Youth

Klinger, Bertoldo (colonel), 242
Kraay, Hendrik, xxi

Labor, 65, 69, 78; aristocracy, 87; and coercion, 114; and conscription, 71, 78; discipline, 76–79, 99, 127, 130, 280; ideas of family honor, 220; length of the work day, 159, 160; and impressment, 84; markets, 72, 78, 130, 131; and nativism, 234; opposition to obligatory hygiene laws, 117; opposition to obligatory military recruitment, 104–6, 114–17, 220, 221, 230, 234; and theories of physical and mental well-being, 141; unrest, 231
Labor organizations, 103, 117; anarcho-syndicalists, 103, 220, 225; Communist Party, 126, 242; and perceptions of praças, 262; and the Sergeants' Conspiracy, 226, 227; Socialist Party, 103, 104, 230; and views of marriage, 119; and the welfare state, 272
Lacerda, Maurício de, 226
Law faculties (Recife and São Paulo), 75, 96, 215; and exemption from the draft, 218
Leisure, 120; and food preparation, 196; and praças, 169, 196
Legitimacy, 1, 2, 73, 119, 153
Leva(s), 128
Levine, Robert M., 165
Liberalism, 52, 65, 68; and conscription, 71, 77, 78, 210, 222, 237, 282; and prisons, 143; and soldiering, 126, 189
Liberal Party: and its representatives, 31, 33, 45, 57–59, 63–65, 69, 70, 71, 73–77, 79, 82, 85–87, 91, 92, 97, 98, 104, 107, 112, 114, 133, 188

Libertos. *See* Slavery
Liga Brasileira de Assistência (LBA), xxiii, 244, 245
Liga Anti-Militarista Brasileira (LAMB), xxiii, 220, 221, 233, 235
Liga de Defesa Nacional (LDN), xxiii, 232, 233, 250, 256, 282
Lima, Pedro de Araújo, 33
Lippe, Wilhelm de Shaumbourg (count), 24, 26, 36, 55, 177, 179, 180, 201
Literacy, 76, 83, 217; among praças, 155, 179, 196, 258, 259
Lombroso, Cesare, 257
López, Francisco Solano, 39, 42
Lott, Henrique (general), 170
Luís, Washington (president), 241
Lusophobia. *See* Nativism

Macedo, Silvino Honório de, 106–8
Maceo, Antonio, 279
Machado, José Gomes Pinheiro (senator), 117, 212, 222, 224, 225, 234
Malandro(s), 173
Maranhão, 25, 33, 34, 142, 271
Marriage, 8, 19, 47, 119; and class, 182; and conscription, 221; and divorce, 260; in penal colonies, 160; promise, 119, 157; rates among praças, 154, 169; and recruitment, 22, 58, 72, 73, 84, 91, 105, 219, 235; among slaves, 274
Married men/women (*casados*), 22, 26, 28, 84, 91, 105
Marson, Izabel Andrade, 47
Marti, José, 279
Martins, Dias, 227
Marx, Karl, xx, 141
Mato Grosso, 21, 51, 53, 67, 86, 97, 107, 115, 129, 144, 165, 171, 184, 191, 192, 196, 240, 241; expedition, 53–55
McCann, Frank D., 207, 239
Medical faculties (Rio and Salvador), 36, 74, 96; and exemption from the draft, 218

Pompéia, Raul, 95
Population: distribution and recruitment, 72, 78, 127, 138; of public disciplining institutions, 299–300
Popular protest, 81–90, 92, 93, 120, 129, 217–22; led by women, 86, 88, 90, 93
Populism, 261, 267, 273
Portugal, 3, 18–20, 22–26, 154
Portuguese, 1–3, 7, 19, 22, 30
Positivism: 96–98, 115, 120, 121, 168, 281; and eugenics, 227, 237; orthodox, 117, 119, 220; Positivist church, 169
Praça(s): 1, 4, 5, 10, 12, 18, 19, 21, 26, 28, 30, 31, 35–37, 44, 46, 47, 52, 56, 57, 61, 63, 67, 68, 84, 86–88, 97, 100, 101, 106, 112, 122; careers and social mobility, 155; and conflicts with national guard and police, 166; duties, 160; family, 196; foreign-born, 154; health, 256; and honor, 197, 198, 202; as laborers, 126; marriage status, 154; and the masculine definite article, 276; in military historiography, 168; and national identity, 261; parentage and birth status, 153; patriotism, 165–68; potential for rebellion, 126, 238; preenlistment occupations, 154, 250, 251, 252; protests in the name of nationalism, 167, 168, 191; racial composition, 155, 282–84; and racial identity, 261; and racial representation, 283; rebels, 223, 241, 242; reservists, 231; and romance, 169; social and geographic origins, 129, 152, 155, 250, 251; surnames, 154; and voting rights, 261
Pracinhas, 276, 283
Prefects, 33–34
Press, the: and conscription, 230, 261

Press gang. See Military recruitment: agents
Prestes, Júlio, 240
Prestes, Luís Carlos, 240, 242
Prestes Column, 240, 242
Prison(s), 12–13, 49, 61, 79, 104; army-administered, 137, 142; capacity, 143; conditions, 139, 181; construction, 138; convicts, 106; and correction, 139; costs, 139; diet, 163; inmate(s), 152; and the Irish system, 138; juveniles, 138, 214; labor, 14, 139; overcrowding, 139, 140, 144; populations, 139, 143, 173; reform, 65, 79; rehabilitation, 139; in small towns, 182; as a trope, 76, 85, 236
Private (soldado): historic use of the term, 9
Private/public spaces. See House and street metaphor
Prostitution, 119, 160, 169, 184, 195, 196, 199, 200, 221, 224, 256, 277; as a trope, 240
Prussia (Prussian), 11, 23, 24, 68, 69, 75, 79, 99, 100, 202, 249
Public education: and the army, 76, 155, 179, 227, 229–32, 258, 263, 264; obligatory, 119, 281
Public health/hygiene: 117, 121, 198, 199, 202, 227, 229, 230, 232, 237, 253, 254, 256; and national defense, 259, 263, 267, 268, 280; and race, 258; and sex, 200, 253, 254; as a trope, 120; and venereal disease, 202, 221, 253, 254
Public relations, 83, 243; and conscription, 228
Public sanitation, 227
Public schools, 75, 119, 121, 151, 155, 209, 256, 271, 281
Public sector employees: and draft registration, 213, 221; and draft rolls, 251; and racism, 260

Volunteer(s) (*cont.*)
  convicts, 51, 143; Dom Obá II,
    167; law students, 215; and na-
    tionalism, 167; new requirements
    for, 235; pressed men listed as vol-
    unteers, 131, 134; requirements for,
    213; and unemployment, 252
Volunteers of the Fatherland (Volun-
    tários da Pátria), 39, 40, 42, 45–47,
    50, 53, 56, 70, 171, 173, 215, 245;
    land grants for, 39, 40, 173
Von der Goltz, Colmar (baron), 99–
    100, 177

War: and the Brazilian army's institu-
    tional role, 138; conventional, 6,
    138; and cross-cultural com-
    parisons, 11; frontline conditions,
    54, 55, 56, 57; and memory, 59,
    283; mobilization, 26, 38, 40, 51–
    53, 57–59, 64, 73, 74, 108, 109, 112,
    279, 280; tactics, 225
Wartime, 21, 34, 38, 59, 73, 74, 82, 94;
    and service conditions for praças,
    163
War of the Triple Alliance. *See* Para-
    guayan War
War minister, 31, 44, 51, 66, 67, 69,
    72, 74, 78, 82, 86, 90, 91, 94, 97,
    106, 113, 134, 140, 141, 168, 173,
    208, 248, 249
War Ministry, 44, 46, 51, 67, 71, 132,
    173; and authority over state mili-
    tary police, 214, 243, 272

Weaponry: and length of enlisted ser-
    vice contracts, 79; Mauser rifles
    213; muzzle-loaded rifles, 79; and
    praça educational background, 155;
    and training difficulties, 162; used
    by praças in violent crime, 195
Weber, Max, 148
Weights and measures, 84, 91, 236
Welfare state, 242, 243, 245, 246;
    and conscription, 261; origins of,
    272
Wilhem II (Kaiser), 214
Widow(s)/widower(s), 47, 73, 137,
    173, 245
Women: and the definition of man-
    hood, 274, 275. *See also* Gender;
    Honor; Military enlisted service;
    Military recruitment; and Popular
    protest
World War I, 6, 225, 226, 230, 232,
    234, 236, 239, 255, 256, 257, 279,
    280, 282
World War II, 12, 243, 244, 255, 258,
    276, 282

Xenophobia. *See* Nativism

Yellow fever, 95, 120
Young Turk(s), 169, 208, 216, 226,
    232, 233, 235, 236, 239, 241
Youth, 230, 231, 232, 233, 236, 243,
    249, 280

Zuavos bahianos (all-black Bahian
    volunteer unit), 53

Peter Beattie is Associate Professor in the Department of History at Michigan State University. He has contributed articles to the *Hispanic American Historical Review* and the *Journal of Social History*. He is currently engaged in research on civil prisons in the state of Pernambuco.

Library of Congress Cataloging-in-Publication Data

Beattie, Peter M.

The tribute of blood : army, honor, race, and nation in Brazil, 1864–1945 / Peter M. Beattie.

p. cm. — (Latin America otherwise)

Includes bibliographical references and index.

ISBN 0-8223-2733-3 (cloth : alk. paper) — ISBN 0-8223-2743-0 (pbk. : alk. paper)

1. Brazil — Armed Forces — Recruiting, enlistment, etc. — History. 2. Draft — Brazil — History. 3. Sociology, Military — Brazil. I. Title. II. Series.

UB325.B6 B43 2001

306.2′7′0981 — dc21   2001028884